T0329043

CAMBRIDGE LIBRARY COLLECTION

Books of enduring scholarly value

British and Irish History, Nineteenth Century

This series comprises contemporary or near-contemporary accounts of the political, economic and social history of the British Isles during the nineteenth century. It includes material on international diplomacy and trade, labour relations and the women's movement, developments in education and social welfare, religious emancipation, the justice system, and special events including the Great Exhibition of 1851.

A Treatise on the Principles and Practical Influence of Taxation and the Funding System

A friend, correspondent and intellectual successor to David Ricardo, John Ramsay McCulloch (1789–1864) forged his reputation in the emerging field of political economy by publishing deeply researched articles in Scottish periodicals and the Encyclopaedia Britannica. From 1828 he spent nearly a decade as professor of political economy in the newly founded University of London, thereafter becoming comptroller of the Stationery Office. Perhaps the first professional economist, McCulloch had become internationally renowned by the middle of the century, recognised for sharing his ideas through lucid lecturing and writing. The present work, first published in 1845, has been hailed as 'the first systematic account of the theory and policy of public finance'. After a general introductory chapter, the book discusses direct and indirect taxation, before considering national debt and how to deal with it. Several other works written or edited by McCulloch are also reissued in the Cambridge Library Collection.

Cambridge University Press has long been a pioneer in the reissuing of out-of-print titles from its own backlist, producing digital reprints of books that are still sought after by scholars and students but could not be reprinted economically using traditional technology. The Cambridge Library Collection extends this activity to a wider range of books which are still of importance to researchers and professionals, either for the source material they contain, or as landmarks in the history of their academic discipline.

Drawing from the world-renowned collections in the Cambridge University Library and other partner libraries, and guided by the advice of experts in each subject area, Cambridge University Press is using state-of-the-art scanning machines in its own Printing House to capture the content of each book selected for inclusion. The files are processed to give a consistently clear, crisp image, and the books finished to the high quality standard for which the Press is recognised around the world. The latest print-on-demand technology ensures that the books will remain available indefinitely, and that orders for single or multiple copies can quickly be supplied.

The Cambridge Library Collection brings back to life books of enduring scholarly value (including out-of-copyright works originally issued by other publishers) across a wide range of disciplines in the humanities and social sciences and in science and technology.

A Treatise on the Principles and Practical Influence of Taxation and the Funding System

J.R. McCulloch

CAMBRIDGE
UNIVERSITY PRESS

CAMBRIDGE
UNIVERSITY PRESS

University Printing House, Cambridge, CB2 8BS, United Kingdom

Cambridge University Press is part of the University of Cambridge.

It furthers the University's mission by disseminating knowledge in the pursuit of education, learning and research at the highest international levels of excellence.

www.cambridge.org
Information on this title: www.cambridge.org/9781108078689

© in this compilation Cambridge University Press 2017

This edition first published 1845
This digitally printed version 2017

ISBN 978-1-108-07868-9 Paperback

This book reproduces the text of the original edition. The content and language reflect the beliefs, practices and terminology of their time, and have not been updated.

Cambridge University Press wishes to make clear that the book, unless originally published by Cambridge, is not being republished by, in association or collaboration with, or with the endorsement or approval of, the original publisher or its successors in title.

TAXATION

AND

THE FUNDING SYSTEM.

NOTICE.

THE Publishers of this work beg to state that it is private property, protected by the late Copyright Act, the 5 & 6 Victoria, c. 45. They beg also to state that any person having in his possession, within the United Kingdom, for sale or hire, one or more copies printed abroad of any English work protected by the Act referred to, is liable to a penalty, which, in cases affecting their interest, they intend to enforce.

The Public are farther informed that the Act 5 & 6 Victoria, c. 47, s. 24, prohibits the importation of all works printed in foreign countries, of which the copyright is not expired. Even single copies, though for the especial use of the importers and marked with their names, are excluded; and the Customs officers in the different ports are strictly enjoined to carry this regulation into effect.

N. B.—The above regulations are in force in all British colonies and dependencies, as well as in the United Kingdom.

A

TREATISE

ON THE

PRINCIPLES AND PRACTICAL INFLUENCE

OF

TAXATION

AND

THE FUNDING SYSTEM.

~~~~~~~~~~~~~~~~~~

BY J. R. M^cCULLOCH, ESQ.,

MEMBER OF THE INSTITUTE OF FRANCE.

———————

" Neque quies gentium, sine armis; neque arma, sine stipendiis; neque
stipendia sine tributis haberi queunt."

TACITI HIST., iv. 74.

———————

LONDON:

PRINTED FOR

LONGMAN, BROWN, GREEN, AND LONGMANS.

———

MDCCCXLV.

London : Printed by WILLIAM CLOWES and Sons, Stamford Street.

PREFACE.

CONSIDERING the importance of taxation, both as regards the interest of the public and of individuals, it appears singular that it should have been the subject of but few publications. The policy of particular taxes has, indeed, frequently engaged the attention of the legislature, and given birth to myriads of tracts, which, however, have been, for the most part, of little value. But, though it had been otherwise, the influence of taxation over public prosperity could not be learned from such desultory discussions. It cannot be advantageously treated of in parts, but, to be properly understood and appreciated, must be considered as a whole, and in a general point of view. Little, however, has been done to set it in this light, or to show the way in which the different parts of a fiscal system act upon each other, and its various bearings and incidences on society. That portion of the 'Wealth

of Nations' which refers to Taxes and Public Debts,
the chapters on the same subjects in Mr. Ricardo's
'Political Economy,' and the treatise of Sir Henry
Parnell on 'Financial Reform,' are the only works
of any eminence on fiscal policy of a comprehensive
character that have appeared in this country. But
the first of these having been published so far back
as 1776, is necessarily in many respects little applicable to the present state of things. Mr. Ricardo's
investigations are too abstract to be of much practical utility ; and the more recent publication of Sir
H. Parnell is but indifferently calculated to supply
the deficiencies of his predecessors : being of limited extent, and including lengthened discussions
on various branches of the public expenditure, his
remarks on taxation are, for the most part, brief and
superficial, and he omits, indeed, all mention of
several of the most important and difficult questions involved in its discussion.

Under these circumstances we cannot be said
to have obtruded ourselves upon a field of discussion already fully occupied. We may have failed
to accomplish our purpose, but the purpose itself
can hardly be objected to. Our work is intended
to supply what is certainly a desideratum in econo-

mical literature, by furnishing the public with a
pretty full exposition of the principles and practical
influence of Taxation and the Funding System. In
this view we have endeavoured carefully to trace
and exhibit the effect of the principal classes of
taxes upon the wealth and well-being of the public.
We have not, however, confined our researches to
the history and influence of the leading taxes imposed in the United Kingdom. These, no doubt,
have engrossed the greater portion of our attention,
but we have also investigated the influence of some
of the more important taxes imposed in other countries. And we are glad to have to state that the
result of these inquiries has been thus far satisfactory, that it shows, that, with one prominent exception, there is but little to object to in the principle
of the greater number of our taxes; that the abuses
and defects with which some of them have been,
and continue to be, chargeable, have seldom been
occasioned by their being essentially unjust, unfair,
or mischievous, but by their having been carried
to excess, or by something defective or wrong in
the mode of their assessment; and that, consequently, they may be amended with comparatively
little difficulty.

The errors which, as we have attempted to show, have been committed in the practice of funding in this country, admit of no remedy. But it is, notwithstanding, of importance that the true principles and proper line of conduct to be followed in respect to such matters should be ascertained; for though the mistakes of a bygone period, and the effects consequent thereon, may no longer be capable of rectification, their repetition may be prevented; and the existing generation, and the generations by which it will be followed, may be taught to avoid and profit by the blunders of the past.

We are not, therefore, wholly without the hope that this work may be of some public utility. If the principles laid down, and the inferences drawn from them, be admitted, they may assist in facilitating the adoption of various salutary reforms, at the same time that they may, perhaps, help to thwart some dangerous projects. At all events, whatever may be thought of this book, the more thoroughly the subjects of which it treats are investigated, the better will it be for the ends of truth, security, and good government. It is no easy matter to ascertain the ultimate incidence and real effect of various taxes; and the loudest clamours have frequently been raised against those that were least objectionable, and conversely. But whether the public form a right or a wrong estimate of any subsisting or proposed tax, or of any financial project, its opinion must necessarily have a powerful influence. It is, therefore, of the utmost consequence that it should be disabused of its errors, that it should learn to look a little below the surface, and cease to mistake appearances and declamation for facts and legitimate reasoning. The more the public mind is enlightened on the subject, the less scope will there be, on the one hand, for misrepresentation and exaggeration, and, on the other, the less excuse for obstinately adhering to vicious systems. The national energies will be less likely to be turned towards vain and perilous schemes, while those that are really beneficial will be more likely to be carried forward. " *Promovere i lumi e la curiosità nelle materie de Finanza e di Commercio, sarà sempre la preparazione migliore di tutti per cominciar le riforme.*"—(Verri, ' Meditazioni sulla Economia Politica,' ediz. 6ᵗᵃ, p. 214.)*

* We have availed ourselves in a few parts of this work of statements in articles we contributed several years ago to the ' Edinburgh Review ;' these have been, however, for the most part rewritten.

Besides this Treatise Mr. M꠵Culloch has published the following works, viz. :—

1. A STATISTICAL ACCOUNT of the BRITISH EMPIRE, exhibiting its Extent, Physical Capacities, Population, Industry, and Civil and Religious Institutions. Second Edition. 2 vols. 8vo. London, 1839.

2. A DICTIONARY, GEOGRAPHICAL, STATISTICAL, and HISTORICAL, of the various Countries, Places, and Principal Natural Objects in the World. 2 thick and closely printed vols. 8vo., illustrated with Maps. London, 1841.

3. SMITH'S WEALTH OF NATIONS; with a Life of the Author, Notes, and Supplemental Dissertations. Second Edition. 1 vol. 8vo., double columns. London, 1839.

4. The PRINCIPLES of POLITICAL ECONOMY; with some Inquiries respecting their Application, and a Sketch of the Rise and Progress of the Science. Third Edition. Edinburgh, 1843.

5. A DICTIONARY, PRACTICAL, THEORETICAL, and HISTORICAL, of COMMERCE and COMMERCIAL NAVIGATION. A new and improved Edition, in one large volume 8vo., illustrated with Maps. London, 1844.

6. The LITERATURE of POLITICAL ECONOMY: a Classified Catalogue of Select Publications in the different Departments of that Science, with Historical, Critical, and Biographical Notices. 1 vol. 8vo. London, 1845.

CONTENTS.

INTRODUCTION.

GENERAL OBSERVATIONS ON TAXATION.

PART I.

CHAPTER I.

CHAPTER II.

CHAPTER III.

CHAPTER IV.

PART II.

INDIRECT TAXES.

CHAPTER I.

CHAPTER II.

CHAPTER III.

CHAPTER IV.

CHAPTER V.

CHAPTER VI.

CHAPTER VII.

PART III.

FUNDING SYSTEM.

CHAPTER I.

CHAPTER II.

CHAPTER III.

REDUCTION OF THE NATIONAL DEBT.

APPENDIX.

ERRATUM.

Page 213, 6th line from top, for "contradictory," read *contradictorily*.

TAXATION

THE FUNDING SYSTEM.

INTRODUCTION.

GENERAL OBSERVATIONS ON TAXATION.

Definitions—Necessity of Taxation—Present System of Taxation originated in
the decline of the Feudal System—Taxes estimated by Values, and not by
Quantities—Improvements in the Arts enable Countries to bear Additional
Taxes—Opposite Effects of Moderate and Heavy Taxes—Fallacy of the
Doctrine that Taxes are restored to the Contributors by the Expenditure
of Government—Erroneous opinion of Locke and Quesnay respecting the
Incidence of Taxes—Maxims laid down by Smith with respect to Taxes—
Observations on these Maxims—Excise Scheme of Sir Robert Walpole—
Expense and Mode of collecting Taxes — Contributions of compulsory
Labour—Corvées—Conscription.

A TAX is a portion, or the value of a portion, of the property or labour of individuals taken from them by government, and placed at its disposal.

A tax may be either *direct* or *indirect*. It is said to be
direct when it is immediately taken from property or
labour ; and *indirect* when it is taken from them by making
their owners pay for liberty to use certain articles, or to
exercise certain privileges.

A tax may be either *general* or *particular* ; that is, it
may either affect all classes indiscriminately, or only one
or more classes.

Taxation is the general term used to express the aggregate of particular taxes. It is also the name given to
that branch of the science of political economy which ex-
plains the mode in which different taxes affect the public
interest, and in which the revenue required for the public
service may be most advantageously raised.

B

It would be superfluous to enter into any lengthened arguments to show the utility, or rather necessity,
of raising a revenue for the use of the public. It is
sufficient to state that the experience of all ages and
countries shows that good order and tranquillity at home,
security from foreign invasion, and the speedy and impartial administration of justice, are indispensable to
the vigorous exercise of industry, the accumulation of
wealth, and the well-being of society; and that where
they are wanting the energies of the population are
prostrated, industry paralysed, and poverty and barbarism universally diffused. The duty of making adequate provision for securing the means by which so
much good may be realized on the one hand, and so
much evil averted on the other, is, therefore, impera-
tive : an expenditure for such objects is most profitable : it is essential, indeed, to the existence of the
body politic, and, being productive of universal advantage, it should be defrayed by the joint contributions
of the society. Hence the fundamental principle that,
in as far as practicable, all the subjects of a state should
contribute to the sums required to maintain its fleets
and armies, with the various functionaries and institutions, necessary for defence against hostile aggression, for
the preservation of internal peace, the promotion of prosperity, and the protection of every citizen in the undis-
turbed enjoyment of his property and rights. It, no
doubt, frequently happens that the public has to contribute larger sums than are necessary for the ends of good
government. Inasmuch, however, as all abuses of this
sort obviously originate either in the misconduct of governments or in something defective in their organization, they do not come within the scope of our inquiries,
and have, in fact, nothing to do with taxation. It is
sufficiently clear that, so long as taxes imposed for necessary and legitimate purposes are judiciously assessed,
and collected in the way least likely to be injurious, their

payment cannot reasonably be objected to. Under such circumstances their expenditure seldom fails to secure an adequate return to the contributors. But, at all events, it is no part of our business to inquire whether the revenue raised by the state exceed its necessary wants, or whether it be judiciously expended. How important soever, these questions do not affect the principles on which taxes should be imposed, nor the mode of their imposition, and are consequently foreign to the nature and objects of this work: and, leaving them to be examined by others, we shall content ourselves with endeavouring to ascertain the influence of taxation over individual and national wealth; and, by analysing the various methods in which a revenue may be raised, and comparing them together, we shall, perhaps, be able to show which is most advantageous, or rather which is least injurious.

The scheme of taxation now in force in modern Europe had its origin in the decline of the feudal system. According to the principles of that system, lands were held as fiefs of the crown, on condition of their possessors performing certain stipulated services; of which the obligation to support the sovereign when he took the field, with a body of retainers armed and maintained at their own expense, was by far the most important. The tenants in chief of the great fiefs, or those who held directly under the sovereign, were either originally invested with, or subsequently usurped, the prerogative of distributing justice in their respective lordships; and in those days the administration of justice, instead of being a source of expense, became, in consequence of the corruption and abuses with which it was infected, a considerable source of influence and emolument. The clergy were supported partly by the produce of their own estates, and partly by a tithe levied upon the estates of others. And the labour of the peasantry, during a few days before and after harvest, sufficed to put the roads and bridges into that state of repair which the depressed situation of commerce, and the little intercourse among the different parts of the country, seemed to require. It was not even necessary to levy a tax for the support of the monarch and his court. The rents of the crown estates, or of the royal demesnes which had not been granted to others, but remained in the immediate possession of the sovereign, and the revenue derived from wardships and other feudal incidents, were generally sufficient to defray this part of the public expenditure. When the feudal system was in its vigour, the demesnes of the crown were, in most countries, very extensive; and the alienations occasioned by the profusion and facility of some princes were compensated by the forfeitures and escheats that were always taking place.

The vicious nature of this system is too obvious to require being pointed out; and it had for a long series of years the most disastrous influence over the peace and prosperity of Europe. But the progressive though slow advance of civilization ultimately occasioned its overthrow. Money payments were gradually substituted for personal services; and the establishment of standing armies in France * by Charles VII., and their introduction into other countries, entirely broke the power and spirit of the feudal aristocracy, and enabled the different governments to introduce a regular plan of administration, and to enforce that system of pecuniary contribution now universally established.

The amount of a tax is not to be estimated by the *bulk* or *species* of the produce which it transfers from individuals to government, but exclusively by its *value*. A heavy taxation consists in the abstraction of a large value, and a light taxation in the abstraction of a small value. When a fall takes place in the cost of producing

* Hallam's ' Middle Ages,' vol. i. p. 118.

any article, its price necessarily declines in an equal degree; and if the value of money continue stationary, its producers are obliged to dispose of a proportionally larger quantity to obtain the means of paying the same amount of taxes. But it is an obvious error to suppose, as is very commonly done, that the burden of taxation is consequently increased. The value paid by the contributors remains the same; and it is by values, and not by quantities, that the weight of taxation is to be measured. If, through improvements in agriculture, machinery, or any other cause, *two* quarters of wheat, or *two* yards of cloth, were produced with the *same* expenditure of capital and labour that is now required to produce *one* quarter or *one* yard, it would be no hardship to give *double* the present quantity of wheat and cloth in payment of taxes.

The want of attention to this principle has led to much erroneous reasoning on the subject of taxation. Even Smith made no sufficient allowance for the influence of improvements in enabling a country to bear additional taxes. Nothing, however, can be more obvious than that the share of the products of its subjects taken by government as revenue may be regularly increased in every country in which the arts are progressive, without really adding to their burdens. Every invention and discovery by which the production of commodities is facilitated, and their value reduced, enables individuals to spare a larger quantity for the use of the state. The sacrifice made in paying taxes consists in the labour, or in the cost of the money or produce required to pay them, and not in the amount of such money or produce. To pay 100*l.* or 1000*l.* to government at this moment will require a cotton-manufacturer to sell not less, perhaps, than fifteen or twenty times the quantity of cottons that would have sufficed to make the same payment in 1760. But as this diminution in the value of his

goods has been occasioned by an equivalent diminution
in the expense of their production, he is not thereby
placed in any respect in a worse situation; nor is he
making any greater sacrifice now than formerly. Governments have, therefore, precisely the same interest
as their subjects in facilitating production; inasmuch as
its increased facility affords the means of adding to the
quantity of produce at their disposal, without really
adding to the weight of taxation; whereas, on the contrary, a diminished facility of production must either
diminish in an equal degree the produce appropriated
by government, or compel it to lay heavier burdens on
its subjects. Public wealth, in short, is merely a portion
of private wealth transferred to government; and the
greater the amount of the latter, the greater, of course,
will be the magnitude of the portion that may be conveniently spared for public purposes.

Though taxation be necessary, it should always be
kept within the narrowest limits. The best taxes, provided they produce the necessary supplies, may, speaking generally, be said to be the lightest, or those of
which the pressure is least felt. But how light soever,
all taxes necessarily at first encroach somewhat on the
means of enjoyment or of accumulation possessed by
the parties by whom they are paid; and whatever may
be their amount, and however imposed, they must necessarily fall either on the revenue of the contributors
or on their capital or stock. Perhaps, indeed, there is
no tax the produce of which is not partly derived from
both these sources. It is, however, abundantly certain
that all taxes, when judiciously imposed, and not carried
to an oppressive height, occasion an increase of industry
and economy, and but rarely encroach on capital. Under
these conditions they operate as motives to restrain
expense, and as incentives to labour and ingenuity,
frequently occasioning the production of more wealth

than they abstract. But the power to make increased exertions, and to save from expense, though not easily defined, is not illimitable. And whenever this limit has been attained—that is, whenever the burden of taxation is not fully compensated by increased production or increased saving—it must encroach on the means of future production, and the country will then begin to retrograde. Taxation, when carried to this extent, is one of the severest scourges to which a people can be subjected. By diminishing capital, or the funds destined to support productive industry, it lessens the national revenue, the only fund out of which taxes can be permanently paid; and lays the sure foundation of public poverty and disgrace, in the destruction of individual fortunes. Like falling bodies, which are precipitated with a constantly and rapidly increasing velocity, a system of taxation acting on capital multiplies pauperism and distress in a geometrical proportion, and destroys alike the desire and the means of reproduction.

It would, however, be an error to suppose that a tax necessarily falls upon capital because it is laid on capital, or on income because it is laid on income. A moderate tax laid on capital may be, and generally is, defrayed out of a saving of income; whereas an oppressive tax laid on income has in most cases to be partly paid from capital. But of all species of taxes, those would seem to be among the worst which necessarily fall on capital, without giving the contributors an opportunity to defray them from revenue. By diminishing the means of reproduction, they in so far diminish the future taxable income of the country. The legacy duty, as will be afterwards seen, has been objected to, though perhaps without much reason, on this ground.

Most of the writers on finance, patronized by European governments, have laboured to show that taxation is never a cause of diminished production; but that, on the contrary, every new tax creates a new ability in the subject to bear it, and every increase of the public burdens a proportional increase in the industry of the people. The fallacy of this opinion, when advanced thus absolutely and without reservation, has been ably exposed by Hume in his ' Essay on Taxes.' It is true, however, as has been already stated, that the desire to preserve their fortunes unimpaired, and to improve their condition, stimulates most men to endeavour to discharge the burden of moderate taxes by increased industry and economy, without allowing them to encroach on their fortunes.

The operation of this principle has been strikingly evinced in the financial history of this country since the commencement of the American war. That contest, and the more recent struggle with revolutionary France, occasioned a vast increase of taxation, and an expenditure that has no parallel in the history of the world. The public debt, which amounted to about 145 millions in 1772, amounted to about 841 millions in 1817; and, in addition to the immense sums raised by borrowing, the gross produce of the taxes levied in the United Kingdom during the late war exceeded the enormous sum of 1300 millions sterling! And yet the rapid increase of population—the wonderful progress and improvement of agriculture, manufactures, and commerce—the extension and embellishment of towns and cities—the formation of so many new docks, roads, and canals—and the infinite variety of expensive undertakings entered upon and completed in all parts of the country during the continuance of hostilities—show clearly that the savings of the mass of the people greatly exceeded the warlike expenditure of government and the unprofitable expenditure of individuals. It may be safely affirmed that no other country could have made such extraordinary exertions without being ruined ; and we owe the power to make them to a variety of causes, but chiefly, perhaps, to that security of property and freedom of industry which we enjoy in a greater degree than any other European nation, and to that universal diffusion of intelligence which enables those who carry on industrious undertakings to press all the powers of nature into their service, and to avail themselves of productive energies of which a less instructed people would be wholly ignorant.

Speculative inquirers have sometimes indulged in conjectures as to what would have been our present situation had the wars which have occasioned the contraction of so large a debt, and the expenditure of such vast sums, not occurred. Dr. Smith appears to have concluded that, in the event of our having enjoyed perpetual peace since the Revolution, almost the whole sums that have been since laid out on warlike enterprises would have been added to the national capital, and that we should in consequence have been incomparably richer, more populous and powerful. " Had not these wars," he observes, " given the particular direction to so large a capital, the greater part of it would naturally have been employed in maintaining productive hands, whose labour would have replaced, with a profit, the whole value of their consumption. The value of the annual produce of the land and labour of the country would have been considerably increased by it every year, and every year's increase would have still more augmented that of the following year. More houses would have been built, more lands would have been improved, and those which had been improved before would have been better cultivated. More manufactures would have been established, and those which had been established before would have been more extended ; and to what height the real wealth and revenue of the country might by this time have been raised it is not perhaps very easy even to imagine." *

* See the edition of the Wealth of Nations by the author of this work, in one vol. 8vo. p. 153.

But this, though a popular, is a very doubtful conclusion. A speculation of this sort is necessarily, indeed,
encumbered with so many difficulties as to admit of little
else than probabilities; though these, we think, go far to
warrant the belief that, but for the contests in which we
have been engaged since the Revolution, the greater
portion of the wealth expended in carrying them on
would never have existed. Smith forgot that an increase of taxation has the same powerful influence
over a nation that an increase of his family or of his
necessary expenses has over a private individual. The
constantly increasing pressure of taxation during the war
begun in 1793, was felt by all classes, and gave a spur to
industry, enterprise, and invention, and generated a spirit
of economy that we should have in vain attempted to excite by any less powerful means. Had taxation been very
oppressive, it would not have had this effect; but it was not
so high as to produce either dejection or despair, though
it was at the same time sufficiently heavy to render a
very considerable increase of industry and parsimony necessary to prevent it from encroaching on the fortunes of
individuals, or, at all events, from diminishing the rate
at which they had previously been increasing. Man is
not influenced solely by hope, he is also powerfully
operated on by fear. Taxation brings the latter principle into the field. To the desire of rising in the world,
implanted in the breast of every individual, an increase
of taxation superadds the fear of being cast down to a
lower station, of being deprived of conveniences and
gratifications which habit has rendered all but indispensable; and the combined influence of the two principles
produces results that could not be produced by the un-
assisted agency of either. Without the American war
and the late French war there would have been less industry and less frugality, because there would have
been less occasion for them. And we incline to think
that those who inquire dispassionately into the matter
will most probably see reason to conclude that the in-

crease of industry and frugality occasioned by these contests more than sufficed to defray their enormous expense,
and that the capital of the country is probably about as
great at this moment as it would have been had they
not occurred.

But we must be on our guard against the abuse of
this doctrine, and must not suppose that, because it holds
in certain cases and under certain conditions, it will,
therefore, hold in all cases and under all conditions.
To render an increase of taxation productive of greater
exertion, economy, and invention, it should be slow and
gradual; and it should never be carried to such a height
as to incapacitate individuals from meeting the sacrifices
it imposes by such additional exertions and economy
as it may be in their power to make without requiring
any very sudden or violent change in their habits. The
increase of taxation should never be so great as to make
it impracticable to overcome its influence, or to induce
the belief that it is impracticable. Difficulties that are
seen to be surmountable sharpen the inventive powers,
and are readily and vigorously grappled with; but an
apparently insurmountable difficulty, or such an increase of taxation as it was deemed impossible to defray,
would not stimulate, but destroy exertion. Whenever taxation becomes so heavy that the wealth it
takes from individuals can no longer be replaced by
fresh efforts, these efforts uniformly cease to be made;
industry is paralysed, and the country declines. Oppression, it has been said, either raises men into heroes
or sinks them into slaves; and taxation, according to its
magnitude and the mode in which it is imposed, either
makes men industrious, enterprising, and wealthy, or
indolent, dispirited, and impoverished.

It must not, however, be supposed that, because the
probability is that the capital of the country is about
as great at present as it would have been had the late
war with France not occurred, we sustain no incon-

venience from the taxes imposed to defray its expense. Undoubtedly they form, and will most probably continue to form for a lengthened period, a heavy drawback on the industry and prosperity of the country. But they do this, not so much by reason of their magnitude compared with our ability to bear them, as by reason of their magnitude compared with the taxes of most other countries, and the consequent temptation they have created to transfer capital and skilled labour to those countries. The decline of Holland may, in fact, be traced to the operation of the principle now referred to. Notwithstanding the vast expense of her revolutionary struggle with Spain, and of her subsequent contests with England and France, the capital of the republic increased prodigiously during the latter half of the 16th and the greater part of the 17th century. But despite this increase, the number and magnitude of the taxes which it became necessary to impose, to defray the interest of her debt and her current expenditure, so reduced the rate of profit, that the Dutch capitalists were tempted to vest very large sums in foreign countries, and that the manufactures and commerce of the republic gradually declined.

But we shall have other opportunities of recurring to the important considerations now merely glanced at; and we only mention them at present lest it might be supposed that, in exhibiting the powerful influence of increased taxation in stimulating industry and economy, we were unconscious of, or had overlooked, the serious inconveniences that usually follow such increase, when not confined within moderate limits.

The effects, now alluded to, of the too great increase of taxation are, for the most part, developed only by slow degrees, and are not in general very sensibly felt till a considerable period after it has taken place. The injurious effects that have been observed immediately to follow certain taxes will, we believe, be almost uni-

formly found to have resulted either from something
vicious in the nature of the taxes, or from their being
suddenly carried to an oppressive height. Taxes of a
definite amount, that admit of being fairly assessed and
collected, without requiring any offensive inquisition into
the affairs of individuals, and without obstructing improvements, may be gradually increased to what might,
à priori, be considered a most oppressive extent, without
any immediate injury to industry, and without occasioning discontent. But taxes that may be increased or
diminished at the pleasure of the collectors, or which
affect only certain classes of properties or persons, or
which cannot be assessed without prying into the circumstances of the contributors, or which discourage improvements, uniformly occasion, even when comparatively
light, the greatest dissatisfaction, and have a most pernicious influence. The extremely vicious nature of the
taxes to which she has been subjected, and not their
magnitude, has been one of the most potent causes of
the decline of industry in Spain, and of the abasement
into which she has sunk.

It should be observed, in estimating the influence of
taxation over the condition of society, that the repeal of
any important tax, if it have existed for a considerable
time, usually occasions a comparatively rapid increase
of accumulation. The habits of the population having
been accommodated to the tax, its withdrawal, unless it
have been imposed on some article in very general demand, makes little difference in the expenditure of most
people. And even supposing it had been imposed on
an article in extensive demand, its consumption by the
upper and even the middle classes will most probably be but little affected; so that, though some part
of the saving effected by the repeal of the tax will no
doubt be absorbed in increased purchases of the article itself, and of other things, the fair presumption is,
that a larger portion will be added to their accumula-

tions. We incline to think that the operation of this principle has been strongly felt in this country since the termination of the war, and that the habits of saving which grew out of the privations it entailed on the bulk of the population have made large portions of the sums saved to the middle classes by the repeal of taxes be added to their accumulations, and have had, in this way, no inconsiderable influence in promoting the increase of capital that has since taken place.

Besides contending that the uniform effect of taxes is to create a new ability in the people to bear them, modern financiers have frequently also contended that they are not really lost to the contributors, but are restored to them through the expenditure of government and its agents! And notwithstanding the gross and almost obvious fallacy which this statement involves, it not unfrequently forms the substance of the answers made to those who complain of the injurious influence of oppressive taxes. To show its absurdity, suppose a farmer is taxed 50*l*., and let us endeavour to ascertain whether the expenditure of this sum by the public functionary, or individual, to whom it has been paid by government, affords any compensation to the farmer for its loss. If the receiver of the tax do not lay it out on articles produced by the farmer, it is obvious it cannot again revert to him, and he can derive no advantage from its expenditure. But suppose, which is the most favourable hypothesis for the statement we are combating, that the tax-receiver comes to the farmer to buy his produce, and let us trace the successive steps and effect of the whole transaction: first of all, then, the farmer sold as much corn, or other produce, as was worth 50*l*.; he next paid away these 50*l*. to a tax-collector; and the person who received the 50*l*. from the tax-collector now comes to the farmer and offers them back to him, on condition of his receiving an equivalent in corn or other produce. This is the way in which the money drawn from the pockets of the public by taxation always reverts to them; and if it enrich any one, it is obvious it must do so by making him pay *twice* for the same sum of money! It is to no purpose to endeavour to escape from this *reductio ad absurdum* by telling us that industry is benefited by every extension of the market, and that the consumption of soldiers and sailors is advantageous, because it increases demand. To benefit industry, the market must be real—not nominal; it must be one in which the demanders have supplied themselves, through their own industry or resources, with the money or other equivalents they offer for commodities. It is absurd to suppose that either individuals or states should receive the smallest benefit from the demand of those whom they have been previously obliged to furnish with the means of buying. This, however, is always the case with the demand of those who live on the produce of taxation; and to keep up useless regiments and overgrown establishments, on pretence of encouraging industry by increasing demand, is quite as irrational as if a shopkeeper were to attempt to increase his business and get rich by furnishing his customers with money to buy his goods.

"To argue," says Dr. Hamilton, "that the money raised in taxes, being spent among those who pay it, is, therefore, no loss to them, is no less absurd than the defence of a housebreaker, who, being convicted of carrying off a merchant's money, should plead that he did him no injury, for the money would be returned to him in the purchase of the commodities in which he dealt."*

It is obvious, therefore, that the services rendered by the various public functionaries who receive taxes form the only return made to the contributors. And it is

* On the National Debt, 3rd ed., p. 35. This sophism is equally well exposed in the 'Lettres d'un Citoyen sur les Vingtièmes,' &c., p. 113, published in 1768.

undoubtedly true that these services are of the highest value, and that, when neither the number nor the salaries of those by whom they are rendered are unnecessarily large, they constitute a full and ample equivalent for the sums expended upon them. But all beyond this—all that is drawn from the people by means of taxes to be expended in maintaining unnecessary functionaries, or in over-paying them—is wholly lost to the tax-payers, or is not in any way compensated to them.

Like all other values, the smaller the sacrifice for which that security, protection, and good government, which it is the object of taxation to procure, may be obtained, the better. A diminution of expenditure, and consequently of taxation, confers an advantage on the public, similar to that which a diminution of the cost of any indispensable or highly desirable article confers on individuals. There is no mystery in the manner in which government is supported and taxation operates. Government is not a producer: its expenditure is not defrayed by its own labour, but by that of its subjects. And hence, the greater the expenses of governments, the deeper must they encroach on the income or capital of their subjects, and conversely, unless, as previously stated, they be met by increased industry or economy, or both. But this is not always to be depended upon; and M. Say, notwithstanding his wish to be epigrammatic, is justified in saying that the best system of finance is to *spend little;* and the best of all taxes, *the least. Le meilleur de tous les plans de finance est de dépenser peu, et le meilleur de tous les impôts est le plus petit.*

Various and very discordant opinions have been entertained respecting the ultimate incidence and effect of particular taxes. Locke in England, and Quesnay and his followers in France and Italy, contended that all taxes, however imposed, fell ultimately on the land. This erroneous opinion originated in their supposing that agriculture is the only productive species of industry; whereas it is in no respect more productive than others. The truth is, that every burden, laid directly or indirectly on any article for which there is any considerable demand, falls ultimately on its consumers. A tax on hats, for example, raises the price of hats, and a tax on leather raises the price of shoes; for were it otherwise, the profits of the hatters and shoemakers would be reduced below the general level; and as they would not certainly be satisfied with less profit than was made by their nieghbours, they would begin to withdraw from such unprofitable businesses, and would continue to withdraw till, through the diminished supply of hats and shoes, their prices had been raised to their former height, or to such a height as would yield the makers the average profits of stock exclusive of the tax. There are natural limits, however, to the extent to which taxes on commodities can be carried; and their effects differ according as they are laid on those required for the consumption of the labouring class, or on those principally consumed by the higher classes. But before proceeding to inquire into the influence of particular taxes, it may be as well, perhaps, to make a few observations on the maxims of Dr. Smith with regard to taxation, which have been much and justly referred to.

First Maxim.—" The subjects of every state ought to contribute towards the support of the government, as nearly as possible in proportion to their respective abilities; that is, in proportion to the revenue which they respectively enjoy under the protection of the state. The expense of government to the individuals of a great nation is like the expense of management to the joint tenants of a great estate, who are obliged to contribute in proportion to their respective interests in the estate. In the observation or neglect of this

c

maxim consists what is called the equality or inequality of taxation."

Second.—" The tax which each individual is bound to pay ought to be certain, and not arbitrary. The time of payment, the manner of payment, the quantity to be paid, ought all to be clear and plain to the contributor and to every other person. Where it is otherwise, every person subject to the tax is put, more or less, in the power of the tax-gatherer, who can either aggravate the tax upon any obnoxious contributor, or extort, by the terror of such aggravation, some present or perquisite to himself. The uncertainty of taxation encourages the insolence and favours the corruption of an order of men who are naturally unpopular even where they are neither insolent nor corrupt. The certainty of what each individual ought to pay is, in taxation, of so great importance, that a very considerable degree of inequality, it appears, I believe, from the experience of all nations, is not near so great an evil as a very small degree of uncertainty."

Third.—" Every tax ought to be levied at the time and in the manner in which it is most likely to be convenient for the contributor to pay it. A tax upon the rent of land, or of houses, payable at the same term at which rents are usually paid, is levied at the time when it is most likely to be convenient for the contributor to pay, or when he is most likely to have wherewithal to pay. Taxes upon such consumable goods as are articles of luxury are all finally paid by the consumer, and generally in a manner that is very convenient for him. He pays them by little and little, as he has occasion to buy the goods; and as he is at liberty, too, either to buy or not to buy as he pleases, it must be his own fault if he ever suffers any considerable inconveniency from such taxes."

Fourth.—" Every tax ought to be so contrived as both

to take out and to keep out of the pockets of the people as little as possible over and above what it brings into the public treasury of the state."*

It is easy, however, to see, notwithstanding their apparent completeness, that the characters of good and bad taxes embodied in the above maxims are not sufficiently comprehensive. It would, no doubt, be in various respects desirable that the inhabitants'of a country should contribute to the support of its government in proportion to their means. This is obviously, however, a matter of secondary importance. It is the business of the legislator to look at the practical influence of different taxes, and to resort in preference to those by which the revenue may be raised with least inconvenience. Should the taxes least adverse to the public interests fall on the contributors according to their respective abilities, it will be an additional recommendation in their favour. But the *salus populi* is in this, as it should be in every similar matter, the prime consideration; and the tax which is best fitted to promote. or least opposed to, this great end, though it may not press quite equally on the different orders of society, is to be preferred to a more equal but otherwise less advantageous tax. Had Smith restricted his maxim to taxes laid directly on property or income, he would have been quite right in saying that they should be proportioned to the abilities of the contributors. Equality, indeed, is essential to such taxes; and whenever they cease to be equal, they become partial and unjust. But in laying down a principle that is to apply to all taxes, equality of contribution is an inferior consideration. The distinguishing characteristic of the best tax is, not that it is most nearly proportioned to the means of individuals, but that it is easily assessed and collected, and is, at the same time, most conducive, all things considered, to the public interests.

* Wealth of Nations, 1 vol. 8vo. p. 371.

The truth is, that the greater number of taxes, including, we believe, every one that is least injurious, are imposed on a totally different principle from that laid down in the first of Smith's maxims. They consist of duties payable by those who use certain articles or exercise certain privileges and by none else. Taxes of this sort, though not proportioned to the abilities of the consumers, cannot be said to be unjust; and provided they be imposed on proper objects, and kept within reasonable limits, they do not appear open to any good objection.

We may refer, in illustration of this statement, to the duties on malt, spirits, wine, and tobacco. These produce a very large annual revenue; and though some of them might be advantageously reduced, they appear—supposing them to be properly assessed—to be, in all respects, unexceptionable. Other duties of this description, such as those on saddle horses, carriages, and livery servants, fall only on the more opulent classes. But this is not the case with the more productive duties; and it must be admitted that the largest portion of the revenue derived from them is paid by the lower and poorer orders. This, however, is not, as has been often alleged, a consequence of the latter being over-taxed, but of their being so very numerous that the produce of taxes to which they generally contribute invariably exceeds the produce of much heavier taxes falling exclusively on the richer classes. The duties now under consideration act, in fact, as a species of improved sumptuary laws, having all the useful with few or none of the injurious influences of these regulations. The articles on which they are imposed are seldom indispensable to the well-being of any one; so that the duties may be partially or wholly evaded by those who prefer exercising a little self-denial to making the increased exertion necessary for their payment. But in nine instances out of ten the influence of the duty is of a compound description, infusing at one and the same time a greater spirit of industry and economy into all classes. Duties laid on articles like spirits, the free indulgence in which is most injurious, are probably the best of any; for while they bring large sums into the public treasury, they help to repress vicious habits and to improve the public morals.

In the case of necessary articles duties of this sort should be cautiously resorted to, and should always be confined within moderate limits. But, even in their case, the injury the duties do to the poorer classes is often more apparent than real; for, as will be afterwards shown, their wages are in most cases increased proportionally to their amount. Without, however, insisting on this circumstance, it is at present enough to state that it rarely happens that the quantity of an article used previously to its being burdened with a moderate duty may not be diminished by the substitution of something else in its stead, or by the exercise of greater economy, without entailing any very serious privation on the consumers.

We confess, therefore, that so long as this species of duties are imposed on proper objects, and not carried to too great a height, we have yet to learn the grounds on which they can be said to be either unjust or oppressive. A revenue must be raised by one means or other; and we are sanguine enough to believe that it will be sufficiently demonstrated in the sequel, that such portion of it as may be raised by the duties now referred to will be the least onerous of any.

Although, however, it be no valid objection to a large class of taxes that they are not proportioned to the means of the contributors, it may be laid down in general that no tax, whether it be proportioned to their means or otherwise, can be a good tax unless it correspond pretty closely with the conditions in the last three maxims of Smith.

The great defect, for example, in the system of taxation in France previously to the Revolution, and in that of most continental countries, consisted not so much in its magnitude, or in the oppressive manner in which it was collected, as in its inequality. The principal taxes were direct, and should, therefore, have been proportioned to the abilities of the contributors. But, on the contrary, those who had the largest fortunes, and who consequently derived the greatest advantage from the protection afforded by government, were expressly relieved from the burden of direct taxation. The nobility and clergy, while they engrossed every situation of power and emolument, were, in as far as possible, exempted from the taille and other heavy and vexatious imposts. And it is no longer a question that the disgust occasioned by this inequality, the impatience of the feudal privileges of the nobility, and the desire of equal rights, were the leading causes of those revolutions which made such tremendous havoc amongst the ancient institutions of the continent.

The mischiefs occasioned by the former inequality of taxation in France were set in a very striking point of view by the late Arthur Young, whose 'Travels in France' contain the most comprehensive and accurate account of the state of that country previously to the Revolution.

" The abuses attending the levy of taxes," says Mr. Young, " were heavy and universal. The kingdom was parcelled into generalities, with an intendant at the head of each, into whose hands the whole power of the Crown was delegated for everything except the military authority, but particularly for all affairs of finance. The generalities were subdivided into elections, at the head of which was a sub-delegate appointed by the intendant. The rolls of the *taille, capitation, vingtièmes*, and other taxes, were distributed among districts, parishes, and individuals, at the pleasure of the intendant, who could exempt, change, add, or diminish at pleasure. Such an enormous power constantly acting, and from which no man was free, must, in the nature of things, degenerate in many cases into absolute tyranny. It must be obvious that the friends, acquaintances, and dependants of the intendant, and of all his sub-delegates, and the friends of these friends, to a long chain of dependence, might be favoured in taxation at the expense of their miserable neighbours; and that noblemen in favour at court, to whose protection the intendant himself would naturally look up, could find little difficulty in throwing much of the weight of their taxes on others, without a similar support. Instances, and even gross ones, have been reported to me in many parts of the kingdom, that made me shudder at the oppression to which numbers must have been condemned by the undue favours granted to such crooked influence. But without recurring to such cases, what must have been the state of the poor people paying heavy taxes, from which the nobility and clergy were exempted? A cruel aggravation of their misery, to see those who could best afford to pay exempted because able! The enrolments for the militia, which the *Cahiers* call *an injustice without example*, were another dreadful scourge on the peasantry; and, as married men were exempted from them, they occasioned in some degree that mischievous population of beings brought into the world for little else than to be starved. The *corvées*, or police of the roads, were annually the ruin of many hundreds of farmers; more than three hundred were reduced to beggary in filling up one vale in Lorraine: all these oppressions fell on the *tiers état* only, the nobility and clergy having been exempted from *tailles*, militia, and *corvées*."*

These, Mr. Young adds, with the feudal privileges of the nobles, and the venal, partial, and scandalous administration of justice, were the principal grievances

* Vol. i., p. 598.

that threw France into a flame, and produced the greatest and most destructive convulsion of which history has preserved any memorial.

The system of taxation generally established in eastern countries has the defect of not corresponding with the second maxim of Smith. The amount of the taxes is fluctuating and arbitrary—not fixed and certain. In despotic countries, every agent of government is a despot in his own peculiar sphere; and though the sum demanded by the Sultan should be defined and ascertained, there are no limits to the extortion and rapacity of his agents. An individual who has paid the tax imposed by the Sultan has no guarantee against being further called upon to pay three or four times as much to the pacha of the province. The security of property is thus completely subverted; and the arbitrary nature of the public burdens is entirely destructive of that spirit of industry which might have supported itself under a much greater weight of equal and well-defined taxes.

The destructive influence of this system of taxation is strikingly exemplified in the wretched state of the Ottoman dominions. Exclusive of the *miri*, or taxes for the public treasury, and of those called *hazné*, appropriated to the peculiar use of the Grand Seignior, the people are subject to contributions in kind for troops passing from one part of the empire to another, to corvées, or contributions of forced labour, compulsory loans, &c. And in addition to these, which may be regarded as contributions for the service of the state, the pachas and their satellites squeeze out of the inhabitants all that they possibly can, without inquiring or caring whether their demands be legal. Hitherto the only criterion of an approved administrator in Turkey has been the amount of tribute remitted to the public treasury, and the magnitude of his douceurs to those in power. Inquiry is seldom or never made into the means by which this revenue is raised. To rob those below him, that he may bribe those above him, is the constant aim and sole object of each petty tyrant through all the gradations of this baleful despotism. Under its blighting influence palaces have been changed into cottages, cities into villages, and the finest, and of old the most flourishing, countries in the world, are reduced to the most deplorable state of depopulation, poverty, and barbarism.*

We need not, under these circumstances, be surprised to learn that, notwithstanding their prejudices, some of the more intelligent Turks have been long aware of the ruinous consequences of the present system of taxation, and of the advantages that would result from its being reformed, and limits set to the *avanias* or extortions of the pachas. Nothing, however, was done in furtherance of these views till 1839, when a *Hatti Scheriff*, or Imperial Decree, was issued, which, could it be carried into effect, would obviate several of the abuses complained of. But it is idle to suppose that this, or any similar project, can, at present, have any considerable practical influence in Turkey. There is neither public virtue nor knowledge in the country to accomplish any substantial reforms. Nothing short of a miracle would suffice for its regeneration. Corruption and venality are everywhere the order of the day, and our conviction is that the abuses that have so long infected every department of the government, and shed their deadly influence over every part of the empire, will not be sensibly abated till foreign force or domestic violence overthrow the religion and government, of which they are the bitter but legitimate fruits.

The establishment of the *warehousing* system, or the granting of liberty to the merchant, on payment of a

* See ' Geographical Dictionary,' art. Turkey.

moderate rent, to deposit imported goods in public warehouses, whence they may be withdrawn at pleasure for
exportation, and where they may be kept without paying the duties laid on them when entered for consumption
till he finds it convenient to dispose of them for that purpose, has made a large branch of our taxation correspond very closely with the third maxim of Smith, the
customs duties being now levied at the time and in the
manner most convenient for the contributors. Previously
to the act of the 43rd of George III., establishing the
warehousing system, the customs-duties on imported
articles, which amount to a very large proportion of the
public revenue, had either to be paid at the moment when
the goods were imported, or a *bond*, with sufficient security, for their future payment, had to be given to the revenue officers. The hardship and inconvenience growing
out of a practice of this sort are obvious. Sureties were
often difficult to be obtained, and the merchant, in order to
raise funds to pay the duties, was frequently reduced to
the ruinous necessity of selling his goods immediately on
their arrival, when perhaps the market was already
glutted. Neither was this the only inconvenience
entailed on the country by this practice; for, the duties
being payable at once, and not by degrees as the goods
were sold for consumption, their price was raised by the
amount of the profit accruing on the capital advanced in
payment of the duties. Competition, too, was diminished
in consequence of the greater command of funds required
to carry on trade under such disadvantages; and a few
rich individuals were thus, in a great measure, enabled
to monopolize the business of importing commodities
charged with heavy duties. The practice had, besides,
an obvious tendency to discourage the carrying trade of
the country, and to endanger the security of the revenue.
For the necessity of paying import duties even on those
commodities which were destined for re-exportation prevented our merchants from profiting by the peculiar

capabilities of our ports for becoming *entrepôts*, by obstructing the importation of most foreign commodities, except those colonial products of which we had a monopoly, that were not likely to be speedily required for home consumption; at the same time that the difficulties attending the granting of a really equivalent drawback to the exporters of such as had paid the duty opened a door for the commission of every species of fraud.

Sir Robert Walpole appears to have had a clear conception of the injurious consequences of this system; and it was the object of the famous *Excise Scheme*, proposed by him in 1733, to relieve the importers of tobacco and wine from the necessity of paying the duties chargeable on these articles till they sold them for home consumption, by making them be deposited, when imported, in public warehouses, under the joint locks of the king and the merchant. The celebrity of this scheme, and the misconceptions that have been so generally entertained respecting it, incline us to think that we shall gratify our readers by laying before them the following passages from the speech made by Walpole on submitting his plan to the House of Commons.

" The duties now payable upon tobacco, on importation," said Sir Robert, "amount to sixpence and one-third part of a penny per pound weight; all which must be paid down in ready money upon importation, with the allowance of ten per cent. upon prompt payment; or otherwise there must be bonds given, with sufficient sureties, for the payment thereof; which is often a great loss to the public, and is always a great inconvenience to the merchant importer. Whereas, by what I am to propose, the whole duties to be paid for the future will amount to no more than fourpence and three farthings per pound weight; and this duty not to be paid till the tobacco comes to be sold for home consumption. So that, if the merchant exports his tobacco, he will be quite free

from all payment of duty, or giving bond therefor, or
finding out proper sureties for joining in such bond : he
will have nothing to do but unload his tobacco on board
a ship for exportation, without being at the trouble to
attend for having his bonds cancelled, or for taking out
debentures for the drawbacks; all which, I conceive,
must be a great ease to the fair trader; and to every
such trader the preventing of frauds must be a great advantage, because it will put all the tobacco-traders in
Britain upon the same footing; which is but just and
equal, and what ought certainly to be accomplished, if
it be possible.

"Now, in order to make this case effectual to the fair
trader, and to contribute to his advantage by preventing
as much as possible any frauds in time to come, I propose, as I have said, to join the laws of excise to those of
the customs, and to leave the one penny, or rather three
farthings, per pound, called the further subsidy, to be
still charged at the custom-house upon the importation
of any tobacco; which three farthings shall be payable
to his Majesty's civil list, as heretofore. And I propose
that all tobacco, for the future, after being weighed at
the custom-house, and charged with the said three farthings per pound, shall be lodged in the warehouse or
warehouses to be appointed by the commissioners of the
excise for that purpose, of which warehouse the merchant importer shall have one lock and key, and the
warehouse-keeper to be appointed by the said commissioners shall have another, in order that the tobacco may
lie safe in that warehouse till the merchant finds a market
for it, either for exportation or home consumption. And
if his market be for exportation, he may apply to his
warehouse-keeper, and take out as much for that purpose as he has occasion for, which, when weighed at the
custom-house, shall be discharged of the three farthings
per pound with which it was charged upon importation ;
so that the merchant may then export it without any

further trouble. But if it be taken out for home consumption, he shall then pay the three farthings charged
upon it at the custom-house upon importation; and then,
upon calling his warehouse-keeper, he may deliver it to
the buyer, on paying an inland duty of fourpence per
pound weight to the proper officer appointed to receive
the same."

Walpole concluded his speech by saying, " I look upon
this as a most innocent scheme; it can be hurtful to
none but smugglers and unfair traders. I am certain
it will be of great benefit to the revenue, and will tend
to make LONDON A FREE PORT, AND, BY CONSEQUENCE, THE
MARKET OF THE WORLD. If I had thought otherwise of
it, I should never have ventured to propose it in this
place."*

Nothing can be clearer than this statement; and no
doubt can now remain in the mind of any one that the
adoption of the scheme would have been highly advantageous to the commerce and revenue of the country.
But so powerful was the delusion generated with respect
to it, that its proposal nearly caused a rebellion. Most
merchants had availed themselves of the facilities that
the system which Walpole's project was intended to
supersede, afforded for defrauding the revenue; and
they dexterously endeavoured to thwart its success, and
consequently the serious check it would have given to
smuggling, by making the public believe that it would
be fatal to commerce. The efforts of the merchants
were powerfully assisted by the spirit of party, which
then ran very high. The opponents of the ministry,
anxious for an opportunity to prejudice them in the
public estimation, contended that the scheme was only
the first step towards the introduction of such a uni-

---

* Tindal's 'Continuation on Rapin,' viii. p. 154, ed. 1769; Coxe's 'Sir R.
Walpole,' vol. i. p. 372, 4to. ed. Had the resolutions with respect to tobacco
been carried, those regarding wine, which were to have been exactly similar,
would have been proposed.

versal system of excise as would be subversive alike
of the comfort and liberty of the subject! In consequence of these misrepresentations, the most violent
clamours were everywhere excited against the scheme.
On one occasion Walpole narrowly escaped falling a
sacrifice to the fury of the mob, which beset all the
avenues to the House of Commons; and after many
violent and lengthened debates the scheme was abandoned.

The disadvantages of the old plan, and the benefits to
be derived from the establishment of the warehousing
system, were ably set forth by Dean Tucker in his
ingenious ' Essay on the Comparative Advantages
and Disadvantages of Great Britain and France with
respect to Trade,' published in 1750. But so lasting was
the impression made by the opposition to Sir Robert
Walpole's scheme, and such is the force of prejudice,
that it was not until 1803 that this signal improvement—
the greatest, perhaps, that has been made in our financial
and commercial policy—was adopted.

The facility and cheapness with which taxes may be
collected should be particularly attended to in their
selection. Every tax should, as Smith has stated in his
fourth maxim, be contrived so as to take out and keep
out of the pockets of the people as little as possible
above what it puts into the public treasury. The reason
of this maxim is obvious. The nett produce of taxation,
or the sum which it yields after the expenses of collection
are deducted, is all that is applicable to national purposes; and taxes which cost a great deal to collect impose a heavy burden on the people for the sake of a
small advantage to government. It is stated by Sully,
in his Memoirs, that the expense of collecting a nett
revenue of *thirty* millions of livres in France in 1598
cost the enormous sum of 120 millions; or, in other words,
that, of a sum of 150 millions taken from the people

by means of taxation, only *thirty* millions found their way into the coffers of the treasury! Under the administration of Necker, a revenue of about 557 millions of livres was collected at an expense of fifty-eight millions; being about 10⅜ per cent.

The expense of collecting the public revenue of Great Britain, for the year ended the 5th January, 1843, amounted to 6*l*. 7*s*. 8¾*d*. per cent. on the gross produce; while in Ireland its expense for the same year amounted to 12*l*. 16*s*. 3¼*d*. per cent., or to twice as much as in Britain. Most part of this difference is to be ascribed to the different situation of the two countries; but a good deal is also owing to the more defective system of taxation established in Ireland. Formerly, however, the cost of collecting the revenue in Ireland was proportionally much greater than at present; the adoption of the plans and suggestions of the commissioners appointed to inquire into the state of Irish revenue having been productive of a material saving in this department.

Taxes may be collected by officers employed by government for that purpose; or government may let them *in farm* for a rent certain, giving the lessees or their servants power to collect them. The answer to the question, which of these modes of collection should be adopted, depends on a variety of circumstances, and, consequently, differs in different cases. Well defined taxes, which may be collected without any inquiry into the private concerns of individuals, may generally, perhaps, be farmed with advantage. In such cases the proceedings of the farmers could not well excite the prejudices of the contributors; and the greater vigilance and economy with which businesses are usually conducted by individuals would most likely enable the farmers to pay, exclusive of their profits, a larger sum to government on account of the tax than it would have much chance of receiving from its own agents. But taxes which are not well defined, or which require an examination into the affairs of individuals for their fair assessment, should be, in all cases, collected by the servants of government. It is probable, indeed, that such taxes might be more productive were they farmed; but this, though an important consideration, is not the only one to be attended to. Taxes which expose private affairs to investigation are always unpopular; and it is obvious that this unpopularity will be immeasurably greater when the investigations are conducted by those who have a personal interest in prosecuting them with the greatest strictness, than when they are conducted by the agents of government, who, in most cases, derive none, and in all cases only a very slender benefit from the increased productiveness of the tax. The mass of the people would assuredly ascribe much of the hardship of such taxes to the vigilance and keenness of the farmers; and would be disposed to believe that a considerable portion of their produce went into their pockets, and that they were not only assessed to defray the charges of the state, but to add to the fortunes of a class who are universally objects of popular indignation. We admit that these suspicions and complaints are in most cases destitute of foundation. The farmers can only enforce payment of a tax according to the provisions in the law imposing it; and if its pressure be either unequal or severe, or the mode of its collection vexatious or troublesome, the fault lies with those who imposed it, and not with the farmers. But, however groundless, the prejudice against the latter will always exist, and should be respected. Perhaps we overrate its influence; but we have very little doubt that, were an income-tax of two per cent., let in farm, established instead of the present income-tax of about three per cent., it would be generally considered as the more oppressive and vexatious of the two. Although, therefore, we are not disposed to concur with Smith in his opinion that *all* taxes should be collected by the officers of government,* still less can we concur with Bentham, who has endeavoured to prove that farming is in every case the preferable mode of collection.† Taxes on stamped paper, houses, windows, horses, carriages, and perhaps also the customs-duties, might be advantageously collected by letting them to farmers; but any attempt to farm taxes on income, excise-duties, or taxes which require an examination of and interference with private affairs, would excite the most violent clamour and irritation, and could not be otherwise than pernicious.

Taxes in most civilized countries have, for a lengthened period, consisted principally of portions of the property of individuals, the amount to be paid being usually fixed or rated in money. Labour taxes, or contributions of personal services for the execution of public works, were, however, at a former period, extremely common in this and other countries, and are still far from being entirely relinquished. But it may be safely affirmed that compulsory contributions of labour are among the very worst species of taxes; being of little advantage to the public compared with the injury they inflict on the contributors. Those who are made to work without pay, and against their inclination, uniformly waste their time and energies; and a heavy loss is frequently also incurred by the interruption of the regular pursuits of the labourers, who may be called away with their teams to assist at public works, at the very period their exertions are most necessary at home. When Turgot entered on his administration, he sent a circular letter to the road surveyors and engineers of the different provinces of France, directing them to transmit estimates, framed on the most liberal

* Wealth of Nations, p. 409.
† 'Théorie des Peines et des Récompenses,' tome ii., p. 203.

D

scale, of the sums of money for which the usual repairs
might be made on the old roads, and the ordinary number of new ones constructed. The average of the different
estimates showed that a money contribution of about 10
millions of livres a-year would suffice for the repair and
construction of the different roads; whereas Turgot
showed that the execution of these repairs and construc-
tions by contributions of forced labour, or *corvées,* cost not
less than 40 millions, or four times as much as the other!*

The practice of making and repairing roads by compulsory contributions of labour was at one time general
throughout Europe; the principle being embodied in the
Roman law, whence it was introduced into the common
law of this and most modern states.   Indeed the obligation to assist in the repair of the roads formed a part
of the *trinoda necessitas,* from which no individual was
exempted, whatever other immunities he might enjoy.†
In 1555 the statute 2 and 3 Philip and Mary, cap. 8,
enacted that two surveyors of roads should be annually
chosen in every parish, and that the inhabitants should
be obliged, according to their respective abilities, to
furnish labourers, carriages, tools, &c., for four (afterwards increased to six) days, to work at the roads in the
parish under the orders of the surveyors. But though
the system established by this act, from its making the
surveyors responsible in some measure for the state of
the roads, was certainly at the time a great improvement,
it was, notwithstanding, for the reasons already stated, in
many respects most objectionable ; and we are assured, by
an unexceptionable judge, that " the six days' duty on the
highways is done so miserably, and so much time is necessarily lost by going to a distance, that nobody can doubt
but any new road or considerable work might be made
by a private man, or an appointed surveyor, with teams

* Say, ' Economie Politique,' ii. 345.
    † The *trinoda necessitas* embraced *expeditio contra hostem, arcium constructio,
et pontium (vel itinerum) reparatio.—Blackstone,* book i., c. 9.

for the purpose, for *a tenth* part of the sum which it would cost if performed by parish-work." * But despite this experience, the construction, repair, and police of the cross or parish roads continued, down to a comparatively late period, to be principally regulated by the statute of Philip and Mary.

The great increase of wealth and population in the latter part of the 16th and during the 17th century compelled in the end recourse to be had to a different system for the construction and repair of the principal roads, especially those in the vicinity of London. It was introduced by the statute 26th Charles II. cap. 1, which imposed tolls, or duties collected at toll gates, (called turnpikes,) on all travellers along the great north road; the management of the road being at the same time vested in trustees authorized to expend the revenue derived from the tolls on its improvement. But, how singular soever it may now appear, this plan was for a lengthened period exceedingly unpopular; and it was not till after the peace of Paris, in 1763, that turnpike-roads began to be extended to all parts of the kingdom; and that the means of internal communication began, in consequence, to be signally improved. The turnpike-roads of England and Wales extend at present to a length of about 24,000 miles.

Turnpikes being erected only on the principal roads, the old plan for keeping up cross or parish roads was not affected by their institution. The individuals subject to the assessment for compulsory labour on the latter were however at a distant period authorized to compound, if they thought fit, with the surveyors, according to certain fixed rates; though in consequence of the difficulties in the way of such compositions, and the ignorance of the parties, the value of the contributions of labour in kind amounted, according to the official returns, previously to the introduction of the existing

* Young's ' Political Arithmetic,' part i., p. 192.

system in 1835, to from 500,000*l*. to 600,000*l*. a-year! But the act passed in the last-mentioned year has entirely superseded the old system, and, instead of contributions of labour, the surveyors are now authorized to impose a rate, on the basis of the poor-rate, for the construction and repair of cross and parish roads.

The system followed in Scotland with respect to the roads was very similar to that of England. An act passed in 1669 compelled the agricultural population of the country to work six days in each year on the public roads. This contribution was commuted in the early part of the reign of George III., for a tax on land, rated according to its valuation in the cess-books. This commutation has been of the greatest advantage. Previously to its taking place, the roads in Scotland were, perhaps, the very worst, and they have since become among the very best, in Europe.

Contributions of compulsory labour or personal service are, however, enforced for other objects, that have attracted less notice (at least from economists) than *corvées*, though, from the magnitude to which they have latterly attained, they are now in many countries of the highest importance, and deserve the most attentive consideration. We allude to the obligation imposed in most states on all individuals, or on those belonging to certain classes, to serve for some fixed period, in the event of their being called upon, in the army or navy or both. This system, which had been partially acted upon for a lengthened period, has been vastly extended since the introduction of the conscription into France; and the armies of that kingdom, with those of Prussia, Austria, Russia, and other continental states, are now recruited by draughts of recruits taken by lot from certain classes of the population. Napoleon said, in reference to the conscription, that it was "*le mode de recrutement le plus juste, le plus doux, le plus*

avantageux au peuple;" and authorities have not
been wanting who have recommended its introduction
into this country, or at least an extension to the army of
the principle on which the militia is recruited.   But the
plan of recruiting by voluntary enlistment is, notwithstanding the deference due to those who maintain the
contrary, the only one consistent with justice, or with any
regard to the rights of individuals, at the same time that
it is in other respects decidedly the best.   We do not
mean to deny that the conscription, provided it be really
equal and impartial, has some advantages on its side;
but they are certainly very much overbalanced by the
oppression and other disadvantages inseparable from it.
Among the individuals subject to a conscription, there
is the greatest discrepancy of tastes and tempers, some
preferring the military profession to every one else,
while others hold it in abhorrence. The system of voluntary enlistment avails itself of these differences : far from
offering violence to any one, it gratifies all, by enabling
those who prefer a military life, and those who prefer
other pursuits, to indulge their tastes without let or hin-
drance.   The conscription, on the other hand, introduces
a species of fatalism, where there should be choice and
discrimination; the chances being equal that the lots
will fall upon individuals most disinclined to enter the
army.   Who would think of forcing people to become
miners, shoemakers, or weavers? and why should the
state attempt to enforce a system productive of still
greater hardship and injustice ? If soldiers could not be
procured otherwise, we should readily admit that necessity formed a valid excuse for the introduction of the
conscription : but such is very far indeed from being
the case; men in abundance may always be found, without any compulsory process, and with very moderate encouragement, ready to undertake any employment how
disagreeable or hazardous soever.   The free and adventurous life of a soldier has, however, many powerful at-

tractions. Even during war, the dangers and privations of campaigns are underrated, and the chances of advancement proportionally exaggerated, in the heated imaginations of the young and the inconsiderate; and unless their pay and other advantages be very decidedly below what the state of society requires, a moderately populous country may always obtain any number of troops by voluntary enlistment.

It is plain, therefore, that the conscription is an unnecessary, as well as a most oppressive burden. Whenever it is resorted to, the population is necessarily exposed to a twofold grievance—that of being liable to be compelled to engage in a service to which they may entertain an unconquerable aversion, and of being underpaid when so engaged.

In addition to its oppressiveness, a conscription is almost always unequal in its operation, pressing with its utmost severity on certain classes of the population, and exempting others. If all ranks and orders were equally subject to its influence, the imputation of partiality would, of course, fall to the ground. This, however, is but seldom the case. The upper classes, in most countries, are exempted from the conscription, and the custom of admitting substitutes is also very prevalent. But wherever an individual chosen by lot to serve as a conscript may send a substitute in his stead, the conscription obviously degenerates into the worst sort of capitation-tax, entailing a mere pecuniary contribution on the wealthier part of the community, instead of one which the lower ranks must pay with their personal service, and probably their blood.

It is not easy to find words sufficient to depict the hardship and injustice of such a system; and yet we regret to have to say that this was the mode in which the militia in this country was recruited during the late war; so that we have a more intimate acquaintance with the principles and practice of the conscription than is generally supposed. It is, however, to be hoped, that no government may ever again attempt to renew the suffering inflicted by the militia-laws on the lower classes during the period now referred to; and it is perhaps doubtful, supposing such an attempt were made, whether it would be patiently submitted to. A conscription is tolerable only when none escape its pressure —when the destiny of rich and poor, high and low, is alike subject to the event of the ballot, *omnium versatur urna:* to attempt to throw it on the poor by exempting the higher classes, or by allowing them to serve through substitutes, is subversive of every principle on which public burdens should be imposed, and of every natural and constitutional right.

The practice of compulsory service has not, however, been confined to the army and militia; in this country, at least, it has been carried to a still greater extent in the case of the navy. It appears to have been, for a lengthened period, taken for granted that the practice of impressment is indispensable, especially at the breaking out of a war, for the manning of the fleet. But it has been shown that such is not the case, and that sailors, like soldiers, may be obtained in sufficient numbers, under a proper system, by voluntary enlistment.* It is needless to dwell on the violence and injustice inseparable from the practice of impressment; but it may, perhaps, be worth while to observe that their liability to this oppressive treatment, by obstructing the entry of young men to the sea-service, and lessening the supply of sailors, tends, especially during war, to raise their wages far above their natural level, to the extreme injury of the king's and of the merchant service. "The custom of impressment," says Sir Matthew Decker, "puts a free-born British sailor on the same footing as a Turkish slave. The Grand Seignior cannot

---

* See note on Impressment in the edition of the ' Wealth of Nations' by the author of this work.

do a more absolute act than to order a man to be dragged away from his family, and, against his will, run his head against the mouth of a cannon. And if such acts should be frequent in Turkey upon any one set of useful men, would it not drive them away to other countries, and thin their numbers yearly? And would not the remaining few double or treble their wages?— which is the case with our sailors in time of war, to the great detriment of our commerce."*

In corroboration of what has now been stated, it may be mentioned that, while the wages of other sorts of labourers and artisans are uniformly higher in the United States than in England, those of sailors are most commonly lower. The reason is, that the navy of the United States is manned by means of voluntary enlist-ment. The Americans are desirous of becoming a great naval power, and they have wisely relinquished a practice which would have driven their best sailors from their service, and have forced them to man their fleet with the sweepings of their gaols.

It has been estimated that there were above 16,000 British sailors on board American ships at the close of last war; and the wages of our seamen, which in time of peace rarely exceed 40s. or 50s. a-month, had then risen to 100s. and 120s.! This extraordinary influx of British seamen into the American service, and no less extraor-dinary rise in their wages at home, can be accounted for only by our continuing the practice of impressment after its abandonment by the United States. Formerly, our seamen were in the habit, on the breaking out of a war, of deserting to Holland; but the difference of language was an insuperable obstacle to this being done to any very considerable extent. In the United States, how-ever, our sailors may always expect to find a safe asylum among those whose language, customs, and habits are identical with their own, and who will anxiously hold out

* Essay on the Causes of the Decline of Foreign Trade, ed. 1756, p. 24.

every temptation to draw them to their service. Nothing less than the abolition of impressment can countervail such inducements to desertion, and effectually reduce the wages of our seamen. And, as impressment is nowise necessary to the manning of the fleet, it is to be hoped that it may speedily be abolished, and that the efforts of the Americans to increase their naval power may not be assisted by our obstinately clinging to a system fraught with injustice and oppression.

PART I.

DIRECT TAXES.

IT is impossible, for the reasons noticed in the previous pages, to regard such taxes as really fall on capital as permanent sources of public income. Capital consists of produce saved from immediate consumption, and employed partly to maintain those who are engaged in the great work of production, and partly to facilitate their labour. Its amount determines the amount of productive industry: and, such being the case, it is plain that whatever has a tendency to diminish capital, or to convert it into revenue, must, by diminishing the means of employing and facilitating labour, and consequently the annual produce of the country, be a fruitful source of pauperism. This, however, would be the precise effect of taxes on capital; and it is for this reason that they should always be regarded in the light of extraordinary resources, and should never be imposed except in cases of necessity. The misapplication and destruction of the means of production which they infallibly occasion would not only defeat every attempt to render them permanent, but would, by impoverishing and exhausting the country, render all other taxes comparatively unproductive. "*Nulle richesse nécessaire aux travaux de la reproduction n'en peut être détournée sans nuire à cette reproduction, à la richesse nationale, et, par suite, aux moyens de puissance du gouvernement.*" *

It is not from capital, therefore, but from revenue, that all permanent taxes should be derived. And as all revenue, except that enjoyed by individuals supported

* Œuvres de M. Turgot, iv., 345.

by taxation, must be drawn from rents, profits, or wages, or from two, or all of these sources, it follows that all taxes which do not fall on capital must, however imposed, ultimately fall on one or more of those species of income. Without further preface, therefore, we shall proceed to trace the incidence and effect of taxes on rent, on profit, and on wages. When we have ascertained the way in which they operate, it will be comparatively easy to investigate the influence of a tax meant to fall equally on all the varieties of income.

CHAPTER I.

TAXES ON RENT.

SECTION I.—TAXES ON THE RENT OF LAND.

Dr. Smith held that taxes on the rent of land, taking the term in its popular and broadest sense, fell wholly on the landlords. No doubt, however, this is an error.

The sum which the occupier of an improved farm pays to the landlord is uniformly derived from two distinct sources, and is consequently divisible into two portions, whereof one is a compensation for the use of the natural and inherent powers of the soil; and the other a compensation or return for the use of the buildings, roads, drains, fences, and other improvements made on the farm. Rent, properly so called, consists of the first only of these portions; the second, though usually included under the term, being obviously the return to, or profit derived from, the capital expended upon the land. There are but few instances in old settled and densely peopled countries in which the rent even of inferior farms is not derived from both these sources; though, from the various ways in which a large class of

improvements are mixed up and blended with the soil,
it is rarely possible for the most experienced agricul-
turist to separate his rent into its proper elements, or
to discriminate, with much precision, between the sum
he pays to the landlord as proprietor of the soil, and
that which he pays him as profit on the capital laid out
on its improvement.

If, however, this distinction were either made or
approximated to with anything like accuracy, government might appropriate, by a special tax, all that portion of the gross rent of the land which consists of the
sums paid for the use of its natural and inherent powers,
without its being in the power of the landlords to elude
the payment of such tax, or to throw any portion of
it on any one else.   This is a consequence of this portion of the rent of land being extrinsic to the cost of
production.   Rent, in the limited sense in which we are
now considering it, originates in the varying fertility of the
soils successively brought under cultivation.   The most
fertile lands in a country, or those that are first brought
into tillage, may be supposed to yield, with a given
outlay of capital and labour, 100 quarters of corn, while
lands of a secondary quality only yield, with the same
outlay, 90 quarters, lands of the third quality 80 quarters, and so on.   It is not necessary, for the elucidation
of this subject, that we should enter into any lengthened
examination of the various questions involved in the
theory of rent.   It is enough to state that it has been
demonstrated over and over again, that the produce raised
on the last or poorest quality of land under tillage is,
speaking generally, uniformly sold at its necessary price,
or at the sum which affords the cultivators the common
and average rate of profit, without including any payment on account of rent.   And supposing that the fourth
or lowest quality of land in cultivation yields 70 quarters, then as the same outlay which produces 70 quarters
on it produces 100 quarters on lands of the first quality,

90 on those of the second quality, and 80 on those of the
third quality, it is obvious that, to place all the cultivators in the same condition, those occupying the best
lands will have to pay their proprietors a corn-rent of
30 quarters (100 — 70), or a corresponding money-rent;
while those occupying the secondary lands will have to
pay 20 quarters (90 — 70); those occupying the third, 10
quarters (80 — 70): and so on, according as cultivation is
extended.

If improvements had been effected on all or any of
these lands previously to their being let, then, of course,
they would have brought an additional rent, which
would have been the interest or profit of the capital
laid out on the improvements. But, to simplify the
question, it is best to keep such considerations for the
moment out of view, and to fix our attention in the
first instance only on the rent paid the landlords for
the use of the natural powers of the soil. Inasmuch,
however, as this rent originates in, and depends wholly
upon, the principles now briefly stated, it is easy to see
that it might be entirely swept off by a tax, without
prejudice to the interests of any class except the landlords. Such tax could not raise the price of corn or other
raw produce; for nothing can affect its price unless it
either affects the cost of its production or its supply.
But a tax on the real rent of land does neither : it cannot, it is evident, have any influence over the cost of
production, for real rent is extrinsic to and independent
on that cost, and consists of the surplus produce remaining after the profit on improvements has been deducted, and the cultivators have been fully indemnified for the expense of cultivation, and have obtained
the common and ordinary rate of profit on their capital;
and though it would vary the distribution of corn, it is
obvious that a tax which has no influence over its production could not affect its supply. The true conclusion consequently is, that the prices of all sorts of farm

produce would continue unaffected, though a tax were imposed absorbing all the real rent of land, meaning by *real* rent the sum paid for the soil only.

It would not, however, be possible for government, supposing it made the attempt, to appropriate, by means of direct taxes, the entire *gross* rent of the land, or the total sum paid, as well for buildings and improvements, as for the soil itself. In whatever degree the rent paid for land may consist of interest of capital laid out upon it, in that degree would a tax on it raise the price of raw produce, and fall ultimately on the consumer. That portion of the gross rent of the landlords which consists of payments for the use of the natural and inherent powers of the soil, originates in the circumstance of land being appropriated and made private property; but it is otherwise with the portion of the gross rent paid for houses, fences, drains, roads, and other improvements. This, it is evident, is a consequence of the landlords being not merely owners of the land, but also of the capital employed upon it, and contributing essentially to its productiveness; and it is easy to see that a tax affecting the profits of such capital will necessarily affect the cost of its produce. Suppose, for example, that the gross rent of a farm is 500*l*. a-year, a half, or 250*l*., thereof, being, in fact, the interest of capital laid out on its improvement. If, in such a case, a tax of 10 per cent. were laid on rent, only a half, or 25*l*., of this tax would be permanently paid by the landlord. In the first instance, no doubt, the whole 50*l*. might fall upon him; but 25*l*. of this payment would, it is plain, be a deduction from the profits of the capital belonging to the landlord, and not from rent properly so called. And the landlords being consequently placed in a comparatively unfavourable situation, no more capital would be expended upon the soil until the price of corn, and other raw produce, was raised by the gradual diminution of its quantity, or the increase of demand, so as to place them in the same situation as other producers; that is, until they obtained the common and ordinary rate of profit from the capital expended on improvements.

It appears, therefore, that, though it may be supposed possible to draw into the coffers of the treasury, by an exclusive tax, that portion of the rent of land which is paid for the use of the soil only, the other portion, which is paid for the improvements made on it, would not be permanently affected by an exclusive tax; and could, speaking generally, only be taxed to the same extent that the profits of capital employed in other departments are taxed.

In a practical point of view, taxes on the rent of land are extremely objectionable. It is, as already stated, quite impossible to separate rent into its elements, or to say how much is paid for the soil and how much for improvements. No two agriculturists ever arrive, in any given case of this kind, unless by accident, at the same conclusion; and the best judges affirm that, generally speaking, the distinction is impracticable. When, therefore, a tax is laid on rent, it is necessarily proportioned to its gross amount, or to the total sum paid to the landlords, without regard to the sources whence it is derived. Inasmuch, too, as it is for the interest of all parties to conceal its amount, it is no easy matter to ascertain even this gross rental. But without laying any stress on this circumstance, a tax on rent is one of the least expedient that can be suggested. It has always been, and will unavoidably continue to be, a formidable barrier to agricultural improvements; for, the return paid to a landlord for capital expended on the soil being included in rent, a tax on it discourages, or, it may be, wholly prevents, fresh outlays of capital on the land, and consequently depresses the most important branch of national industry. Instead of being carried from other employments to agriculture, capital is then carried from agriculture to them. Landlords and occupiers no longer wish to have their farms look well, but to have them look ill; and it may be said of farms as of individuals—

Pauper videri vult Cinna, et est pauper.

A tax of this sort discourages those virtues and that expenditure on the land which all wise governments endeavour to promote. We doubt, indeed, whether it be possible to suggest any impost more at variance with sound principle, or more adverse to the progress of improvement.

But supposing that the distinction previously alluded to could be made, or that rent could be readily discriminated into its elements, and the sum paid for the use of the soil separated from that paid for the use of the capital expended upon it, the imposition of a peculiar tax on the first-mentioned portion would appear to be most unjust. If direct contributions for the public service be resorted to, they should, in as far as possible, be universal and proportioned to the means of all classes of contributors; and government should never swerve from this fundamental principle by yielding to exaggerated and fallacious estimates of the advantages to be derived from laying taxes on certain classes of individuals, or descriptions of income. All sorts of property that have been lawfully acquired should be considered as equally sacred and equally entitled to protection. It is no doubt true, as has been stated by Mr. Ogilvie and others, that landlords, as such, are not producers, but merely receivers of income which would otherwise belong to the state. But a right of property in land has everywhere been coeval with the establishment of civilized societies; and to attempt to invade it, whether by depriving landlords of any of the advantages fairly

resulting from its possession, or by making them contribute more than their fair share to the exigencies of the
state, would be barefaced oppression and robbery. "Rent,"
to use the words of Mr. Ricardo, "often belongs to
those who, after many years of toil, have realized their
gains, and expended their fortunes in the purchase of
land or houses; and it certainly would be an infringe-
ment of that security of property which should ever be
held sacred, to subject it to unequal taxation." * We
may, indeed, be assured that, in taxation, as in everything else, justice is the only safe policy, the permanent
interest of all men and all communities. *Nihil est quod
adhuc de republicâ putem dictum, et quo possim longius
progredi, nisi sit confirmatum, non modo falsum esse illud,
sine injuriâ non posse, sed hoc verissimum, sine summâ
justitiâ rempublicam regi non posse.* †

As rent must unavoidably arise in the progress of
society, it has been suggested, by those who would, perhaps, object to any attempt to throw any peculiar burden
on the landlords in old settled countries, that it would be
good policy for the governments of countries like the
United States, which have large tracts of fertile and
unappropriated land, to retain the property of such land,
and to let it by public auction, in such portions and for
such number of years as might be deemed advisable.
This, however, would be a very questionable course of
policy. It would certainly hinder many of those expensive improvements in drainage and planting, and in the
construction of houses, roads, bridges, &c., necessary to
the comfort of the inhabitants, and to the full development of the productive powers of the soil, effected by in
dividuals who have the absolute property of the land,
and are able to bequeath it to others. These consequences might, it is true, be in part, though they never

* Principles of Political Economy, 3rd ed., p. 230.
† Cicero, ' Frag. de Repub.,' lib. ii.

E

can be fully, obviated by increasing the length of leases, so as to encourage the outlay of capital. But, in whatever way it may be let, there can be no manner of doubt that a right of private property in land is the best stimulus to its improvement. Those to whom it belongs, will be more disposed than any one else to avail themselves of every suggestion that may be likely to increase its value; and even those landlords who are most care-less in this respect endeavour, by enforcing rules as to management, to keep their farms in good condition, especially towards the termination of a lease. This last is a matter of infinitely more importance than is generally supposed, and much of the prosperity of agriculture depends at all times on the attention which it receives. But if the lands of an extensive country belonged to government, the presumption is that the tenants would act on the principle, if we may so call it, that

> He that havocs may sit;
> He that improves must flit! —

and, however inattentive in other respects, would take care that, previously to the termination of their leases, their farms should be in such a state that there would be little chance of their being removed or their rents raised. It may be supposed, perhaps, that these inconveniences might be obviated by employing inspectors to enforce conditions as to management. But in an extensive country this would be next to impracticable, without incurring an enormous expense; and though this were not the case, the jobbing and favouritism to which it would inevitably give rise would, in no long time, make the inspection be regarded by everybody as an unmixed nuisance. It is idle, therefore, to think that a right of private property in land can ever be advantageously dispensed with. Its establishment is, in fact, the grand source of civilization. It inspires us with the love of country and of posterity; and by asso-

ciating the destiny of the landlords with what is im-
perishable and susceptible of indefinite improvement,
teaches them to look forward to a remote futurity, and
to form projects, and engage in undertakings in which
tenants for an ordinary term of years would never dream
of embarking. The plans of the latter are circumscribed
by the duration of their leases. They are merely, as it
were, possessors of a *rente viagère;* their only object being
to make the most of the land during the term for which
they are to hold it, without thinking or caring about the
state in which they may leave it. The proprietor, on
the contrary, combines, in his plans, the future with
the present; and is anxious as well for the continued
amelioration, as for the immediate productiveness of
his estate. The importance of a right of property in
land is, indeed, so very obvious, that it has been recog-
nized from the earliest periods. The author of the book
of Job places those who removed their neighbours' landmarks at the head of his list of wicked men; while other
ancient writers ascribe the origin of laws and government
to the partition of the land. *Ex agrorum divisione inventa
sunt jura;** and we may be assured that the amount of
wealth, conveniences, and enjoyments in a country with
a right of property in land, will always incomparably
exceed their amount where no such right is established.

It has, however, been alleged that if landlords should,
under an equal system of taxation, pay 10 per cent. of
their incomes, it must, after all, be immaterial whether
it be taken from them by a tax on rent or by any
other means, the grand point being to make sure that
they pay this much, neither more nor less But although it be immaterial to the revenue how the sum
is raised, the previous statements show that it is very
far from being immaterial to the landlords or to the
public. In taxation the direct is not always, nor even

* Macrob., Saturnal., lib. iii. c. 12.

most frequently, the best road. Taxes should in all
cases be imposed so as to interfere as little as possible with the progress of industry. But in this respect taxes on rent are peculiarly objectionable. Where
they do not exist, a landlord who has a farm worth 50*l.*
or 100*l.* a-year may, by laying out capital on its improvement, which produces merely the ordinary rate of
profit, make it worth 200*l.* or 300*l.* a-year; but the
chances are twenty to one that he will not so much as
think of anything of the kind, if he be compelled to share
his increased rent, or the increased produce of the land,
with a tax-gatherer. Taxes, whether on the one or the
other, unavoidably retard, and, indeed, frequently arrest the progress of agricultural improvement. They
are, therefore, even when least oppressive, most inexpedient; and when carried to any considerable extent,
they go far to dry up what is the most prolific source
of national wealth. But if the sum that the landlords
should pay be drawn from them by means of taxes on
expenditure and luxurious gratifications, little if any
harm is done to industry, and their interests, as well as
those of the public, are equally promoted.

It is the greatest imaginable error to suppose that
the only thing to be attended to in taxation is the
realizing of a certain amount of revenue. This, no
doubt, is the problem to be effected, but as much depends on the mode in which it is brought about as
on the thing itself. In taxation, as in surgery, a necessary and even simple operation may, if performed
unskilfully, be fatal. The skill of the financier is exhibited in carefully weighing the consequences of different plans; and in endeavouring to assess and collect
the necessary sums, not by what may appear to be the
most direct methods, but by such methods, whether
direct or indirect, as may occasion the least inconvenience to the contributors and the least harm to
industry.

It is unnecessary, after what has been already stated, to take up the reader's time by entering into any lengthened discussions respecting the theory of Quesnay and the Economists, who contended that all taxes, however imposed, fell ultimately on the land; and who, consistently with this opinion, recommended that all existing taxes should be repealed, and replaced by a single tax (*l'Impôt Unique*), laid directly on the net produce or rent of the land! Quesnay and his followers appear to have been led to this extraordinary conclusion by supposing that the earth, because it furnishes the matter of which all articles are made, is the only source of wealth. But until labour has been employed to appropriate matter, and to fashion and prepare it for our use, it is destitute alike of utility and value, and is not and never has been considered as forming wealth. Notwithstanding their extreme variety, all the operations of industry have for their end and object the giving of utility to matter spontaneously furnished by nature; and it has been repeatedly shown, that the labour employed in manufactures and commerce is in all respects as creative of utility, and consequently of wealth, as the labour employed in agriculture. It is not, therefore, land, but *labour*, that is the real source of wealth and value : and there neither is nor can be any reason why corn, cattle, or other farm products, should be taxed in a greater or less degree than other goods manufactured at home or imported from abroad.

It may be further observed, in explanation of the economical theory, that Quesnay, and even Adam Smith, regarded the rent of land as a peculiar product, originating in and depending upon the special bounty of nature to the agriculturists. But in this they were entirely wrong. Nature is unpolluted by any taint of favouritism, and is equally bountiful to her children, whether they cultivate the land, fashion its products into articles of use or ornament, or convey them from where they are abundant to where they are scarce : she works for us at all times and in all places. It is true that without her helping hand the labours of the husbandman would avail nothing : she unfolds the germ, feeds and ripens the growing plant, and brings it to maturity. But what could the manufacturer or artisan do, did not nature supply him with the products of the forest, the field, and the mine, whereon to exert his industry ? and did she not lend him her streams, the agency of fire, the elasticity of steam, and the great law of attraction, to put his machinery into motion, to give efficiency to his labour, and all but omnipotent strength to his feeble arm ? Without the polarity of the magnet, the action of the winds, and the buoyancy of the seas and rivers, how could the ships and goods of the merchant be conveyed to the remotest corners of the world ? Nothing, indeed, can be more completely erroneous than the allegation that "nature does nothing for man in manufactures." * Her creative agency is indispensable in every department of industry, and is felt alike in all ; and, however ingenious, any theory that assumes the contrary must be entirely fallacious and unfounded. Probably, however, it was hardly necessary to say so much in elucidation of what is so very clear. It is sufficient to state that rent, in so far as it does not consist of the interest or profit of capital laid out on the land, is a mere consequence of one piece of land being more fertile or better situated than another ; and that it depends in no degree on the superior productiveness of agricultural industry.

It is singular that the practical absurdity of their proposal for the consolidation of all taxes into a single tax on rent did not lead the Economists to suspect the principles whence they deduced their conclusions. At this moment the gross rental of the landed property of England and Wales may be estimated at about

* Wealth of Nations, p. 161.

33,000,000*l.*, and that of Scotland and Ireland at about
16,000,000*l.* or 17,000,000*l.*, making together 49,000,000*l.*
or 50,000,000*l.* But the ordinary expenditure of the
country, including poor-rates, tithes, and such like burdens, certainly exceeds 68,000,000*l.* a-year; so that
unless a method should be found of taking a greater
from a less, the *Impôt Unique* is here, at least, an impos
sibility! After the whole landed property of the kingdom had been confiscated, it would be necessary to raise
several millions a-year by additional taxes.

We have, however, already seen that, supposing
an attempt had been anywhere made to give effect
to the project of the Economists, it would necessarily
have failed from the impracticability of laying a special
tax on that portion of the rent of land which consists of
the interest of the capital expended on buildings and
improvements. We are wholly unable, as formerly stated,
to discriminate between the portion of rent now referred to, and that which is paid for the use of the
natural and inherent powers of the soil. But there
can be no reasonable doubt that in all improved
countries the former portion far exceeds the latter.
Those who reflect for a moment on the many hundreds,
or rather thousands, of millions that have been expended in fencing, draining, manuring, and otherwise
improving the land of Great Britain, and in the erection
of farm buildings, must be satisfied that the return for
this capital, though miserably inadequate, very greatly
exceeds the other portion of the gross rental of the
kingdom. It is a vulgar error to suppose that the
income of the landlords depends merely on the circumstance of land being appropriated and of varying degrees
of fertility. In all populous and improved countries it
arises in a far greater degree from their being capitalists
as well as owners of the soil, or from their letting means
and instruments for the profitable cultivation of the land,
along with the land itself. The real or ground rent of a

highly improved farm, especially if it be of rather inferior land, does not, perhaps, bear so great a proportion
to its total rent as the ground-rent of a cotton-factory
bears to the total sum for which it would let.

The former celebrity of the doctrines of the Economists, and the references which are still frequently made
to them, will perhaps be deemed a sufficient apology for
these remarks. They were hardly, indeed, necessary to
enable any one who may have paid any attention to what
had been previously advanced to detect the fallacy of
the principles on which the Economists constructed their
system, and the contradictory nature of their conclusions.
Still, however, the observations now made may have
their use, if, as we hope may be the case, they should
tend still better to illustrate the inexpediency of taxes
on rent.

But notwithstanding the many inconveniences that attach to such taxes, they are necessarily, in countries in
a low state of civilization, and where manufactures and
commerce have made little progress, nearly the only
sources of revenue. In most Eastern countries the government is, as it were, head landlord; the tax paid by
the occupiers being in general equivalent to a pretty
high rent. But in European countries the proprietors
have luckily been able to oppose a more effectual resistance to the encroachments of their rulers; and even
in those parts of Europe in which the land-tax is heaviest,
it seldom amounts to more than a reasonable per centage
on the rent. During the feudal system the obligations
of military service, with the different payments to the
sovereign, under the heads of aids, reliefs, fines on alienation, purveyance, wardship, primer-seisin, scutages,
hydages, escheats, and so forth, due by the proprietors
of estates held directly of the crown (who in their turn
exacted similar payments from their sub-tenants), fell
wholly on the land, and were, in effect, so many land

taxes. These revenues, added to the rental of the crown estates, were, for a considerable period, adequate to defray the expenses of government. But after the advantage of maintaining a regular military force began to be appreciated, money payments began also to be substituted for knights' service; and, when once introduced, were gradually extended, and in the course of time were made to affect personal as well as real property. During the Commonwealth several of the incidents belonging to the feudal system were dispensed with; and the money required for the service of the state was principally raised by subsidies, or assessments of so much a-month on real and personal property, and partly by excise-duties (imposed, for the first time, by the Long Parliament), and other subordinate sources. The right of the crown to the various items of feudal revenue was revived at the Restoration; but their oppressive operation, and the advantages that had resulted from their partial suspension, were so sensibly felt, that measures were immediately taken for their total abolition. This was effected by the Act 12 Chas. II. cap. 24, which suppressed the court of wards and liveries, with wardship, aids, fines on alienation, and other feudal incidents, converting all tenures held of the king into free and common soccage. Blackstone says this statute was a greater acquisition to the property of the kingdom than even Magna Charta itself; inasmuch as the latter only pruned the luxuriances which had grown out of military tenures, whereas this statute extirpated them root and branch.*

But, however advantageous to the nation, it is at the same time obvious that this statute was more especially advantageous to the landlords. The taxes, and grievances which it abolished, directly affected them only; and such being the case, it is plain, as the crown could not afford

* Commentaries, book ii., cap. 5.

to lose the feudal revenues, that compensation should
have been made for their loss, and that of the services
abolished by the statute, by a corresponding land-tax.
An arrangement of this sort, which had been suggested
during the reign of James I., would have been of signal
advantage to the landlords, by substituting a fixed and
equal for a fluctuating and unequal burden; and while it
benefited them, it would not have been injurious to any
one else.   But instead of being commuted in the way
now stated, it was decided, at the passing of the above-
mentioned act, that the deficiency in the hereditary revenue, caused by the abolition of wardships and other
feudal incidents, should be made good by imposing, and
assigning to the crown in perpetuity, certain excise-
duties on beer, ale, and other liquors, and on licences!
So that what had previously been a burden affecting
the landlords only, was thus dexterously transferred
from their shoulders to those of the community in general.*

We are not, however, to understand from this that all
direct taxes on land, for public purposes, ceased with the
Act 12 Chas. II. cap. 24.   It relieved the land from the
burdens that grew out of feudal tenures ; but the assessments granted for the public service, during the reign of
Charles II., were, to all intents and purposes, land-taxes.
These continued to be levied down to the æra of the
Revolution, and subsequently.   In 1692 a land-tax, at the
rate of 4s. in the pound of the rental of estates, manors,
and other real property, was granted to the crown.   The
valuation, according to which this tax was assessed, was
loose and unequal in the extreme.   It was, indeed, in
a great measure left to the different proprietors to
assess themselves, and those in the counties most warmly
attached to the revolutionary establishment returned
their estates much nearer to their fair value than the
others.   But such as it was, a tax at the rate of 1s. in

* St. John on the ‘Land Revenue,’ p. 138; Blackstone, *ubi supra*.

the pound on this valuation was found to produce nearly
500,000*l.* a-year. Though the tax was continued by
annual acts, no change has ever been made in the
valuation on which it was originally assessed. For a
while its amount varied from 2*s.*, to 3*s.* and 4*s.* in the
pound;* but without ever exceeding the latter sum. At
length it came to be considered as a fixed or invariable
tax of 4*s.* per pound on the valuation of 1693; and in
1798 the Act 38 Geo. III. c. 60 made it perpetual at
that rate, giving, at the same time, power to the landlords, of which many have availed themselves, to redeem
it on certain conditions.† The different degrees of improvement that have since taken place in different parts
of the country have, in some instances, tended to correct
the inequalities in the assessment of the land-tax, and
in others to increase them.

It is admitted on all hands that the land-tax, of which
we have thus briefly sketched the history, has been but
little burdensome, and has in nowise obstructed improvements. But this circumstance is not, as has been
supposed, inconsistent with the remarks previously made
regarding the influence of taxes on rent. The latter
necessarily vary with the varying amount of rent; and
have consequently, exclusive of their injustice, the in-
curable defect of obstructing the outlay of capital on
the land, and preventing improvements. Such, however, is not the case with the existing land-tax. As
previously noticed, it was originally assessed, in most
instances, on a very low valuation; and (which is of infinitely more importance) a limit was fixed, beyond which
it has never been carried; and for a lengthened period
its amount has been fixed and constant. It has not,
therefore, except in so far as it may have diminished
the means of the proprietors, had the smallest influence

* It was as low as 1*s.* per pound in 1731 and 1732.

† At present (1844) the land-tax redeemed amounts to 737,285*l.* a-year, and
the unredeemed to 1,069,904*l.* a-year. For several years past, little or no progress has been made in its redemption.

in discouraging improvements; neither has it interfered
in any way with the cultivation of estates; it is never, indeed, taken into account, or so much as referred to, in
estimating the probable influence of new modes of management or of the outlay of additional capital on the
soil; and is, in fact, to be regarded as a stationary quit-
rent payable to the state, without being either directly or
indirectly injurious to individuals. We may regret, perhaps, that the land-tax was not more equally assessed,
and its limits considerably extended, after the Revolution. Whatever hardship, or even injustice, might have
been occasioned in 1693 by raising the range or limit of
the assessment, supposing it had been fairly made, from
two to four, five, or even six millions, would have been
obviated very many years ago, and the country now
would have been in possession of a large revenue, raised
without inconvenience or prejudice to any one. But such
advantages can no longer be realized. The land-tax has
been placed on its present footing for about a century and
a half; so that, whether it were unwisely or unfairly limited
when first imposed, has long ceased to be a matter of any
practical interest. New rights, new interests, and new
generations have grown up under the established system; the lapse of time having completely obviated or
sanctioned any defects in its original constitution. The
landlords have long stood, in respect of taxation, on the
same footing as the rest of the community; and can with
justice be subjected to such taxes only as are laid on merchants, manufacturers, and other capitalists. It is obvious, therefore, that all projects for laying peculiar burdens on the land, however varnished or disguised, should
no longer be looked upon as projects for the imposition
of equitable taxes, but for the confiscation of a portion of
the property of the landlords! If such flagitious schemes
be ever entertained, they will form a precedent that will
justify the repudiation of the public debt and the subversion of every right.

It must, therefore, always be borne in mind that the land-tax owes its innocuousness partly, no doubt, to its moderation, but principally to its being fixed and invariable. Even in this country we have had some striking instances, in the assessment of the poor and other local rates, of the pernicious influence of taxes proportioned to the rent. In the parish of Cholesbury, in Bucks, the poors'-rate, which amounted in 1801 to 10*l.* 11*s.* a-year, had increased, in 1832, to no less than 367*l.*, notwithstanding the population had continued all the while nearly stationary! It would be foreign to our objects to inquire into the circumstances which led to so flagrant an abuse of the principle of a compulsory provision for the poor. But, however it originated, it did not merely put a stop to all improvement, but actually induced the proprietors of the parish to abandon their rents, the occupiers their tenancies, and the clergyman his glebe.* Happily the evil does not seem to have attained to such a height in any other part of the country. But notwithstanding the low rate at which rents have been usually valued in assessments for the poor and other local burdens, the influence of the latter in discouraging improvements has been dwelt upon by all agricultural writers from Arthur Young downwards; and, conjoined with tithe, has been the principal cause of the slowness of agricultural improvement in most parts of England, during the last seventy or eighty years, as compared with its progress in Scotland. The more, indeed, that their operation is inquired into, the more clearly it will appear that taxes proportioned to the rent or'to the net or gross produce of the land are the bane of every country in which they exist. They never can be otherwise than unequal; and when carried to any considerable height they hinder the spread of agricultural improvement, and exercise a most pernicious influence over the public prosperity.

* Report of Commissioners of Poor Law Inquiry, p. 64, 8vo. ed.

The act imposing the land-tax, 4 Will. & Mary, cap. 1, also imposed a duty of 4s. per pound on pensions and offices, and of 24s. per 100l. on personal property. It would, however, appear that the commissioners to whom the levy of the tax was entrusted, in no long time all but wholly abandoned the assessment on personal property, most probably from the difficulty of learning its amount, and contented themselves with assessing it on what was fixed and tangible. In illustration of this, we may mention that while the perpetual assessment charged by the act of 1798 on lands and tenements in Essex, one of the most heavily burdened counties, was fixed at 88,638l. 10s. 2¾d., the assessment on personal estate amounted to no more than 1l. This portion of the tax was, indeed, wholly abandoned in 1833, having been repealed by the act 3 Will. IV. cap. 12. The sum assessed on offices and pensions is but inconsiderable.*

But if, notwithstanding its pernicious influence, it be deemed necessary, either for public or local purposes, to impose a land-tax which shall not be fixed, but capable of indefinite increase, the best way to effect this would appear to be to make a valuation of the net annual value of the land; and to assess the tax accordingly, with and under the condition, that whatever additions or deductions may be made to or from it in time to come, should be proportioned to this original valuation. A tax imposed in this way would be far less objectionable than if it were made to vary with the rent or with the net or gross produce of the soil. Thus suppose that two farms are rated in the original valuation at 100l. each; if the tax were 5 per cent., they would, of course, pay 5l. each; and in the event of its being increased at any future period to 7½ or 10 per cent., they

---

* See the evidence of John Wood and William Garnett, Esquires, in the Second Report of the Commons Committee on the State of Agriculture in 1836, pp. 255—270.

would pay 7*l.* 10*s.* or 10*l.* each; though, in the meantime, one of the farms may have become, under this equal
rate, through the judicious outlay of capital or otherwise,
worth 200*l.* a year, while the value of the other may have
undergone no corresponding change. But even under a
system of this sort the increase of the rate of assessment
would discourage improvements; for one is always disinclined to lay out capital on anything subject to a rate of
taxation that may be indefinitely increased, and from which
there is no escape. Certainly, however, the discouragement
in this case would not be so great as if the basis of the
assessment were variable; and the rate might be proportioned, not to the old, but to the new or improved value
of estates.

Exclusive, however, of the disinclination to improve
occasioned by variations in the rate of assessment, a project of this sort is liable to much obstruction from the
difficulties in the way of making the primary or original
valuation that is to serve for its basis on an equitable
principle. Suppose it were found that two farms were
fairly let each for 100*l.* or 500*l.* a year; it might,
perhaps, be concluded that nothing more was required
to be known respecting them, and that they should
be respectively valued at the same sum: and yet a
proceeding of this sort might involve extreme injustice.
One of the farms, though naturally bad land, may belong
to an active intelligent proprietor, by whom it has been
highly improved, so that its rent consists principally of
the return to the capital expended upon it, a considerable
portion of which will most probably require to be perpetually renewed. The other farm may belong, on the contrary, to an indolent, careless landlord, who has done nothing for its improvement, its rent being wholly a consequence of its naturally superior soil or situation. Surely
it is obvious that, by valuing these farms at the same
sum, a grievous injustice would be done to the owner of
the first, who would be burdened, in all time to come,

with a tax not proportioned to the value of his land, but to the amount of stock, whether lasting or perishable, expended upon it! This is a difficulty inseparable from all attempts to tax rent, or to make its amount a basis for taxation. In enacting a land-tax founded upon a valuation of this sort, the legislature would, in fact, enact that perpetual premiums should be given to those who had been idle and improvident, and perpetual fines imposed upon those who had been industrious and diligent.

It has been attempted to obviate these revolting consequences, by directing those employed to value the land to make their estimates depend rather upon what it might be worth intrinsically than upon its worth when highly improved; and to deduct from the rent a sum adequate to insure the farm buildings, and to replace them and similar outlays on the land when they may be supposed to be worn out. But, though some of the more striking instances of hardship may, no doubt, be got rid of in this way, it is to be feared that the cure will sometimes be but little better than the disease. We have already seen how impossible it is to say what any estate owes to nature, and what to improvements; and it is obvious, that valuations made out in the way now stated, can have but slender claims to the public confidence. They depend on no fixed principle, but on the worst of all securities, the good faith, intelligence, and discretion of the valuers! so that full scope is given for every sort of abuse, whether originating in error or in corrupt motives. But when, despite its inequality and other bad consequences, the imposition of a tax on land, or on the rent of land, is determined upon, the preferable plan is to estimate the value of the land or the rent as fairly as practicable; and having done so, to make the assessment perpetual at a *low* per centage upon such valuation, without ever varying the latter or the rate. Variations in the rate are least pernicious; but all uncertainty, either as to the valuation or the rate, inevitably discourages the employment of capital on the land, and depresses the most important department of national industry.

Hitherto the sums levied in this country on account of the poor, highway, and other local rates have, as previously seen, been mostly raised by assessments on land and other fixed property, especially the former. It is probable, however, owing to the conflicting statutes and decisions with respect to these rates, and the discrepancy in the practice followed in their assessment in different parishes and districts, that a statute providing for their consolidation and for their uniform assessment and collection will, at no distant period, be enacted. And should such be the case it will, we apprehend, be found most advisable that a general valuation of the land should be effected, with as much care and attention as the circumstances will admit; and that the rate for the local burdens referred to should in time to come be proportioned to this valuation without taking any account of the improvements that may subsequently be effected. In a case of this sort the limitation of the rate is unluckily impracticable; but we shall do what is next best, if we declare that the valuation on which it is to be raised shall be a perpetual *maximum;* and that though it may, under certain circumstances, be susceptible of being reduced, it shall not, under any circumstances, nor in any case whatever, be susceptible of increase. It is, of course, to be understood that this limitation of the valuation applies only to land; for it will be afterwards seen that but little inconvenience arises from varying the assessments in the case of buildings, and such like descriptions of property.

It may be said, perhaps, that a tax proportioned to a permanent valuation of the land, must, in the course of no very long time, become unequal, not merely from the influence of improvements in certain districts and not in others, but from changes of situation, originating in the opening of new channels of commerce, and the shutting

F

up of the old, the growth and decay of manufactures in particular localities, and so forth. But though these circumstances would undoubtedly alter the value of property and vitiate the valuation, the consequences that would attend the periodical revaluation of the land are such that no policy of that sort should ever be thought of. Proprietors of estates subject to a variable land-tax have, in fact, only a modified right of property in them, government being entitled to claim an indefinite share of their produce. Such persons are consequently without that feeling of security which is the foundation of all enterprise and improvement; and it were idle to suppose that they should make the same outlays on their estates that they would make if they held them in absolute property under an invariable tax, or, which is next best, under a tax *proportioned to a valuation that cannot be augmented.*

It is obvious, too, that in so far as estates may be improved by the contingencies alluded to above, their proprietors would have nothing to object to the limitation of the valuation, which, on the contrary, would be highly advantageous to them. The proprietors of estates that had fallen in value in consequence of these contingencies would, however, have reason to complain, were they to continue to be assessed in all time to come on valuations made when their estates, owing to circumstances which no longer exist, bore a comparatively high value; and therefore it would be right and proper to enact, that though the valuation should be wholly unsusceptible of increase, it might, under certain circumstances, be reduced. If a dock, a harbour, a ferry, or a factory existed on the estate of A when it was valued, and if, owing to some change of circumstances, such dock, &c. has been transferred to some other locality, it would be unjust that this estate should continue to be assessed on a valuation made when it enjoyed advantages of which it has been deprived without any fault of the proprietor. It

would, however, be quite another thing if the decline in
its value had been a consequence of the adoption of a
worse or more slovenly system of management; and to
reduce the valuation in such a case would be to give a
premium to sloth extravagance, or ignorance, or to all
three. And hence, supposing this system were adopted,
whenever application was made to have a valuation reduced, it should be referred to a jury to decide whether
the value of the property had been reduced by circumstances over which the landlord had no control, and which
he could not have prevented; and in such case, and such
case only, it would be expedient and equitable that the
property should be revalued.

By adopting a system of this sort, or by making the
valuation a perpetual *maximum*, we should do the most
that can be done, with a variable rate of assessment, to
hinder the tax from obstructing improvements; while by
allowing, under certain circumstances, the valuation to be
reduced, we provide against the hardship and injustice
that might otherwise arise when estates fall in value
from contingent and unavoidable circumstances,

The injurious operation of oppressive, and especially
of variable, land-taxes is strikingly exemplified in our
Indian dominions. The land-tax has always constituted
the principal part of the revenue of Hindostan, and of
most other Eastern countries. The British government,
like the governments by which it was preceded, may, in
truth, be regarded as the real proprietor of the greater
part of the vast dominions subject to its authority in
India; its rights as such being, however, in so far modified that the cultivators have an hereditary and transferable right of occupancy so long as they pay the share of
the produce demanded by government. The value of this
right to the rural population varies in different districts, according to the nature of the country and the resistance they have been able to make to the exactions of

their rulers. But in most parts the tax on land is quite
enormous; and being, except in Bengal since the introduction of the perpetual settlement by Lord Cornwallis,
variable as well as exorbitant, it has been an insuperable
obstacle to improvement, and has either reduced the inhabitants to the most abject state of poverty or retained
them in that state.*

SECTION II.——TAXES ON THE RENT OF HOUSES.

With the exception of those in peculiarly fine or
fashionable situations, the greater part of the rent of
houses usually consists of a return for the capital laid
out on their erection, or, as it is usually termed, of *building*-rent, a comparatively small part only being *ground*-
rent, or rent payable for the land on which they are
erected. It is evident, therefore, from the principles
already established, that, if the supply of houses were
as easily diminished and increased as the supply of raw
produce, a tax on their rents would fall entirely on the
occupiers and ground landlords, in the proportion that
the profits of the capital laid out on them bore to the
rent of the land on which they stood. But as the supply of houses is not susceptible of speedy diminution,
the builders would have no means of immediately raising rents when a tax was laid on them; and unless the
population and demand for houses were rapidly increasing, a considerable period would necessarily elapse before they would be able to relieve themselves of the
tax. Houses, however, though slowly, are yet certainly
perishable; and as no more of them would be built,
after they had been taxed, until the increasing demand
had raised their rents so as to indemnify the builders
for the tax, and to elevate their profits to the common
level, it is clear that, in the end, the tax would be

* See the note on this subject in the Appendix.

thrown wholly on the occupiers and ground landlords in the proportions already mentioned.

Taxes on houses have been for a lengthened period ordinary sources of revenue in this country, having been introduced by the Act 7 Will. III., cap. 18; and we are inclined to think that when these taxes are assessed according to the rent, they are among the least exceptionable that can be devised. Houses are occupied either wholly as residences, or they are used partly as such and partly for the purpose of carrying on some sort of business or profession. Now, with respect to the first of these descriptions of houses, or those used wholly as residences, they may, speaking generally, be taken as a pretty fair index of the incomes of their occupiers; and it may in consequence be presumed that taxes laid on them in proportion to the rent would be, in fact, pretty nearly proportioned to the abilities of the parties. But it is not necessary that the same rate of duty should be imposed on all descriptions of houses. It is generally, no doubt, best to avoid as much as possible graduated or cumulative taxes. Inasmuch, however, as those occupying one class of houses may resort to another in the event of their thinking the tax too high, there appears to be less objection to increasing the rate of duty on houses in proportion to their value, than on most other things. At all events, there can be no solid objection to the tax, provided it be equally imposed. It is neither unfair nor unjust for government to lay it down that individuals using certain articles, or occupying houses of a certain value, shall be charged with certain duties.

With respect to the other description of houses, or those used partly only as residences, and partly also as shops or places of business, there is more difficulty; and, on the whole, the better plan would seem to be to exempt the shop or place of business from the tax, and to assess the latter on that portion only of the building that is used as a dwelling-house. In ordinary cases, a shop-tax, being an increased charge upon the shop-keepers, would, no doubt, in the end be thrown upon their customers or the public. But in the numerous cases in which the rent of shops may be regarded, from the peculiarity of their situation, as a species of mono-poly rent, the tax would ultimately have to be borne, in a great measure, by the ground-landlords. But by ex-empting shops and places of business from the tax, and confining it to buildings or parts of buildings used as dwelling-houses, these difficulties are avoided, and it may be easily and fairly assessed.

Being impressed with the force of these considera-tions, we cannot help regarding the abolition of the late house-tax as an ill-advised concession to vulgar and unfounded clamour. A tax on houses interferes with no department or branch of industry; the subject on which the tax is laid is obvious, and cannot be concealed; and it is never any very difficult matter to determine the value of houses with sufficient precision for its fair assessment. In these respects a tax on houses has many advantages as compared with the greater number of excise-duties, and still more as compared with taxes on property or income. The inquisitorial pro-ceedings indispensable in assessing the latter, and which are at the same time so ineffectual to the discovery of truth, and so justly complained of, are wholly unneces-sary in the case of taxes on houses: these are easily assessed; and, except in the mere fact of payment, a tax on them involves nothing that should occasion irri-tation.

In 1836, the year before its repeal, the late house-tax produced 1,262,754l.; farm-houses, and all houses under the value of 10l. a-year, were, however, exempted from the tax; and it was contended that, in the event of the tax being continued, it would have been proper to exempt a still greater number of houses. But it would be difficult to show any good reason why any description of houses should be exempted from a house-tax. The occupier of a 10*l.* house has been intrusted with the elective franchise, and it does not appear at all unreasonable that the parties to whom such a valuable privilege has been given should contribute their fair proportion of the tax on that description of property that has been made the test of their ability to exercise the franchise. Sundry reasons may, however, be alleged to show that it would be expedient to charge the duty on houses under 10*l.* a-year on the proprietor, and make it payable by him or his agent. This would obviate the alleged hardship of assessing a tax of this kind on common labourers, and would, besides, be advantageous by discouraging the building of cottages, except when they are really required.

It appears, from the returns under the late census, that there were in Great Britain, in 1841, 3,444,848 inhabited houses. Of these, however, not more than from a fourth to a fifth part are supposed to be worth above 10*l.* a-year. But as the old tax on this small portion, with the further deduction of farm-houses, produced about 1,260,000*l.* a-year, it is easy to see that had the tax been extended to the lower description of houses, and the rates increased on the superior houses, it might have been rendered a most productive source of income. In further corroboration of what is now stated, we may observe, that the rental of the dwelling-houses assessed to the poor-rate in England and Wales, in 1840—41, amounted to 23,386,401*l.* and adding to this sum one-fifth part for Scotland, the gross house-rental of Great Britain will have been about 28,000,000*l.* a-year. Now supposing that a tax of 10 per cent. (which would have been anything but oppressive) had been imposed on this rental, it would have produced 2,800,000*l.* a-year; and had the better class of houses been charged at higher rates, the produce would have been still greater.

A prejudice was raised against the late house-tax from

a notion that it was unfairly assessed, and, in proof of
this, it was said that not a few of the middle class of inns
and hotels paid a larger amount of house-duty than was
paid by some of the most splendid baronial residences.
But no one could honestly pretend that there was any
unfairness in this, seeing that the house-duty was assessed not by what a house cost, but by the rent which
it fetched, or which it would have fetched had it been
actually let. Everybody knows that the baronial residences referred to would not let at all, and that no
one, except their owners, would occupy them unless
he were tempted by the offer of a considerable annual
allowance. Being a tax depending on the rent, how
could the house-duty be levied on houses that were worth
nothing ? which none would inhabit unless enticed by a
considerable bonus?   This objection might, however,
have been obviated by charging the tax on superior
houses, partly only in proportion to their rent, and partly
also in proportion to their cost.

The window-tax, which was imposed at the same time,
and by the same Act as the house-tax, is, in all respects,
more objectionable than the latter, and should, consequently, have been repealed in preference. The number
of windows in a house affords no criterion of its value
or of the probable means of those by whom it is occupied. "A house of 10l. rent in a country town may
sometimes have more windows than a house of 500l. rent
in London; and though the inhabitant of the former is
likely to be a much poorer man than that of the latter,
yet, so far as his contribution is regulated by the window-
tax, he must contribute more to the support of the
state." * In most cases, too, a tax on windows makes
houses be built on improper principles, and with less
light than may be desirable for health as well as convenience. A tax on houses is free from these inconve-

* Wealth of Nations, p. 382.

niences; it is proportioned to their value and most commonly also to the fortune of the occupiers, and it interferes in no sort of way with the taste or plans of the builder.

The *contribution mobilière*, imposed in France in 1791, by the Constituent Assembly, on movable property, and intended to balance the *contribution foncière*, which falls exclusively on land and other fixed property, consisted principally of an assessment on the occupiers of houses in proportion to their rents; those parties whose revenues were derived wholly or in part from land, being either wholly or proportionally exempted from the tax. Assuming that the annual value or rent of the houses occupied by different individuals afforded on the whole the best practical test that could be found of their fortune or of their ability to bear taxes, the Assembly selected it as the principal evidence on which to assess the *contribution mobilière*; the grounds for doing so being ably set forth in the Report of the Committee of the Assembly, which preceded the introduction of the tax. The *contribution mobilière* has since undergone various changes and modifications. In 1831 government proposed that it should be established at the rate of 6 per cent. on all habitations; and had this proposal been carried into effect, it would have formed an important source of revenue, which, though no change had been made in the rate, would have increased with the increasing wealth of the country. The Chambers, however, modified the project in so far as to fix a principal for this tax and for the *contribution personnelle* (a direct tax on labour) of 34,000,000 fr., or nearly 1,400,000*l.* sterling, distributed among the departments in certain proportions; and this principal, with the *centimes additionnels*, produced, in 1837, 55,646,396 fr., and in 1842, 56,235,340 fr. In consequence of this arrangement the amount of the tax differs in different parts of the kingdom; and though it is to be newly distributed once in ten years, it can never be made a really equal burden.*

The fixing of the principal or basis of the assessment of the house-tax appears to be an error. A tax proportioned to the rent of land is most objectionable from its obstructing the progress of agricultural improvement. But a tax proportioned to the rent of houses is not open to any such objection. Suppose it were fixed at 10 per cent., its utmost effect would be to make parties who might have occupied houses worth 100*l.* a-year, had there been no tax, occupy houses worth only 90*l.* But the fair presumption is, that in most cases the parties would endeavour, without resorting to inferior houses, to defray the tax by greater exertion and increased economy in other things.

In addition to the tax on rent, charged upon the occupiers, houses are assessed in France to the *contribution foncière*, and they are further charged with duties on doors and windows. House taxes are also imposed in the Netherlands, Austria, Prussia, and most other Continental States; and they are everywhere, we believe, reckoned among the least questionable modes in which a revenue can be raised.

CHAPTER II.

TAXES ON PROFITS.

A TAX proportioned to the net profits realized by those engaged in every department of industry, provided it were fairly imposed, would fall wholly on profits.

Such a tax would equally affect all capitalists. When five or ten per cent. was laid on the profits of the farmer or manufacturer, five or ten per cent.

* Macarel, ' De la Fortune Publique,' iii. pp. 230—353.

would be laid on the profits of the merchant, the ship-owner, and all the other employers of capital or labour. It is evident no individual could hope to evade a tax of this sort by changing his business; and it would not, therefore, occasion any transfer of capital from one employment to another; neither would it occasion any variation in the supply and demand of commodities, nor in their money price. For, as the tax falls on profits and not on capital, the means of producing would not be impaired by its imposition; the means of purchasing possessed by those whose incomes were derived from profits, previously to the imposition of the tax, would indeed be diminished; but as the means of purchasing possessed by the government and its dependents, who receive the tax, would be proportionally augmented, the aggregate demand of the society would continue the same; and hence, as the tax would neither lessen the quantity of capital in the country, nor the power to purchase its produce, it is obvious it would not, supposing the value of money to be stationary, occasion any variation in the money prices of commodities.

An equal and universal tax on profits would, therefore, in the first instance, reduce them in the same proportion. And as the power to accumulate capital, and consequently to feed and employ additional hands, is always proportioned to the rate of profit, it follows that the tendency of taxes on profits, and their ultimate effect, if they be carried to such a height as to prevent their being balanced by increased exertion and economy, is to check the accumulation of capital and the progress of population.

But it is material to bear in mind that these conclusions are true only on the supposition that the tax is made to affect all profits to the same extent. Practically, however, this is impossible. There are no means by which to measure the rate of profit in different businesses. Generally, indeed, it can only be guessed at even by those who carry them on; and were an attempt made to tax profits, the great majority of individuals would underrate their amount, and, in the far greater number of businesses, it would be quite impossible for government officers to form anything like an accurate estimate of their magnitude. It would, in consequence, be necessary to adopt some general rules for assessing the tax; and the vice of these is, that, being bottomed on assumed average rates, they invariably, even when most accurate, make those engaged in unsuccessful speculations pay a great deal too much, while those engaged in peculiarly successful speculations pay only a comparatively small portion of what they should pay were the tax fairly assessed. In truth, profits never can be ascertained; and consequently never have been and never can be taxed in proportion to their amount: and though it be important to know how a tax on profits would operate were it equally imposed, it must be kept in mind that this is altogether impracticable, and that the supposition is made merely to illustrate a principle.

A tax laid only on the profits of a particular business would have a different effect: it would, sooner or later, raise prices, and would not, therefore, permanently fall on the producers, except in as far as they were themselves consumers of their own produce. Suppose, for example, that a tax of 10 per cent. is laid on the profits of the shoemaker, and on none else: the slightest consideration will show that this tax must, in the end, add proportionally to the price of shoes; for, when first imposed, the shoemakers will make less profit than the untaxed parties engaged in other businesses, and they will, in consequence, gradually contract or leave their business, until, through the diminution in the supply of shoes, their price is raised so as to yield them the common and average rate of profit, exclusive of the tax. For the same reason, if an exclusive tax on the profits of the hatter, or clothier, or farmer, be not partially or wholly countervailed by an increased facility of production, it will make, in the end, a proportional addition to the price of hats, cloth, or agricultural produce. In these cases the producers can raise prices, and consequently can throw the burden of the tax on the consumers; because they can withdraw from the businesses in which profits are taxed, and engage in those in which they are not taxed. But when the profits realized in all kinds of businesses are equally taxed, they are deprived of this resource; and have no means either of raising prices or of evading the tax.

It must, however, be observed, that, though a tax on the profits of those engaged in a particular line of business, or in the production of a particular article, will, in the end, be defrayed by those who purchase the services of the parties or the article, the rise of price by which this transfer of the tax to the consumers is effected may so narrow the demand for the products or services of the taxed class as to be very injurious to their interests. Were a peculiar tax of ten or twenty per cent. laid on the profits of the hatters, it would, no doubt, for the reasons already stated, ultimately occasion a corresponding rise in the price of hats, and be thrown wholly on the public. But if this rise should, by occasioning (as it would most probably do) the substitution of caps and other articles for hats, materially lessen the demand for the latter, the business of the hatters would, it is plain, be proportionally diminished; and it is likely that they would be driven in considerable numbers from their employment. This result might, it is true, be partially or wholly obviated were any considerable discovery or saving of labour or expense simultaneously made in the business carried on by the hatters or taxed class; and it is farther true that the imposition of the tax would make them endeavour to neutralize its influence by increased economy, without adding to the price of their products.

But, unless when some discovery or saving of the kind now alluded to is made, it is the climax of error to suppose, because taxes on those engaged in peculiar businesses are in the end identified with the price of their products or services, and thrown upon the consumers, that they are not, therefore, injurious to those on whom they are directly imposed. In point of fact, there are but few instances in which, for a while at least, they do not lay the latter under very considerable difficulties; while, in a good many others, their influence is, in this respect, of an abiding character. We shall afterwards show that the malt-tax is, for the reasons now glanced at, especially injurious to the agriculturists.

Hence it appears, that when the demand for any article is narrowed by a tax, some of its producers, including most probably those who are least prosperous, begin to withdraw their capital and industry to other businesses; and when this has gone on for awhile, and the level of price and profit been restored, the influence of the tax on those who still continue in the business may perhaps be but little sensible. But though this result will, in most cases, be ultimately brought about, it is not always an easy matter to effect an equalization of profit in the way now pointed out. The transference of capital and labour from one business to another is usually a troublesome and costly, and sometimes even an impossible proceeding. Fixed capital, employed in a particular department of industry, is frequently wholly unsuitable for any other; and any tax which should throw a portion of such capital out of employment would occasion a loss to its proprietors from which they would have no means of escaping. When, indeed, a country is fast increasing in wealth and population, taxes on the profits of particular businesses, or on commodities, supposing they are kept within due bounds, seldom entail more than a temporary hardship on the producers, and are either met by increased efforts of skill and economy,

or partly by these and partly by the increasing wealth
and demand of the country. But in stationary or retrograde countries their influence would, most likely, be
very different; and, if taxes happened to be imposed on
the profits of those engaged in businesses that require
the agency of a peculiar description of fixed capital, the
chances are, that they would not only diminish the businesses, but also destroy a portion of the capital or stock
of those engaged in them.

It is easy to see, from these principles and considerations, that an equal tax on the profits of agriculture
and other businesses would not occasion any diminution
of rent. When farmers are taxed equally with other
producers, they have no motive to withdraw capital
from the land, and no variation will take place in the
price of corn; nor, as rent consists in the excess of
the produce obtained by the capital first applied to the
land over that which is obtained by the capital last
applied, will it be affected by such tax. But Mr.
Ricardo contends that, if the tax, instead of being general and equal, were laid exclusively on the profits of the
farmer, it would occasion an increase of rent. No rent,
as has been seen in the preceding chapter, ever enters
into the cost of producing that portion of the required
supply of raw produce which is raised by the agency of
the capital last laid out on the land. It is plainly impossible, therefore, that its raisers could indemnify themselves for any burdens laid on them by making an equivalent deduction from rent. And hence, when a tax is
laid exclusively on the profits of agricultural capital, the
price of raw produce must sustain in the end a corresponding rise; for, in the event of its not rising, the producers of that portion which pays no rent would abandon
their business, and the necessary supplies would not be
obtained. Inasmuch, however, as the rise of price which
is required to remunerate those who raise corn that pays

no rent, after a tax is imposed on profits, must be *universal*, it must raise rent. Thus, on the supposition that *five* equal capitals, applied to soils of various degrees of fertility, respectively yield 100, 90, 80, 70, and 60 quarters, their *corn* rents would be 40, 30, 20, and 10 quarters; and if the price required to remunerate the cultivators of the *fifth* and worst quality of land, which pays no rent, were 2*l.* a-quarter, the *money* rent of the *first* quality would be 80*l.*, of the *second* 60*l.*, of the *third* 40*l.*, and so on. Suppose, now, that a tax is laid exclusively on the profits of agricultural capital, and that, to remunerate the cultivators of the worst land, the price rises from 2*l.* to 2*l.* 10*s.* a-quarter; it is plain, according to Mr. Ricardo, that the rent of the *first* quality would be raised to 100*l.*, the second to 75*l.*, the third to 50*l.*, and so on; being an increase of 20*l.* on the rent of the *first*, of 15*l.* on the rent of the *second*, of 10*l.* on the third, &c. Hence he concludes, " to tax the profits of the farmer, and not those of any other capitalist, would be highly beneficial to the landlords. It would, in fact, be a tax on the consumers of raw produce, partly for the benefit of the state, and partly for the benefit of the landlords." *

But in making this statement Mr. Ricardo has tacitly assumed, first, that a rise of price consequent to a tax does not occasion any diminution of consumption; and, second, that foreign corn is excluded from our ports, or loaded with a duty sufficient to countervail that which is laid on the profits of the farmers. Now, with respect to the *first* of these assumptions, it is certainly unfounded. Every rise of price is accompanied by a diminution of consumption. In the case supposed, the landlords might probably lose about as much by the diminution of demand, and the consequent contraction of tillage, as they would gain by the rise of price; and it is needless to add that they would be serious losers by the discouragement such a tax would give to the outlay of capital on

* Principles of Political Economy, 3rd edit., p. 241.

the land. As regards the *second* assumption, it may be either well founded or not. But if foreign corn be freely admitted, or if it be burdened with a less amount of duty than is laid on the British farmers, it follows, seeing that the market is in part supplied by parties not subject to the tax, or to any equivalent impost, that prices will not rise in proportion to its amount. Under these circum-stances, the occupiers of the poorest lands will inevitably be driven from their farms, and rents will, in consequence, be proportionally reduced. And hence, in the event of any peculiar tax being imposed on the land, it is neces-sary, if we would do justice to all parties, that an equi-valent duty should be laid on the importation of foreign agricultural produce. At present, however, it is needless to insist further on this point, seeing that there will be a better opportunity for its elucidation when we come to investigate the incidence and influence of tithe, which is a tax of the kind now alluded to.

The *taille*, which existed in France previously to the Revolution, was one of those oppressive and unequal burdens that grew out of the feudal system, having been imposed after the expulsion of the English in the reign of Charles VII. Without entering into minute particu-lars, it may suffice to state that it was said to be either *real* or *personal**—the first being assessed on lands be-longing to copyholders, or held by a base tenure; while the second and most important branch was, in fact, a tax on the profits of those who occupied lands belonging to others, whatever might be the tenure under which the proprietor held them: no landlord holding directly of the crown was subject to the taille, provided he did not retain above a certain portion of his estate in his own occupation. And this exemption, though it became in no

* The personal taille extended to other individuals besides those engaged in agriculture, but it is of its operation on the latter only that we have now to treat.

G

long time most objectionable, and led in the end to the
most ruinous consequences, was originally founded on
a not unfair principle. The taille was imposed to enable
the sovereign to keep up a standing army, instead of
the feudal militia, which had previously constituted the
only force of the kingdom; relieving by this means, at
least to a certain extent, the occupiers of the land or
peasantry from the obligation of personal service : but as
the principal landlords, or those holding directly from
the crown, continued, notwithstanding the institution
of a standing army, liable, as before, to personal service,
it appeared no more than reasonable that the taille,
or tax raised to pay the troops, should be paid by
the former. But the expenses of the state having
continued to increase, they were partly and principally provided for by increasing the taille; so that,
as Turgot has shown, the exemption of the nobles
from the tax for the support of the standing army gradually extended itself to the taxes imposed for other
objects; till at length the revolting spectacle was exhibited of the wealthiest and most exalted order in
the state being relieved from all those direct taxes imposed for its support, that fell with their full weight on
the other and less opulent classes.* A privilege of
this sort could hardly have been tolerated, even though
it had been enjoyed only by the old nobility, to whom
the people had been accustomed to look up with respect. But after patents of nobility began to be
openly sold, and any tailor or cheesemonger who chose
to pay the stipulated price might get himself enrolled
in the privileged class, the abuse shocked every unprejudiced individual, and became quite insupportable. It
is indeed true that the exemption in question was of
little or no real value to those in whose favour it was
established. Few, however, seem to have been aware of

* Œuvres de M. Turgot, viii., p. 230.

this; while those subject to the taille were not merely
borne down by its pressure, but were disgusted with
its injustice and the partiality of government; and
supposing they had been fully aware of the worthless-
ness of the privilege conferred on the upper classes, they
would most probably have been rendered only the more
indignant, inasmuch as they would have felt that the public prosperity was sacrificed in a vain and unavailing effort
to exempt the richest individuals from contributing to
the necessities of the state! It may, perhaps, be thought
not a little surprising that the nobility did not themselves
relinquish so odious and so useless a privilege. One
would suppose that no very lengthened experience
could have been required to satisfy them that whatever
crippled the means and paralysed the industry of the
tenants of estates could not fail to fall in the end on the
landlords, and, consequently, to be more injurious to them
than to any other class; and this was most particularly
the case with the taille. Its amount and pressure differed
widely in different provinces, and also in different parts of
the same province. But, owing partly to the vicious
nature of the tax, and partly to the impossibility of
assessing it with anything like fairness, it was, even when
lightest, an all but intolerable grievance. The abuses
in its collection were of the most flagrant description.
" The proportion," says Adam Smith, " in which the
taille is assessed in the different provinces varies from
year to year, according to the reports which are made to
the King's council concerning the goodness or badness of
the crops, as well as other circumstances which may
either increase or diminish their respective abilities to
pay. Each generality is divided into a certain number
of elections; and the proportion in which the sum imposed upon the whole generality is divided among those
different elections varies likewise from year to year, according to the reports made to the council concerning
their respective abilities. It seems impossible that the

council, with the best intentions, can ever proportion, with tolerable exactness, either of these two assessments to the real abilities of the province or district upon which they are respectively laid. Ignorance and misinformation must always more or less mislead the most upright council. The proportion which each parish ought to support of what is assessed upon the whole election, and that which each individual ought to support of what is assessed upon his particular parish, are both in the same manner varied from year to year, according as circumstances are supposed to require. These circumstances are judged of in the one case by the officers of the election, in the other by those of the parish; and both the one and the other are, more or less, under the direction and influence of the intendant. Not only ignorance and misinformation, but friendship, party animosity, and private resentment, are said frequently to mislead such assessors. No man subject to such a tax, it is evident, can ever be certain, before he is assessed, of what he is to pay. He cannot even be certain after he is assessed. If any person has been taxed who ought to have been exempted, or if any person has been taxed beyond his proportion, though both must pay in the mean time, yet, if they complain, and make good their complaints, the whole parish is reimposed next year, in order to reimburse them. If any of the contributors become bankrupt or insolvent, the collector is obliged to advance his tax, and the whole parish is reimposed next year, in order to reimburse the collector. If the collector himself should become bankrupt, the parish which elects him must answer for his conduct to the receiver-general of the election. But as it might be troublesome for the receiver to prosecute the whole parish, he takes as his choice five or six of the richest contributors, and obliges them to make good what had been lost by the insolvency of the collector. The parish is afterwards reimposed, in order to reimburse those five or six. Such reimpositions are always over and above the taille of the particular year in which they are laid on." *

Some of the many mischievous consequences inseparable from such a system of taxation have been already noticed, while others are too obvious to require entering into details. It may, however, be further necessary to a right understanding of the operation of the taille, and of all similar taxes, to observe that the assessments were usually made, not so much with reference to the rent paid by the occupiers, or the amount of their produce, as with reference to the presumed value of their stock and other property; so that they were tempted, even when they had the means of getting better, to employ inferior animals and implements, and otherwise to counterfeit poverty! Hence, though the tax had been freed from its extreme inequality and uncertainty, it could not have failed to be in the last degree ruinous to agriculture.

" The taille," says Arthur Young, " being professedly levied according to every one's substance, has the mischievous effect of all land-taxes, even when levied honestly and fairly; for a farmer being taxed in proportion to his profit—his success, his merit,—what surer method can be taken for annihilating the one and the other? The farmers are really poor, or apparently poor, since a rich man will affect poverty to escape the rise of the tax, which professes to be in proportion to his power of bearing it : hence poor cattle, poor implements, and poor dunghills, even on the farms of men who could afford the best. What a ruinous and detestable system ; and how surely calculated to stop the current of public wealth!"†

The greatest statesmen of whom France has to boast have participated in the opinions thus forcibly expressed; though, owing to the false pride and prejudices of the nobles, and the vicious constitution of the

---

* Wealth of Nations, p. 385.   † Travels in France, vol. i. p. 405.

government, the taille could neither be suppressed nor thoroughly reformed otherwise than by a revolution. " *M. de Sully regardait avec raison cet impôt comme violent et vicieux dans sa nature, principalement où il était personnelle. Une expérience constante lui avoit prouvé qu'il nuit à la perception de tous les autres subsides, et que les campagnes avaient toujours dépéri à mesure que les tailles s'étaient accrues. En effet, dès qu'il y entre de l'arbitraire, le laboureur est privé de l'espérance d'une propriété, il se décourage ; loin d'augmenter sa culture, il la néglige pour peu que le fardeau s'appesantisse.*"* And such also was the opinion of Colbert, Vauban, Turgot, and, in fact, of all the most eminent authorities on such subjects.

The taille, even had it been limited to some definite proportion, as a tenth, a fourth, or a third part of the rent, would, by hindering the outlay of capital on the land, have been most inimical to the public interests. Owing, however, to the growing necessities and profusion of the government, its amount was constantly on the increase, and it continued progressively to absorb a larger share of the produce of the soil. To prevent the cultivators charged with this ever-increasing burden from relinquishing their farms, those who left one part of the country for another were obliged to pay for a certain period the taille due on the lands they had left; those who left the country to establish themselves in towns being also subjected, but for a much longer period, to the same burden.—(*Encyclopédie*, XV. 843.) But even this nefarious attempt to chain, as it were, the cultivators to a single spot, and to prevent them from removing to some less over-taxed district, very generally failed of its object. The inability to pay the taille nullified the law; and, in the central and poorer provinces, or country of the *petite culture*, where the taille was

* Forbonnais, ' Recherches sur les Finances,' i. p. 107.

most oppressive, large tracts of inferior land were not unfrequently abandoned by the occupiers.

Even had the mode of its assessment been less arbitrary and less opposed to sound principle, the distinctive character of the tax would have rendered it in no ordinary degree injurious. It was of its essence to be partial and unfair; and, as it affected those only who rented lands or were owners of lands held by a base tenure, its payment was considered as involving some degree of degradation, and as being, in fact, a mark and a consequence of the ignoble or rather servile condition of those on whom it fell. The few who made anything by farming were thus rendered anxious to withdraw from so discreditable a business; while rich merchants and capitalists were prevented from buying and improving estates. Not only, therefore, did the taille hinder a large part of the capital generated on the land from being laid out upon it, but it turned from it all the capital that had been accumulated in other employments! And if we add to this its direct influence in discouraging industry, it may well be doubted whether any means could have been devised better fitted to retain agriculture in a rude and infant state, to depress rents, and to extinguish emulation and industry amongst the farmers. Considering the lengthened period during which France was subject to this tax, and the additions that were constantly being made to it, the wonder is—not that her agriculture was in an extremely backward and depressed state at the Revolution, but that it was so far advanced as it really was.

The present French land-tax, or *contribution foncière*, affects all lands, however occupied. It consists of a certain proportion of the net produce of the land—that is, of its produce exclusive of the expenses of cultivation, but inclusive of rent. The *contribution foncière* was imposed by the Constituent Assembly in 1791, and was intended to supply the place of the *taille, vingtièmes,* and other taxes on land that were then abolished. Its total amount was originally fixed at 241,000,000 fr., or 9,640,000*l.* sterling; and a committee was appointed to apportion it among the different departments. The amount of the various taxes to be replaced by the *contribution foncière,* that the provinces had previously been in the habit of paying, formed the only ground on which this committee was able to proceed in distributing the tax; and, as there had been very great differences, owing to the peculiar privileges and franchises enjoyed by certain provinces, in the pressure of the former system of taxation, these differences were perpetuated in the new system; and, in consequence, it was found that the proportion which the *contribution foncière* bore to the net produce of the soil was *twice* as great in some departments as in others.

This inequality necessarily gave rise to much dissatisfaction, to appease which large abatements were made in 1797, 1798, 1799, and other years, from the amounts originally assessed on the overburdened departments: the loss of revenue that was thus occasioned being made up by imposing *centimes additionnels;* that is, by making additions to the tax proportioned to its *principal,* or to the original assessment in the instances in which it remained unaltered, and to the new assessment in the instances in which abatements had been granted. With the view, also, of getting the tax more equally assessed, government ordered a *cadastre,* or survey, to be made of the whole kingdom, exhibiting the extent and value of every separate property, and even of every field. This immense undertaking was zealously prosecuted for many years; but after about 30,000,000 fr. had been expended in carrying it on, it was found that it would still require a lengthened period, and a great additional outlay for its completion; and it began, also, to be doubted whether it would be good policy further to disturb the distribution of the tax among the different departments, seeing that, how unequal soever at first, the burden had become accommodated to and mixed up with the value of property in each. In conformity with these sentiments it was enacted, in 1821, that a further deduction of 19,619,229 fr. should be made from the principal of the tax paid by the more heavily taxed departments, that no changes should be made in future in its distribution, among the different departments, and that the *cadastre* should thenceforth be employed only in apportioning with greater correctness the quota payable by each department over its surface.

The *contribution foncière* affects houses, mills, and all sorts of fixed property, as well as land; and almost the only additions made to its amount since 1821 consist of the tax imposed on new buildings, on forest-land brought into cultivation, land gained by embanking, &c.

It appears from the official returns that, in 1837, the principal of the *contribution foncière* amounted to 155,200,083 fr., of which 123,005,340 fr. were assessed upon land, and 32,194,743 fr. upon houses and buildings; but, including the *centimes additionnels*, its total produce that year amounted to 263,239,065 fr.; and as the tax was assessed on 49,621,769 hectares* (equivalent to 122,622,487 acres) of land, and 6,775.236 houses, &c., it follows that, at an average, each hectare paid 4 fr. 20 c. (equivalent to 1 fr. 70 c. per acre), and each house, or other building, 8 fr. 5 c. The *contribution foncière* amounted in 1842 to 268,270,150 fr.†

It is obvious that France has gained immensely by the substitution of this tax for the taille and other

---

* Exclusive of 2,905,008 hectares, which include forests belonging to the state, roads, rivers, lakes, burying grounds, &c., exempted from the tax.

† For further information as to the *contribution foncière*, see Macarel, ' De la Fortune Publique,' iii. pp. 1—228.

burdens which affected landed property previously to the Revolution. The produce of the *contribution foncière* differs but little from that of the old taxes; and, while it is collected at half the expense, it has the inestimable advantage of pressing equally on all descriptions of proprietors and cultivators,—so that the jealousies and animosities that formerly subsisted between the privileged classes and the mass of the people have wholly disappeared.

It further appears from the above statements that the *contribution foncière* is now assessed, in part at least, in the way in which we have previously seen that a variable land-tax is least objectionable. The principal of the tax is fixed; the variations in its amount being made by adding to or deducting from it so many *centimes additionnels*. Unluckily, however, this principle is not carried out to its full extent; for, though the sum to be paid by each department be fixed, the assessment of this sum within its limits is left to the discretion of the local authorities. In consequence the principal sum assessed on estates is liable to perpetual variations, at the same time that they may all be subjected to an indefinite amount of *centimes additionnels*. But, apart from the latter circumstance, it would obviously be of much importance were the principal of the tax payable by each department distributed at once and for ever among the various properties within its boundaries. This would get rid of the greater portion of the uncertainty growing out of the tax. Its basis would then be fixed; and the subsequent variations would only affect the rate of assessment.

Undoubtedly, however, it were far better, were all uncertainty, either as to the rate or the basis of the assessment, put an end to by following the precedent of the English land-tax—that is, by definitively assessing the sums to be paid by every different property, and declaring that such sums shall be invariable and payable in all time to come. It is abundantly certain that a measure of this description, even though 25,000,000 fr. were added to the amount of the tax, would be one of the greatest boons which can be conferred on France. However heavy in the mean time, the *contribution foncière* would, after its limitation, have comparatively little influence in preventing or retarding improvements; and the fair presumption is, that agriculture, which is almost everywhere the principal branch of industry, and which in France is of incomparably more importance than all other employments put together, would be prosecuted, in time to come, with a vigour hitherto unknown.

It has been argued, in opposition to this proposal, that it would be wrong to exclude government from participating in the advantages arising from the future progress of agriculture; and that, in the event of the amount of the tax being fixed, it would be proportionally diminished by any fall that might afterwards take place in the value of money. These objections do not, however, appear to be entitled to much weight; and it is unnecessary, perhaps, to do more than refer, in answer to them, to England and Bengal; and to the advantages that have resulted from the limitation of the land-tax in the one and the establishment of the perpetual settlement in the other. Their experience is conclusive of the question; but we may shortly observe that it is nugatory to suppose that government should not derive the greatest advantage, under the proposed limitation, from the improvement of agriculture. This could not fail to improve the condition of the great bulk of the people, who would consequently pay a comparatively large amount of indirect taxes. At this moment the total revenue of France amounts to about 1100 or 1150 million francs, of which not more than 268 or 270 millions are raised by the *contribution foncière*. If, therefore, the limitation of the latter should give, as it certainly would, a powerful stimulus to agriculture, on which so great a portion of the population is dependent,

it is all but obvious that the revenue would gain instead
of losing by the measure. For the improved condition
of the cultivators, resulting from the encouragement
given to agriculture, would afford them proportionally
greater means of contributing to those indirect taxes
which are the principal sources of revenue, and which are
at present principally paid by them. It is idle, indeed,
to imagine that the condition of the agriculturists of any
country, and especially of one in which this class so greatly
preponderates as in France, can be considerably improved
without an increase of the revenue derived from duties on
commodities. It may, speaking generally, be assumed,
that the more people have to spend the more they will
spend. The fixity of the *contribution foncière* would make
improvements be undertaken that would not otherwise be
thought of; and the system of indirect taxation would
assure to government a participation in their advantages.

The same reasoning applies to the supposition of a
fall in the value of money after the *contribution foncière*
had been limited. Such fall would, in so far, improve
the condition of the occupiers of land ; and their increased
consumption of other things would afford the same or a
greater amount of revenue to government.

There cannot, therefore, as it appears to us, be any
reasonable doubt of the many advantages that would
accrue from fixing the amount of the *contribution foncière*
exigible in future from all properties. When thus
limited, it would cease to be an obstacle to improvements, and the agriculturists would have that perfect
security of which they are at present deprived. And,
provided means were at the same time devised for putting a stop to the endless division and subdivision of the
land, occasioned by the present law of succession, the
prosperity of agriculture would be ensured.

A large proportion of the produce of the *contribution
foncière* is absorbed in provincial expenses, or those incident
to the administration of the departments and communes.

Thus, of 268,270,250 fr., the total produce of the tax in 1842, no fewer than 78,507,990 fr. were retained to defray local expenditure.

We have entered into these details, partly because of the light which they appear to throw on the nature and operation of an important description of taxes, and partly because they are but little understood in this country. So little, indeed, do we know of the mode in which the public revenue is raised in France, that a notion seems to be generally entertained that it is principally derived from the land, and that a very large proportion of the territorial produce of the country is appropriated by government. Nothing, however, can be more completely unfounded than such a notion; and, how much soever it may be at variance with the popular opinion on the subject, it is certain that, including tithes, poor-rates, and other county rates, the land of England is twice as heavily taxed as that of France.

In Austria and Prussia the land-tax furnishes a large proportion of the public revenue. The governments of both countries have laudably exerted themselves for a lengthened period to introduce a regular plan of assessment, and to make all lands, whether held by nobles or others, contribute equally to the wants of the state. But notwithstanding the efforts to equalise the assessment, it still differs very widely in different provinces, and sometimes even in different cantons of the same province. The principle generally followed is to assess the tax on the net produce of the land, supposing it to be in a medium state of improvement; the net produce including, as in France, the rent, but excluding the seed and all expenses of cultivation.*

* For full details as to land-tax of Austria, see the valuable work of Tegoborski, " Des Finances et du Crédit Publique d'Autriche," i. pp. 143—195.

CHAPTER III.

TAXES ON WAGES.

In every discussion respecting the influence of taxes on wages, or on the necessaries consumed by the labourer, it is indispensable to distinguish between the *natural* or *necessary* rate of wages, or the rate required to enable the labourers to subsist and continue their race, and the *market* rate, or the rate paid them at any particular period.

The natural or necessary price of labour, like that of everything else which may be indefinitely increased or diminished, is determined by the cost of its production. The capacity of the labourer to support himself, and to rear as many children as may be required to keep up the supply of labourers, does not, it is plain, depend on the sum of money he receives as wages, but on the quantity of food, necessaries, and conveniences essential to his support, for which that money will exchange. The natural rate of wages must, therefore, depend on the cost of producing the food, and other necessaries, required for the maintenance of the labourer. A rise in the market rate of wages does not always coincide with a rise in the price of necessaries; but they can seldom be far separated. However high the price of necessaries may rise, the labourers, speaking generally, must always receive such a quantity as may enable them to support themselves and continue their race : were wages to fall below this necessary level, they would be left destitute, and the consequent diminution of their numbers would sooner or later raise wages to their old level, or to one not very different from it : and on the other hand, were wages to rise considerably above this necessary level, a proportional stimulus would be given to population, and the increase of labourers would, in the long run, lower wages.

In considering the influence of taxes, or of variations in the price of the articles used by the labourer, on wages, it is necessary to inquire whether the latter are rated by the day or other specified portion of time, or by the piece. In this country they are partly rated in the one way, and partly in the other; and though, from household servants being mostly paid by time, the generality of persons are most familiar with wages so rated, it may be doubted whether the sums paid on their account greatly exceed those paid to labourers by the job or the piece. This distinction has been little, if at all, attended to by writers on Political Economy; and it may appear to a careless observer as if it were immaterial, in estimating the influence of taxes on wages and necessaries, whether workpeople are employed in the one way or the other. But a little consideration will serve to show that this is very far, indeed, from being the case, and that it is indispensable, in reasoning upon such matters, that the distinction in question should be kept steadily in view.

This, however, is not the only distinction to be attended to in these discussions. It is further indispensable, if we would form any accurate conclusions respecting the influence of taxation on wages and necessaries, to ascertain whether the labourers (however hired) subject to such taxes live in the houses of their employers, or apart from them in their own lodgings, and on their own account. It is evident that taxes on the articles consumed by domestic servants do not fall on them, but on their masters. Probably, indeed, such taxes, when carried beyond their proper limits, may make fewer servants be employed; but, except in so far as they operate in this way, the duties on sugar, tea, beer, soap, and other articles used by household servants, are wholly paid by those with whom

they live. Hence the importance of distinguishing in
these investigations between such labourers and those depending on their own resources. Everybody knows that
the class of domestic servants in this and other civilized
countries is very large indeed; but, how large soever, it
is apparent that a proportionally large share of the taxes
which are said to fall wholly on the lower classes, is neither
assessed upon nor paid by them, and in most cases hardly
even affects them indirectly. The following remarks will,
therefore, refer to those labourers only, whether engaged by
time or by the piece, who do not live with their employers,
but who provide themselves with lodging and subsistence.

The opinion of those who contend that the rate of
wages does not depend on the cost of the articles consumed by the labourers, but on the demand for their exertions compared with their numbers, has obviously
originated in their confounding the principles which
govern the market price of labour, at a particular period,
with those which govern its natural or necessary price.
But though the market price of labour at any given
period depends on the state of its supply as compared
with the demand, it is easy to see that the supply will
cease to be brought to market unless the rate of wages be
generally sufficient to maintain and bring up labourers;
that is, if we may so speak, unless the cost of their
production be paid. From whatever point of the political compass we may set out, this is the principle to
which we must always come at last. To set this in a
clearer point of view, let it be supposed that, owing to a
scarcity, the price of bread is doubled: it is plain, inasmuch as the same number of labourers would be seeking
for employment after the rise as before, and as there is
no ground for supposing that a scarcity should increase
the demand for labour, that wages would not be advanced; the labourers would, in consequence, be forced
to economize, and the rise of price would thus have the

effect of lessening consumption, and of distributing the
pressure equally throughout the year. But suppose that
the rise, instead of being occasioned by a deficient crop,
has been occasioned by an increased difficulty of production, and that it will be permanent, the question is, will
wages continue at their former rate, or will they rise?
In this case the probability is that they will rise ; but the
mode in which the rise will be effected will differ most
materially in the case of labourers paid by time, and of
those paid by the piece. It is plain that the situation
of both classes will be changed very much for the worse
by the rise of prices; and those hired by the day, week,
&c., who, previously to the rise, had only enough to subsist upon, will be reduced to a state bordering on desti-
tution. Under such circumstances, an increase of mortality can hardly fail to take place; while the greater
difficulty of providing subsistence will interpose a powerful check to matrimonial connexions and the increase of
population. By these means, therefore, the number of
labourers in this class, or the ratio of their increase, or
both, will in all likelihood be diminished; and this diminution will continue until wages have been raised to
their natural rate; that is, as Smith has defined it, to
such a rate as may enable them to obtain "not only the
commodities which are indispensably necessary for the
support of life, but whatever the custom of the country
renders it indecent for creditable people, even of the
lowest order, to be without."

But the piece-work labourers have another resource. If
A be hired to execute any given work, by which, when using
ordinary diligence, he makes 3s. or 3s. 6d. a-day, he may,
perhaps, be able, by using greater diligence, to make 4s. or
4s. 6d. a-day ; and may in this way be fully able to meet the
increased burdens he is called upon to sustain. It is obvious, too, that every fall of wages, however brought about,
unless it be so very great as to prostrate all their energies, will not merely stimulate the labourers by piece-work

H

to redouble their exertions, but will make them exert
themselves to discover new and more easy methods of
accomplishing their tasks.   What is true of necessity is
true of taxation : if not carried to an extreme, it undoubtedly occasions fresh displays of industry, frugality, and ingenuity.

Dr. Smith contends that the labouring classes contribute
nothing of consequence to the public revenue; and Mr.
Ricardo has expressed his concurrence in this opinion.
But, notwithstanding the deference due to their authority,
the previous statements show that this opinion must be
received with very great modification.   Had it been restricted to the case of household servants, it would have
been very nearly correct ; but it may be, and we believe
most frequently is, very wide of the mark when applied
to the case of out-of-door labourers, whether working by
time or by the job.   Those hired in the former mode cannot, it is true, meet the burden imposed by additional taxes,
or by a rise of prices, by increased exertion ; but they may
be in a condition to meet it in whole, or in part, by increased frugality, without changing their habits as to marriage ; and it is only in the event of their inability to do
this that it will affect their numbers, and be, in the end,
wholly or partly compensated by a corresponding rise of
wages.   But that large class of labourers who work by the
piece, and by whom manufactures of all sorts are principally carried on, may, and certainly do, in all cases, make
large contributions to the public revenue.   A tax on any
article consumed by them, provided it be not excessive,
never fails to make them more industrious.   Were their
powers already tasked to the utmost such, of course, would
not be the case.   But, though far from being so comfortable as might be wished, they are not, fortunately. reduced
to this miserable state either here or any where else : they
have still ample room for the exercise of greater industry.
frugality, and ingenuity ; and so long as this is the case,
they will continue to contribute in the most effectual man-

ner to the revenue. We have great doubts whether the taxes on tobacco, spirits, and tea, have added anything to the wages of labour; and whether all the large sums contributed to them by out-of-door labourers be not wholly the result of the greater industry and frugality occasioned by their desire to command these gratifications.

If a specific quantity of certain articles were necessary for the subsistence of labourers, the rate of wages, it is plain, could not be reduced for any considerable period below that quantity or the sum of money that would buy it. But there is no such absolute standard of natural wages. The articles which are deemed necessaries, and the quantity of such articles required by the labourer, depend, in a great degree, on custom and habit, and are, in consequence, extremely variable. The people of Hindostan principally subsist on rice, those of Ireland on potatoes, and those of England on bread and beef. In one country it is discreditable for the lowest orders to be without comfortable clothing, including shoes and stockings, while in others, with a different climate, or with different habits, the clothing of the people may be comparatively scanty and inferior, and shoes and stockings be used only by the rich. In many provinces of France and Spain a certain allowance of wine is considered indispensable; and in England the labouring class entertain nearly the same opinion with respect to beer and porter. The differences of public taste at different periods in the history of the same countries are equally striking. The articles which custom and habit render necessary for the comfortable subsistence of the English and Scotch labourers of the present day are as widely different from those which were judged necessaries by their ancestors in the reigns of Elizabeth, James I., and Charles I., as they are from those which form the ordinary subsistence of the labourers of France and Spain. Despite the depressing influence of heavy taxes and other circumstances, the

H 2

standard of natural wages has been raised, and the poor have been taught to form more elevated notions respecting the quantity and the species of the articles which it would be discreditable for them to be without.

The natural rate of wages is not, therefore, fixed and unvarying; and though it be true that the market rate of wages can never, when reference is made to periods of considerable duration, be sunk below its contemporary natural rate, it is no less true that the natural rate has a tendency to rise when the market rate rises, and to fall when it falls. The reason is, that the supply of labour in the market can neither be speedily increased when wages rise, nor speedily diminished when they fall; and the powerful influence which fluctuations in the market rate of wages have over the condition of the labouring classes, especially the portion which is engaged by time, principally depends on this circumstance. If the supply of labour were suddenly increased when wages rise, that rise would be of little or no advantage to the existing labourers. It would increase their number, but it would not enable them to mount in the scale of society, or to obtain a larger supply of necessaries and conveniences. And, on the other hand, if the supply of labour were suddenly diminished when wages fall, that fall would merely lessen the number of labourers, without having any tendency to degrade their habits or to lower their condition. But, speaking generally, no rise of wages can be countervailed by an increased supply of workmen coming into the market until eighteen or twenty years after it has taken place; for there are few or no branches of industry in which an active and skilful labourer can be bred in a shorter period. During all this interval, therefore, the labourer is placed in an improved situation. He has a larger supply of food; he has better clothes and a better habitation; he is rendered more attentive to cleanliness; and as he rises in the scale of society, he naturally uses more prudence and circumspection in the forming of matrimonial connexions. In short, his opinions respecting what is necessary for his decent and comfortable subsistence are raised, and the natural rate of wages is, in consequence, proportionally augmented.

The principle now stated may, however, be modified in practice, if foreign labourers, or labourers from a different part of the same country, be permitted freely to immigrate into the country, or portion of the country, where wages have risen. There can be no doubt, for example, that any considerable increase of wages in England would give an increased stimulus to immigration from Ireland; and that the English labourers would, in consequence, be deprived, in part at least, of the advantages which the increase would otherwise confer on them.

It is equally impossible suddenly to diminish the number of labourers when wages fall. Such diminution cannot, as already stated, be effected otherwise than by an increase of mortality, or by a decrease in the number of births, or both. But unless the fall were very sudden and extensive, it would require a considerable number of years to render the effects of increased mortality very apparent; and it is so difficult to change the habits of a people, that, though the demand for labour were to decline, it would, notwithstanding, continue for a while to flow into the market with nearly the same rapidity as before. Nor would the amount of population, or the rate of its increase, be materially diminished, until the misery occasioned by the restricted demand on the one hand, and the undiminished supply on the other, had been very generally felt.

In whatever way, therefore, a fall of the wages of labourers hired by time and supplying themselves with food and other accommodations may be counteracted, and their restoration to their old level brought about — whether it be by increased mortality, or a decreased number of births, or both, it can never be the work of an instant. It must always require a considerable time before it can be effected; and there is in consequence an obvious risk lest the habits of the labourers should in the mean time be degraded. When wages are reduced, or necessaries are raised in price, the poor, unable to meet the difficulty by greater diligence, are obliged to economise; and should the coarse and scanty fare that is thus, in the first instance, forced upon them by necessity, become in the end congenial from habit, no check would be given to population, and the natural rate of wages would be permanently reduced. In such a case the cost of raising labourers would be diminished; and this cost determines the natural rate of wages, with which the market rate must generally correspond. A fall of wages is therefore as peculiarly injurious to the labourers as a rise of wages is peculiarly beneficial to them. Its obvious tendency is to degrade the condition of all the great class engaged by time, and to add, in the first instance, to the privations of the other class : and wherever the labourers can bear to retrench, or to descend from a higher to a lower station, it will most likely sink them in the scale of society, unless their desire to preserve their place should occasion a greater prevalence of moral restraint, and a slower increase of population.

It is true, indeed, as has been stated by Mr. Malthus, that, to whatever extent wages fall, the labourers possess the means of raising them to their former or to a higher level; that, if they understock the market with labour, wages will continue high, notwithstanding the means of employment should be diminished; and that if they overstock the market with labour, wages will be low, even though these means should be very considerably increased. But a principle of this sort, though easily stated, is most difficult to act upon. The conduct of the bulk of individuals is influenced by circumstances peculiar to the narrow sphere in which they move, and which directly affect themselves, and not by considerations having reference to society. Even supposing that a considerable proportion of the population should acquiesce in the abstract truth of the principle stated by Malthus, their acquiescence would, most likely, have little or no practical influence. An individual sees what would be of advantage to society; but to secure that advantage the co-operation of vast numbers is required; and as he is *one* only among several millions, he justly thinks that all that he could do would be of no consequence whatever in bringing about a general result, and that consequently he should act as he considers best for himself without regard to others. Ninety-nine out of every hundred persons proceed on this principle. Combination to bring about a general and remote result is in such cases impossible. If you satisfy any one that his peculiar interests, or those of his near connexions and dependents, will be advanced by his abandoning one line of conduct and following another, there is some probability that he will make the change. But to effect this you must address yourself to his selfishness, and not to his patriotism. If you tell him that by making the change he will benefit society, the chances are a hundred to one (unless his vanity be of the most inordinate description) he will pay no attention to your statements, and will not be in the slightest degree influenced by them. And it were idle to suppose that it should be otherwise. All ordinary individuals must be too conscious of their own insignificance, and have too little interest in the well-being of those to the vast majority of whom even their existence is unknown, to think of sacrificing or postponing their own gratification or advantage for that of the public. Hence the extreme difficulty of changing the habits of any people, even when they are decidedly prejudicial. And if, owing to any alteration of the circumstances under which society is placed, the progress of population should require to be slack-

ened, we may be assured that the change will be effected
slowly and with much difficulty; and not till the influence of the circumstances to be countervailed has been
very widely and sensibly felt. Prospective considerations
have comparatively little influence over the labouring
classes; they always operate with the greatest force
on the middle and upper classes: wherever, indeed,
the bulk of the people are in a depressed condition,
these considerations have comparatively little practical
influence; and it is not till their circumstances begin to
improve, and their prospects are brightened, that they
begin seriously to weigh and reflect upon the consequences
of improvident unions.

Dr. Smith has said that, "while the demand for
labour and the price of provisions *remain the same,* a direct tax on the wages of labour can have no other effect
than to raise them somewhat higher than the tax."*
And he further supposes that, to whatever extent the
wages of manufacturing labour may be increased by
a tax, the burden will ultimately fall, not on the
manufacturers or merchants, but on the consumers, by
an increase in the price of commodities; and that, to
whatever extent the tax may raise the wages of agricultural labour, it will really fall, not on the farmer or the
consumer, but on the landlord.

It is, however, easy to see that these conclusions are
incorrect. The immediate influence of taxes over wages
does not depend on the circumstance of the demand for
labour continuing stationary, but on the mode in which
the produce of the tax is expended. And it is now
admitted on all hands, that, when wages rise, either
from being taxed, or any other cause, that rise does
not raise the price of commodities, or lower rent, but
forms a deduction from the profits or incomes of those
who employ labour.

* Wealth of Nations, p. 390.

To illustrate its operation, suppose that a tax of ten per cent. is imposed on wages, or that all labourers are made to hand over ten per cent. of their earnings to collectors appointed by government: seeing that no part of this tax is taken from the employers, it is clear it cannot in any way diminish their means of hiring labour. Its effect must, therefore, depend on the mode in which it is expended. If the produce of the tax be laid out in hiring additional troops or sailors, it is easy to see that it can be productive of no immediate injury to the labourer; for were such the case, the agents of government would enter the market for labour with means of purchasing, derived (not from the employers, but) from the labourers themselves; and, in consequence of this greater competition, wages would be raised in exact proportion to the additional means in the hands of government, or, in other words, to the amount of the tax. An example will render this apparent: suppose that the labourers in a particular country receive as wages 2,000,000*l.* a-year; and suppose, further, that government wish to increase the military force, and that, to get the means of doing so, a tax of ten per cent., or of 200,000*l.*, is laid on wages. The unavoidable consequence will be, that the employers will still come into the market for labour with the 2,000,000*l.* expended by them on wages, while the agents of government will also come into the same market with the 200,000*l.* derived from the tax; so that, between the two, wages will be raised in exact proportion to the tax.

But if the tax were laid out, not, as has been supposed, in hiring additional troops, but in increasing the pay of those already embodied, or of the other functionaries employed by government, its effect would be different. In this case there would be no additional demand for labour. The individuals receiving the tax would, indeed, have a greater demand for the produce of

labour; but their greater demand, being merely equivalent to the diminished demand of the labourers by whom
the tax had been paid, would make no real addition to
the total demand of the country. And thus it appears
that when the produce of a tax on wages is employed to
hire fresh individuals for the service of government, it
raises, by taking so much labour out of the market, the
price of the remainder in proportion to its amount.
But when its produce is employed to increase the wages
of public functionaries or of troops already embodied, the
quantity of labour in the market is not lessened, and it
must in consequence fall, in the first instance, wholly on
the labourers. But, even in this last case, a tax on
wages might not, and it is most probable would not, continue to be paid entirely out of wages. Such tax,
when first imposed, could hardly fail, by lessening the
comforts, and perhaps also the necessaries, of the labourer,
to check the progress of population, as well by retarding
the period of marriage as by increasing the rate of
mortality; and in consequence of the diminution of
labourers arising from these causes, wages might be
raised so as to throw the tax either wholly or partially
on the employers.

But, for the reasons already stated, there are very
considerable obstacles to a rise of wages in the way now
pointed out; and should their reluctance to change their
habits as to marriage lead the poor to submit to a lower
standard of comfort, wages would be permanently reduced, and their condition changed in so far for the
worse. It will be afterwards seen that the influence of
direct taxes on wages, as well as of those which affect
them indirectly by being laid on the articles consumed
by the labourers, depends most materially on the condition of the country at the time when they are
imposed; and that burdens which, in an advancing
society, might be productive only of some trifling temporary inconvenience, might, in a stationary or retro-

grade society, be permanently and in the highest degree adverse to the interests of the labouring class. But, without reference to the state of society, it is always best to guard against whatever has any tendency to lower the habits of the bulk of the people, or to reconcile them to an inferior scale of living; and on that ground we should be disposed to consider direct taxes on wages as most objectionable, unless their produce were expended on the employment of additional troops, or in removing labour from the market. And even in the cases in which taxes on wages are so expended, it seems very questionable whether they should be resorted to. It would be exceedingly difficult to convince the labourers that the produce of a tax on wages, however laid out, ever reverted to them. They would see the immediate sacrifice they were called upon to make, but they would see no more. If their condition were not deteriorated, it would be ascribed to causes which the tax would not be considered as promoting, but as counteracting. Such taxes would therefore be in no ordinary degree unpopular. And, besides, it is clear that, if they are expended so as to raise wages—and otherwise they should on no account be imposed—they may as well be laid directly on the employers. If the latter do not pay such taxes at first, they must pay them at second hand. And though their effects were in other respects somewhat different, a prudent administration would rather choose to tax the employers directly than to tax them indirectly, by laying burdens in the first instance on the labourers that will ultimately fall on them. It is true that the plan of directly taxing the employers is of no real advantage to the labourers; but neither is it injurious to the former; and the circumstance of its tending to lessen popular irritation, and to facilitate the imposition of the tax, should make it be preferred.

It is obvious, from what has been stated, that the real injury inflicted on the labourers by a tax on wages,

expended in the way now supposed, consists not in its
immediate, but in its remote effects.   By falling on profits its tendency is to diminish the power to accumulate
capital; and when carried so far as to have this effect, it
cannot fail, unless the stimulus previously given to
population be at the same time diminished by the more
powerful operation of moral restraint, to depress the
condition of the labourers, and lower the natural rate of
wages.

Without undervaluing the mischievous influence of
taxes on necessaries over the condition of the inferior
classes, it may be doubted whether their depressed situation
in this country is to be ascribed to them.   Indeed, the
taxes laid directly on necessaries amongst us are small
compared with those laid on them in most continental
states.   In Holland, Prussia, and Austria duties are imposed on corn when ground at the mill ; and in the countries now referred to, and in France, duties *(octrois)* are
laid on butchers' meat and most other articles brought
into all considerable towns, and on salt, beer, houses, &c.
It must be admitted, however, that the taxation affecting
food in this country is heavier than it appears to be from
the operation of the corn laws ; and it must further be
admitted that our industry and means of enjoyment are
seriously crippled by the high duties laid on the importation of butter, cheese, sugar, and other products, in
the view of protecting branches of industry carried on at
home or in the colonies.   But while we admit the influence
of these and such like circumstances, we much fear that
the unprosperous condition of the bulk of the manufacturing and other labourers is principally a consequence of
different and, for the most part, less obvious and more
deeply seated causes.
Without entering at any length on this difficult inquiry,
which is, indeed, foreign to the objects of this work, we
may shortly observe, that our proximity to Ireland, and

the vast influx of workpeople, or rather of pauper hordes
from thence, has powerfully contributed to reduce wages
on this side the channel, partly by increasing the competition for employment; but more by familiarizing the English and Scotch labourers with a lower standard of comfort,
and teaching them to be contented with all sorts of cheaper
and inferior accommodations. We believe that this has
done and is continuing to do great injury to our work-
people. But we apprehend, how paradoxical soever the
statement may at first sight appear, that they have sustained still greater injury from the late extraordinary
extension of the manufacturing system. In the first instance, no doubt, this system, which originated in the
wonderful inventions and discoveries of Watt, Arkwright,
and others, occasioned a great rise of wages, and a proportional improvement in the situation of the labouring class.
This would necessarily have led, under any circumstances,
to an increase of population; but its influence in this
respect was prodigiously augmented by the circumstance
of the increased demand for labour not being confined
to that of males, nor even of adults, but of its comprising
that of young persons of both sexes and of the tenderest
years. In consequence a family became in the manufacturing towns a source of wealth to their parents instead of
a burden; and the population of Lancashire, the West
Riding of Yorkshire, and of the manufacturing districts
generally, being exposed to the full action of this powerful
stimulus, has increased with the rapidity of the most
prosperous colony. Unluckily, however, a tendency of
this sort, when once impressed upon a population, can
only, as already shown, be countervailed slowly and with
extreme difficulty; and notwithstanding the condition of
the labouring classes has been for a lengthened period
far from prosperous, population is still increasing with
great, or rather, we may almost say, appalling rapidity.

The restrictions imposed of late years on the employment of children and young persons in factories can hardly

fail to do something to arrest the progress of population; and it is much to be regretted that they were not enacted at an earlier period. But, considering the vast extent to which the manufacturing system has attained, the immense number of persons depending upon it for support, and the competition to which we are exposed, any further interference with it is become a matter pregnant with danger, and requiring the utmost caution and deliberation. It is impossible at this moment to cast the horoscope of this system, to foresee its revolutions, or to estimate its future influence over society. We confess, however, that our anticipations are not of the most agreeable kind. It appears to be, of its essence, that most sorts of employments should be conducted on a large and continually increasing scale, in great establishments, with the assistance of highly improved and expensive machinery; providing, in this way, for the exaltation of a few individuals by the irremediable helotism of the great majority. And this conclusion would seem to be consistent not only with the nature of manufacturing industry, but with the fact, that though there has been a vast increase of production, and of wealth and comforts among the upper classes engaged in business during the last twenty or thirty years, and a considerable diminution of taxation, the condition of the workpeople during that period has certainly not been in any degree improved, but has rather, we incline to think, been sensibly deteriorated. There may, however, be, and we trust there are, countervailing principles at work, of which we cannot at present trace the operation: and at all events we are, whether for good or for evil, too far advanced in manufactures to think of seriously checking their progress. It is obvious, too, that if we interfere with the mode in which they are carried on, we must do so in an empirical manner; and having no experience of the means by which the injurious consequences with which we are threatened may be averted, or those of an opposite tendency be secured, our interference will, to say the least, be as likely to produce mischief as any-thing else. We do know, however, that we may open additional markets for our manufactured goods, and that we may lighten the burdens of the industrious classes, by suppressing prohibitory regulations, and repealing or modifying injudicious or oppressive taxes; and it is the bounden duty of government to do this much. But, when this has been done, it had better pause. And how unphilosophical soever it may seem, the safest course will then probably be to fold our arms, and to leave the *dé-nouement* to time and Providence.

Taxes of so much a-head, or poll-taxes, upon the labourers employed in the cultivation of the ground were formerly common all over Europe. When they are pay-able to the landlord, as is the case at this moment in Russia, Hungary, and some other countries, they are to be viewed as the rents of the possessions held by the contributors; but when they are paid, as has been the case in France, England, and Holland, to government, they are really taxes on wages. The latter description of poll-taxes have seldom been very productive, and have uniformly been submitted to with great reluctance. They seem to have been first imposed in England in the reign of Edward III.; and their augmentation, in the early part of the reign of his grandson, Richard II., was the principal cause of the discontent and irritation that broke out in the famous rebellion headed by Wat Tyler. Poll-taxes proportioned to the rank and station of the individuals were afterwards imposed in the reigns of Henry VIII., Charles I. and II., and, lastly, in that of William III., when they were finally abolished.

It is unnecessary to dwell at any length on the policy of these taxes. When confined to the labouring classes, they are, to all intents and purposes, taxes on wages. But when they are made to include every description of persons, and are varied according to their rank and station, they partake of the nature of an income-tax. It is obvious, however, that such taxes must always be extremely unequal, and therefore extremely objectionable. Two individuals may be of the same rank, and may fill the same station, at the same time that the income of the one may be ten or twenty times greater than the income of the other. Surely, however, it is unnecessary to say that nothing could be more unjust, or contrary to sound principle, than to impose an equal direct tax on these persons. A man's rank or station is no test of his income. But, as it is the only test that can be resorted to in the imposition of a graduated poll-tax, it shows conclusively that it can never be fairly assessed, and consequently that it should not be adopted.

The *taxe personnelle*, or poll-tax, existing at present in France, consists of the value of three days' labour due by all individuals of both sexes in the enjoyment of civil rights, and not classed as paupers. The principal sum to be paid is fixed by the council general of each department, under the condition that it shall not be under 50 c. a day, nor above 1 fr. 50 c.; but this principal may be indefinitely augmented by the imposition of *centimes additionnels*.

Having thus endeavoured to trace and exhibit the effects that would result from the imposition of taxes separately affecting rent, profits, and wages, we shall now proceed briefly to inquire into the effects that would result from the imposition of taxes proportioned to the property and income of individuals. The influence of indirect taxes on wages, or of taxes on the articles consumed by the labourer, will be inquired into in a subsequent chapter.

CHAPTER IV.

TAXES ON PROPERTY AND INCOME.

A GOOD many of the statements made, and principles laid down, in the previous chapters, apply directly, and others indirectly, to taxes on property and income. But, besides the importance of the latter as sources of public revenue, the mode of their assessment, and their probable influence as compared with other taxes, involve so many considerations and questions so delicate, that it seems necessary to submit them to a separate and somewhat lengthened examination.

Whatever difficulties may occur in estimating the incidence and practical operation of taxes on property and income, there can, at all events, be no question in regard to the principle on which they should be imposed. It is agreed on all hands that they should be made to square with the first of Dr. Smith's general maxims, or be assessed so that they may fall on different individuals " *in proportion to their respective abilities, or in proportion to the revenue which they respectively enjoy under the protection of the state.*" Thus far everything is obvious; but when we propose acting on this principle, sundry difficulties present themselves. Shall we take the properties of different individuals as evidences of their ability to bear taxes, and assess property only? Shall we estimate the value of different sorts of property by the same standard, and subject the owner of a capital of 1000*l.* to the same rate of taxation as the owner of a capital of 10,000*l.* or 100,000*l.*? Or, supposing income to be assessed, we have then to inquire whether the incomes of professional men should be as

I

heavily taxed as those of landlords and capitalists? and
whether the same proportional charge should be made
on incomes of 100*l*. or 500*l*. a-year, as on those of 1000*l*.
or 5000*l*.? These are not questions of easy solution;
and yet it is indispensable that they should be disposed
of one way or other before we can form anything like a
correct appreciation of the influence of taxes on property
and income.

If the choice lay only between a tax on property
and a tax on income, we incline to think that the
latter should be preferred. It will be afterwards seen
that it is all but impossible to ascertain incomes with
anything like accuracy, or to tax them fairly after they
are ascertained. But whatever errors may be made
in estimating and assessing income would be at least
equalled, and probably exceeded, by those that would be
made were it attempted to estimate and assess property.
Let any one fancy himself appointed to value the property
of some one of his neighbours engaged in agriculture,
or in any department of trade or manufacture, and a
very little reflection will satisfy him that the task is one of
no common difficulty. Suppose, for example, that it were
required to estimate the stock of an individual engaged
in farming: in this case, the property to be valued is
mostly all obvious, and it might be supposed that there
would be little difficulty in the matter; and yet, in point
of fact, the difficulties would be next to insuperable. In
the first place, no two individuals would form the same
estimate of the value of any article; and, in the second
place, how are they to decide as to what is to be deemed
stock, and what not? Is all that is upon the farm in the
month of March or the month of August to be deemed
stock, and subjected to taxation? and if not, what deductions are to be made, at each period, to arrive at the
true amount of stock or farming capital employed? Suppose that a field has been recently limed, marled, or other-

wise manured, at a heavy expense,—is the worth of this improvement to be taken into account in estimating the farmer's stock? And if this question be answered (as we think it should be) in the affirmative, how is the value of those manures to be ascertained that have been recently ploughed down and incorporated with the soil? But, supposing the other difficulties to be got over, how are the assessors to deal with the debts that the proprietor or occupier may be under? It is clear they should be deducted from the supposed amount of his capital, and that he should not be obliged to pay duty on what really belongs to another. Although, however, it does not well seem how this concession could be refused, it is easy to see that by making it a wide door would be opened for fraud and evasion; and that it would be no easy matter to distinguish between real and fictitious debts. Were an attempt made to calculate the stock of any individual engaged in trade, the difficulties would be much greater. It is to no purpose referring to books; for, were they used for such an object, it would be the easiest thing in the world to construct them so that they should yield no information, or such only as was false and misleading. In fact, it would be found that, in nine instances out of ten, except in the cases of funded property, money lent on mortgage, and a few others, nothing better than the declarations of the parties concerned could be obtained; and we look upon every system of taxation as radically vicious that sets the interest and the duty of individuals at variance—that tempts them to balance between the loss of property and the commission of perjury.

But, admitting that it were possible, which it obviously is not, to form a tolerably fair estimate of the property of individuals, its adoption as a standard by which to determine the amount of taxation would be singularly inexpedient. It is necessary to look as well at the practical operation as at the apparent justice of a principle. On a superficial view, nothing seems fairer, supposing the property of individuals were known, than to tax them proportionally; and yet few things would, in reality, be more unfair or more mischievous.

The productiveness of their property is quite as important an element in measuring the ability of individuals to bear taxes as its amount. A has a farm, a house, or a shop, worth 500*l.* a-year, let to a substantial tenant who pays his rent punctually: B also has a property of the same kind and of the same value, but it happens to be let to a bad tenant, unable to pay the rent. In like manner, one ship-owner has a ship at sea, making a profitable voyage, while that of another is in port unemployed. The furnaces of one iron-master are in blast, while those of others are out of blast: and so in fifty other instances. And such being the case, could anything be more unjust—more completely at variance with the principle of proportioning taxes to the ability of the contributors—than to subject parties placed under such different circumstances to the same rate of taxation? Hence, if we would keep this principle in view, it is plain that the productiveness as well as the amount of the property belonging to individuals must be taken into account in subjecting them to taxes. Property, taken by itself, is no accurate test of the capacity to bear taxes: that depends quite as much on income as on property; and to leave the former out of view in assessing taxes of this description would be like leaving the influence of currents or of contrary winds out of view in estimating the course of a ship.

But, besides being unfair, taxes on property would have other practical consequences of the most mischievous kind. If a tax be laid on income, it creates an inducement to conceal its amount; but it does not tempt any one to employ inferior instruments or processes in carrying on his employment. This, however, is the inevitable effect of taxes on capital or property. The moment they are established, every one attempts to elude their pressure, by concealing a portion of his property, or employing it in some underhand manner. Those engaged in industrious occupations endeavour to carry them on with the least amount of capital. An indisposition is generated to lay out fresh capital on works or improvements, seeing that it will be taken as an evidence of increased wealth, and will consequently expose the parties to additional taxation. The object, under such circumstances, is not to appear rich, but to appear poor; and the reality too often corresponds with the appearance. We have already seen that this was one of the worst consequences of the taille in France; and such, in a greater or less degree, must necessarily be the effect of all taxes proportioned to the capital or property of individuals. Had any such tax existed during the last half-century in England, it is quite impossible that the progress either of manufactures or agriculture could have been half so great as it has been.

Hence it appears that it is only in certain cases—and those probably not the majority — that the property belonging to, or employed by, individuals affords anything like a true criterion of their ability to bear taxes. But, even if the mere amount of property were in all cases sufficient to go by, the preceding statements show, first, that it is next to impossible to determine the amount of capital belonging to the great bulk of individuals; and second, that, supposing it were determined, it would be most unwise to adopt it as a standard of taxation. The impossibility of ascertaining its amount renders taxes proportioned to the property or capital of individuals about the most unequal that can be imagined; while, from their pernicious influence over industry, they become the most prolific sources of poverty and dissatisfaction.

Probably, however, it will be said that we mistake the views of those who propose that a tax should be laid

on property; that it is not meant that it should be universal, or that property engaged in industrious undertakings should be subjected to its operation; but that
it should be assessed only on what is called realized property, or on lands, houses, the public funds, mortgages,
and such-like securities; and that, when so restricted,
the tax would not have the effects previously ascribed
to it.   But, though this be partly true, we contend that
the limitation of the tax in the way now stated would
be flagrantly unjust, and that its operation, if so limited,
would be still more disastrous than if it were extended
to all sorts of property.   There is no foundation for the
notion that land is held by those only who have withdrawn from active life; it is often purchased as a means
of investing capital, and cultivated with no other view
than that of profit.

Suppose two individuals have each 500*l.* or 5000*l.*, and
that the one vests his money in land, the other in a ship;
could anything be more unjust than to tax the property
of the former, and to allow that of the latter to escape?
Would this be making them contribute to the wants of
the state " in proportion to the revenues they respectively enjoy under its protection?" It has been said, in
vindication of this inequality, that the properties are of
a different description; that the land will last for ever,
whereas the ship will be speedily worn out.   And no
doubt this is true; but it is also true that, while the land
will not yield more, probably, than 200*l.* a-year to its
owner, the ship will, at an average, produce 500*l.* or
600*l.*, or more; and by accumulating the surplus a sum
will be provided sufficient to replace the ship when she
is worn out.   Insurance effectually provides against all
risk of loss by accident, so much so, that the capital
vested in a ship or a cotton-mill may be rendered substantially as secure as if it were vested in land.

The greatest possible misconception prevails among
the great majority of the manufacturing, mercantile, and

moneyed classes, with respect to the situation and circumstances of the owners of land.   The possessors of great estates are but few in number.   Inasmuch, however, as they fill high stations and stand prominently forward, they engross the attention of the careless observer, and prevent his fixing his eye on the mass of obscure petty landowners who make up the great bulk of the class.   The land belonging to opulent proprietors bears, in fact, no sort of proportion to that which belongs to persons of middling and very small fortune.   Nothing can be a greater mistake than to suppose, as is generally done, that the landowners are an extremely opulent and an extremely indolent body.   These may be the characteristics of a few individuals amongst them; but it would be quite as wide of the mark to affirm that they are generally applicable to the entire class as that they are universally applicable to the classes of manufacturers and traders. We have made some inquiries upon this point, and we are convinced that, if the landlords of England and the master manufacturers be compared together, the latter will be found, speaking generally, to be the richer, but hardly the more industrious, of the two.   In the majority of English counties property is subdivided to a far greater extent than is commonly supposed; and there are few that lead a more laborious life, or are more under the necessity of abstaining from luxurious indulgences, than the owners and occupiers of small landed properties.*   At this moment the entire landed rental of England and Wales may be taken at about thirty-four millions.   Now, as this has to be divided among, at least, 200,000 proprietors, it gives to each an average income of about 170*l.* a-year.   And seeing that a few have much more, it follows that many must have a great deal less.   However little conversant with national statistics, those acquainted with the situation of

---

* Land is not nearly so much subdivided in Scotland, but even there it is much parcelled in some districts.

the " statesmen," or small landed proprietors, of Cumberland and Westmoreland; the yeomen of many of the midland and southern counties; the copartners of Lincolnshire, &c., will have little difficulty in admitting what has now been stated. In extensive districts of Lincoln the smaller class of properties vary from 1 to 50 acres. Arthur Young, in his survey of the county, says that their proprietors are very happy; adding, however, that he was told " The little proprietors work like negroes, and do not live so well as the inhabitants of the poor-houses." *

We are very far, however, from saying or insinuating that this should be considered as anything like a fair representation of the general condition of the smaller class of proprietors in England. But assuredly there are few classes to whom industry and self-denial are more indispensable. Indolence or extravagance would speedily sink them to the condition of labourers. It is only, indeed, by persevering exertion and economy that they preserve their place in society and bring up their families.

But though the landlords were generally as rich and luxurious as is imagined, or at least represented by the demagogues in manufacturing towns, the plan for laying exclusive taxes on their property would be too grossly partial and unfair to entitle it to much attention. When, however, instead of being rich, the great majority of landlords are either poor or in but very indifferent circumstances, the iniquity of the proposal becomes still more glaring. To suppose that it should be established by law would be a libel on Parliament; and to suppose that such a law, if enacted, would be submitted to, would be a libel on the people of England. Many of our richest merchants, bankers, manufacturers, ship-owners, traders, &c., do not possess a single acre of land, and some of them have little or no funded pro-

* Survey of Lincoln, 2nd edit., p. 20.

perty; and is it to be endured that the property of such persons should enjoy a total exemption from that direct taxation which is to fall with its full weight on the individual struggling to support himself and his family on some 5, 10, 50, or 100 acres of land? Surely those who imagine that, if attempted, such enormous injustice would be tolerated, mistake altogether the character and feelings of Englishmen.

It is a still greater mistake to suppose that funded property is principally held by the *fruges consumere nati*, or by those who take no active share in industrious pursuits. The very opposite supposition would be a good deal nearer the truth. Every one, we believe, will allow that those engaged in the businesses of banking and insurance have a fair claim to be ranked amongst the industrious classes; and yet the capitals of bankers and of insurance companies are principally vested in the funds; so that a tax on the latter would really be a tax on the property of some of the most useful and industrious classes of the community. It should also be kept in mind that a large amount of funded property is always held by those who have had capital thrown on their hands which they have not been able to employ in any active pursuit, and which they have vested in the mean time in the funds for the sake of the interest. A tax on the funds would tempt many such persons to keep their idle capital at their banker's or in their strong-box; it would do an injury to the industrious classes, without securing any corresponding advantage to the state.

But this is not all. Those who are so very fond of indulging in declamatory invectives against the fundholders, and who endeavour to prejudice them in the public estimation by representing them as "leviathans of wealth," either know nothing of the matter or speculate upon the ignorance of their readers or hearers. The truth is, that the great majority of fundholders, like the majority of landholders, are persons of very slender

means. The facility of vesting small sums in the funds,
and the circumstance of none of the London banks
having, till very recently, allowed interest on the balances in their hands, have occasioned an immense influx
of small depositors to the funds. The official statement
for 1842 shows that the total number of warrants issued
to receive dividends at the Bank of England in the
quarters ended the 10th of October and 5th January,
amounted to 282,349; and of these no fewer than 85,991
were warrants to receive sums under, and not exceeding,
5*l*. ! Above 45,000 warrants were at the same time issued for sums under, and not exceeding, 10*l*.   It is,
perhaps, still more singular that only 210 warrants were
issued for sums of 2000*l*. and upwards.   It will be observed, too, that the dividends due to the Equitable
and other insurance companies, to the Banks of England, Scotland, and Ireland, and to a great number
of other associations, are all paid upon single warrants,
as if they were due to so many private individuals;
whereas they are really paid to the managers of the
institutions in question, merely because they act as
agents or trustees for a vast number of other persons to
whom they are distributed.

It is idle, therefore, to talk about taxing the funds in
order to get at "the overgrown fortunes of the moneyed
class."   At best this is but a robber's pretext.   But
the statements now made show that a tax on the
funds would fall principally on the lower and middle
classes.   It would, without materially abridging the
comforts of the rich, aggravate in no ordinary degree the
difficulties of the industrious part of the community;
and unless the tax were extended to every other description of property, it would be an undisguised breach
of the public faith.

But suppose that we are wrong in the previous statements; that all the lands, funds, and mortgages of the
empire are held by rich individuals not engaged in busi-

ness; and that they may be, not unjustly, burdened with an exclusive tax,—its imposition would, notwithstanding, be most unwise. What object have industrious persons in view? what is it which inspires them with courage to undertake, and resolution to overcome, the most irksome and laborious tasks? The hope that they may be able to realize a fortune in land, funds, or mortgages! But were the state, in its fancied wisdom, to enact that these sorts of property should be exclusively loaded with a heavy direct tax, it is clear that either the process of accumulation would be effectually checked, or, which perhaps is the most probable result, the accumulations, when made, would be carried to foreign countries, where taxes were imposed on some less partial and oppressive principle. It is useless to inquire which of these consequences would be most injurious. It is sufficient to know that either would be ruinous. If we are to have a property-tax, it must be made to affect all who possess property. It is not easy, indeed, to exaggerate the mischievous consequences of such a tax; but they would certainly be very inferior to those that must follow any attempt to assess it exclusively on the property of particular classes.

A tax on income is free from some of the inconveniences now pointed out; but many are inherent in it that should forbid its adoption, except under very peculiar circumstances, or when most other available sources of revenue are exhausted or closed. From a variety of causes, which, as they will readily occur to every one, it is useless to specify, property or capital, though engaged in industrious undertakings, may not yield, perhaps, for a lengthened period, any return to the proprietor. While this untoward state of things continues, a tax on income would not affect its possessors; their capital would continue unimpaired; and when the peculiar circumstances that rendered it unproductive

were obviated, it would yield as large a revenue as ever
to its owners, and consequently furnish as large a tax
to the state.   But a tax on property would operate
very differently, and would, as already seen, affect capital, whether it were productive of profits or not.   Hence
the stock of all individuals, when it happened either to
be employed unproductively or not employed at all,
would be diminished by a tax on property.   This equal,
or rather most unequal tax, would frequently fall where
no tax ought, if possible, ever to fall—on capital, without
giving the contributors any opportunity of defraying it
out of revenue.   It would not be very far from being
as often proportioned to the disability as to the ability
of those on whom it was laid.

A tax on income is free from this inconvenience.   Those
who have no income, or who have their capital so employed that it affords no profits, escape the tax :* in this
respect, therefore, it has a decided advantage over a tax
on property; but in other respects it is nearly as objectionable as the latter.

It is true that an income-tax is, at first sight, apparently the fairest of all taxes.   It seems to make
every one contribute to the wants of the state in proportion to the revenue which he enjoys under its protection; while, by falling equally on all, it occasions no
change in the distribution of capital, or in the natural
direction of industry, and has no influence over prices.
It were much to be wished that any tax could be imposed having such effects; but we are sorry to be obliged
to state that none such has hitherto been discovered;
and those who expect that an income tax, however imposed, should operate in the way now stated, will cer-

---

* We have stated, conformably to the maxim, *ex nihilo nihil fit*, what would
appear to be the plain, common-sense view of a tax on income, viz. that before a
party can be subjected to it, he must have an income to tax.   But, unless there
be something *sui generis* in the case of the Messrs. Fielden, this would not
appear to be necessary.   See notice of this case in the Appendix.

tainly be very much disappointed. An income-tax would, no doubt, have the supposed effects, were it possible fairly to assess it. But the practical difficulties in the way of its fair assessment are not of a sort that can be over-come. And the truth is, that taxes on income, though theoretically equal, are, in their practical operation, most unequal and vexatious.

The difficulties in the way of assessing income are of two sorts : 1st, the difficulty of ascertaining the incomes of different individuals; and, 2nd, supposing their amount to be known, the difficulty of laying an equal tax on in-comes derived from different sources.

1. It would be useless to dwell at any considerable length on the first of these heads. Incomes arising from the rent of land and houses, mortgages, funded property, and such-like sources, may be learned with tolerable precision; but it neither has been, and, we are bold to say, never will be, possible to determine the incomes of farmers, manufacturers, dealers of all sorts, and professional men, with anything like even the rudest approximation to accuracy.

Most persons have the greatest dislike to the payment of direct taxes; and though occasionally a few individuals may be found who, either from a wish to be thought richer than they really are, or from a desire to quiet the suspicions of their creditors, return their incomes beyond their real amount, the vast majority endeavour to conceal and underrate them. The strength of the motive to such concealment depends, of course, on the amount of the tax; and those who might willingly make a *bonâ fide* disclosure of their incomes, did it amount to only 3, 4, or 5 per cent., might take every possible means to conceal them did the tax amount to 10, 12, or 15 per cent. But, how low soever the rate of duty, a great many individuals will always endeavour to evade or elude its pressure. And it is next to impossible to defeat the machinations of such persons by instituting an examination into the state of their affairs. In very many cases such examination can lead to no satisfactory results; and the commissioners employed to assess the tax must either accept the returns sent by those parties whose revenues are not derived from visible and easily appreciated sources, when verified by their oath, or they must be authorized to assess them according to their own notion of what is right and proper. If the former criterion be adopted, everything is made to depend on the honour of the parties, so that the tax will then fall with its full weight upon men of integrity, while the *millionnaire* of " easy virtue" may well-nigh escape it altogether. Hence it may be truly said to be a tax on honesty and a bounty on perjury and fraud; and were it carried to any considerable height, or to 10, 12, or 15 per cent., it would undoubtedly generate the most barefaced prostitution of principle, and would do much to sap that nice sense of honour which is the only sure foundation of national probity and virtue.

But whatever may be the consequences of making the amount of the assessment depend on the oath of the contributors, the fair presumption is that they will be still worse when it is left to the discretion of the commissioners to fix its amount. Even when most inclined to do what is right, the commissioners cannot fail frequently to do that which is wrong; and while a wide door is opened for the exercise of favouritism and preferences, the honest, though erroneous decisions of the commissioners may be ascribed to the basest motives. It is in fact impossible, do what you will, to assess large classes of incomes with any considerable fairness. The parties will not disclose them, and it is not in the power of any one else to learn their amount.

To be aware of the all but insuperable difficulties that have to be encountered in attempting to learn the real incomes of individuals, one has only to look into the clauses in the Act 5 & 6 Victoria, cap. 35, imposing the present income-tax, which refer to the assessing of incomes derived from trades and professions, and to those relating to appeals. They are framed to meet, in as far as practicable, every case, and give the commissioners the most ample means of ascertaining the incomes of individuals by authorising them to demand papers and answers to written and *vivâ voce* questions, which the parties may be called upon to verify on oath, to examine witnesses, &c. And yet, notwithstanding these investigations and the moderation of the tax, everybody knows that evasion and concealment are extensively practised; and that, while some are taxed to the full amount of their incomes, or perhaps even more, the greater number, being either less honest or more fortunate in their appeals, succeed in evading a portion of the duty.

2. But supposing it were possible (which it plainly is not) to get over this fundamental objection, and that means were devised for easily ascertaining the incomes of different individuals with something like precision, we should have made but a very small progress towards the fair assessment of the tax. On one point, indeed, there can be no difficulty. Property-taxes should undoubtedly be laid on all sorts of property, and income-taxes on all sorts of income. But the question immediately occurs, whether should the tax be of the same magnitude on all sorts of income? And if this question be answered in the negative, we have next to inquire into the principle on which distinctions should be made.

Those who say that an income-tax should be laid equally on all incomes, from whatever source derived, contend that the hardship of such a proceeding is not real, but apparent. The incomes of lawyers, physicians, clergymen, and other professional men, must, they affirm, always bear a certain relation to the incomes of the landlords, manufacturers, and other classes; but if the former were not taxed to the same extent as the latter, this relation would be subverted; the condition of professional men would be relatively improved; and it is alleged that, under such circumstances, there would be a greater influx of entrants into professional businesses, whose competition would depress the incomes of those engaged in them, so as to place them once more in their natural position, with respect to landlords, capitalists, &c., on whom the full weight of the tax is supposed to fall. On this ground it is contended that the tax should be made to press equally on all incomes, and that there is no in-justice in making the same deduction from the fees of a lawyer or physician that is made from the rent of a landlord or the profit of a capitalist; for, supposing the former were partially or wholly exempted from the tax, he would be as much injured by the greater competition that would grow out of such exemption as by being subjected to its full amount.

But these statements, though in some degree true, are in the main fallacious. Professional fees, when once fixed, are not easily altered. Notwithstanding the heavy fall of prices and profits since the peace of 1815, the fees of professional men have not materially varied; nor did they vary materially during the previous period of depreciation. We doubt whether the imposition of a peculiar tax, of a moderate amount, on professional incomes, or their total exemption from a tax laid on incomes arising from other sources, would have any sensible influence over fees. If it were very heavy, it might, and most probably would, in the long run, affect them to a greater or less extent; but its operation could not be in any case immediate; and unless the tax exceeded all reasonable bounds, there is but little ground for thinking that it would very materially affect them.

But suppose it were really true that professional incomes vary at the same time and in the same degree as other in-comes, this would not justify the laying the same tax on them all. A landlord receives 500*l*. a-year of rent, and an attor-ney or an apothecary makes 500*l*. a-year by his business. But though the income of each be at present the same, their ability to pay taxes is materially different; for the income of the first arises from a comparatively lasting source, whereas that of the latter is dependent on his life and on his health. And hence, in order to lay the same burden on both parties, we should calculate the *present value* of the income enjoyed by each, and lay the same tax on it ; or, which would come to the same thing, we should deduct from the income of the professional man such a portion as would effect an insurance on his life for a sum equivalent to the present value of his income, and assess the tax on the remainder. This is the only way in which, supposing incomes to be known, it is possible fairly to tax them. It would, however, be extremely difficult to proceed in this way. To illustrate the principle : suppose that a clergyman, A, forty years of age, has an income of 1000l. a-year, and that it is required to decide how much he should contribute to a tax of 10 per cent. on all incomes considered as perpetuities. Here we are met at the very outset by the difficulty of deciding by what standard we should estimate A's expectation of life. If we take the Northampton table, we shall obtain a certain result, if we take the Carlisle table we shall have another, and if we take Mr. Finlaison's table we shall have a third result, all differing considerably from each other. But suppose that the Carlisle table is selected ; A's expectation will be 27·61 years. Having got thus far, we have next to decide upon the rate of interest at which the present value of A's annuity or income is to be estimated. Everybody knows that the answer to the question which we are endeavouring to solve depends materially on the assumed rate of interest ; and there would be endless disputes respecting the rate that should be fixed upon. In the event, however, of 4 per cent. being selected, the present value of A's income would be 16,500l., yielding a perpetual revenue of 660l. ; so that he should contribute 66l. to the tax.

This is the way in which taxes on income should be assessed, if they are to be imposed with any pretensions to fairness. It may be objected, perhaps, that the fundamental supposition on which the income is valued and the tax imposed, viz. that A, being at present forty years of age, will live other twenty-seven years and a half, is quite gratuitous ; that it is merely an average rule deduced from observations made on a large number of individuals ; and that, for any-

thing we can affirm to the contrary, A may die to-morrow.
But all this may be admitted without impeaching the principle laid down above; for the difference between A's actual
income of 1000*l.* and the corresponding perennial income of
660*l.*, that is, 340*l.*, will, if accumulated for twenty-seven
years and a half, at 4 per cent., produce 16,500*l.*, and an
insurance office would transact with A on this footing, or on
one not very different.

These statements show how taxes on professional incomes
should be imposed, if it were meant to render the tax really
equal; and they also show how very difficult, or rather how
impossible, it would be, fairly to assess such incomes, even
if there were any means of learning their amount with anything like precision. It is to no purpose to talk about establishing uniform rates of deduction. Unless wholesale injustice is to be perpetrated, uniformity in cases of this sort
must be rejected: each must be judged of separately. The
income of two lawyers may be the same, but, if their ages
differ, they cannot be fairly taxed to the same extent; nor,
when interest is 4 per cent., should the tax be the same as
when it is 3 or 5 per cent.

It was proposed during the discussions respecting the
present income-tax to charge incomes derived from annuities in the public funds proportionally to the duration of
such annuities; and, abstractly considered, nothing could be
fairer than this proposal, inasmuch as it is palpably unjust to
lay the same rate of duty on an income that will terminate in
five or ten years, or at the death of the party, as on one that
will last for fifty or sixty years, or is perpetual; but it is plain,
had this proposal been entertained, that the principle must
have been carried infinitely farther. Professional men should,
in so far as this tax is concerned, be regarded as holders of
life annuities, and this also is clearly the case with clergymen, officers in the army and navy, clerks of all descriptions,
whether in public or private offices, widows with annuities,
owners of entailed estates, and a host of others. Although
therefore it be unjust to lay the same rate of duty on a

terminable as on an interminable funded income, it would be still more unjust to make abatements in favour of one class of annuitants and not of others. And, therefore, it would seem that parliament did right in rejecting the proposal now alluded to. It was felt that practically it would be impossible fairly to carry out the principle which it embodied; and that it was better to make all who were placed under similar circumstances suffer alike, than to make concessions in favour of a single class which had no better right to them than the others.

To get rid of the extreme difficulty that would otherwise have to be encountered in assessing an income-tax on the incomes of farmers and other occupiers of lands, tenements, and so forth, it is usual to assume that the farmer's income amounts to some portion or multiple of his rent, and to assess him accordingly. Thus, under the old income-tax, the incomes of the tenants of land in England were supposed to amount to three-fourths, and in Scotland to half the rent; and under the existing tax the incomes of the tenants in England are taken at a half, and in Scotland at a third part of the rent. Hence, under the present law, the occupier of a farm rented at 1000*l.* a-year is supposed in England to have an income of 500*l.*, and in Scotland of 333*l.* 6*s.* 8*d.* a-year, and is taxed on such. We have no doubt that this is, on the whole, the very best plan that could be devised for assessing such incomes, and yet it may lead to consequences that seem not a little revolting. Farming, like other businesses, and, indeed, in a still greater degree than many others, is exposed to vicissitudes; and it may be safely laid down that at all times a considerable number of occupiers of land are losing by their business. But the tax makes no exception in favour of such unfortunate cases. It sweeps with undistinguishing severity its equal, or rather most unequal, demands from all; and, Procrustes-like, compels the tenant who has made, and he who has lost, 500*l.* by his farm, to contribute the same sum!

Owing to the practice of remitting or drawing back the duties laid on commodities consumed at home, when they are sent abroad, absentees get their revenues transmitted to them free from taxation, and consequently avoid contributing their fair share of the public expenditure. Some stress has been laid, but without much reason, on the supposed influence of an income-tax in obviating this inconvenience. Except in so far as absentees escape those taxes they would have to defray were they resident at home, their absence is immaterial; and, considering the small proportion which the revenues of absentees bear to the revenues of the resident population, there are no grounds for thinking that the burdens of the latter are sensibly increased by the absence of the former. But, when an income-tax of any considerable magnitude is imposed, if it lessen, on the one hand, the temptations which operate on certain classes to go abroad, it must, on the other hand, act as a new stimulus to the investment of capital in foreign countries, where it may escape the tax and the investigations connected with its assessment. Surely, however, it can hardly be necessary to say that, while the residence abroad of individuals is little if at all injurious, the transferring of capital to other countries is a most serious calamity. And any measure that should discourage the former, by stimulating the latter, would be like stopping up the spigot that the bung-hole might be opened.

The best defence of the existing income-tax, and indeed of income-taxes in general, was made by Sir Robert Peel in the debates in 1842. He contended, that the deficiency in the revenue, which then exceeded 2,000,000*l.* a-year, made the imposition of new taxes indispensable; and without attempting to conceal or gloss over the injustice and hardship of the income-tax, he argued, that it was as little open to those objections as any other tax calculated to raise a considerable amount of revenue that could be imposed in its stead, and that, on the whole, the balance of advantage seemed to be in its favour. It is not to be denied that there is much force in these statements. The sacrifice of the house-tax to vulgar clamour, and of the greater part of the post-office revenue to unfounded notions of public convenience, may be truly said, by occasioning the deficiency in the revenue, to have given birth to the income-tax. It would also, we admit, be no easy matter, in the present state of the country, to point out any tax or taxes fitted to produce four or five millions a-year, against which several formidable objections might not be urged, and this diffi- culty is increased by the fact of the renewal of a tax that has been recently repealed being always a peculiarly ungracious and unpopular proceeding. Perhaps, however, were the house-tax placed on a right footing, it might be revived and made, in no very long time, a productive source of revenue; and there can be little doubt that the existing arrangements respecting the post-office might be so modified as to double the revenue derived from it, without improperly lessening the facilities of correspondence. We are far from supposing, as has sometimes been done, that we have arrived at or very near the limits of indirect taxation; and we shall afterwards endeavour to show that considerable addi- tions might be made to the revenue by modifying some of the existing duties and commercial regulations, not only without any increase, but with a considerable diminu- tion, of the pressure on the public. Neither can we help thinking that in the discussions in question Sir Robert Peel overrated the inconveniences attached to duties on expendi- ture. Though unequal in their incidence, we have already seen that they are neither unfair nor unjust ; they are not, in fact, intended to fall on all individuals, but only on those who indulge in taxed articles; and then only according to the extent to which they indulge in them, so that in most cases it is their own fault if they be over-taxed. But no such excuse can be made for the unequal pressure of taxes on income. The existing income-tax has been imposed on the principle of making all individuals subject to its operation contribute the same portion of their incomes, how different

soever the sources whence they may be derived, and, consequently, falls with disproportioned severity on those possessed of perishable incomes; and yet this hardship cannot
be obviated without the entire abandonment of the tax; the
practical difficulties in the way of its equitable apportionment being altogether insuperable.

Taxes on income are also in other respects exceedingly
objectionable. They require a constant interference with, and
inquiry into, the affairs of individuals, and in this way, independently of their inequality, keep up a perpetual feeling of
irritation. It is farther to be observed that while such inquiries can never be made effectual to their object, they are
not of a description that are easily justified. What right
has the public to know the means or resources of those who
make no claim on it for support? Why compel those who
strive by rigid economy to make a decent appearance to
declare their condition? to expose themselves to the *magnum
pauperies opprobrium*? Such inquiries and disclosures must
necessarily always be hateful to the parties, and cannot fail
to excite their disgust. Luckily, however, the great majority
of taxes on expenditure are free from these defects; and
we believe we may safely affirm that the excise duties,
which produce nearly fourteen millions a-year, are collected
without provoking a tenth part of the irritation and fraud
occasioned by the income-tax, though it produce little more
than five millions. Even in the case of a house-tax, calculated to produce three or four millions a-year, we incline to
think that the irritation would be trifling compared with that
excited by the income-tax; and, at any rate, it would have
comparatively little foundation. The amount of the tax
might be objected to ; but the assessment would be easily
made, and, when once made, it would not be subject to perpetual change, nor would it involve any inquiries into the
condition or circumstances of the occupiers.

Although, therefore, we admit the inequality, and perhaps,
in a few cases, even the injustice, of taxes on expenditure, we
contend that in these respects the worst of them are less
objectionable than the most carefully devised income-tax;

while the greater facility with which they are assessed, and the greater willingness with which they are paid, should in all ordinary cases give them a preference.

But it is said that this difficulty of taxing the incomes of professional men, and of the classes alluded to above, is a good reason for exempting them wholly from the tax, which should fall only on the incomes of those possessed of real property. We take leave however to dissent entirely from this conclusion. The difficulty of assessing the incomes in question may be a sufficient reason for rejecting an income-tax altogether; but it is assuredly no reason for making it partial, and consequently unjust. Professional men, and annuitants of all descriptions, contribute to taxes on commodities. And if these be repealed, and an income-tax, from which professional and other terminable incomes are exempted, be imposed in their stead, an obvious injustice will be done to the other classes, who will be saddled with the whole of a burden of which they have hitherto borne a part only, and which should press equally on all ranks and orders. It is plain, however, in this, as in the previous case, that, were the classes already alluded to exempted from the tax because of the admitted impossibility of fairly assessing their incomes, vast numbers of incomes derived from real property would have equal claims to be exempted, because of their being quite as evanescent as those of clergymen or lawyers, and still more difficult to assess. It is needless to say that no proposal for exempting the owners of cotton, woollen, or flax mills, breweries, distilleries, ships, warehouses, houses, &c., from taxes laid on the property or incomes of landlords, fundholders, mortgagees, &c., would be tolerated, or could be thought of for a moment. But in fairly assessing the incomes of the owners of ships, mills, and similar property, most of the difficulties would have to be encountered that make the fair taxing of professional incomes so impracticable, with others peculiar to the cases in question. An estate, abstracting from the buildings and improvements made upon it, may be regarded as a lasting source of revenue; but ships,

houses, factories, mills, &c., are all perishable, and, before
the latter can be taxed in the same ratio as the former, the
degree of their durability must be determined, and the income arising from them reduced to a perpetuity. Suppose,
for example, that a tax of 10 per cent. is imposed on revenue arising from lands, funds, and mortgages, and that it
is required to lay a really equivalent tax on income arising
from houses, shops, warehouses, mills, ships, canals, and
such-like property : in this case we should have to begin by
estimating the present value of the shop, mill, ship, or other
property yielding the revenue proposed to be taxed. Having
done this, we should next have to estimate the probable
duration of such property; and then, in order to get the
nett or taxable income, we should have to deduct from the
gross income such a sum as would suffice, being accumulated
at the ordinary interest of the day, to replace the shop, mill,
&c., when it was worn out. An income-tax, imposed on fair
principles, and made to press with the same severity on all
classes, according to their ability to bear it, must be assessed
in the way now mentioned. But the difficulties in the way
of such a course are obviously insurmountable. There
would evidently be great room for doubt, evasion, and fraud
in the valuation of the property; and though this were got
over, how is its probable duration to be ascertained ? The
power to determine a point of this sort could not be intrusted
to officers; for if so, it would open a door to every sort of
abuse. Neither is there any standard to which to refer in
estimating durability, seeing that it must vary in every case
from a thousand peculiar and almost inappreciable circumstances. Although, therefore, it were conceded that taxes
on income are, in principle, the best of any, the above statements are sufficient to show that this circumstance should
go for little in the way of recommending them. It is of very
trifling consequence whether a tax be theoretically good or
bad; it is in a practical point of view only that we have to
deal with it; and however well it may look in demonstrations
on paper, if it be impossible fairly to assess it, it should,
unless in peculiar cases, be rejected.

Even as applied to the rent of land, an income-tax is in most instances extremely unfair. Two estates yield the same rent, but one is naturally very inferior to the other—its deficiencies having been compensated by the execution of expensive improvements. Where, then, would be the justice or the policy of laying the same tax on the rental of both estates? A half, or perhaps three-fourths, of the rent of the one consists of the interest of capital laid out on improvements, most of which are as little durable as either shops or cotton-mills. Hence the hardship of laying the same tax on the rent of an improved as on that of an unimproved estate; and yet, as already seen, we can adopt no other criterion; for all the tax-collectors of the empire, even if they were assisted by as many farmers, would not be able to resolve the rent of an improved farm into its constituent parts; that is, to separate what is really paid for the natural and inherent powers of the soil from what is paid for the capital expended on improvements.

We have thus seen, in the first place, that it is not possible to acquire any accurate information in regard to the magnitude of the incomes enjoyed by some large and important classes; and we have next seen that, though such information were obtained, the sources whence different incomes arise are so very various, and so very different in their degrees of durability, that all attempts to subject them to a really equal tax must prove utterly abortive. The truth is, that such tax is a desideratum which is not destined ever to be supplied. After the legislature has done all that can be done to make it equal, it will be most unequal. To impose it only on certain classes of incomes, or to impose it on all incomes, without regard to their origin, is alike subversive of sound principle. Nothing therefore remains but to reject it, or to resort to it only when money must be had at all hazards; when the ordinary and less exceptionable means of filling the public coffers have been tried and exhausted; and when, as during the late war, Hannibal is knocking at your gates, and national independence must be secured at whatever cost. An unreasoning necessity of this sort is the only satisfactory justification of taxes on property or income.

When, however, the circumstances of a country are either such, or supposed to be such, as to require the imposition of an income-tax, some point must be fixed for its commencement. It has sometimes been said that it should affect all incomes. But were it imposed on this sweeping principle, it would really be, in as far as the labouring class is concerned, a tax on wages; and we have previously seen that there are but few cases in which it would be wise to impose a direct tax on them, or possible to collect it. Generally, however, it is admitted that the wages of ordinary labour should be exempted from the tax; but the difficulty is to specify the limit where it should begin to take effect, and whether it should be charged indifferently on all incomes from the same point. The old income-tax, as remodelled in 1806, fell with its full weight on all incomes, whatever might be their amount, derived from fixed or funded property. Professional incomes under 50*l.* were, however, exempted from the tax; and when between 50*l.* and 150*l.* they were entitled to certain abatements. Under the existing income-tax the assessment on all sorts of incomes begins at 150*l.* a-year; and provided the propriety of exempting the smaller class of incomes from the burden be conceded, we do not know that any better point could be selected whence to commence the assessment. To nothing, indeed, is the present tax so much indebted for its comparatively easy working as to the *minimum* taxable income being fixed at 150*l.* This exempts vast numbers of persons, comprising all those most sensible to the pressure of the tax, and least familiar with the methods of getting any over-assessment rectified, from its operation; and has, in consequence, prevented it from becoming a topic for popular declamation and invective.

But though the limitation of the tax to incomes exceeding 150*l.* a-year be, in a practical point of view, an unexceptionable arrangement, it is not to be denied that it involves a principle which may easily be abused and perverted to the most dangerous purposes. The question—where shall the assessment begin ?—presents, in fact, one of the most serious difficulties with which income-taxes are encumbered. Any attempt to tax all incomes, how limited soever, would certainly miscarry ; while, if you once begin to make exemptions, it is impossible to say where you ought, or will be permitted to stop. What conclusive reason can be assigned for fixing upon 150*l.* in preference to 200*l.* or 250*l.* for the commencement of the tax? And when such is the case, is there no risk lest a minister, who may happen to be unpopular with the upper classes, or who may wish to court the applause and conciliate the support of the lower and more numerous portion of society, should be tempted to avail himself of this latitude of selection ? and by carrying the principle of exemption to excess, convert the tax into an engine of misgovernment, by employing it to advance his own interests and those of his party, at the expense of the rights and interests of others ?

The income exempted from the tax, whatever it may be, should be held to be indispensable for subsistence, for otherwise there can be no good reason for its being exempted. And consistently with this principle it was proposed, during the debates on the tax in 1842, to deduct 150*l.*, the sum assumed in the Act as the minimum of necessary income, from all incomes subject to the tax, and to assess it on the surplus only ; so that a person with an income of 160*l.* would, had this proposal been adopted, have been assessed on 10*l.* only, a person with an income of 300*l.* on 150*l.*, and so on. We regret that this equitable proposal was not agreed to. It was, perhaps, the only one of the numerous amendments offered at the time, the adoption of which would have materially improved the Act. No doubt it would have rendered the tax somewhat less productive; but to obviate this the point of commencement might have been fixed a little lower, or the rate might have been increased a little, or both these measures might have been resorted to. This would have placed all classes on the same footing, and would, in all

cases, have exempted what the statute presumes to be necessary income from the tax.

The difficulty of distinguishing between those who should
and those who should not be charged is another inconvenience attending taxes on property and income, unless
they be made to fall with their full weight on every one.
Thus, under the existing tax, the assessors, having no means
of learning whether individuals have 130*l.*, 140*l.*, or 150*l.*
a-year, must, to make sure that the tax is not evaded by
those who should pay it, serve notices on a great number of
parties not liable to the assessment, who, in consequence,
must either establish the meanness of their circumstances
to the satisfaction of the commissioners, or submit to pay
the tax! In the case of funded property, the tax on all
dividends, whatever their amount, is deducted, it being left
to those who are not worth 150*l.* a-year to prove the fact
before they are entitled to claim restitution of the sum
deducted on account of the tax.* This is obviously no
small grievance; and every body knows that many persons
pay the tax who should be exempted rather than encounter
the trouble and expose themselves to the questions they
would have to answer in substantiating their claim to be

* The subjoined official return shows the extent to which this grievance
operates :—

    A Return, showing the Number of Claims of Exemption under the Property
    Tax Act received at the Tax Office up to the 20th of May, 1844; the
    Number on which the Duty has been repaid; the Amount of Duty repaid;
    the Number of Claims in which Orders have been issued by the Board of
    Taxes for discharging the Property of the Claimants from Assessment;
    and the Number of Claims now remaining in the Tax Office for Exami-
    nation and Inquiry.

Number of Claims received.	Number of Claims on which Duty has been repaid.	Amount of Duty repaid.	Number on which Orders have been issued discharging the Property of the Claimants from Assessment.	Number of Claims remaining in the Office for Examination and Inquiry.
82,854*	75,500	£. *s.* *d.* 69,101 9 3	49,370	1,354

    * Of these about 6000 claims have been found defective, and returned to the Surveyors
for correction or amendment.

exempted. And yet this, like the other grievances that grow out of the tax, cannot be obviated. No one doubts the impracticability of assessing a tax of this sort on the poorer classes ; some point must be specified where it is to begin ; so that the difficulty of distinguishing between those who are and those who are not liable to its operation may be truly said to be inherent in it.

It has been contended, by Say and some other economists, that if taxes on income be resorted to, they should be imposed on a graduated scale, and. made to increase according to the increase of the incomes subjected to their operation ; and the countenance which has been so frequently and cordially given to proposals for the introduction of property and income taxes by the more dangerous class of politicians has originated in their supposing that they might be made to embrace a plan of graduation. And, though in the last degree objectionable, it is not to be denied that there is something exceedingly plausible in this plan. A tax of 10*l.* is said to be more severely felt by the possessor of an income of 150*l.*, or of a property of that amount, than a tax of 100*l.*, or 1000*l.*, by the possessor of an income or of a property of 1500*l.* or 15,000*l.* ; and it is argued that, in order fairly to proportion the tax to the ability of the contributors, such a graduated scale of duty should be adopted as should press lightly on the smaller class of properties and incomes, and increase according as they become larger and more able to bear taxation. We take leave, however, to protest against this proposal, which is not more seductive than it is unjust and dangerous. No tax on income can be a just tax unless it leave individuals in the same relative condition in which it found them. It must of course depress, according to its magnitude, all those on whom it falls ; and it should fall on every one in proportion to the revenue which he enjoys under the protection of the state.* If it either pass entirely over some classes, or press

* That is, of course, supposing all revenues reduced to the same denomination, or to perpetuities.

on some less heavily than on others, it is unjustly imposed.
Government, in such a case, has plainly stepped out of its
proper province, and has assessed the tax, not for the
legitimate purpose of appropriating a certain proportion of
the revenues of its subjects to the public exigencies, but
that it might at the same time regulate the incomes of the
contributors; that is, that it might depress one class and
elevate another. The toleration of such a principle would
necessarily lead to every species of abuse. That equal taxes
on property or income will be more severely felt by the
poorer than by the richer classes is undeniable; but the
same is true of every imposition which does not subvert the
subsisting relations among the different orders of society.
The hardship in question arises out of the order of Providence; for it is one of the evils of poverty, and to attempt
to alleviate it by adopting such a graduated scale of duties
as has been proposed would really be to impose taxes on the
wealthier part of the community for the benefit of their less
opulent brethren, and not for the sake of the public revenue.
Let it not be supposed that the principle of graduation may
be carried a certain extent, and then stopped.

> Nullus semel ore receptus
> Pollutas patitur sanguis mansuescere fauces.

The reasons that made the step be taken in the first instance, backed as they are sure to be by agitation and clamour, will impel you forwards. Having once given way,
having said that a man with 500*l.* a-year shall pay 5 per
cent., another with 1000*l.* 10 per cent., and another with
2000*l.* 20 per cent., on what pretence or principle can you
stop in your ascending scale? Why not take 50 per cent.
from the man of 2000*l.* a-year, and confiscate all the higher
class of incomes before you tax the lower? In such matters
the maxim of *obsta principiis* should be firmly adhered to
by every prudent and honest statesman. Graduation is not
an evil to be paltered with. Adopt it and you will effectually
paralyse industry and check accumulation; at the same time
that every man who has any property will hasten, by carry-

ing it out of the country, to protect it from confiscation. The savages described by Montesquieu, who to get at the fruit cut down the tree, are about as good financiers as the advocates of this sort of taxes. Wherever they are introduced security is at an end. Even if taxes on income were otherwise the most unexceptionable, the adoption of the principle of graduation would make them about the very worst that could be devised. The moment you abandon, in the framing of such taxes, the cardinal principle of exacting from all individuals the same proportion of their income or of their property, you are at sea without rudder or compass, and there is no amount of injustice and folly you may not commit.

In order to furnish the means of defraying the cost of the war begun in 1793, Mr. Pitt proposed, in 1797, to treble the amount of the assessed taxes, or duties on houses, windows, horses, carriages, &c. This plan, however, did not answer the expectations of its projectors, and next year it was abandoned, and a tax on income substituted in its stead. According to the provisions of the act imposing this tax, all incomes of less than 60*l.* a-year were exempted from assessment; an income of from 60*l.* to 65*l.* was taxed one *one hundred and twentieth* part; and the rate of duty increased through a variety of gradations, until the income reached 200*l.* or upwards, when it amounted to a *tenth* part, which was its utmost limit; a variety of deductions being at the same time granted, on account of children, &c. The commissioners to whom the assessment of this tax was intrusted were chosen by the freeholders of counties and the electors of boroughs, nearly in the same way as their representatives in parliament, only that a smaller qualification was sufficient to enable any one to be elected a commissioner. The services of the commissioners were gratuitous; and they were sworn to secrecy with respect to the affairs of individuals. They were authorized to call for returns from every person whose income they supposed to exceed

60*l.* a-year; and in the event of their being dissatisfied
with these returns, they were empowered to call for written
explanations, and ultimately for the oath of the party.   But
this examination was rarely necessary, except in the case
of incomes derived from wages, from capital employed in
manufacturing and commercial business, or from the interest of loans; the rental of landlords being, in most
cases, learned from the terms of the agreements with their
tenants; while the profits or incomes of the latter were,
as already stated, estimated in England at *three-fourths*,
and in Scotland at *half* the rent.   The commissioners
were assisted, or rather overlooked, by the tax-surveyors
appointed by government, who were required to see the
provisions of the act strictly enforced, and whose duty it
was to scrutinize all returns of income, to challenge such
as they considered fraudulent, to object to the deductions allowed by the ordinary commissioners, and to bring
the matter under the review of the commissioners of appeal,
whose sentence was final.   Infinite fraud and evasion were
practised; and nothing could be more arbitrary than the
rule for estimating farmers' incomes.   But the exigencies
of the country at the time made this and its other defects be little thought of; and, on the whole, the provisions of the act were enforced better than could have been
anticipated.

This tax was repealed in 1802, after the peace of Amiens,
having produced, at an average, about *five millions and a
half* annually.

In 1803 the income-tax, under the name of property-
tax, was again revived.   The assessment began, as before,
on incomes as low as 60*l.* a-year, and gradually increased
until the income reached 150*l.* a-year, when it amounted
to 5 per cent., which was its highest rate.   An addition
was made to this tax in 1805; and in 1806, during the
short-lived administration of Mr. Fox and Lord Grenville,
the assessment was raised to 10 per cent. on all incomes,
however small, arising from land or capital.   Professional

incomes under 50*l.* were exempted from the tax; and incomes of that sort exceeding 50*l.* and under 150*l.*, the limit at which they became subject to the full assessment of 10 per cent., were allowed deductions, varying inversely as their magnitude. This tax was finally repealed in 1816, and would hardly have been submitted to, but for the well-founded conviction that it was indispensable for carrying on the desperate struggle in which we were then engaged.

We subjoin, from a parliamentary paper presented to the House of Commons, in 1823, a return of the total *gross* and *nett* assessments to the property or income tax, for the year ending 5th April, 1815:—

	Gross Assessment.	Nett Assessment.
	£.	£.
A. Lands, Houses, Manors, Tithes, Canals, Mines, Ironworks, &c.	5,923,486	5,923,189
B. Profits from the Occupancy of Lands, &c.	2,734,451	2,176,228
C. Dividends on Public Annuities, and other Securities	2,885,505	2,885,505
D. Profits and gains of Trade	3,831,088	3,146,332
E. Salaries, Pensions, &c.	1,174,456	1,167,678
Totals	16,548,985	15,298,982

The following is the return of the value of the several species of property on which the assessment was made for the years 1813 and 1814, ending 5th April, 1814 and 1815, viz.—

Schedules.	1813.	1814.
	£.	£.
A.	56,701,923	60,138,330
B.	36,336,883	38,396,144
D.	36,080,167	38,310,935
E.	11,380,748	11,744,557
C. Not stated, but estimated at	30,000,000	30,000,000
Totals	170,499,721	178,589,966

The present Income-Tax Act, the 5 and 6 Victoria, c. 35 (22 June, 1842), imposes a duty of 7d. per pound sterling (2l. 18s. 4d. per cent.) on all incomes, from whatever source derived, of 150l. a-year and upwards. As already seen, the incomes or profits of the occupiers of land, &c., are assumed to amount, in England, to a half, and in Scotland to a third, part of the rent; and are assessed on that hypothesis. We subjoin an official

Return of the Nett Amount of Duty collected under each Schedule of the Property Tax Act, during the Year ended the 5th of April, 1843.

Schedule A.	£2,150,412 10	9
„ B.	298,763 0	0
„ C.	812,982 13	1
„ D.	1,466,985 9	8
„ E.	260,657 11	3
Total for England and Wales .	4,989,801 4	9
Total for Scotland	394,324 10	3*
Grand Total for Great Britain .	5,384,125 15	0

Schedule A comprises in this, as in the former Act, the assessment upon lands, houses, tithes, manors, mines, quarries, canals, ironworks, &c. ; and it is to be regretted that no account has been published of the amount of income assessed under each head of the Schedule. But taking the returns as they stand, they must have been assessed in England and Wales as follows:—

Schedule A having produced 2,150,412l. 10s. 9d., at 7d. per pound, must have been assessed on . . .	£73,728,430
„ B, 298,763l., at 7d. per pound, must have been assessed on	10,243,303
„ C, 812,982l. 13s. 1d. do. do. do. . .	27,873,691
„ D, 1,466,985l. 9s. 8d. do. do. do. . .	50,296,645
„ E, 260,657l. 11s. 3d. do. do. do. . .,	8,936,830
	171,078,899

The rents payable by the occupiers assessed under Schedule B must have amounted (as they were charged only on

---

* The amount of duty collected in Scotland is not distinguished in Schedules.

the half) to 20,486,606*l*. And, perhaps, we may not be far wrong if we estimate the total landed rental of England and Wales at the present moment at about double that amount, or at from 40 to 41 millions sterling. By far the greatest increase of property since 1815 has been in houses, warehouses, factories, and property of that description.

Of the total amount of income assessed to the tax, the portion charged under Schedules C and E, amounting to 36,810,521*l.*, consisting principally of dividends on the public debt, and of salaries and pensions to public servants, is of quite a different character from the other portions, and is not to be regarded in the same point of view. It is not an original or independent, but a secondary or derivative income, and consists, in fact, of a portion of the income of others transferred to the holders by means of taxation. But we shall endeavour, in a subsequent part of this work, fully to clear up this important distinction; and we only mention it now to prevent an erroneous estimate being formed from these returns of the magnitude of the national income.

PART II.

INDIRECT TAXES.

CHAPTER I.

ADVANTAGES AND DISADVANTAGES OF INDIRECT TAXES.

THOUGH most governments have had recourse to direct taxes, they have rarely, at least in Europe, formed the sole or even principal source of the public revenue. Indirect taxes have with few exceptions been the greatest favourites both of princes and subjects; and there are very sufficient reasons for the preference of which they have so generally been the objects. The burden of direct taxation is palpable and obvious. It admits of no disguise or concealment, but makes every one fully sensible of the exact amount of his income taken by government. We are all, however, extremely averse from parting with property, except we obtain some more acceptable equivalent in its stead. And the benefits derived from the institution of government, though of the highest importance, being neither so very obvious nor striking as to be readily felt and appreciated by the bulk of the people, there is, in the great majority of cases, a strong disinclination to the payment of direct taxes. For this reason governments have generally had recourse to those that are indirect. Instead of exciting the prejudices of their subjects by openly demanding a portion of their incomes, they have taxed the articles on which these incomes are usually expended. This ingenious plan conceals the amount of taxation, and makes its payment appear in some measure voluntary. The tax being generally paid, in the first instance, by the producers, the purchasers confound it with the natural price of the commodity. No separate demand being made upon them for the tax, it escapes their recollection; and the article which they receive seems the fair equivalent of the sacrifice made in acquiring it.* Such taxes have also the advantage of being paid by degrees, in small portions, and at the time when the commodities are wanted for consumption, or when it is most convenient for the consumers to pay them.

Besides their greater facility of imposition, indirect taxes have been supposed to have the further and exclusive advantage of acting as stimulants to industry. " Dans la perception directe," says the Marquis Garnier, " l'impôt se montre sans nul déguisement; il vient sans être attendu, à cause de l'imprévoyance si ordinaire au commun des hommes, et il apporte toujours avec lui de la gêne et du découragement. Mais l'impôt indirect, en ajoutant successivement un surcroît de prix aux articles de consommation générale et journalière, au moment où tous les membres de la société ont contracté l'habitude de ses consommations, rend ses divers articles un peu plus coûteux à acquérir ; c'est-à-dire, qu'il donne lieu à ce qu'il faille, pour se les procurer, un surcroît proportionné de travail et d'industrie. Or, si cet impôt est mesuré de manière à ne pas aller jusques à décourager la consommation, ne semble-t-il pas, dans ce cas, agir comme un stimulant universel sur la partie active et industrieuse de la société, qui l'excite à un redoublement d'efforts, pour n'être pas obligé de renoncer à des jouissances que l'habitude lui a rendues presque nécessaires, et qui, en conséquence, donne un plus grand développement aux facultés productives du travail et aux ressources de l'industrie ? Ne doit-il pas en résulter, qu'après l'impôt il y a la même somme de travail et d'industrie qu'auparavant pour

---

* Nero was supposed to have abolished the duty of 4 per cent. on the slaves sold in Rome, when he really did no more than order it to be paid by the seller instead of the buyer. " Remissum," says Tacitus, " specie magis quam vi ; quia cum venditor pendere juberetur, in partem pretii emptoribus accrescebat." (Annal., lib. xiii., cap. 32.)

fournir aux besoins et aux jouissances habituelles des hommes qui composent la classe laborieuse, plus la somme de travail et d'industrie qui a dû pourvoir au surcroît de prix destiné à l'impôt ? Or, cet impôt, ou ce surcroît de produit que se paye, étant dépensé par le gouvernement qui le recueille, sert à alimenter une nouvelle classe des consommateurs, qui forment des demandes que l'impôt les met à portée de payer."*

The truth of the greater part of this statement cannot be disputed. It is, however, essential to observe that the effect ascribed by Garnier to indirect taxes, of stimulating industry, depends on the circumstance of their not discouraging consumption ; or, which is the same thing, of their being so moderate that the contributors may defray them by increased exertion and economy. Were this not the case, they would have a precisely opposite effect, and, instead of acting as a stimulus to production, would certainly occasion its decline.

We believe, however, that a moderate tax on income, provided it could be fairly assessed, would have nearly the same effect in stimulating economy as moderate taxes on expenditure. But we doubt whether a fairly assessed income-tax, supposing it were possible, would have anything like the same influence in stimulating fresh efforts of industry, invention, and enterprise as taxes on expenditure. Suppose that the price of an article in extensive demand is 5s., and that it is burdened with a duty of 1s., or of 20 per cent.: the producers know that, if they raise the price of the article to 6s., the demand for it, and, of course, also their business, will be very materially contracted: they therefore have a novel and powerful motive to task their invention to discover improved and cheaper methods of producing the article, so that the operation of the tax may be (as it very frequently is) neutralized or defeated.

It is perhaps unnecessary to add anything to what has been previously stated (pp. 8, 10, &c.) in illustration of the prin-

* Préface à la Traduction de la Richesse des Nations, t. i., p. 66, éd. 2de.

ciple now referred to ; but it is so strikingly exemplified in
the case of the farmers and occupiers of land, that we may,
perhaps, be excused for again shortly adverting to it. In so
far as the parties now referred to are concerned, the rents
they have to pay may be looked upon as a tax, and it is
well known to practical men that, of all the sources of
improvement, none is more prolific than an increase of rents.
Arthur Young states, over and over again, that he never
knew an instance of good cultivation associated with low
rents; and he says that, when he heard gentlemen boast-
ing that they never raised their rents, he thought it would
have been more to the point had they boasted that their
tenants were without industry, and their lands not half cultivated !

It is unnecessary, however, to travel beyond the limits
of financial history for examples of the influence of taxes
in stimulating ingenuity and invention. Previously to 1786
the duties on spirits distilled in Scotland were charged
according to the quantities supposed to be actually produced : but as this mode of assessing the duty was found
to open a door to extensive frauds, it was resolved to substitute in its stead a licence-duty proportioned to the size
of the still used by the distiller. Stills being all of the
same shape, and the quantity of spirits that each could produce in a year according to its cubic contents having been
accurately calculated, it was supposed that this plan would
effectually prevent smuggling, and that the officers would
have nothing to do but to inspect the stills that had been
licensed, to prevent their size being increased.* On the first
introduction of this apparently well-considered system, the
licence-duty on each still was fixed at the rate of 30s.
a-gallon ; but the principle on which the duty had been assessed was very soon subverted. The stills in use down to

---

* See an able tract entitled " Resolutions of the Landed Interest of Scotland
respecting the Distillery, with Reasons why the Duty on Spirits should be
levied by an Annual Licence-Duty on the Still." (By Sir John Dalrymple,
Bart.) Edinburgh, 1786.

this period were very deep in proportion to their diameter, so that after being charged they required at an average about a week before the process of distillation was completed. No sooner, however, had the new mode of charging the duty been introduced, than it occurred to two ingenious persons, Messrs. John and William Sligo, distillers, Leith, that, by lessening the depth of the still and increasing its diameter, a larger surface would be exposed to the action of the fire, and they would thus be enabled to run off its contents in a much less time. Having adopted this plan, they found that it answered their expectations, and that they were able to distil the same quantity of spirits in a few hours that had previously occupied a week. Messrs. Sligo had the exclusive possession of this important invention for about a year : but the secret was not of a description that could be long concealed ; and the moment it transpired the plan was adopted by the other distillers. In consequence, in 1788 Government raised the licence-duty on the still from 30s. to 3l. a-gallon ; but this increase having redoubled the activity of the distillers, the duty was again raised in 1793 to 9l. a-gallon, in 1795 to 18l., and in 1797 it was carried to the enormous sum of 54l. a-gallon! Still, however, the ingenuity of the distiller had outrun the increase of the tax ; and it was proved, before a Committee of the House of Commons in 1798, that distillation had been carried to such perfection, that stills had occasionally been filled and discharged once every *eight* minutes! This, it was supposed, must be the maximum of velocity, and the licence-duty was consequently laid on the still on the hypothesis that it could at an average be run off in that time, or that it could be filled and emptied once every eight minutes during the season. But the ingenuity of the distillers was not yet tasked to the highest ; and it was ascertained that, towards the latter end of the licence-system, stills of forty gallons had been, at an average, filled and run off in the almost incredibly short space of *three* minutes, being an increase of 2880 times on the rapidity of distillation that had obtained when the licence-system was first introduced in 1786!

Now, surely it will not be alleged, had a duty of 5 or 10 per cent. been laid on their income or capital, that Messrs. Sligo would have been half so likely to make this important discovery. Being assessed on the still, the duty had the double effect of fixing attention specially on it and of operating as a powerful stimulus to its improvement.

The same principle holds in the case of duties laid on commodities imported from abroad. All the energies of the merchant are immediately employed to discover new markets, or means of importing the goods at cheaper rates, so that the operation of the duty may in as far as possible be defeated by a reduction in the cost of the articles on which it is laid. In the stimulus thus given to invention and economy we find the explanation of what Garnier calls the most surprising phenomenon of Political Economy, "*l'accroissement rapide et prodigieux de la richesse chez les nations les plus chargées d'impôts sur les articles de la consommation générale.*"

But, notwithstanding the facility with which they may be imposed, and their powerful influence (while confined within reasonable limits) in stimulating industry and economy, it must not be supposed that taxes on commodities or on expenditure are, in all respects, unobjectionable. It may be said of taxes as of poems,—

> Whoe'er expects a faultless tax to see
> Expects what neither is, nor was, nor e'er shall be.

The disadvantages incident to this class of duties have, however, been much exaggerated. It is alleged, for example, that they alter the natural distribution of capital and industry, and force them into less advantageous channels, because, as already seen, when a tax is laid on any description of commodities, the producers, unless they can otherwise neutralize its influence, raise their prices by diminishing the supply of taxed articles in the market, and employing a portion of their capital in some more profitable business. But, if at all sensible, this disturbing action is experienced only when a duty is first imposed; for capital being distributed, after a short while, so as to suit the new state of things, the influence of the duty is, in this respect, at an end. It is not, however, by any means a necessary consequence that the prices of articles on which a duty has been laid will be raised proportionally to its amount, or, indeed, that they will be raised at all, and in the latter case the distribution of capital will not be affected. Provided the duty be not oppressive, its influence in stimulating those engaged in the production of the taxed articles to new efforts of industry and economy may enable them to sell the commodities at their old price or at one but little higher. And supposing it were otherwise, and that prices were raised proportionally to the tax, the effect would be confined to the home-market, inasmuch as the granting of an equivalent drawback, or the remitting of the duties on the articles when exported, hinders the foreign market from being affected by the tax.

Duties on commodities being usually paid by the producers before they are sold to the consumers, they not only, it is said, increase prices by their amount, but also by the amount of the profits of the various parties by whom they have been advanced. But though this circumstance undoubtedly operates to increase prices, its influence has been excessively overrated by Sir Matthew Decker, Say, Sismondi, and others. The latter has calculated that a tax of 4000 francs, paid originally by a manufacturer whose profits were 10 per cent., would, if the manufactured commodity only passed through the hands of five different persons before reaching the consumer, cost the latter 6734 francs. This calculation proceeds on the supposition, that he who first advances the tax receives from the next manufacturer 4400 francs, and he, again, from the next 4840 francs; so that at each step 10 per cent. is added to its value. "But this," as Mr. Ricardo has justly observed,

" is to suppose that the value of the tax would be accumulating at *compound* interest; not at the rate of 10 per cent. per annum, but at an absolute rate of 10 per cent. at every step of its progress. M. Sismondi's statement would be correct, if five years elapsed between the first advance of the tax and the sale of the taxed commodity to the consumer; but if one year only elapsed, a remuneration of 400 francs, instead of 2734, would give a profit at the rate of 10 per cent. per annum to all who had contributed to the advance of the tax, whether the commodity had passed through the hands of five manufacturers or fifty." *

It is certainly true that duties on commodities encourage smuggling. " They tempt," says Smith, " persons to violate the laws of their country, who are frequently incapable of violating those of natural justice, and who would have been in every respect excellent citizens, had not the laws of their country made that a crime which nature never meant to be so." † In consequence of this tendency, high duties require the employment of a great number of revenue officers; and, by exposing the producers of taxed articles to considerable inconvenience and hardship from domiciliary visits, force them to indemnify themselves by making a corresponding addition to the price of their goods. But this, after all, is not so much a consequence of duties on commodities, as of their abuse, or of their being carried to an oppressive extent. If they be confined within reasonable limits, the temptation which they create to engage in smuggling transactions may be very easily obviated. And it will be afterwards seen that duties so restricted are uniformly more productive than those which are carried to such a height as to hold out any great encouragement to smuggling.

It is true that duties on commodities do not always fall on individuals in proportion to their means of paying them; and that, while they press severely on persons with large families, or who occupy prominent stations, they may be

* Principles, &c., 3rd edit., p. 459.   † P. 378.

almost wholly avoided by rich misers and those in obscure stations. But though not proportioned to the means of the parties, nor intended to be so, it has been already seen that they are imposed on a fair principle, and involve no real injustice. Their payment is to a considerable extent voluntary; and the fact that they sometimes press but lightly on those who might best afford them is of very little importance. Such persons will, in consequence, accumulate more and more capital, which must, directly or indirectly, be laid out on industrious undertakings, and will most likely afford those engaged in them additional means of consuming. But whether this be so is immaterial. Two generations of misers do not often follow in succession; so that the probability is, that the more liberal expenditure of those who are to come will fully compensate for the parsimony of their fathers. In matters of this sort, practical considerations are entitled to the utmost regard. The perfect equality of taxation is impossible. All attempts to assess individuals in proportion to their incomes must necessarily miscarry; and will most likely be, in the end, productive of more evil than good. Nothing, therefore, remains but to adopt the best practicable taxes, and these, for the reasons already stated, appear to be duties on commodities or on expenditure. If duties be laid on sugar or wine, those who abstain from their use will, no doubt, escape them : surely, however, those who use such articles have no good right to complain of this, seeing that they may also, by being as self-denying as the others, exempt themselves from the duties.

It is sometimes said that direct taxes are preferable to those that are indirect, because they fall principally on the wealthier classes, whereas indirect taxes fall, it is alleged, principally on the lower and poorer portion of the community. But it may be doubted whether this be a fair statement. It is true that a duty on spirits, tobacco, beer, or other articles consumed by the inferior classes, produces a greater amount of revenue than a duty on carriages, horses, French wines, livery servants, or such-like articles, used principally by the rich. But we have seen (*ante*, p. 20) that this is not a consequence of the duties pressing more heavily on the lower classes, but of their immense preponderance in point of numbers; and that we can draw no fair conclusion in regard to the influence of taxation over different classes by merely looking at the aggregate sums which they respectively contribute to the revenue.

Independently, too, of these considerations, it has been shown, in treating of taxes on wages (and the same thing will be more fully established in the following chapter), that taxes on the necessaries consumed by the labourers most commonly bring about, in the end, a corresponding rise of wages, and either fall on their employers or are defrayed by an increase of industry and economy. No doubt, however, there are cases in which such taxes occasion a nearly corresponding decrease in the comforts of the labourers; and, speaking generally, they should be resorted to with extreme caution, and should always be confined within the narrowest limits.

But whatever may be the incidence of taxes laid directly on wages, or on necessaries, there is not, we apprehend, much ground for supposing that the condition of the labourer would be sensibly improved by repealing such taxes, and replacing them by an equivalent tax on property or income. Without repeating what has been already said respecting its inequality and mischievous influence, let it be supposed that the taxes on tea, sugar, and soap, producing above ten millions a-year, are repealed, to be replaced by a tax on property or income. In this case we believe it may be safely affirmed that from a half to two-thirds of the indirect taxes now referred to are paid by parties who would not be directly affected by a property or income tax, commencing at the same point as the existing income-tax. And, taking this for granted, it follows that from 5,000,000*l.* to 6,600,000*l.* would be added, in the event of the supposed commutation taking place, to the taxes falling at this moment upon the upper classes, whose means of employing labour, or of buying its produce, would, of course, be diminished in a corresponding degree. Whatever, therefore, the labourers might gain on the one hand by such a measure as this, they would necessarily lose about as much on the other. Their interests are in this respect identical with those of their masters; and it is a contradiction to suppose that you can improve their condition by repealing the taxes that fall on them, to lay them directly on their employers. If you add 100*l* or 1000*l* a-year to the taxes falling on a capitalist, do you not lessen, directly or indirectly, his demand for labour, or for the produce of labour, to that extent?

It is, also, abundantly certain that any considerable increase of the direct taxes falling on the upper classes would be most injurious to the labourers, by giving additional force to the motives which induce people to reside abroad, and to employ their capital in other countries. Capital has already a strong tendency to leave this country, to seek more profitable investments in the colonies and among foreigners. And this tendency, which originates, in part, at least, if not principally, in our heavy taxation, would be vastly increased were any considerable additions made to the direct taxes falling on the upper classes. The burden which now falls indirectly on them, and of which they have no clear idea, would then be rendered obvious; and as they could no longer hope to elude or mitigate its pressure, by abstaining from the use of taxed articles, they would be tempted to withdraw their property beyond the sphere of its influence.

It has been sometimes said, by those who are hostile to indirect taxes, that they are too easily augmented, and that the probability is, had the revenue been principally raised by direct taxes, that it would not have attained to anything like its present magnitude. Facility of imposition is not, however, a defect, but one of the principal recommendations of a tax; and if taxation has been carried to an undue extent, the excess must be sought for in something else than this; in the prejudices, pride, and warlike propensities of the public, and in the errors and misconduct of successive governments. But when a great national effort has, whether wisely or not, been determined upon, the question is, in what way may the necessary funds be raised with the least injury to the public? It will be afterwards shown that, notwithstanding the various drawbacks incident to direct taxation, it should have been employed to a decidedly greater extent during the American war and the late French war; not, however, that it might have been substituted for indirect taxation, but that it might have co-operated with the latter; so that the necessity of resorting to heavy loans; and of funding so great an amount of debt, might have been partly or wholly obviated. The waste, extravagance, and mismanagement that may be found in the conduct of public affairs is wholly beside the question. The produce of the best tax, or description of taxes, may, like most other things, be misapplied or employed to advance improper purposes; surely, however, that is no reason why it should not be preferred to others. It is conceivable that a military force may be employed to establish tyranny at home; but would it be prudent, because of the bare possibility of such a contingency, to disband the army, and to trust for protection against internal faction or foreign aggression, to the ill-combined efforts of an undisciplined rabble? No wise or just government will ever raise by indirect taxes, or in any other way, a shilling more than is necessary for the public security and well-being; and the greater the facility with which the necessary supply may be raised the better.

CHAPTER. II.

TAXES ON NECESSARIES AND LUXURIES.

WITH regard to the influence of taxes on the price of commodities, it has been shown that, if a duty be laid on one
commodity and not on others, its price, unless some corresponding facility be at the same time given to its production,
will sustain an equal rise; for if it did not rise to this extent,
the profits of the producers would sink below the common
level, and their business would be abandoned. But it depends on the circumstance of the commodity being of the
class denominated luxuries, whether a tax on it will fall
wholly on the consumers. Taxes on necessaries consumed by
landlords and capitalists are defrayed by them; but taxes on
necessaries consumed by labourers have the same influence
as taxes on wages; and we have seen that, in very many
cases, such taxes are not really defrayed by the labourers;
but occasion an equivalent rise in the rate of wages, and
are thus, in fact, paid by their employers.

It seldom happens that wages in fully peopled countries
exceed the amount required to furnish the labourers with
the necessaries and conveniences which the custom of the
country renders it discreditable for them to be without.
And such being the case, the probability is, if taxes be imposed on necessaries, that they will be defrayed partly by
increase of exertion and economy, and partly by an increase
of wages arising out of the check which the altered situation
of the labourers will most probably give to population:
and in so far as the latter result may take place, the taxes
will in the end fall on the employers of work-people making
an equivalent deduction from their incomes or their profits.
At the same time, it would be wrong in a matter of this
kind to lay any considerable stress on theoretical principles or à priori conclusions; and in truth, the practical

influence of taxes on necessaries depends principally on their
amount, and on the state of the country in which they
are imposed.   In thriving countries, where the population
is not in excess, and there is a brisk and growing demand
for labour, a moderate tax on corn or other necessaries
might be but little injurious, inasmuch as the additional
foresight and economy it could hardly fail to bring along
with it would, in no long time, enable the labourers either
to get an equivalent increase of wages, or to discharge the
tax by an increase of frugality, without its making any
very sensible encroachment on their comforts.   But in a
declining society, or when the demand for labour is stationary or retrograde, a tax on necessaries would have a very
different effect ; and if it were heavy, or even considerable,
would infallibly entail the severest privations on the labouring class.   Under such distressing circumstances the
tax would, for a while at least, fall wholly on them ; and
though it might, perhaps, discourage marriage, and add
new strength to the principle of moral restraint, it would
at the same time, by increasing their privations and lowering their opinions of what is necessary to their decent subsistence, certainly help permanently to degrade their condition.   Hence it is that taxes on necessaries should always
be introduced with extreme caution, and be confined within
moderate limits.   But when they have been introduced, and
levied for a considerable period, they become, whether they
be really borne by the labourers or by their employers,
identified with the wages of the former, in the same way
that a tax on a commodity is identified with its cost.   They
are then, also, in a great measure forgotten by the labourers,
the majority of whom are hardly, perhaps, aware of their
existence.

If we exclude tea and sugar from the list, the tax on soap
is now almost the only one directly imposed in this country
on a necessary used by the poor.   But other and more important necessaries are taxed indirectly, by means of duties
and restrictions on their importation.   It will be afterwards

M

seen that the influence of the subsisting restraints on the importation of corn have been ludicrously overrated; still, however, it is not to be denied that they increase its price considerably, especially in unfavourable seasons. The duty of 21s. a cwt., or of 2¼d. per lb. on foreign butter, is also far too heavy. It is necessary to bear in mind, in estimating its influence, that it does not merely add 2¼d. per lb. to the price of the 250,000 cwts. of butter annually imported, but, also, to all the immense quantity which is produced at home; for, were it not for the duty, foreign butter would be sold here for 2¼d. per lb. less than it costs at present; and as there cannot be two prices of the same article in the same market, the price of native butter would be proportionally lowered. The duty of 11s. a cwt. on foreign cheese has the same influence, and is liable to the same objection. And though, from their being identified with the price of the articles, the duties in question have not called forth much remark, they certainly exercise a powerful influence; and their reduction to 5s. a cwt. would be an important boon to the labouring part of the population, without being productive of any considerable loss of revenue.

The admission, in 1842, of foreign live cattle, sheep, fresh provisions, and fish, which had previously been prohibited, on payment of moderate duties, is both in a commercial and economical point of view a highly advantageous measure. It is, indeed, true, from there not being any such discrepancy between the prices of provisions in our markets and those whence they may be imported as had been supposed, that this measure has not had the influence over prices here that was anticipated. But we incline to think that it will lead, in the end, to a considerably increased importation of bacon and other articles; and, at all events, it affords a security against their further rise, and has happily prevented the clamour, abuse, and agitation to which the continuance of the prohibition would most likely have given rise.

But whatever may be the influence of taxes on necessaries over wages and the condition of the labourers, their repeal, after they have been imposed for a considerable period, is always of singular advantage to them. For the progress of population having been determined by the circumstances under which the labouring classes have been placed, will be but little and only slowly modified by the change ; so that if there be no glut of unemployed labour in the market, and no means of easily importing additional labourers, their condition will be most materially improved. —The capital that is to employ them and their number being the same, they will necessarily get the same wages after taxes have been repealed that they got previously ; and these wages will, of course, purchase a greater quantity of the article or articles the duty on which has been abolished or lowered, or of other things.

It will be afterwards seen that the changes recently made in the regulations under which the sugar-trade has been carried on, coupled with the farther changes which are understood to be in contemplation in relation to the duties on sugar, will materially reduce the price of that most important article ; and that the like effect would follow from the reduction of the present exorbitant duty on tea to something like a reasonable amount. And as such measures could in nowise lessen (though they might and would extend) the demand for labour, whatever sum a labourer's family may at present have to expend upon tea and sugar, whether it be 40s. or 50s. a-year, they would continue to have that sum to expend upon them or on whatever else they fancied. And the demand of the consumers of tea and sugar being in a great degree formed upon and adapted to the existing prices, the presumption is that some considerable portion of the sum which is at present expended by them upon these articles, would after their fall be expended on other things; so that the reduction would not merely be advantageous to them, and to the large class who are now all but wholly denied the use of tea, but also to great numbers in their capacity of producers.

The operation of this principle is strikingly exhibited in

the case of fluctuations in the price of corn. This being
the article most indispensable to subsistence, when its price
rises, through a scarcity, a prohibition of importation, the
imposition of a duty, or any other cause, the poorer and
more numerous classes endeavour, by reducing their outlays
on less necessary articles, to get as much bread as possible.
And it accords with universal experience, that any material
rise in the price of corn is invariably, *cæteris paribus*, accompanied by a diminished demand for butcher's meat, tea,
sugar, beer, coarse cotton and woollen goods, and, in short,
for all the articles which principally enter into the consumption of the lower and least wealthy classes. And it equally
consists with experience that the opposite results invariably
follow when the price of corn falls; and that there is then a
more extensive and brisker demand for other things. Hence
the vast importance of good harvests, or of an equable
supply of corn at moderate prices, not merely to the well-
being of the labourers, but to that of the manufacturers and
producers generally. The distress of the latter in bad years
is not owing so much, perhaps, to the increased cost of their
food, as to the falling off in the demand for their services
occasioned by the diminution in the demand for their peculiar products. The revenue returns may be referred to in
corroboration of this statement; the produce of the excise
and customs duties on the great articles of consumption
being invariably greatest in plentiful years.

It is probable that in the event of the condition of the
labouring class being very materially improved by a reduction of taxation, the number of marriages would be increased, so that in the long run the rate of wages would
most likely be, to some extent, reduced. But this is a contingent and uncertain consequence. And as no increased
supplies of labour could, under the supposed circumstances,
come into the market for many years, the labourers would,
in the mean time, acquire improved habits, and would
most probably continue to preserve a large portion of the
advance they had gained.

But, except in peculiarly flourishing countries, where there is an increasing demand for labour, the policy of laying taxes on necessaries appears very questionable. The public necessities may, indeed, be such as to require the imposition of these, or of still more objectionable taxes; but, wherever it is possible, they had better be avoided. It is, however, quite different with moderate taxes on the luxuries or enjoyments of the labourer. No good objection can be made to them; and when they are not carried to excess, or to such a height as to defeat their object, by encouraging smuggling, they are productive of a large amount of revenue, without being injurious to the contributors. The duties on spirits and tobacco, and perhaps, also, malt liquor, are of this description. They are paid without being grudged, because they are identified with the cost of the articles, and because the taste for them is at once strong and deeply rooted. We beg, however, to protest against being reckoned of the number of those who think it would be good policy, were it practicable, to proscribe such indulgences. The taste for them may not, perhaps, be in all respects the most desirable; but it is incomparably better that it should exist and become more powerful, than that it should be suppressed without another of a preferable description being previously substituted in its stead. Men who, either from the pressure of taxation or any other cause, are confined to the mere necessaries required for their subsistence, are uniformly indolent, without enterprise, and without any wish to improve their condition. The enjoyment of superfluities by the lower classes is the best test of civilization, and the wish to possess them is the grand stimulus to industry and invention. But when the taste for them is widely diffused and engrafted, as it were, upon the habits of the people, duties, fitted to raise a large amount of revenue, may be laid on them without materially diminishing their consumption or the wish to possess them; while, by taxing the more questionable description of luxuries, such as ardent spirits, more heavily than others, the public taste may be gradually diverted into more wholesome channels. Dr.

Smith, no doubt, says that the trade which a workman carries on with the alehouse "is not necessarily a losing trade;"* and so long as he confines his demands within proper limits, this, perhaps, is true; but it is, at all events, a trade which is very apt to be, and *is* very frequently, abused; and there is nothing more likely to prevent such abuse than the laying of pretty smart duties on spirits and all sorts of intoxicating articles.

Sugar and tea are to be regarded in this country partly as necessaries and partly as luxuries, though, perhaps, they belong more to the former than to the latter class. But supposing the duties on them to be reasonable in amount, and properly assessed, they would appear to be, in most respects, unexceptionable.

We are supported in our view of the influence of taxes on the luxuries of the poor by the authority of Smith: "The high price of such commodities (tobacco and spirits) does not necessarily diminish the ability of the inferior ranks of people to bring up families. Upon the sober and industrious poor, taxes upon such commodities act as sumptuary laws, and dispose them either to moderate or to refrain altogether from the use of superfluities which they can no longer easily afford. Their ability to bring up families, in consequence of this forced frugality, instead of being diminished, is frequently, perhaps, increased by the tax. It is the sober and industrious poor who generally bring up the most numerous families, and who principally supply the demand for useful labour. All the poor, indeed, are not sober and industrious, and the dissolute and disorderly might continue to indulge themselves in the use of such commodities after this rise of price in the same manner as before, without regarding the distress which this indulgence might bring upon their families. Such disorderly persons, however, seldom rear up numerous families, their children generally perishing from neglect, mismanagement, and the

* Wealth of Nations, p. 217.

scantiness or unwholesomeness of their food. If by the strength of their constitution they survive the hardships to which the bad conduct of their parents exposes them, yet the example of that bad conduct commonly corrupts their morals, so that, instead of being useful to society by their industry, they become public nuisances by their vices and disorders. Though the advanced price of the luxuries of the poor, therefore, might increase somewhat the distress of such disorderly families, and thereby diminish somewhat their ability to bring up their children, it would not probably diminish much the useful population of the country."*

There can be no question respecting the incidence of taxes on the luxuries consumed by the rich. Duties on coaches, carriage-horses and hunters, packs of hounds, champagne, and such-like articles, fall wholly on those by whom they are used, and cannot be shifted to any one else. Owing, however, to the limited proportion which the more opulent classes bear to the middle and lower classes, duties on the luxuries principally used by the former seldom yield a large amount of revenue. Contrary, also, to what might, perhaps, be supposed by most persons, such duties, unless confined within reasonable limits, cease to be productive and lead to results that are always to be deprecated. It has been said, that as rich people can pay, there can be no harm in laying heavy duties on the articles consumed by them. Duties, however, should, speaking generally, be proportioned to the value of the articles on which they are laid, and not to the means of those who it is presumed will most likely buy them. Neither does it by any means follow that because a man *can* pay he *will* pay. On the contrary, it is found whenever articles principally used by the higher classes are loaded with oppressive duties, that they either give up using the taxed articles, or resort to enjoy them to other countries. In illustration of this statement we may mention, that "In 1767, 1,500,000*l.* were borrowed upon a duty on ladies' chip

---

* Wealth of Nations, p. 394.

hats; the duty was made large in proportion to the value
that it might be productive; the consequence was, that
chip hats were discontinued, and the tax produced nothing."*
The same may be said of the tax laid on hair-powder in
1797; and similar results follow in the case of disproportionally heavy taxes on articles the taste for which is less
fluctuating and capricious. Thus from 1821 to 1824, both
inclusive, when the rate of duty on French wines was 13s. 9d.
per imp. gallon, the consumption amounted to 171,838 gallons a-year at an average. In 1825 the duty was reduced
to 7s. 3d. per gallon; and during the subsequent four years
the average annual consumption was 360,450 gallons!
In these respects, indeed, there is no difference in the practical influence of oppressive duties, whether they be laid on
the articles used by the higher, the middle, or the lower
classes: they are uniformly pernicious and unproductive,
whereas moderate duties are as uniformly productive and
innocuous, if not advantageous.

CHAPTER III.

AD VALOREM TAXES.

It had been, we believe, uniformly supposed, down to the
publication of the edition of ' The Wealth of Nations,' by
the author of this work, that an equal *ad valorem* duty on
all commodities, by affecting them to the same extent, would
not in any degree modify or change the relation or proportion which they previously bore to each other.† But it must
be observed that, though an equal *ad valorem* duty would
affect commodities in the same proportion, it would not
affect the profits of their producers in the same, but in a very
different proportion; and it is by the degree in which the
latter are affected that the relation of commodities to each

---

* Eden's Letters to the Earl of Carlisle, 3rd edition, p. 119.
† See Mill's ' Elem. of Polit. Econ.,' 2nd ed., p. 271.

other is determined. If all classes of producers employed the same proportions of fixed and circulating capital,* an equal *ad valorem* duty would affect them all equally, and the values of their commodities, as compared with each other, would not be affected by its imposition. But this is not the actual state of things; different sorts of commodities are produced by the agency of very different proportions of fixed and circulating capital; and hence, were an equal *ad valorem* duty laid on them all, it would not affect profits equally, and would consequently cause a transfer of capital from one business to another, and a variation in the value of commodities, raising some and sinking others. To illustrate this, assuming that profits are 10 per cent., let it be supposed, in the first place, that A advances 1000*l*. in wages at the commencement of the year, and that he receives the produce, which must, by the supposition, be worth 1100*l*. at the end of the year; in the second place, let it be supposed that B has a capital of 11,000*l*. vested in a highly durable machine, which is capable of performing its work without any, or with but very little, manual labour; the annual produce of this machine being, it is obvious, under the circumstances supposed, wholly made up of profits, and necessarily selling for 1100*l*.; and lastly, let it be supposed that an equal *ad valorem* duty of 10 per cent. is laid on commodities. Now, it is plain that in this case A and B will each bring, at the end of the year, commodities worth 1100*l*. to market, and will therefore be respectively taxed 110*l*. But 100*l*. only of the value of A's goods consists of profits, the rest consisting of the capital expended in paying the wages of those by whom they were produced; whereas the whole value of B's goods consists of profits: hence it is clear that, while the duty would swallow up the whole of A's profits and 10*l*. of his capital, it would only take 10 per cent. of B's profits. We have

---

* It is, of course, taken for granted that the fixed capitals are of the same degree of durability, and that the circulating capitals are returnable in the same periods.

purposely chosen a case that sets the unequal operation
of the tax in a striking point of view; but whenever there
was any considerable difference in the proportions of fixed
and circulating capital employed in producing different
commodities, an equal *ad valorem* duty would operate in
the way now pointed out. Such a duty would, therefore,
be among the most unequal and injurious that could be imposed. It would cause an immediate derangement in all the
channels of industry, and in the value of most descriptions of
commodities. Capital would be driven from employments
principally carried on by hand to those principally carried
on by machinery; and while the value of commodities produced by the former would rise, the value of those produced
by the latter would fall, until they had been adjusted so as
to yield the same rate of profit to the producers.

It has also been contended, by those who supposed an
ad valorem duty did not change the relation of commodities
to each other, that it notwithstanding occasioned a universal
rise of price proportioned to the duty. * Mr. Mill contends that this result is brought about, not by any change in
the production of commodities, but by an increased rapidity
of circulation. But it may, we think, be shown, admitting
(for the moment) that it has no influence over their relative
values, that an *ad valorem* duty would not have the effect
ascribed to it. Suppose an *ad valorem* duty of 10 per cent
is laid on commodities, and let us endeavour, by tracing
its operation, to discover whether it would really have any
influence over their price, assuming, for the moment, that it
has no influence over their relative values. The duty must
either be laid upon those who buy commodities, or upon
those who sell them. Suppose that A goes to buy a commodity, and has got twenty shillings in his pocket; if the
government officers take two shillings of this sum, A will, of
course, have only eighteen shillings to offer for the commodity for which on former occasions he paid twenty shil-

* Ricardo's 'Principles of Political Economy,' 3rd ed., p. 281.   Mill's
'Elements,' 2nd ed., p. 272.

lings; but as the government agents will come into market
with the money they have got from him, the obvious result
will be, that he will get nine-tenths of the commodity for his
eighteen shillings, and that the officers will get the other
tenth for their two shillings; so that there is no room or
ground for any, even the smallest, change taking place in
its price. Suppose now that the duty, instead of being laid
on the buyer, is laid on the seller : in this case, the person
who received the twenty shillings from A would have to pay
two of them to a tax-gatherer; and though when he went
to market he would have only nine-tenths of the money in
his pocket which he would have had but for the duty, yet,
as the government agents would, as before, go to market
with the other tenth, the same result would take place, and
prices would not be affected.

Probably, however, it may be inquired, does not this
suppose that money is also taxed? And would it not
follow, unless the same duty that is laid on other things
were laid on bullion when imported, that the supply of gold
and silver in the country would be increased, and that prices
would, in consequence, be raised? These questions must,
however, be answered in the negative. A measure which
does not alter the value of any article as compared with
others produced at home, cannot raise its value as compared
with those produced in foreign countries; for if the exporters
of goods could exchange them for a greater quantity of
foreign products in consequence of the tax, they would
realise more profit than the sellers in the home-market, an
inequality which, as every one knows, could not continue for
any considerable period: and even supposing it were otherwise, and that the articles sent abroad really exchanged for
more than previously, because of the equal duty laid on
them, the increase of their price, by proportionally diminishing the foreign demand, would prevent the importation of a
greater aggregate quantity of bullion than formerly.

But it was unnecessary, perhaps, to say so much with
respect to a statement resting on an imaginary hypothesis;

the previous investigation having shown that, instead of an equal *ad valorem* duty leaving the values of commodities exactly where it found them, it would occasion the greatest fluctuations.

It may also be observed that, though the determination of the question, with respect to the incidence of equal *ad valorem* duties on all commodities, be of considerable theoretical importance, it can never be brought to any practical test. Equal *ad valorem* duties might perhaps be imposed with considerable fairness on some of the principal commodities imported from abroad; but it is quite out of the question to suppose that such duties, even were they as desirable as the reverse, should ever be imposed on the infinite variety of commodities produced within any extensive country. The greatest imaginable number of officers would not suffice either to assess or to collect such duties.

Even as respects commodities brought from abroad, the obstacles in the way of assessing *ad valorem* duties are not easily overcome. It is very difficult to learn either what most articles cost or what they are worth at the present moment. If the determination of such a point were left to the importer, he would, in order to save the duty, be disposed to undervalue the articles; while if it were left to the officer, he might overvalue them. It has sometimes been the practice, when articles are entered at value and charged with *ad valorem* duties, to authorise the officers, if they suspect the articles are undervalued, to take them on account of government at the price entered, adding a reasonable profit for the merchant. But a plan of this sort is very liable to abuse, and especially to collusion between the importers and the officers. Probably no *ad valorem* duty was ever so fairly assessed and easily collected as that on tea previously to the abolition of the East India Company's monopoly. All sorts of tea were then exposed to public sale in London; a duty of 96 per cent. being charged upon such as sold under 2*s.* per pound, and of 100 per cent. on such as sold at 2*s.* per pound and upwards; so that there was no room whatever for fraud or favouritism. But after the abolition of the Company's monopoly, when everybody might import teas into the outports as well as into the metropolis, and dispose of them at pleasure, the former system for the assessment of the duties could no longer be acted upon; and it will be seen in the sequel that the difficulties in the way of distinguishing the varieties of tea, and of assessing specified duties thereon, were either such, or alleged to be such, as to occasion the abandonment of the latter, and the imposition of the same duty on all sorts of tea.

It has often been proposed to impose *ad valorem* duties on wine; and were it practicable it would be a very desirable arrangement. There is the greatest difference in the qualities and values of different wines; and it is against all principle to subject inferior wines to the same rate of duty that is laid on the finest Champagne and Burgundy. But, however desirable, the difficulties in the way of assessing *ad valorem* duties on wine with any degree of fairness are such that it is not very likely they should ever be overcome. It is often no easy matter to discriminate between entirely different kinds of wine, and it is still more difficult to discriminate between different varieties of the same wine. Were the attempt made a great deal would have to be left (where nothing ever should be left) to the discretion of the officers; and there is good reason to think that the frauds thence arising would more than countervail any advantage to be derived from the adoption of the principle.

Where the practice of charging *ad valorem* duties is at all common, it is not unusual to fix an arbitrary value on most articles, and to rate the duty accordingly. But, however accurate at first, valuations of this sort must in no long time, owing to the changes that are perpetually occurring in the cost and value of commodities, become very wide of the mark; though as perfect accuracy in matters of this sort is unattainable, we incline to think, wherever the differences between articles subjected to *ad valorem* duties are distinctly

marked, that this is the preferable plan for their assessment.
The valuations might be revised every ten or twelve years,
and the discrepancies between them and the real value of the
goods would, in that case, be seldom very considerable. It
will always, however, be found to be next to impossible fairly
to assess *ad valorem* duties in the cases in which they would
otherwise be most desirable ; that is, in the case of articles of
the same species, such as corn, wines, teas, sugars, silk goods,
&c., the qualities and values of different varieties of which,
though distinguished with difficulty, differ very greatly.

CHAPTER IV.

TAXES ON RAW PRODUCE.

THE question respecting the ultimate incidence of taxes on
the raw produce of the soil is one of considerable nicety and
difficulty. If land yielded no surplus to its possessors above
the common and ordinary profit of the capital employed in its
cultivation, the imposition of a tithe or other peculiar tax
on its produce would obviously occasion an equivalent increase of price. For, as there neither is nor can be any
reason why the agriculturists should content themselves with
a lower rate of profit than is realized in other employments, as
soon as a tithe was imposed they would set about transferring
a portion of their stock to some more lucrative business ; and
this transfer would continue until the diminution of supply
raised prices to their proper level, and restored the equili-
brium of profit. In such a state of things tithe would indis-
putably form an equivalent addition to the price of raw
produce. But after various qualities of soil have been brought
under cultivation, and rents have, in consequence, been generally introduced, it is not so easy to trace the incidence and
influence of tithes and other taxes on the produce of the
land. They then appear to occasion a diminution of rent
rather than a rise of prices. Farms that are tithe-free bring
a higher rent than those which are titheable; and it is

naturally concluded that, were tithes abolished, the depressed rents would rise to the level of the others.   For
this reason tithe was long considered as consisting, in advanced societies, of a portion of the rent of the land of
which the clergy and lay impropriators were the rightful
owners, and that it had no influence over prices.   " Taxes
upon the produce of land," says Smith, " are in reality
taxes upon rent, and, though they may be originally advanced by the farmer, are finally paid by the landlord.
When a certain portion of the produce is to be paid away
for a tax, the farmer computes, as well as he can, what
the value of this portion is, one year with another, likely to
amount to, and he makes a proportional abatement in the
rent which he agrees to pay to the landlord.   There is no
farmer who does not compute beforehand what the church-
tithe, which is a land-tax of this kind, is, one year with
another, likely to amount to." *

Conclusive, however, as this statement appears on a first
view, it is in most instances destitute of any good foundation.
It has been repeatedly demonstrated that a very considerable
portion of the raw produce raised in every extensive country
is produced by means of capital laid out on the land in the
view merely of obtaining the customary rate of profit at
the time, without its yielding any rent.   It must also be
observed that the cost of producing this portion of the required supply of raw produce determines the price of the
rest; for it is produced under the most unfavourable circumstances; and unless its producers were repaid their expenses and profits, it would not be brought to market,
and a scarcity would ensue.   But when a tithe is imposed,
it affects, of course, the producers of this portion, in common
with the others.   Inasmuch, however, as they pay no rent,
they cannot throw the burden of tithe on a landlord; and
as they would not continue in their business unless they
obtained the same rate of profit as their neighbours, it ap-

* Wealth of Nations, p. 377.

pears unavoidably to follow that the price of corn must rise
proportionally to the tithe, which will, in that case, fall
wholly on the consumers.

This last is Mr. Ricardo's theory, and no doubt can be
entertained of its accuracy, provided—1st, that the tithe
extends to all or nearly all the lands of a country; and,
2nd, that foreign corn is excluded or burdened with a tax
equivalent to, or greater than, the tithe. We shall submit
a few remarks in illustration of this :—

1st. There cannot, as already seen, be any doubt that a
tithe universally imposed, by raising the cost of cultivating
inferior lands, which pay little or no rent, and affecting all
capital expended on improvements, must, when foreign corn
is excluded, or admitted under a duty exceeding the tithe,
occasion a corresponding rise of price, and fall wholly on the
consumer. When, however, a considerable portion of the land
of a country is exempted from tithe, its operation is somewhat
different, inasmuch as it then encourages cultivation as much
on the untithed as it discourages it on the tithed lands; so
that it has a double effect, increasing the price of raw produce to the public by the addition it makes to the cost of
cultivating the tithed land, and adding proportionally to the
rent of that which is untithed.

According to the returns obtained under the late Income-
Tax Act, the total annual value of the land of England and
Wales in 1813 was estimated at 29,476,853*l.*, of which lands
of the annual value of 7,904,378*l.* were wholly tithe-free,
while lands of the annual value of 856,184*l.* were tithe-free
in part, and other lands, of the annual value of 498,823*l.*,
paid only a low modus. So far, therefore, is it from being
true that all, or nearly all, the land of England and Wales
pays tithe, that it appears that about a third part is exempted from this burden; and if to the tithe-free land of
England and Wales we add Scotland, it will be seen that
half the cultivated land of Great Britain is unaffected by
tithe. Under these circumstances the tithe will obviously
extend cultivation over the lands which are tithe-free to

about the same extent that it contracts it on those which it affects; and will consequently occasion a rise, probably of about 5 per cent., in the price of corn, and a corresponding increase in the rents of the tithe-free lands.

2nd. But it is easy to see that these conclusions would be, not modified merely, but altogether changed, in the event of foreign corn being admitted at all times duty-free. In that case, prices here (so long at least as we continued to be a generally importing country) would be determined by the prices at which corn could be imported; and the owners and occupiers of the tithed portions of the country being no longer able, by restricting cultivation and raising prices, to indemnify themselves for the burdens laid exclusively on their lands, these would in future fall wholly on them; so that in this respect the practical effect of the opening of the ports to the free importation of corn, without any duty, would be to throw a burden from the shoulders of the public, by whom it has hitherto been wholly borne, to those of the landlords. It is true certainly that the proprietors of the tithe-free lands would continue, even with open ports and no duties, to receive, so long as tithe is charged on the others, a comparatively high rent; but this rent would, under the supposed circumstances, be identical with what it would be were tithe abolished; whereas, at present, it is higher from tithe increasing the price of corn.

As legally and constitutionally settled, tithe is a tenth part of the gross produce of the land, subject to none of the expenses of cultivation or of severance. Hence the burden which it imposes, though nominally the same, becomes really greater according as the increase of population forces recourse to inferior soils, and as more costly and expensive crops are cultivated. It has been observed in all countries subject to tithe that it uniformly increases more rapidly than rent, and that the severity of its pressure is progressively augmented. Its apologists allege, indeed, that it has the same effect, in as far as the interests of the farmers are concerned, as an equivalent amount of

N

rent. But this is a most fallacious statement. Rent, when once fixed, continues the same during the currency of the lease or agreement. Though an industrious and enterprising farmer should raise ten or twenty times the quantity of produce raised by a sluggard, his rent would not, therefore, be increased; and he would reap, as he ought, all the advantages of his greater industry and intelligence. Such, however, is not the case with tithes, unless they are commuted or limited to a rent certain. Where this is not the case they are invariable to the sluggard, while they become more and more oppressive to the industrious man, and increase with every fresh outlay of capital and labour. This, however, is a matter in which the interests of the landlords are still more sensibly affected than those of the tenants; all expensive improvements usually undertaken by the former being prevented till prices rise so as to yield not only the common rate of profit on the necessary outlay, but also to indemnify them for the tithe. Practically, therefore, tithe operates as a premium on idleness, and as a heavy and constantly increasing tax on industry. It obstructs the progress of improvement; and by preventing the cultivator from deriving the entire advantage of superior skill and increased exertion, discourages his efforts and contributes to render him indolent and indifferent. A farmer pays his rent willingly to the landlord; but he considers the clergyman as an interloper, who, without having contributed in any way to raise the crop, claims a tenth part of its gross amount. The occupier of a farm subject to this galling charge seldom believes that he is realizing the same rate of profit from the capital he employs as his neighbours in tithe-free farms; and we are told by Mr. Stevenson, the well-informed author of the Agricultural Survey of the County of Surrey, that it is the common opinion that a farm tithe-free is better worth twenty shillings an acre than a tithed farm equally favoured in soil and situation is worth thirteen shillings. In this way, tithes contribute indirectly as well as directly to raise prices; indirectly by generating an indisposition to apply fresh capital to the improvement of the soil, and directly by the positive addition which they make to the expense of cultivating bad land.

Dr. Paley, who cannot surely be reckoned unfriendly to the real interests of the church, says that, "of all institutions adverse to cultivation and improvement, *none is so noxious as that of tithes.* A claimant here enters into the produce who contributed no assistance whatever to the production : when years, perhaps, of care and toil have matured an improvement, when the husbandman sees new crops ripening to his skill and industry, the moment he is ready to put his sickle to the grain, he finds himself compelled to divide the harvest with a stranger. Tithes are a tax not only upon industry, but upon that industry which feeds mankind, upon that species of exertion which it is the object of all wise laws to cherish and promote." *

"Tithe," says Dr. Smith, "is always a great discouragement both to the improvements of the landlord and to the cultivation of the farmer. The one cannot venture to make the most important, which are generally the most expensive, improvements; nor the other to rear the most valuable, which are generally too the most expensive, crops, when the church, which lays out no part of the expense, is to share so largely in the profit. The cultivation of madder was for a long time confined by the tithe to the United Provinces, which, being Presbyterian countries, and upon that account exempted from this destructive tax, enjoyed a sort of monopoly of that useful dyeing drug against the rest of Europe. The late attempts to introduce the cultivation of this plant into England have been made only in consequence of the statute which enacted that five shillings an acre should be received in lieu of all manner of tithe upon madder."† In further illustration of the principle stated above, we may mention that the cultivation of flax and hemp in Ireland

---

* Paley's Works, ii., p. 105, ed. 1819.
† Wealth of Nations, p. 377.

never succeeded until a low *modus* had been fixed by law; since which it has made a considerable progress.

Mr. Howlett, vicar of Dunmow in Essex, has made some statements in his valuable tract on tithe, which strikingly illustrate the oppressive nature of that impost when levied on expensive crops, and which also show the impossibility of its being deducted from rent. He says, it frequently happens that the tithe of an acre of hops is worth 3*l.* or 4*l.* after the charge for drying and the duty are deducted; while, perhaps, the rent of the land is not more than 40*s.* or 50*s.*; and he adds that he had known the tithe of an acre of carrot-seed worth from six to eight guineas grown on land not worth 20*s.*!* But even in the case of wheat and other corn crops, the result is not materially different; the value of the tithe being, in very many instances, equal to, and frequently much greater than, the rent.

We may not, perhaps, be considered as travelling out of our way in observing that the *moral* seems to be as bad as the economical influence of tithes. The clergy cannot be blamed for exacting payment of the share of the produce of the land appropriated for their support; and it is admitted, on all hands, that they rarely carry their claim for tithes to its full extent, and are in general less rigorous in their demands than lay impropriators. But, notwithstanding their forbearance, a provision of this sort is most objectionable. The influence and usefulness of a clergyman depend, in a great measure, on his possessing the esteem and affection of his parishioners; and these he can with difficulty acquire, when his stipend consists of tithe, without the sacrifice, which perhaps he can ill afford, of a portion of his income. " The rate of tithe," says the author of the 'Agricultural Survey of Clare,' is a tolerable barometer of the love or dislike of parishioners; where it is higher than usual, you may be certain of finding a turbulent divine, who will have *his rights*, regardless whether he is

* Inquiry concerning the Influence of Tithe, p. 3.

liked or disliked. If, on the contrary, tithe is moderately exacted, the love and respect of his neighbours follows of course." A system of this sort sets the kindly feelings and the interest of the clergy in opposition to each other, and has done much to paralyse their exertions and to lessen their usefulness. Mr. Grattan said in the House of Commons that " the tithe system made the clergyman's income fall with his virtues and rise with his bad qualities, just as it made the parishioner lose by being ingenuous and save by dishonesty." It is difficult, indeed, to conceive how any better plan could have been devised for making the clergy the unwilling instruments of endless litigation and implacable animosities.

A just sense of the injurious influence of tithe in obstructing agricultural improvement, and involving the clergy in contests with their parishioners, had long excited a general wish among well-informed individuals for its commutation; and this is now in the way of being effected, under the provisions of the Act 6th and 7th Will. IV., cap. 71. This act directs that the average value of the tithes in each parish, during the seven years ending with 1835, should be ascertained, and distributed into equivalent quantities of wheat, barley, and oats, which are made a fixed and invariable rent-charge upon the land : and it is further enacted that the clergy and lay impropriators shall receive the value of these quantities in all time to come, according to the average prices of corn in England and Wales during each previous seven years. Commissioners have been appointed to carry the act into execution; and the tithes in a great number of parishes have already been commuted conformably to its stipulations.

Recently, however, this act has given rise to a good deal of discussion; and it has been alleged that it unjustly aggravates the pressure of tithe on some districts, and lessens it on others. Down, it is said, to the passing of this act it was the practice in all parts of the country, as it is still the practice where its provisions are not acted upon, either to

acquit the burden of tithe by a payment in kind, or by a
money-payment under a special agreement with the tithe-
owner; and as there is a very wide difference between the
price of corn in different parts of the country, such, for example, as Kent and Essex on the one hand, and the northern
and Welsh counties on the other, it is obvious that a landlord
or farmer, burdened with a rent charge of 100 quarters as
tithe in Westmoreland, would, when free to act as he thought
best, stipulate for a very different money-payment on its
account from what would have to be made for an equal
amount of tithe in the Isle of Sheppey or the Isle of Thanet.
The Commutation Act has, however, we are told, wholly
overlooked this important difference; and has, by making
the prices of the quantities of corn payable to the tithe-owners
depend on the average prices of the kingdom, materially
increased the burden of the tax on the poorer and more
backward districts, and diminished it on the richer and more
improved.   It has been affirmed that the increased pressure
of the payments on account of tithe, occasioned by the circumstance now mentioned, had a considerable influence in
exciting the recent disturbances in Wales; and, whether such
were really the case or not, it would appear to be abundantly
certain, inasmuch as the prices of corn in the principality
are very decidedly below the average prices of the kingdom,
that, by taking the latter for a standard by which to com-
mute the corn-rents payable instead of tithe, a very considerable addition has been made to the pecuniary payments which
the Welsh have to make on this head.

But notwithstanding the plausible nature of these statements, and the sanction given to them by some high authorities, they may, we think, be shown to be destitute of any
good foundation.   They appear to take for granted that the
quantity of corn payable as rent by the landowner on account
of tithe that has been commuted, has been determined by
the quantity (and not by the value) of the produce taken as
tithe in each particular case.   And were such the case the
objections made to the operation of the act in the more

backward parts of the country would be perfectly well founded : but the real state of the case is quite otherwise ; and as this is a matter of some difficulty and of considerable practical importance, which appears to have met with less attention than it deserves, we may be excused, perhaps, for endeavouring to set it in its true light.

We need not, however, trace the various steps indicated by the act. It is sufficient to state that the value of the tithe payable by an estate, supposing it not to have been determined by a lease, but to have been taken in kind, is ascertained by the prices at which the produce taken as tithe has been sold for in the nearest markets. And supposing the value of the tithe thus ascertained to be 100*l.*, this sum is divided into three equal parts of 33*l.* 6*s.* 8*d.*, each of which is converted into an equivalent in corn according to the *average prices of the kingdom* during the preceding seven years : and supposing those prices to be such that the 33*l.* 6*s.* 8*d.* will be worth 12 quarters of wheat, 20 of barley, and 24 of oats, these will be the quantities by which the rent due by the landowner on account of tithe will be determined in time to come.

It seems plain, under these circumstances, which are those that take place in practice, that there can be no injustice in converting the fixed quantities of 12, 20, and 24 quarters of wheat, barley, and oats into money according to the average prices of the kingdom. Had the value of the tithe as ascertained in the first instance been converted into equivalent quantities of wheat, barley, and oats according to the prices of the district, the quantities of corn forming the basis of the future rent to be paid by the tithe-owner would have been proportionally greater; but, inasmuch as these quantities were determined by the higher average prices of the kingdom, justice requires that they should in future be commuted by the same standard.

To illustrate this, suppose the prices in any market of Wales to be 40*s.* a quarter for wheat, while the average price of the kingdom is 50*s.* : in this case it is alleged that

by taking the latter for a standard in converting the corn-rent
due for tithe into money, the Welsh landowner or occupier
has to pay 10*s.* a quarter more on account of tithe than formerly. But in making this statement it is forgotten that
the quantity of corn to be converted into money was itself, as
already seen, determined by the higher price of the kingdom.
In the case now under consideration let it be supposed that
the tithe payable by an estate in Wales previously to the
commutation cost 150*l.* a-year, all legal deductions being
made : this sum will, under the new act, be converted into
quantities of wheat, barley, and oats respectively worth 50*l.*
according to the average prices of the kingdom : in future,
therefore, the landowner will be charged with 20 quarters
of wheat (20 at 50*s.* = 50*l.*) and with barley and oats in
proportion ; but, it is plain, had the conversion been made
according to the prices of the district, the wheat-rent to be
paid in future would have been 25 instead of 20 quarters
(25 at 40*s.* = 50*l.*), so that his position, by taking local
prices for a standard, would have been neither better nor
worse than it is : whatever he might, under such circumstances, have gained by the lower rate at which the corn-rent
would henceforth be converted into money, he would unavoidably have lost a precisely equal sum by the greater amount
of such corn-rent.

But though there be no foundation whatever for the opinion that the Commutation Act has been injurious to the
more backward parts of the kingdom in the way previously
stated, we are not surprised that it should have occasioned
dissatisfaction. The truth is that fixed money-payments are
but little suited to persons in the depressed condition of the
greater number of Welsh tenants. In bad years they could
formerly, if they pleased, fall back upon a payment in kind,
and could higgle with the parson or other tithe-owner for a
reduction of his charge. But now the sum payable as tithe
is fixed and ascertained, and the remedy for recovery being
simple, the burden appears to the majority of poor occupiers
to be materially augmented.

Owing also to the moisture of their climate, the Welsh had formerly in dealing with parsons and other tithe-owners a powerful resource in threatening to allow their land to " run to grass," as they call it; and when it is in grass it is of little importance to the farmer whether it be broken up a year or two sooner or later.   But this resource is now, also, cut off; and the consequence is, that the burden of tithe, though really reduced, seems to many to have become more oppressive than ever.

We believe, also, that the plan of making the payments of every year depend on the average of the preceding seven years is most unwise.   Under its operation the farmer has frequently a high payment to make when prices are low, and conversely.   Common sense would, however, dictate that the payments to be made in any given year should correspond with the prices of that year.   This is the plan followed in Scotland ; and there is every reason to think that its adoption in England would considerably facilitate the easy working of the commutation project.

In Scotland, as in the other divisions of the empire, the Romish clergy, exclusive of the large landed estates of which they obtained possession, were entitled to a tithe of the produce of the lands belonging to others.   But, at the Reformation, the estates of the clergy, and the tithes payable to them, were either seized upon or granted by the crown to certain lay proprietors, who have received the name of *titulars*. The reformed clergy, who were thus left without any fixed or legal provision, loudly condemned this appropriation of the church property; for though they had abjured the spiritual errors of the Romish church, they never so much as dreamed of renouncing what they believed to be their right to succeed to her revenues.   And as the tithes in possession of the titulars or lay impropriators were more rigorously exacted than they had been by the clergy, the complaints of the latter were re-echoed by a large proportion of the farmers and smaller proprietors.   In consequence of these complaints,

and of the extreme distress of the clergy, various efforts
were made to secure some provision for the latter out of the
wreck of the church property, and to put a stop to the rapa-
cious exactions of the titulars. After much fluctuating
legislation on the subject, the whole matters in dispute were
referred to Charles I., by whom they were finally arranged
and settled, by a judgment pronounced in 1629, which was
ratified by an Act of the Scotch Parliament in 1633. This
statute ordained that landlords should be entitled to get
their estates valued, and that the whole sum which could
ever be drawn by the clergy from them should not exceed a
fifth part of their valued free rent, and that, when once
made, this valuation should not be subject to any future
revision or modification. The clergy were not, however, to
be entitled to the immediate or unconditional possession of
the *fifth* part of the free rent of the land that was thus set
apart for their maintenance, for it was remitted to a committee of the Scotch Parliament (and, since the Union, the
same power has been lodged in the Court of Session), to
grant the clergy such portions of this *fifth* part of the valued
free rent as they might judge suitable for their support.
When a clergyman has got the whole of this *fifth* part, the
teind or tithe of his parish is said to be exhausted, and he
has no further claim of any sort on the land. This is now
the case in a considerable number of Scottish parishes; and
by a late statute a sum of about 10,000*l*. a-year is given to
make up the stipend of clergymen in such parishes to 150*l*.
a-year, exclusive of glebes and houses.

The valuation of the rent of Scotland according to which
the clergy are now paid was principally executed in the
reigns of Charles I. and II. Even at the time it was understood to be very low; and the subsequent rise of rent has
been so very great that, instead of getting a fifth, the clergy
are not at present receiving more than its *twenty-fifth* or
thirtieth part. On a few estates which were not valued so
early, the case is a little different; but we believe we are
warranted in affirming that the provision for the clergy does

not, in any instance, amount to a tenth part of the nett rental of the land.

At the same time that the provision for the clergy was fixed on this footing it was also enacted that all individuals who paid tithes to lay impropriators should be entitled to buy them up on paying the proprietor *six* years' purchase of their estimated annual value—a power of which the payers have universally availed themselves.

These arrangements have been productive of the greatest benefit, and have contributed, in no ordinary degree, to the advancement of agriculture. The landlords and occupiers of farms in Scotland have not been restrained from laying out capital, or making the most expensive improve. ments, by any fear of a clergyman or lay impropriator demanding a share of the produce. And what is of equal, and perhaps greater importance, the salutary influence of the clergy has not been in any degree weakened by the mode in which they are provided for, and squabbling and unseemly altercations between them and their parishioners, with respect to stipends, have been all but entirely unknown.

The influence of tithe and other taxes on the price of raw produce has been urged as a reason why an equal duty should be imposed on such produce when imported from abroad. But foreign corn must be paid for, either directly or indirectly, by the exportation of some species of manufactured commodities; and it is, therefore, clear that the home producers of corn have no claim to a protecting duty on the importation of foreign corn, unless the tithe, and other taxes falling on raw produce, exceed those which fall on manufactured goods. Heavy taxes, provided they be equally distributed, do not render a particular class less able to withstand the competition of foreigners than others, and cannot, therefore, entitle it to a protecting duty. But if higher duties be laid on a particular description of commodities, the case is different. If, for example, while the duty on commodities generally was 10 per cent., a duty of 20 per cent. were laid on a particular article, its price must rise 10 per cent. more than the others, in order to maintain its producers in the same relative situation as before. But in the event of the ports being opened to the importation of foreign goods free of duty, the producers of the heavily-taxed commodity would, it is plain, be deprived of the means of limiting its supply, and consequently of raising its price, so as to indemnify them for the excess of tax with which they are charged. The 10 per cent. extra duty would then really operate as an equivalent bounty on the importation of the commodity; and unless it were defeated by a protecting duty of 10 per cent., the home producers would be placed in a relatively disadvantageous situation, and would, perhaps, have to abandon their business.

Now it may, we apprehend, be easily shown that the agriculturists are actually in this situation; and farther, that the peculiar burdens they have to sustain would be very materially increased, were the ports open to the importation of corn without any duty. No branch of manufacturing or commercial industry is subject to a tax at all similar or equivalent to tithe. We have already seen that under the existing regulations it operates partly to increase prices, and partly to raise the rents of the untithed lands; and we have further seen that under a system of free trade without duties the present incidence of tithe would be completely changed; and that it would no longer raise either prices or rents, but would fall wholly on the landlords and occupiers. But we are not to attempt to bring about what is believed to be a great national improvement, by shifting a burden borne by the public to a peculiar class. This would be flagrant injustice, to be vindicated only by the most overwhelming necessity. Luckily, however, we have not to deal with any such unreasoning principle; and hence the obligation, in the event of the ports being opened, of imposing a duty on foreign corn sufficient to countervail the tithe.

Should the country continue to prosper, and the rent of

land to rise, the incidence of tithe, now that it has been commuted, will be wholly changed, and it will come to be entirely defrayed by the landlords without in any degree affecting the prices of corn. The tithe will, also, fall exclusively on them should anything occur to check the progress of agriculture, or materially to lower rents and prices. But, in the former case, the pressure of the tithe would be comparatively light, whereas in the latter it would be comparatively heavy : indeed in this case the rent payable to the tithe-owner might be so very oppressive as not merely to put a stop to all improvement, but even to make it for the land-owner's interest to abandon the land. The pressure of a fixed burden becomes, it is evident, progressively less as the wealth of those who have to bear it is increased, and progressively greater as it is diminished. But at present, or while the Commutation Act is only in the course of being carried into effect, the former incidence of tithe can be little changed ; and there can consequently be no doubt, for the reasons already stated, that a corresponding duty should be laid on foreign corn when imported.

When the commutation is completed, the fixed and in-variable corn-rent that will then be laid on the land, will be a novel and strongly-marked feature in the economical condition of the kingdom. Had tithe been commuted a century or even half a century since, it would have been a very different matter. But considering the very advanced and peculiar situation of the country at the æra of the commutation, and the fact that our average prices have been for many years considerably above those of the contiguous continental states, it is pretty evident that the fixed rent due to the tithe-owners may easily come to have a very serious operation on the interests of agriculture, and consequently on those of the public. We have every confidence in the national resources, and in the elasticity and buoyancy of the national industry. But we are not on that account to shut our eyes to possible contingencies. And at all events the fact of the land being burdened with a fixed corn-rent, ascertained when cultivation was far advanced, is far too momentous to be forgotten or overlooked in dealing with restrictions on importation.

Exclusive of tithe, the land is burdened with an extra weight of other taxes. Poor-rates and county-rates of all descriptions have always fallen much heavier on it than on any other species of fixed property; and though, within the last few years, some of the more striking anomalies in their assessment have been removed, they still continue to press with disproportioned severity on the land. Moneyed fortunes, also, and funded and other moveable property are exempted from all local burdens. An individual may have 100,000*l.* engaged in trade, or vested in the public funds, in mortgages, or in stock of the Banks of England or Scotland, without being subject to tithe, or to any of those taxes for the poor, and other local objects, that fall on the owner of the smallest patch of land, as well as on most other descriptions of fixed property. There may be reasons to justify this exemption; but the fact of its existing proves sufficiently that land and other fixed property is peculiarly affected by taxation.

It will be afterwards seen that the malt-tax, though of course it falls directly on the consumers, is, in its indirect operation, particularly injurious to agriculture; and, being a grievance peculiar to this department, it would entitle the agriculturists, had they no other claims to urge, to a countervailing duty on the importation of foreign corn.

Such being the case, the agriculturists are clearly justified in demanding, in the event of the free importation of corn being permitted, that it should be burdened with a fixed or constant duty sufficient to countervail the peculiar charges that would fall on the land, were the ports unconditionally opened. It is impossible to refuse them this, without trampling on every fair principle. Such protection is not given to the agriculturists as a favour, but to keep them where they have a right to be kept—on the same level as the other classes of their countrymen. If they be relieved from these peculiar burdens, the necessity for the countervailing duties will of course cease, and they may, and indeed should, be repealed forthwith; but the equalization of taxation at home should, in all cases, precede the repeal of duties on importation. It is not possible, perhaps, to form any very accurate estimate of what the countervailing duty should amount to; but it would not, we apprehend, be difficult to show that, by fixing it at 5*s.* or 6*s.* a quarter on wheat, and other grain in proportion, the justice of the case would be satisfied, and the interests of the agriculturists and those of the public conciliated and most effectually promoted. A duty of this amount would preserve all parties in the same relative situation after the opening of the ports as previously; and would treat them, as they should ever be treated, with equal and impartial justice.

It has been objected to a fixed duty on foreign corn, that it could not be collected in years when there was any unusual deficiency in our harvests, the prices of corn, even without any duty, being then oppressively high. But, though it may seem paradoxical, it is certainly true that prices in such years would not be sensibly influenced by the payment of a moderate duty, and that they would be quite as high were it repealed or suspended as they would be were it allowed to exert its full influence. It is easy to see that such would be the case. At present, if there were no duty, and no restrictions of any kind on importation, foreign corn of about the same quality as British corn might, in ordinary years, be imported from Dantzic and other corn-shipping ports, and sold to the miller for about 48*s.* or 50*s.* a quarter.* If, then, a fixed duty of 6*s.* were laid on imported corn, the price would have to rise to 54*s.* or 56*s.* a quarter before it would answer the foreigner to send corn to this country. But he would begin to export as soon as it attained this level; and if the price rose to 55*s.* or 57*s.*, its exportation would be peculiarly advantageous. The

* For proofs of this, see Art. Corn Laws and Corn Trade in ' Commercial Dictionary.'

moment, however, that it is ascertained that any serious deficiency has taken place in our harvest, the price of corn, as every body knows, rises far above this limit, most probably ranging, according to the presumed deficiency, from 65*s*. to 85*s*., 90*s*. and upwards, a quarter. But when such is the case, the duty ceases to have any perceptible influence over price, which is then wholly determined by the proportion between the supply and demand, without reference to the cost of the corn. Under such circumstances, the duty becomes, in fact, a deduction from the profits of the foreigner, so that its suspension would only add to the latter, without depressing prices.

An objection has been made to this reasoning, founded on the different distances from which corn has to be brought in dear years. It is admitted that the duty would have no direct influence in such seasons over the prices or supplies of corn brought from the contiguous markets ; but it is contended, that by obstructing importation from great distances, it would tend by lessening the supply to raise prices generally. But this statement is more ingenious than correct. The practical influence of a duty of 6*s*. a quarter, in the way now stated, would be quite inappreciable. Every person engaged in the corn trade knows, that when prices are 65*s*., 75*s*., or 85*s*. a quarter, the fact of there being or not being a duty of 5*s*. or 6*s*. on importation would have no perceptible influence over the quantities imported. The circle whence corn is brought in years of scarcity is too vast, and its margin too ill-defined, to be either sensibly expanded or circumscribed by adding 5*s*. or 6*s*. to, or deducting the same sum from, our prices.

It appears, therefore, however much the conclusion may be at variance with popular prejudices, that a fixed duty on corn would be most onerous when prices were about the level at which importation can take place, or but a little higher. It would then, like the generality of customs duties, fall wholly on the importers, or on the consumers here. But when prices rise considerably above the level of profitable importation, the duty has no sensible influence over them, and falls wholly on the foreigner. Hence the repeal or suspension of the duty when prices are high, would be most impolitic; it would be sacrificing revenue, not for the benefit of our own people, but for that of the growers and dealers in Poland and other exporting countries.

Whatever amount of duty may be laid on foreign corn, for the equitable purpose of countervailing peculiar burdens laid on the corn raised at home, an *equivalent drawback* should be allowed on exportation. " In allowing," says Mr. Ricardo, "this drawback, we are merely returning to the farmer a tax which he has already paid, and which he must have to place him in a fair state of competition in the foreign market, not only with the foreign producer, but with his own countrymen who are producing other commodities. It is essentially different from a bounty on exportation, in the sense in which the word bounty is usually understood; for by a bounty is generally meant a tax levied on the people for the purpose of rendering corn unnaturally cheap to the foreign consumer: whereas what I propose is, to sell our corn at the price at which we can really afford to produce it; and not to add to its price a tax which shall induce the foreigner rather to purchase it from some other country, and deprive us of a trade which, under a system of free competition, we might have selected."*

Besides being indispensable to meet the justice of the case, we are firmly persuaded that nothing would do so much to promote and secure the interests of agriculture and of the public as the opening of the ports, under such a duty as has been suggested, accompanied by an equal drawback. The granting of the latter is of more importance than is commonly supposed. Thanks to the spread of agricultural improvement, we now grow, in moderately favourable years, nearly as much corn as is sufficient for our supply; and in unusually productive years, such as 1822 and 1833, the home

* Protection to Agriculture, p. 53.

supply is so very abundant, that the market is overloaded.
This abundance is, however, under the peculiar circumstances of the case, a serious loss to the farmer; for, owing
to our ordinary or average prices being above those of the
Continent, the market cannot be relieved by exportation till
they have fallen to a ruinously low level.   Nine-tenths of the
agricultural distress, of which we have heard so much at
different periods since the peace of 1815, originated in the
way now mentioned.   Such revulsions would, however, be in
a great measure obviated by granting a drawback of 5s. or
6s. a quarter, inasmuch as it would, by facilitating exportation in unusually plentiful years, hinder prices from then
falling to the extent they now necessarily do.   Such a plan
would, by checking all tendency to extremes, render agriculture and commerce comparatively secure; and would, in
this way, promote the prosperity of both.

   Taxes on raw produce, by raising the price of the articles
required for the food of the labourer, usually, also, raise
wages and lower profits.   Such taxes, therefore, fall with
double weight on capitalists; affecting them both as employers of labour and as consumers.   Indeed, one of the
principal disadvantages of taxes on raw produce consists
in their tendency to lower profits.   "With a permanently
high price of corn," says Mr. Ricardo, "proportional wages
would be high; and as commodities would not rise on account of the rise of wages, profits would necessarily fall.   If
goods worth 1000l. require at one time labour which costs
800l., and at another time the price of the same quantity of
labour is raised to 900l., profits will fall from 200l. to 100l.
They will fall, not in one trade only, but in all.   High
wages equally affect the profits of the farmer, the manufacturer, and the merchant; nor is there any other way
of keeping profits up than by keeping wages down.   In
this view of the law of profits, it is at once seen how
important it is that so essential a necessary as corn,
which so powerfully affects wages, should be sold at a

low price; and how injurious it must be to the community generally, that, by prohibitions against importation, we
should be driven to the cultivation of our poorer lands to
feed our increasing population." *

Exclusive of tithes, taxes on commodities are most commonly divided into two great classes; one consisting of
external or frontier, and the other of internal duties. The
first class, called in England customs duties, are principally
charged on commodities brought from foreign parts, on
their importation, and sometimes, also, on native commodities when exported. The second class, which are here
called excise duties, are charged on certain articles produced
within the country, and intended for home consumption. In
addition to these great sources of indirect taxation, duties are
sometimes laid on the paper, or other materials, required in
certain writings, on licences to exercise certain privileges, to
carry on certain businesses, &c.

CHAPTER V.

CUSTOMS OR FRONTIER DUTIES, OR DUTIES ON THE IM-
PORTATION AND EXPORTATION OF COMMODITIES.

These, like other duties, are, speaking generally, paid by the
consumers of the taxed commodities. When a government
lays a duty on the foreign commodities which enter its
ports, the duty, in ordinary cases, or when there is no
sudden and extraordinary demand for the articles on
which it is laid, falls entirely on its own subjects by whom
they are purchased. The circumstance of the products
imported from the French, Americans, and other foreigners
being subject in this country to certain rates of duty,
lessens our demand for them; but otherwise it is of no consequence to the foreigners. They sell their goods indif-

* On Protection to Agriculture, p. 43.

ferently for exportation to us, or for home consumption, for a sum sufficient to defray the cost of their production, including profits; the duties imposed on them in our ports making a further addition to their cost which is wholly paid by our people.   Any one, indeed, who reflects that the duties on tobacco, spirits, tea, most sorts of wine, and various other articles brought from abroad do not merely equal, but in general very greatly exceed their price in the foreign markets, will at once perceive how contradictory it is to suppose they should fall on the foreigner.   And for the same reason, when a government lays a duty on the commodities which its subjects are about to export, it does not fall on them, but on those by whom they are bought.   If, therefore, it were possible for a country to raise a sufficient revenue by laying duties on exported commodities, such revenue would be wholly derived from others, and it would itself be entirely relieved from the burden of taxation.   There can, however, be little doubt, were one state to attempt to raise a revenue in this way, that others would speedily do the same; and as the imports are always equal to the exports, and generally, indeed, exceed them, what a country gained on the one hand, by a policy of this sort, she would most likely lose on the other.   It is further necessary, in imposing duties on commodities about to be exported, to take especial care not to lay them on such as may be produced with nearly the same facility by others; for the duties, by increasing the cost of the products on which they are laid, might, in such cases, put an entire stop to their exportation, and throw the trade into the hands of the foreigner.   It is only when commodities in extensive demand happen to belong exclusively to particular countries, or to be produced in them at a decidedly cheaper rate than they can be produced elsewhere, that reasonable duties on their exportation may be advisable.   The teas of China, the coal of England, and the superior wines of France, have been said to belong to this description of articles.

But even in cases of this sort the greatest caution is required in imposing export duties. It may be laid down, in general, that they should, at the outset, be adopted by way of experiment only, and be confined within the narrowest limits, and that their increase should depend wholly on circumstances. There are few, or rather no articles that can be considered indispensable; and if the government of a country which is fortunate enough exclusively to possess any article in extensive demand were, in the view of drawing by its means a large revenue from foreigners, to load such article with a heavy export duty, the chances are ten to one the demand for it would be so much lessened that the heavy duty would be less productive than a lighter one. Tea on being exported from China might bear, perhaps, a duty of 3*d.* or 4*d.* per lb., but were it carried much beyond this, it would, by causing coffee, cocoa, and other articles to be substituted for tea, certainly diminish the demand for the latter, and deprive the Chinese of the many advantages derivable from its export, and of the greater revenue which a lower rate of duty would have afforded.

The duty on cinnamon exported from Ceylon may be referred to in illustration of the mischievous consequences resulting from carrying duties on exports, even when the exporting country has great facilities of production on her side, to an unreasonable extent. Ceylon, as most part of our readers must be aware, enjoyed for a lengthened period a monopoly of the growth of cinnamon, its culture being confined to certain gardens in the vicinity of Columbo, the produce of which was raised and sold on account of government. This system was much and justly complained of; and it was contended that the preferable plan would be to throw open the culture of cinnamon, laying at the same time a moderate duty on its exportation. At length, after a great deal of discussion, the monopoly was suppressed in 1833, and the culture declared free. But all the good that would otherwise have resulted from this judicious measure was more than neutralized by the cinnamon being charged on its exportation with an exorbitant duty of about 3*s.* per lb. This duty was sure, by

keeping up and even increasing the former high price of cinnamon, to prevent the trade from extending; but it has done
more than this: it has led to the introduction and successful
cultivation of the cinnamon plant in Java, Guiana, and the
West Indies; and it has also led to the general substitution
of cassia in the place of cinnamon.   We endeavoured to
show, at the time ("Commercial Dictionary," Art. *Cinnamon*), that such would most probably be the result of the
duty.   Unfortunately, however, it was allowed to spread
its upas-like influence over the trade, which it has well
nigh annihilated, till 1842, when it was reduced to 1*s.* per lb.
It is still, however, decidedly too high; and it may be safely
affirmed that the trade will never attain anything like the
value and importance to which it might and would have
attained but for the duty, unless the latter be reduced to 3*d.*,
or at most 4*d.* per lb.

Of late years coal has been almost the only article of British
produce that has been charged with any considerable duty on
exportation; and a good deal of difference of opinion has been
entertained in regard to its policy.   It has sometimes been
contended that, as our manufacturing prosperity is materially
dependent on abundant supplies of coal, and as these, though
vast, are not inexhaustible, it is wrong, by allowing coal to be
exported, to accelerate the period when posterity may be reduced to difficulties by the scarcity of this most valuable
mineral.   We are not, however, disposed to attach much
weight to these considerations.   It has been sufficiently demonstrated that we have in South Wales and other parts of the
kingdom, a supply of coal amply sufficient to permit of the
consumption being continued on its present gigantic scale for
upwards of 2000 years.   This, therefore, is clearly a case in
which it would be absurd to deny ourselves any immediate
advantage to be derived from the exportation of coal, in the
view of guarding against so distant an evil as the exhaustion
of the mines.   Indeed, the fair presumption is, that long
before the supplies of coal can begin sensibly to decline, such
improvements will have been made in the arts as will enable

industrious undertakings to be carried on with a much less expenditure of fuel than is now required, and as will, in fact, go far to supersede it. But whether these anticipations should or should not be realized, we may, at all events, postpone for the next 500 or 1000 years the consideration of the question respecting the probable influence of the exhaustion of the mines, in deciding upon the propriety of allowing the exportation of coal.

The policy of permitting its exportation has, however, been impugned on other grounds, that are less easily disposed of. It is contended that a supply of British coal is of the greatest consequence to several branches of manufacture carried on in the neighbouring continental states, and that in permitting its exportation we give up one of our principal advantages as a manufacturing people, and put, in so far, our rivals in the same situation with ourselves. And were such the case, sound policy would either dictate that the exportation of coal should be wholly put a stop to, or that it should be charged on being shipped with a high duty. It is, however, alleged, by those interested in the coal trade, that the possession of our coal is not necessary, nor even of any considerable consequence, to the foreigner ; and that by prohibiting its exportation, or loading it with a heavy duty, we should encourage the working of foreign mines, at the same time that we discouraged the working of our own, and deprived ourselves of the revenue derivable from a moderate duty on coal, without securing in return any corresponding advantage. It is not very easy to judge between these conflicting statements, or to say how much of truth and of exaggeration may be in each. On the whole, however, it seems sufficiently clear that English coal, though not by any means indispensable, is of very considerable advantage to the foreigner; and, such being the case, there can be no doubt that we have done wisely in laying the moderate duty on its exportation, imposed by the tariff Act of 1842. The total prohibition of exportation would, there is reason to think, be more injurious to ourselves than to the foreigner : but it

would be most impolitic, considering its nature and importance, to allow coal to be exported duty free. Should the
foreign demand for it continue to increase, the duties may,
perhaps, be advantageously raised.

But, apart from those peculiar considerations which have
to be attended to in estimating the influence of duties on articles like coal that may assist in production, enough has been
already said to show that duties of this sort should never be
resorted to without mature consideration, and that they should,
on no account, be carried to such a height as materially to
diminish exportation. Taxes which have this effect labour
under the double disadvantage of being at once unproductive, and hostile in the extreme to the public interests.

The principle that duties on imports fall on the consumers
does not hold in the event of any unforeseen and extraordinary demand taking place for imported products. The
duties on tea, sugar, coffee, wine, &c., are uniformly, it may
be said, paid by those who buy them. Suppose, however,
that owing to any circumstance or combination of circumstances, the demand for one or other, or all of these articles
were suddenly doubled or trebled; in such case the duty
would fall on the sellers or foreigners, for the price they
would then receive for their products would not depend in
any degree on their cost, but on the supply as compared with
the demand; and would be so very great as to yield them
an extraordinary profit, and make them send us all the produce they could possibly spare without regard to the duty.
But having so very recently endeavoured to exhibit the
working of this exceptional principle in the case of a duty on
corn, almost the only one in which it is ever very likely to be
exemplified, it is needless to enter into any further details
with respect to it.

During the middle ages, and down to the 16th century,
customs duties were charged indifferently on all sorts of
commodities, whether exported or imported; the duty on
wool sent to the Netherlands, France, &c., having been

formerly, in fact, the principal item in the customs revenue of this country. But since the ascendancy of the mercantile system it has been otherwise. To encourage the exportation of domestic produce, and to discourage the importation of foreign produce, was, according to its professors, the only sound commercial policy; and it is to the prevalence of this system in modern times, and its influence over financial and economical legislation, that the almost total exemption of exported commodities from duties, and the ruinous extent to which they have been heaped on those allowed to be imported (for many have been wholly prohibited), are, in a great measure, to be ascribed.

The reader will not expect that we should enter into any lengthened reasonings to show the advantages of commercial freedom and the disadvantages of the mercantile or restrictive system of policy. This would be inconsistent alike with the objects and limits of this work, and it would, besides, be wholly unnecessary. It has been demonstrated, over and over again, that, speaking generally, restraints on the freedom of commerce, or on the territorial division of labour among different nations, are adverse to the progress of real opulence and lasting improvement; and that the advantage which they sometimes confer on particular classes of persons or businesses is uniformly accompanied by a more than corresponding loss to the public. Providence, by giving different soils, climates, and natural products to different countries, has evidently intended that they should be mutually dependent upon and serviceable to each other. If no artificial obstacles were thrown in the way of their intercourse, every people would naturally engage, in preference, in those employments in which they have a superiority, exchanging such parts of their produce as they could spare for the productions they could more advantageously procure from others. By exciting industry, rewarding ingenuity, and using most efficaciously the peculiar powers bestowed by nature, an unrestricted commerce distributes labour as best suits the genius and capacities of every people.

It makes mankind acquainted with numerous productions of which they would otherwise be entirely ignorant; and while it gives them new tastes and new appetites, it affords the means and excites the desire of gratifying them. It enables each particular people to profit by the inventions and discoveries of all the rest; and, by bringing the home producers into competition with foreigners, it stimulates their industry and invention, and forces routine to give way to emulation. By its means, also, the division of labour is carried to the farthest extent; the mass of necessary and useful products vastly augmented, and opulence generally diffused. To suppose, indeed, that commerce may be too free, is equivalent to supposing that labour may be rendered too productive; that the objects of demand may be too much multiplied, and their price too much reduced: it is like supposing that agriculture may be too much improved, and the crops made too luxuriant!

But notwithstanding the overthrow of the mercantile system, the statements already laid before the reader, and the competition that prevails among different countries in all departments of industry, render it in the highest degree improbable that duties on exports should ever be made productive of any considerable amount of revenue. Hence it is satisfactory to know that moderate duties on imports are among the most productive and least objectionable taxes. They are collected with the greatest facility, involving no inquiry into the circumstances of individuals, as is the case with taxes on income or property, nor any interference of any sort with the processes carried on in the arts, as is the case with certain excise duties. By allowing imported goods to be lodged in bonded warehouses, the revenue is protected without compelling the importer to pay the duties till the goods be withdrawn for consumption; and little or no additional capital being required by the merchant, little or no addition is made to the price of the goods through the previous advance of the duties. It is, no doubt, true that, if duties on imports be carried to such a height as to oppose any very serious obstacle to commercial transactions, or to give an overpowering stimulus to smuggling, they become exceedingly injurious. It must be admitted, too, that finance ministers have seldom been sufficiently alive to the import- ance of moderation in imposing these duties; and that, partly from a wish to make them subservient to purposes of pro- tection, and partly from mistaken views in regard to the nature of taxation, they have often carried them to an oppressive extent. Happily, however, this abuse is not of the essence of customs duties; and, supposing them to be kept within reasonable limits and judiciously assessed, it is impossible to imagine any better taxes.

Owing, principally, to the vast increase of the commerce, wealth, and population of the country, but partly also to the increase of the rates, the progress of the customs duties has been quite extraordinary. The revenue derived from these duties in 1596, in the reign of Elizabeth, amounted to no more than 50,000*l.* In 1613 it had increased to 148,075*l.*, of which 109,572*l.* were collected in London. In 1660, at the Restoration, the customs produced 426,582*l.*; and, at the Revolution, in 1689, they produced 781,987*l.* During the reigns of William III. and Anne, the customs revenues were considerably augmented, the nett payments into the Exche- quer in 1712, being 1,315,422*l.* During the war termi- nated by the peace of Paris, in 1763, the nett produce of the customs revenue of Great Britain amounted to nearly 2,000,000*l.* a-year. In 1792 it amounted to 4,407,000*l.*; and in 1815, at the close of the late war with France, it amounted to 11,360,000*l.* In 1843, the gross customs revenue of the United Kingdom amounted to 22,850,169*l.*, collected at an expense of 1,254,136*l.*, being at the rate of 5*l.* 9*s.* 9¼*d.* per cent.; and notwithstanding the exorbitant duties on brandy, hollands, tobacco, sugar, and a few other articles (which would certainly be more productive were they effectually reduced), it might be easily shown that no equal amount of revenue was ever raised in any country or period of time with so little difficulty and inconvenience; and there are no grounds for supposing that it could have been so easily or advantageously collected in any other way.

Independently of the influence which oppressive customs duties have in stimulating smuggling, those which are imposed for the purpose of protection, though they bring little or no revenue into the public treasury, frequently lay heavy burdens on the country. When the importation of an article is prohibited or loaded with an oppressive duty, the fair inference is, that it might be imported more cheaply from abroad, the prohibition and the duty being otherwise quite unnecessary. Now suppose, in illustration of this statement, that an article which is prohibited or burdened with a protective duty costs the public 1,500,000*l.* a-year, and that were the prohibition repealed, or the duty fixed at a moderate amount, it might be obtained for 1,000,000*l.* a-year: in this case the prohibition or duty imposes an annual tax or burden on the public of 500,000*l.* It is material also to observe, that this heavy burden is not productive of any corresponding advantage. It may be supposed, perhaps, that it adds to the demand for labour, and that, were the article imported, the parties engaged in its production would be deprived of employment. This, however, is not the case. When a commodity is brought from abroad that has previously been produced at home, those engaged in its production are exposed to difficulties and privations in having to change their business, in the same way that the parties who produce an article by manual labour may be forced to withdraw from their employment in the event of its being produced at a lower price by new or improved machinery. But the aggregate amount of labour is not affected by such changes; and while the inconveniences resulting from them are but of temporary duration, and affect only a few individuals, the greater cheapness of the commodities is a permanent national advantage. We may, by repealing prohibitions and oppressive duties, change to some extent the species of labour in demand; but if so, we shall, at the same time, render it more productive, without lessening its amount. Should our imports during the current year amount to five or ten millions more than they did last year, we must provide for their payment, either directly or indirectly, by exporting an equally increased amount of our peculiar products. And hence, if exportation be desirable, importation must be so also; for the two are indissolubly connected, and to separate them even in imagination, implies a total ignorance of the most obvious principles. Commerce, whether carried on between individuals of the same or of different countries, is bottomed on a fair principle of reciprocity. Every sale supposes an equal purchase, and every purchase an equal sale. In whatever degree, therefore, an unrestricted trade might lead us to import products from other countries, it would, in the same degree, render them customers for our commodities, would promote our manufactures and extend our trade.

It is further to be observed, that the mere freedom of dealing with each other does not necessarily lead to an intercourse between different places: that is a consequence of those who carry it on feeling that their interests are promoted by it. If either party imagined themselves injured by this traffic, it would be as absolutely put an end to, in so far at least as they are concerned, as if they were separated from the others by impassable mountains or morasses. And when such is the fact, when it is the promotion of their own interests, and nothing else, that leads individuals to engage in commercial enterprises, what is there to fear from giving the same freedom to the intercourse with foreign countries that is given to the intercourse between different parts of the same country? Though the trade between France and England were as free as that between London and Newcastle, it would most undoubtedly continue to be as limited as at present, unless the English as well as the French found it for their advantage to extend their dealings.

The truth therefore is, that prohibitive and protective regulations, if they have any effect, force capital and industry into less productive channels than those into which they would otherwise flow; and that they increase the cost and price of produce without in any degree increasing the demand for labour. We shall refer to one or two instances in illustration of the practical working of the protective system.

It has been already seen that, in consequence of the pressure of peculiar burdens on the land, justice to the agriculturists requires, in the event of the ports being opened, that an equivalent countervailing duty should be laid on foreign corn when entered for consumption. The subsisting corn duty is not, however, imposed on this equitable principle. It is not a fixed duty, but varies inversely as the home price, increasing when the latter decreases, and diminishing when it increases. It is so very high as virtually to prohibit importation when the home price is under 55*s*. or 57*s*. a quarter; and even when the home price is 60*s*. and 65*s*. the duty is 12*s*. and 8*s*. But, however important, it would be useless, seeing how much this subject has recently been discussed, to enter into any lengthened statements with regard to it. It will be sufficient shortly to state that, though most absurdly exaggerated, there can be no reasonable doubt that the influence of the present corn laws is decidedly injurious, especially in bad or indifferent years. We do not, however, think that the circumstance of the duty virtually excluding foreign corn when the price is below 50*s*. a quarter is of much consequence; for it very rarely happens that it would be possible to import corn of about the same quality as English corn, were it charged with a low duty of 5*s*. or 6*s*. when prices here are under 50*s*. or 55*s*. a quarter. The mischievous influence of the duty is occasioned by its high range when the home price is between 50*s*. and 63*s*., and by its uncertainty. It goes far, indeed, except under peculiar circumstances, to prevent importation when prices are under 60*s*.; and though they are often below that limit, that is not a consequence of importations, but of the home supply of corn being such that our prices in favourable years do not differ materially from those of the continent. But when the crops are below an average, the duty has a powerful influence, and makes, at least, a corresponding addition to the price of corn. It is, however, more than doubtful whether this rise in such years, though it entails severe privations on the labouring classes, be of any advantage to the agriculturists. Steadiness of price is always most conducive to their interests; and this would, undoubtedly, be best secured by admitting corn at all times under a moderate fixed duty, accompanied by a corresponding drawback. Under such a system prices could rarely, except in very bad years, rise much above their average level; while, in very abundant years, the drawback would come into operation, and would contribute to hinder their sinking so low as to be injurious to the farmer. And it is material, also, to bear in mind that under a fixed duty there would be nothing adventitious to disturb the plans and combinations of the merchant. His business would not then, as at present, be conducted by fits and starts, to suit the variations, which can neither be perceived nor appreciated beforehand, of the sliding scale. We should not then see, as in 1842, large quantities of foreign corn poured into the market, on the eve of harvest, and when prices were falling, merely that it might escape the increased duty to which it would have been subject had it been kept in the warehouse. Under such a system we should be supplied with foreign corn when it was really wanted, and with the quantity wanted; and should not, as now, be at one time glutted with forced importations, and at another be exposed to the difficulties and privations occasioned by scarcity and high prices.

It is sometimes said that however objectionable in principle, the corn laws could not be placed on the footing proposed, without producing a heavy fall of price, and inflicting the most serious injury on agriculture and the agriculturists, especially since they have been, or speedily will be, burdened with a fixed payment on account of tithes, proportioned to the produce obtained under the protective system. But while we fully admit the importance of these considerations, and the necessity of keeping the commutation for tithe constantly in view, we feel confident that the more the matter is inquired into the more clearly it will appear that there is no real room or ground for the apprehensions in question. The average price of wheat amounts at present to about 57s. or 58s. a quarter, and there is no chance whatever of its being reduced, were importation allowed under a 5s. or 6s. duty a d drawback, below 52s. or 54s., which, indeed, is considerably above its price in all seasons in which the crops are reasonably good.*   It should also be borne in mind by those who would form a correct judgment on this important question, that prices have fallen above 30s. a quarter since 1815 ; that. notwithstanding this immense fall, agriculture has made an astonishing progress in the interval ; that rents, at an average of Great Britain, are higher now than at any former period ; and that despite the vast addition in the interval of about 5,350,000 souls to the population of England and Scotland, the imports of foreign corn have not been materially increased, and sometimes do not take place for years together.   And when such results have taken place in the teeth of a fall of 30s. a quarter, surely it would be something worse than ludicrous to affect to apprehend that any real injury should be done to agriculture by a further fall of 3s., 4s., or 5s. a quarter.   In the case of corn, as in most others, it will be found that there is no difference between what is equitable and what is useful ; the measures that would do justice to all parties being, at the same time, best fitted to promote their prosperity.

In addition to their peculiarly mischievous operation in bad years, we incline to think that the subsisting restraints on importation raise the price of corn in ordinary seasons, taking all sorts into account, about 2s. 6d. a quarter higher

* See 'Commercial Dictionary,' art. CORN LAWS and CORN TRADE *passim.*

than it would be under the proposed plan. And supposing the total quantity of corn annually produced in Great
Britain and Ireland to amount to 62,000,000 quarters,
the total average rise of price will, on this hypothesis,
amount to 7,750,000*l.* But so great a quantity of corn
is consumed by the agriculturists themselves, in food, in
seed, the keep of horses, &c., that not more than a half, perhaps, of the whole quantity produced is brought to market.
Hence, if we are nearly right in this and the previous estimate, it will follow that the restrictions cost the classes not engaged in agriculture in ordinary years 3,875,000*l.*, exclusive
of their other pernicious consequences. Of this sum from a
fourth to a *fifth* part, or from 968,700*l.* to 775,000*l.*, may go
to the landlords as rent; and this is *all* that the agriculturists can be said to gain by the system, for the additional
price received by the farmer on that portion of the produce
which exceeds rent is no more than the ordinary return for
his capital and labour. His profits, indeed, like those of
other capitalists, instead of being increased, are diminished
by this system; and though, nominally at least, it somewhat
increases the rents of the landlords, it is, notwithstanding,
abundantly certain that it is anything but advantageous to
them. It would require a far larger sum to balance the
injury which fluctuations of price occasion to their tenants,
with the increase of poor-rates, and the damage done to their
estates by over-cropping when prices are high, than all that
is derived from the restrictions.

It appears, therefore, that the substitution of a fixed and
moderate duty on corn instead of the present fluctuating
system of duties, would be a very decided improvement in
our domestic policy; and that, while it materially lightened
the pressure on the national resources, it would not inflict any
hardship upon, or do any injustice to the agriculturists. Such
a measure would, also, be of singular advantage by putting an
end to the seeming opposition between their interests on the
one hand, and those of the manufacturing and commercial
classes on the other. These interests are really identical;

P

and it is the merest error to suppose that either can be benefited by anything calculated to depress the other. The placing of the corn laws on a proper footing would be in accordance with this principle; it would also terminate a most pernicious system of agitation; and would contribute powerfully to advance the moral and political as well as the material interests of the empire.

The duties on sugar form one of the most productive sources of the customs revenue; and are not only deserving of especial attention from their importance in this respect, and their influence over the condition of the people, but also from their setting the mischievous influence of the protective system in a striking point of view.

The duty on sugar from British possessions amounted, for some years previously to 1840, to 24*s.*, and since then to 25*s.* 2¼*d.* a cwt. (24*s.* plus 5 per cent.); the duty on foreign sugar being, during the same periods, 63*s.* and 66*s.* 2*d.* (63*s.* plus 5 per cent.). The latter was intended to be, and has, in fact, been completely prohibitory. And, however objectionable in principle, so long as our foreign dependencies furnished sugar sufficient, not only to supply the markets of the United Kingdom, but to leave besides a considerable surplus for exportation to others, the prohibitory duty on foreign sugars was productive of little practical inconvenience. Latterly, however, it became most oppressive in its operation. In consequence of the measures connected with the emancipation of the slaves, the imports of sugar from the West Indies declined from 4,103,746 cwts. in 1831, to 2,509,701 cwts. in 1843. And though, owing to the immigration of hill-coolies, and other circumstances, the exports from the Mauritius have not declined in anything like the same proportion, and there has been a great increase in the imports from India, they have not sufficed to balance the deficiency in the West Indian supplies. On the one hand, therefore, we have had a rapidly increasing population, and on the other we have had that population confined by an oppressive duty to a market for sugar, the supply of which has been progressively diminishing !. The consequences have been such as every man of sense might have anticipated from the outset. The business of refining for the foreign market, and our export trade in sugar, have been all but annihilated; while the average Gazette price of muscovado sugar, admissible to the English markets, amounted during the three years ending with 1842 to more than double the price of foreign sugar in bond, of equal or superior quality ! We beg, in illustration of what is now stated, to subjoin an

Account of the Quantities of Sugar retained for Consumption, of the Nett Produce of the Duties thereon, and of the Prices of British Sugar (ex duty) and Brazil Sugar in bond, in 1840, 1841, and 1842, with the Average for these three Years.

Years.	Quantities.	Nett Revenue from Duties on Sugar.	Average Prices of British Muscovado Sugar.	Average Prices of Brazil Sugar (Brown & Yellow).
	Cwts.	£.	s. d.	s. d.
1840 . .	3,594,834	4,449,070	49 1	21 6
1841 . .	4,057,628	5,114,390	39 8	20 9
1842 . .	3,868,466	4,874,812	36 11	18 3
Total .	11,520,928	14,438,272	125 8	60 6
Average of 3 Years .	3,840,309⅓	4,812,757⅓	41 10⅔	20 2

Now, it appears from this statement, that while the price of British sugar (exclusive of duty) amounted, during the three years ending with 1842, to 41s. 10½d. per cwt., the price of Brazil (and Cuba) sugar was only 20s. 2d. per cwt. ! And hence it follows, that had the present prohibitory duty of 66s. 2d. on foreign sugar been reduced to the same rate (25s. 2d., or 24s. plus 5 per cent.) as that on British sugars, the people of the United Kingdom might have bought the same quantity of sugar for 20s. 2d. that cost them 41s. 10⅔d., that is, they might have got more than 2 lbs. of sugar for the same sacrifice it has cost them to get 1 lb. The aggregate loss to the public from this preposterous arrangement of the sugar duties has been quite enormous. It appears from the above account that the average consumption of sugar, during each of the three years ending with 1842, amounted to 3,840,309⅓ cwts., which, at 41s. 10⅔d., cost 8,040,646l.

19*s.* 4½*d.* ; while, had we been allowed to go into the foreign market for sugar, we might have got the same quantity for 3,872,311*l.* 18*s.* 2½*d.*, being a saving in one year of no less than 4,168,335*l.* 1*s.* 5*d.*, and on three years of 12,505,055*l.* 4*s.* 3*d.* But it may, perhaps, be said, that had our ports been open to the free importation of Brazilian and other foreign sugars, the price of the latter would have been raised; and so, probably, it would : though, considering the vast extent and productiveness of the field from which sugar may be brought, we doubt whether this effect would be very sensible. But, supposing that the opening of our ports had raised the price of foreign sugar from 20*s.* 2*d.* to 25*s.* a cwt., still the saving would have amounted to 3,240,260*l.* 6*s.* a year!—which consequently may be taken as the amount of the burden which the restriction on the importation of foreign sugar has latterly imposed on the country.

Under these circumstances, the reduction of the duty on foreign sugars had obviously become a matter of the expediency or rather necessity of which no doubt could be entertained. But the reduction to be of any real utility required to be on a large scale ; and there were, owing to the peculiar situation of the West Indian body, and their influence in parliament, great difficulties in the way of such a measure. These, however, have been overcome; and the act of last session, the 7 and 8 Victoria, c. 28, has reduced the duty on foreign sugar from 63*s.* to 34*s.* a cwt., leaving a discriminating duty of 10*s.* a cwt. in favour of our own sugars. And, considering the difficulties under which the planters in the West India Islands have been placed by the measures forced on them in connexion with the emancipation of the slaves, and the obstacles that have been thrown in the way of their obtaining supplies of free labour from Africa and the East Indies, the preference given them by the above statute does not appear to exceed what the justice of the case demands.

But besides being embarrassed by the peculiarities in the condition of our own sugar-growing colonies, this question is farther embarrassed by those incident to the condition of

Brazil, Cuba, and other countries in which slavery still exists. Great Britain has, at a great sacrifice, abolished slavery in her colonies, and made every effort in her power to suppress the trade in slaves. And having done this, it is contended that were she to admit slave-grown sugar to her markets, she would be acting contradictory; and be, in fact, encouraging that slavery in Brazil, Cuba, and Louisiana she has suppressed, at an immense sacrifice, in Jamaica, Deme-rara, and the Mauritius. And, consistently with this view of the matter, the reduction of the duty on foreign sugar effected by the 7 and 8 Victoria, c. 28, applies only to that which is produced by free labour; so that slave-grown sugar continues, in effect, to be excluded.

But, however specious, we are not disposed to attach much weight to these considerations. The consistency of our policy in relation to slavery can be but little affected by our conduct in this particular; and the additional encou-ragement we should give to slavery by admitting slave-grown sugars to our markets would be extremely inconsider-able. The raw material of our most important manufacture has always been and continues to be almost wholly produced by slaves; and when such is the case, when Manchester, Glasgow, Paisley, Bolton, Preston, Bury, and a host of other great towns, depend for existence on supplies of slave-grown cotton, it really looks more like affectation and hypo-crisy than anything else to be so very squeamish about im-porting a few thousand tons of slave-grown sugar. And after all we do the very thing we pretend to deprecate. The encouragement to slavery in Cuba and Brazil consists in the purchase of their sugar, and has nothing to do with the mode in which it is disposed of. We send manufactured goods to the Havannah and Rio and exchange them for sugar: and having done that, we carry the sugar to Ham-burgh and Petersburgh and exchange it for wool and flax; so that we in effect transmute the slave-grown sugar into other things, and consume it under its new form! We do not employ it to sweeten our tea or coffee; but we clothe ourselves with wool and flax, manure our lands with bones, and manufacture our paper of rags, which are all bought by it. But suppose we had been a little more Quixotic, and that after getting the sugar we had thrown it into the sea, the result, as respects Cuba and Brazil, would have been the same: they have got value for their sugar. We, the people of England, give, by buying it, all the encouragement in our power to the slavery that exists in these countries. What we shall do with the sugar is our own affair; and whether we use it, sell it to others, or destroy it, is, as far as slavery is concerned, quite immaterial. But it is by no means immaterial as respects our trade with slave-holding countries; for, while this ostentatious display of mock humanity fails to excite any feeling save that of derision, the preference we give to others tempts them to lay heavy discriminating duties on our products, and to depress and embarrass our trade. And even were it as desirable as it is the reverse, it may be doubted whether it be in our power to exclude slave-grown sugar. Certificates of origin will, we apprehend, turn out to be rather a slender security for this result. But supposing them to be effectual, the consequence will be that, a larger quantity of Java and Manilla sugar being consumed in England, less of it can be sent to the Continent, where, by means of our policy, a corresponding market will be opened for slave-grown sugar!

It were really, therefore, to be wished that we should cease to rave, as we have done for the last twenty years, about slavery; and that we should buy sugar as we buy cotton and other things without inquiring how, or by whom, it is produced. We may be assured that we should give as little encouragement to slavery by so doing as we give by our present system; while we should give considerably greater facilities to our trade.

But whatever policy may be pursued in regard to slave-grown sugar, the important measure of last session has paved the way for the consideration of the whole question with regard to the duties on the sugars admitted to consumption.

Had the duty on British sugars been reduced before an effectual reduction was made in the prohibitory duty on foreign sugars, the measure would not have redounded, in any degree, either to the advantage of the consumers or of the revenue, but would have been wholly intercepted by the planters. But now that the principle has been established of admitting foreign sugars under a discriminating duty of 10s. a cwt., a reduction of the duty will be followed by a corresponding fall of price, and will proportionally benefit the public.

Under these circumstances there can be no reasonable doubt that a reduction of the duties on British sugars to 10s. or 12s. a cwt., and of those on foreign sugars in the same proportion, would be a signal boon to the bulk of the population. Most probably too a reduction of this amount would not occasion, within a year or two, any diminution of revenue. Mr. Huskisson stated in his place in the House of Commons in the debate on the sugar duties on the 25th of May, 1829, that "In consequence of the present enormous duty on sugar,* the poor working man with a large family, to whom pence were a serious consideration, was denied the use of that commodity; and he believed he did not go too far when he stated *that* TWO-THIRDS *of the poorer consumers of coffee drank that beverage without sugar.* If then the price of sugar were reduced it would become an article of his consumption, like many other articles, woollens for example, which are now used for their cheapness, which he was formerly unable to purchase." (Speeches, iii. 455.) But the reduction of duty in 1829, being only 3s. a cwt., was too trifling to have any sensible influence; and even if it had been greater, its effect would have been wholly defeated by the increase in the price of sugar (occasioned by the monopoly). Mr. Huskisson's observations continue therefore to be in all respects as applicable at this moment as in 1829. The duty is now as then "enormous," and "the poor man is denied the use of sugar." Indeed the entries for consumption in 1828

* The duty then was 27s. a cwt., and it is at this moment 25s. 2d.

amounted to 3,601,419 cwts., whereas they only amounted in 1840, notwithstanding the immense increase of population in the interval, to 3,594,834 cwts., and in 1841 and 1842 the increase was but inconsiderable.

A reduction of the duties to 10s. or 12s. a cwt.* would (under the new regulations in regard to the trade) certainly occasion a vast increase of consumption which would tell not only on the sugar revenue, but would have a powerful indirect influence over that derived from coffee and tea, to the extensive use of which sugar is indispensable. A cheap supply of sugar would also be of the greatest advantage to the lower and middle classes by enabling them to turn fruit to far better account than they can do at present. Indeed, with the exception of corn and butcher's meat, there is no article of which an abundant supply at a reasonable price is so very desirable as sugar; or which would be so important to the well-being of the bulk of the people and the commerce of the empire.

In France, the results of the protective system, in the case of sugar, have been, if possible, even more injurious than in England. To encourage its manufacture, sugar from beetroot was, for a lengthened period, exempted from duties; and in consequence of this encouragement the business extended itself so rapidly, that its produce amounted in 1838 to 39,199,408 kilogs. But while this increase inflicted a serious injury on the revenue and the colonies, it was of no advantage to the consumer; for, as the greater portion of the sugar required for the home supply was furnished by the colonies, and paid a high duty, the beet-root growers sold their sugar at the price necessary to indemnify the planters for the peculiar burdens with which they were charged.

* Any reduction which should not bring the duty to, at most, 12s. a cwt., would be of little or no consequence. The highest authority on such subjects says, " The reduction must be no half-measure. Ten shillings per cwt. is spoken of as the intended concession, thereby making the duty 15s. a cwt., but nothing less than a reduction of the duty to *a penny per lb.* (9s. 4d. per cwt.) will have the desired effect of at once protecting and relieving the consumer, annihilating fraud, enocuraging the colonies, and infusing stability and confidence into this important branch of trade."— (James Cook, Esq., of the firm of Trueman and Cook.)

Alarmed by the heavy and rapidly increasing loss of revenue that was thus occasioned, and roused by the well-
founded complaints of the planters, government imposed,
in 1838 and 1840, considerable duties on beet-root sugar.
These, however, gave satisfaction to no party; for, while the
beet-root growers alleged they would be ruinous to them,
the colonists contended that they were evaded, and that
justice and a due regard to their interests and those of the
revenue required that the duties should be equalised.   At
length, in 1842, government proposed, in order to get rid
of the difficulties in which the system had involved the
country, to grub up the plantations, paying the planters
40,000,000 fr. (1,600,000*l.*) as an indemnity for their loss!
And, harsh as it may appear, we incline to think that this
proposal was, on the whole, the best that could have been
made, inasmuch as it would have terminated the matter
at once on an equitable principle.   It was not, however,
adopted; but in the course of next session (1843) it was
resolved to add to the duty on beet-root sugar about 5 fr.
per cwt. a year, till the duty on it is equalised with the
duty on colonial sugar.   This system came into operation
on the 1st of August this year (1844), and in August, 1848,
the equalisation of the duties will be effected.   And there
can be little doubt that, if carried out, this project will annihilate the growth of beet-sugar in France quite as effectually as if the plantations had been grubbed up.   Such is the
present state of a project that has cost France an immense
sum; and such is the invariable result of all attempts to
bolster up and protect, by dint of custom-house regulations,
branches of industry for the successful prosecution of which
a country has no real or acquired advantage.*

It is hardly necessary to state that care should be taken,
in imposing customs duties, to assess them principally on
articles of consumption; and that, if exacted at all, they

* For a full account of the sugar trade, and of the duties on sugar, see
‘ Commercial Dictionary,’ art. Sugar.

should be made to press lightly on articles required for the successful prosecution of any manufacture or other employment which it is deemed advantageous to carry on at home. The expediency of keeping this principle steadily in view, is so obvious as hardly to require illustration. The duties of about 3*s.* a cwt. on cotton wool, and of 1*d.* and ½*d.* per lb. on sheep's wool, though not in any degree oppressive, have been much and perhaps justly objected to. It would however appear, from the comparatively stationary state of the woollen manufacture, that of the two the duty on sheep's wool was the most objectionable; and it, therefore, was judiciously repealed in the course of the present year (1844). The continued extension of the cotton manufacture seems to show that it has been little, if at all, obstructed by the duty. Undoubtedly, however, it must sensibly affect the price of the coarser and heavier descriptions of fabrics, in the production of which the foreigner has, in other respects, the greatest advantages on his side. And independently of this, so large a portion of our population is dependent on the cotton trade, and its prosperity is so essential to the prosperity of the empire, that it seems very difficult to vindicate the policy of charging the material with any duty, however light.

But, though apparently obvious, the policy of exempting the materials of manufacture from all or any but inconsiderable duties, has been lost sight of on several occasions. Previously to 1824, for example, the duties on foreign thrown, or organzine silk, amounted to no less than 14*s.* 7½*d.* per lb.; those on raw silk, from Bengal, being at the same time 4*s.* per lb.; and on silk from France, and elsewhere, 5*s.* 7½*d.* per lb.! With such exorbitant duties on the material, no one need be surprised at the little progress made by the manufacture; and that though foreign silks were excluded, it was generally in a languid and sickly condition. Mr. Huskisson was fully aware of their pernicious influence; and in 1826, when he repealed the prohibition against importing silk goods, he reduced the duty on raw silk to 3d. per lb., and that on organzine to 7s. 6d.; and they have since been reduced, the former to 1d., and the latter to 1s. The influence of this change has been most beneficial; and notwithstanding the injury done to the manufacture by the competition and substitution of cottons, it has been more improved and extended since 1826, than in the course of the previous century.

The duties on timber are another instance in which the principle of not taxing the materials and means of manufacture has been lost sight of; and it is not going too far to say that these duties have been, for many years past, from their magnitude and the mode of their assessment, among the most objectionable in our tariff. If, indeed, there be one article more than another of which it is of importance that a manufacturing nation, like Great Britain, with a great warlike and mercantile navy, should have a large supply of the best quality, and at the lowest price, that article is timber. Without good and cheap timber you cannot have good and cheap ships, houses, and machinery. And yet, singular as it may seem, we burdened for a lengthened period this indispensable article with an oppressive duty; while, by making the duty on timber from the north of Europe 55s., and that on timber from our North American possessions only 10s. a load, we forced the importation of the latter, notwithstanding it be, speaking generally, of an inferior quality! And though materially modified, we regret to say that this attempt to force the employment of dear and bad timber is still far from being abandoned; for, in 1842, when the duties on Baltic timber were reduced to 24s. and 30s. a load, those on Canadian timber were reduced to 1s.! But timber either is or is not a fit subject for taxation: if the former, it is impossible to justify the repeal of the duty on the worst species of timber; and if the latter, it is clear the duty on the best timber should have been repealed as well as that on the worst, or rather in preference to it. The truth is, that our regulations in regard to this important trade are so very absurd, that they would almost make one suppose that it was deemed a matter of state policy to inoculate our ships and houses with dry-rot. This is a case in which, if principle or common sense had any weight, differential taxes would be out of the question. A duty on timber, if there is to be one, should be equal, and fixed at a low limit; leaving it to the wants of the consumer, and the sagacity of the merchant, to determine the varieties to be imported, and the best markets whence to import them.

The influence of the high duty, and other restrictions on the importation of iron into France, may also be referred to in illustration of the mischief arising from the want of respect for the principle referred to above. Everybody knows that a cheap and abundant supply of iron is indispensable to the perfecting of machinery, and to the progress of arts and manufactures: but while the government of France has been endeavouring, for many years back, to encourage manufactures, it has at the same time gone far to nullify its efforts, by preventing or greatly narrowing the importation of foreign iron. The greater part of the iron produced in France is smelted by means of wood, and costs from a third to a half more than the iron smelted by pit-coal in this country; and it is quite certain, that, while this discrepancy continues, the attempts of the French to rival us in manufactures must prove total failures. Instead, however, of opening their ports to the free importation of British and other foreign iron, they either exclude it or burden it with heavy duties; and thus, for the sake of the forest proprietors, and of those who have capital vested in forges and iron-works, they lay as it were the industry of the country under a species of proscription, compelling the agriculturists and manufacturers to use inferior tools and machines, costing nearly double the price of the superior articles used by their foreign competitors! Were we anxious for the depression of industry in France, we should wish nothing more than that this system should be persevered in; but we disclaim being actuated by any such feeling. The progress of France in wealth and civilization cannot fail to redound to the advantage of surrounding nations; and we are desirous that her ingenious and industrious inhabitants should be allowed fully to avail themselves of all the advantages of their admirable situation and varied means of production.

But, however objectionable, this much may be said in explanation of the prohibitions and heavy import duties imposed in this and other European countries, that the mercantile system of policy, of which they are the fruits, grew up in a comparatively unenlightened period, before the true principles of commercial intercourse had been elucidated; and that, notwithstanding the strenuous opposition of interested and powerful parties, many prohibitions and oppressive duties have been abolished or reduced, and a considerable advance made almost everywhere towards a more liberal and advantageous system. In America, however, it has been otherwise. The prohibitive system is there of recent origin, and has not grown up in obscurity and ignorance under the fostering shade of false theories, but in a period of general illumination, and in the teeth of the plainest principles, long after the ' Wealth of Nations ' had been in universal circulation, and every statesman in Europe had admitted the soundness of its doctrines. America is not merely a city of refuge for the poor and persecuted inhabitants of the old world, but also for the exploded errors and pernicious sophisms of the mercantile school. The tariffs and the banking system of the United States would discredit any people of the fifteenth or sixteenth century. They divert industry into insecure and unproductive channels, while, by occasioning alternate gluts and scarcity of money, they shake all confidence in engagements, diffuse a gambling spirit, and weaken the sense of honour and the obligations of good faith.

Every one at all acquainted with the condition of America,

with her boundless tracts of fertile and unappropriated land, her scanty population and high wages, knows that agriculture and its immediately dependent employments *must* for a long series of years be the most profitable species of industry in which the bulk of her people can engage. At the same time there can be no question that such branches of manufacture as are suited to her peculiar situation will gradually grow up in the Union, without any artificial encouragement, according as population becomes denser, and the preponderating advantages at present on the side of agriculture are diminished. But to force by means of duties and prohibitions the premature growth of manufactures, is in reality to force a portion of the industry and capital of the country into those businesses in which it will be least productive.

Such, however, has been the policy, if we may so call it, of the American legislature. From 1816 downwards they have been endeavouring to bolster up a manufacturing interest by imposing heavy duties on foreign manufactured goods. But it is admitted on all hands that the articles produced under this system in America cost, at an average, from 20 to 50 per cent. and upwards more than they might be imported for. The aggregate annual amount of the pecuniary sacrifice that has thus been imposed on the Union has been estimated, apparently on good grounds, at from 35,000,000 to 40,000,000 dollars; but taking it at the former sum it is equivalent to above 8,000,000*l.* a year! And this heavy burden—a burden more than twice as great as the whole public expenditure of the Union—is incurred for no purpose of public utility, and is productive of nothing but mischief. The whole effect of the scheme is to divert a certain amount of the national industry from the production of the cotton, rice, wheat, tobacco, and other equivalents sent to foreigners in exchange for manufactured goods, to the direct production of the latter. And as this species of industry is nowise suitable for America, a tax or payment of 8,000,000*l.* a-year is imposed on the Union that the manufacturers may be enabled to continue a losing business! We leave it to others to decide whether the absurdity of such a system or its costliness be its most prominent feature.

It appears, therefore, that we are not always, nor even generally, to estimate the pressure or influence of customs duties by the amount which they bring into the coffers of the treasury. They may, according to the mode in which they are imposed, be oppressive without being productive, and productive without being oppressive. If they be imposed for the purpose of protection, or if, while imposed for the legitimate purpose of raising revenue, they be carried to such a height as to occasion smuggling, they may keep or take large sums out of the pockets of the people, while they add but little to the revenue. In Spain, the customs duties would appear, estimated by their produce in the official accounts, to be moderate in the extreme; and yet, if we look at the overpowering stimulus which their excess gives to the practice of smuggling, which carries fraud and violence into every corner of the country, it will be found that they are really most oppressive. But, as previously stated, these are not legitimate consequences of customs duties, but originate in their wilful abuse. They should never be imposed in the view of bolstering up or protecting any branch of industry, unless it be affected by peculiar burdens; they should never be carried so high as to give any irresistible temptation to the practice of smuggling; and they should press as lightly as possible on the articles necessary for the successful prosecution of domestic industry. Provided these conditions be kept in mind in their imposition, we are not aware of any tenable ground on which customs duties can be objected to. Indeed they appear, when rightly assessed, to possess in a very high degree all the distinguishing attributes of good taxes.

When a customs or excise duty is imposed on any article for which another article may be conveniently substituted, it is necessary, to make the duty effectual, that it should be extended to the latter. It would not, for example, be possible to raise any considerable revenue by taxing one variety of tea, or one variety of spice, or of sugar, or of wine, without taxing the other varieties, inasmuch as the tax, by increasing the price of the variety on which it was laid, would discourage its consumption, and encourage the consumption of the others. The substitution of chiccory for coffee exemplifies what has now been stated. Our readers, no doubt, are generally aware that the roots of chiccory (*cichorium intybus*, wild endive), when dried and ground, bear a strong resemblance to ground coffee; and that they have been extensively employed in Prussia and other parts of the Continent as substitutes for the latter. A few years since, ground chiccory began to be brought into this country for the adulteration of coffee; and to prevent the loss of revenue and the frauds that its continued importation would have occasioned, it was soon after charged with the same duty as coffee.

Nothing, however, was said in the act imposing a duty on foreign chiccory respecting what might be raised in England, the plant having hitherto been cultivated here merely for its herbage. But soon after the importation of chiccory powder was stopped, it was found that it might be profitably raised in various parts of the country; and so rapidly has the culture of the plants and the preparation of the powder extended, that it has been stated by the best authorities that from 3,000 to 4,000 tons a-year of the latter have been latterly produced! And as the whole of this quantity was substituted for and sold as coffee, the demand for the latter, and the revenue, were proportionally affected.

An arrangement of this sort could not, however, be of long continuance. Justice to the consumer of coffee and the revenue required that, if the duty on coffee was to be maintained, an equal duty should be laid on all articles used either as substitutes for it, or (which is the usual method of employing chiccory) as means for its adulteration. And consistently with what has now been stated, notice was given in the course of the present year (1844), that government had determined to lay a duty on chiccory grown or manufactured at home. But owing, probably, to the difficulties in the way, this has not as yet been done : and it is alleged that, from the facility with which chiccory may be grown, the imposition of a duty would lead to smuggling and evasion; and that the better plan would be to destroy the chiccory-grounds and mills (which cost but little), compensation being at the same time made to their owners.

The course now suggested has, as our readers are aware, been adopted in the case of tobacco. This plant was early introduced into England; and though its cultivation was prohibited by James I., who had a horror of the drug, and Charles I., it appears to have speedily made considerable progress. The rapid increase in the consumption of tobacco brought from the plantations having soon after attracted the attention of the government financiers, a duty was laid on it in 1643. It then, of course, became necessary to consider how tobacco of native growth should be treated; and the Lords and Commons, by whom the duty on plantation tobacco was imposed, being aware that to make it effectual they must either prohibit the growth of tobacco at home or burden it with a corresponding duty, adopted the latter alternative. The facility, however, with which the duty on native tobacco was evaded, soon satisfied the republican leaders that more stringent measures were required to render the importation of tobacco a prolific source of revenue; and in 1652 an act was passed prohibiting its growth in England, and appointing commissioners to see its provisions carried into effect. This act was confirmed at the Restoration, by the 12 Charles II., c. 34, which ordered that all tobacco plantations should be destroyed. These measures were believed, at the time, to have been brought about by the solicitations of the planters; but their real intention was not so much to conciliate or benefit the latter, as to facilitate and secure the collection of a revenue from tobacco; and, considered in this point of view, their policy seems unexceptionable.

These measures did not, however, extend to Scotland and
Ireland, in which the culture of tobacco was authorized
down to a comparatively recent period. Its cultivation in
the former, after being long very trifling, began about the
middle of last century rapidly to increase; and various regulations were from time to time enacted for the assessment
and levy on the native of the same duty that was paid by
plantation tobacco. It was, however, again found that this
could not be done, and that either the culture must be suppressed or the revenue be seriously injured by the introduction of native tobacco into consumption which had escaped
the duty. Under these circumstances the English precedent
of 1652 was followed; and by carrying out the provisions
of the 22 Geo. III., c. 72, passed for the purpose, the
tobacco plantations of Scotland shared the fate of those
of England.

But though proscribed in Britain, the tobacco culture continued to be legal in Ireland; and began, especially during
the present century, to be rather extensively carried on in
some parts of that country. But it has there, also, been
suppressed by the act 2 Will. IV., c. 20, the vigorous
enforcement of which, despite the clamour it occasioned,
was highly creditable to government.

Duties on imports and exports have been levied in almost
every country which has had any foreign commerce. The
Athenians laid a tax of a *fifth* on the corn and other merchandise imported from foreign countries, and also on several
of the commodities exported from Attica.* The *portoria*,† or
customs payable on the commodities imported into and
exported from the different ports of the Roman empire,
formed a very ancient and important part of the public

---

* Anacharsis's Travels, iv., p. 375, Eng. Trans. The quantity of corn usually
imported from the countries on the Euxine into Athens amounted to about
400,000 medimni. See Clarke on the ' Connexion between the Roman and
English Coins,' p. 58.

† " Huic vero proprie *vectigalis* denominatio convenit, quippe pro vehendis
mercibus (unde *vectigal*) soluto." (Burman. ' De Vectigalibus Pop. Rom.,'
cap. v.)

revenue. They were imposed, as Tacitus has observed, when the spirit of liberty ran highest among the people. *A consulibus et tribunis plebis institutæ, acri etiam populi Romani tum libertate.* (*Annal.* lib. xiii. cap. 50.) The rates at which they were charged were fluctuating and various, and little is now known respecting them. Cicero informs us (in ii. Ver. cap. 75) that the duties on corn exported from the ports of Sicily were in his time 5, per cent. Under the imperial government the amount of the *portoria* depended as much on the caprice of the prince as on the real exigencies of the state. Though sometimes diminished, they were never entirely remitted, and were much more frequently enlarged. Under the Byzantine emperors they were as high as $12\frac{1}{2}$ per cent.*

Customs duties existed in England previously to the Conquest; and appear to have derived their name from having been immemorially or customarily charged on certain articles when conveyed across the principal ferries, bridges, &c., within the kingdom, and on the exportation of others to, and their importation from parts beyond seas. It is expressly stipulated in Magna Charta that foreign merchants shall have safe and sure conduct to come into England and to carry on traffic in it without being subject to any unusual tolls, but only to the ancient and rightful customs (*antiquas et rectas consuetudines*). It is worthy of mention, that the customs referred to in this clause were let in farm, in 1202, the fourth year of King John's reign, for 1000 marks; and that in 1206, the customs revenue, including the profit accruing to the king from fairs and markets throughout England, produced only 4,958*l*. 7*s*. $3\frac{1}{2}d$.†

These statements sufficiently establish the error of Blackstone,‡ and those who suppose that the king's first claim to the customs was established in the reign of Edward I. They

---

* Burman. 'De Vectigalibus Pop. Rom.' cap. 5.

† Chief Baron Gilbert's 'Treatise on the Exchequer,' App. i. p. 268; Sinclair, 'Hist. Pub. Revenue,' i. 100; Chitty's 'Commercial Law,' i. 693, &c.

‡ Com., book i. cap. 8.

certainly formed a part, however unimportant, of the revenue of his predecessors. But that able and politic prince,
by rendering the levy of the old duties more effectual, and
by procuring the sanction of parliamentary authority to the
imposition of new duties, was the first who made the customs
revenue of any very material consequence. The duties in
Edward's reign, and in the reigns of his immediate successors,
were principally laid on wool, woolfels (sheep-skins), and
leather, when exported.   These were called *magna costuma;*
but, in accordance with the barbarous policy of the times,
extra duties, or *parva costuma,* were laid on all articles when
imported or exported by aliens.   The duties of *tonnage* and
poundage, of which mention is so frequently made in English
history, were customs duties; the first being charged on wine
by the tun, while the latter was a per centage duty on other
articles, the values of which were usually fixed or rated at
certain specified amounts. When these duties were granted
to the Crown they were denominated *subsidies;* and as the duty
of poundage had continued for a lengthened period at the
rate of 1*s.* per pound, or 5 per cent., a subsidy came, in the
language of the customs, to denote an *ad valorem* duty of
5 per cent.   The new subsidy, granted in the reign of William III., was an addition of 5 per cent. to the duties on
most imported commodities.

The various customs duties were collected in a book of
rates published in the reign of Charles II.; a new book of
supplementary rates being again published in the reign
of George I. But notwithstanding the issue of this new
book, and the improvement effected by the 8th Geo. I.,
cap. 15, which relieved a great many articles of native produce from the duties with which they had been previously
charged, the customs duties and regulations became towards
the middle of last century extremely numerous and unintelligi-
ble.   After the Revolution the practice of affixing a certain
rate or value to each article of merchandise and charging the
duty accordingly, was gradually abandoned; and the contrary practice grew up of charging the duties at so much per lb.,

CUSTOMS OR FRONTIER DUTIES.

gallon, yard, or other quantity, or at an *ad valorem* rate on their
value as deduced from the invoices and declarations of the merchants. Hence the mode of assessing the duties in the second
book of rates differed in very many instances from the mode
generally adopted in the first; and the inconvenience thence
arising was greatly aggravated in the course of time by the
passing of an immense number of new acts imposing additional duties without any reference to those already existing,
sometimes in one way and sometimes in another, and frequently, also, under conditions and limitations at variance
with those previously enacted. The confusion that was thus
occasioned was further increased by the practice of specially
appropriating the duties to certain services, and the consequent necessity of each being separately calculated from the
others.

The uncertainty and embarrassment growing out of such
a system may be more easily imagined than described. In
Saxby's work on the customs, published in 1757, intended as
a guide to assist merchants and others in transacting their
business, the duties are classed in no fewer than *thirty-nine*
principal divisions; and these again are broken down into
an endless number of subdivisions, having reference to different articles, &c. Need we wonder that under such circumstances it became hardly possible, even for the most
experienced merchants, to tell the exact amount of duty
affecting any article, or the course to be followed either in
entering or clearing out vessels; so that they were obliged
to leave it entirely to the clerks of the custom-house to state
the amount of duties, and to direct them how to proceed, so
as to avoid the forfeiture of their goods and ships. It would
be idle to take up the reader's time by pointing out the injury
which such a state of things must have done to commerce;
and the innumerable opportunities it afforded for all sorts of
abuses.

But despite the magnitude of the evil, and the incessant
complaints to which it gave rise, the difficulties in the way
of any efficient change were so great that it continued without

amendment till after the close of the American war. In 1787, however, Mr. Pitt introduced and carried his famous measure, the 27 Geo. III. cap. 13, for the consolidation of the customs duties. This was accomplished by abolishing all the then subsisting duties, and substituting in their stead single duties on each article, amounting as nearly as could be calculated to the total amount of the various duties with which it had previously been chargeable. A more simple and uniform plan was then, also, introduced for transacting business at the custom-house.

During the late war the customs duties again became very numerous and complicated; and great practical inconvenience was also experienced from the multiplication of statutes relating to trade and navigation. The inconveniences occasioned by this state of things having been set in a striking light in the Reports of a Committee of the House of Lords on Foreign Trade, in 1820, Mr. Huskisson soon after took the most efficient measures to have them obviated. In this view the customs duties were again consolidated in 1825 by the Act 6 Geo. IV. cap. 111; and acts were at the same time passed, consolidating and simplifying the laws relating to British shipping and navigation, the colony trade, warehousing, smuggling, &c. These acts, which are drawn up with laudable brevity and clearness, were principally compiled by the late Mr. J. D. Hume of the Board of Trade, and do honour to his industry and talent for arrangement. The last consolidation of the customs duties was effected in 1842, by the Tariff Act of that year.

CHAPTER VI.

EXCISE OR INLAND DUTIES.

THE excise,* the next great branch of the revenue, consists principally of inland duties on articles produced or manufactured at home; but exclusive of these, the duties on li-

* Apparently from the Latin *excidere*, to cut off.

cences, auctions, and post-horses are placed under the management of the excise, and are consequently included in the excise duties.

It is said that the first attempt to introduce excise duties into England was made in 1626 by a commission under the Great Seal. But Parliament having remonstrated against the measure, the commission was cancelled. This description of duties had, however, been previously established in Holland; and the large revenue which they afforded, pointed them out to the leaders of the popular party in the great civil war as the most likely means by which they could raise funds to carry on the arduous contest in which they had embarked. They were, consequently, introduced by a Parliamentary ordinance, issued in 1643, which imposed duties on ale, beer, cider and perry, and on the makers and venders thereof. The Royalists soon after followed the example set by the Republicans ; though, as the duties were from the outset exceedingly unpopular, both parties took especial care to ascribe their introduction to necessity, and to pledge themselves to their abolition at the close of the war. But they were soon found to be far too productive to be voluntarily abandoned. And after the nation had been accustomed to them for a few years, and they had been gradually increased, Parliament did not hesitate to declare, in 1649, that "the impost of excise was the most easy and indifferent levy that could be laid upon the people."* And it is worthy of remark, that the regulations embodied in Cromwell's Excise Act of 1657, authorizing officers to make searches, and directing the giving of notices, &c., are very similar to those now in force.

The same reasons that had made the excise be continued down to the Restoration secured its existence subsequently to that event. A portion of its produce was, at the same time, as already seen (ante, p. 58), assigned in perpetuity to the crown, in compensation for its relinquishing the hereditary revenues arising from wardships and other feudal

* Blackstone, book i. cap. 8.

prerogatives which were then abolished. And, notwithstanding Blackstone says, that "from its first original to the
present time its very name has been odious to the people of
England," * it has since continued progressively to gain
ground; and has for a lengthened series of years furnished
a very large portion of the public revenue.†

We believe, however, that the prejudice to which Blackstone alludes, did not originate so much in any dislike to the
duties themselves, as in circumstances connected with their
imposition.   Originally the duties were let in farm, which
is always a most unpopular proceeding.   And down to a
very recent period there was hardly a single duty the assessment of which was not made the subject of numerous lengthened, obscure, and contradictory statutes, so that it was
hardly possible for any trader, however desirous to comply
with the law, to avoid getting into serious scrapes.   The
duties being frequently, also, carried to an oppressive extent,
smuggling was practised ; and when a party was prosecuted,
whether for an intentional or unintentional infraction of the
law, or for attempting to defraud the revenue, the case might
be laid before judges (without the intervention of a jury)
in whose decision the public had little confidence.   No
wonder, therefore, that the excise should have been unpopular.   The obnoxious practice of letting the duties to farmers has, however, been long abandoned; and of late years
the laws and regulations connected with their assessment
have been much simplified.   In this respect, indeed, considerable improvements might still be made; and nothing
should be omitted to render the rules for assessing the duties
brief, clear, and level to the comprehension of every one,

---

* Com., *ubi supra.*

† Johnson's prejudice against the excise is well known. In his Dictionary
he defines it " A hateful tax levied upon commodities, and adjudged not by
the common judges of property, but wretches hired by those to whom excise is
paid." Boswell mentions that Mr. Murray (afterwards Lord Mansfield), then
Attorney-General, being consulted by the Commissioners of Excise, gave it as
his opinion that the definition was actionable, adding, however, that it would
be more prudent not to prosecute.—Boswell's 'Life of Johnson,' i., 228,
Pickering's ed.

and calculated to interfere as little as possible with the details and processes of manufacture. And, supposing their assessment were sufficiently simplified, and that they were in all cases reduced to a reasonable amount, but little objection could be made to them because of the summary jurisdiction exercised by the commissioners and justices. On the contrary this practice has some material advantages. When parties are prosecuted in the Court of Exchequer for offences against the revenue, their case is, of course, submitted to a jury. But in this court, as in others, delays frequently take place, and the expenses are always very considerable ; whereas in cases of summary jurisdiction, or those adjudged by the commissioners and justices, there is little or no delay and little or no expense. And considering that all parties who fancy themselves aggrieved by the decision of the commissioners are entitled (4 Vict. c. 20, § 26) to appeal, at a very trifling cost, to a Baron of Exchequer, who rejudges the case ; while those who suppose themselves aggrieved by a sentence of the justices may appeal to the quarter-sessions (7 & 8 Geo. IV. c. 53, § 82), there really appears to be more to approve than to object to in the summary jurisdiction.

The excise duties formerly imposed on salt, leather, candles, beer, and other less important articles, have been repealed within these few years; and, with the exception of the duty on glass, which interferes with the manufacture, we are not sure that there is one of the existing duties that can be fairly objected to on principle, though the rate of duty might, perhaps, in one or two cases be advantageously reduced. We subjoin an account of the articles subject to excise duties in Great Britain and Ireland in 1843, with the rates of duty, and the nett produce of the duties in that year :—

I.—An Account of the Articles subject to the Excise Duties in England and Scotland in 1843, specifying the Rates of Duty on each, and the Nett Produce of the Duties.

Articles.	Rates of Duty.	Nett Produce of Duty in England.	Nett Produce of Duty in Scotland.	Nett Produce of Duty in Great Britain.
		£.	£.	£.
Auctions.. {	Estates, Houses. &c... 7d. in the £, and 5 per cent. Furniture, &c......... 1s. ditto ditto Sheeps' Wool......... 2d. ditto ditto First Sales of Foreign } ¼ per cent. ditto Produce......... }	249,583	21,094	270,677
Bricks.... {	Small .... 5s. 10d. per 1000, & 5 p. cent. Large .... 10s. ditto ditto	348,177	7,104	355,281
Glass..... {	Flint................ 2d. per lb. ditto Plate................ 3l. per cwt. ditto Crown .... 3l. 13s. 6d. per cwt. ditto German Sheet...... 3l. 13s. 6d. ditto ditto Common Bottle ...... 7s. ditto ditto	544,105	29,958	574,063
Hops......	Hops................ 2d. per lb. ditto	308,366	..	308,366
Licences...	Inserted at the end	826,803	102,334	929,137
Malt ..... {	From Barley......... 2s. 7d. per bush. & 5 per cent. From Bear or Bigg, } 2s. ditto ditto (Scotland only) }	4,149,941	333,806	4,483,747
Paper	Paper of all kinds .... 1¼d. per lb. ditto	491,581	118,549	610,130
Post-Horse Duty	For every Horse let for } hire to travel post .. } 1½d. per mile .... For every Horse to go } no more than 8 miles } 1s. 9d., or 1-5th of the sum from place of letting } charged. For ditto, and not to } 1s. per mile............... bring back........ } For every Horse let for } 2s. 6d., or 1-5th of the sum hire for every day, } charged. not exceeding 3 days } Exceeding 3 days and } 1s. 9d., or 1-5th of the sum not exceeding 13 days } charged. Exceeding 13 and less } 1s. 3d., or 1-5th of the sum than 28 days ...... } charged.	145,841	16,361	162,202
Post-Horses' Licences }	.... 7s. 6d. per annum	3,909	322	4,231
Soap...... {	Hard................ 1¼d. per lb. and 5 per cent.. Soft................ 1d. ditto ditto	808,683	83,580	892,263
Spirits.... {	England............ 7s. 10d. per gallon .... Scotland.. .... 3s. 8d. ditto	2,608,798	1,406,538	4,015,336
Sugar	Sugar .... 1l. 4s. per cwt. and 5 per cent.	3,956	..	3,956
Vinegar ...	Vinegar .... 2d. per gallon & 5 per cent. *	25,304	157	25,461
	Total	10,515,047	2,119,803	12,634,850

Rate per cent. at which the Nett Produce was collected, £6. 8s. 6d.

---

* This duty was repealed in the course of the present year (1844).

Rates of Duty on Licences.

	Per Annum.				Per Annum.		
	£.	s.	d.		£.	s.	d.
Auctioneers	5	5	0	Soap Makers	4	4	0
Brewers of Table-beer, according				Distillers or Rectifiers	10	10	0
to the quantity brewed,				Dealers in Spirits not being Re-			
from 10s. 6d. to	2	2	0	tailers	10	10	0
Ditto of Strong-beer, ditto				Makers of Stills (Scotland only)	0	10	6
from 10s. 6d. to	78	15	0	Chemists, or any other Trade re-			
Retail Brewers, not to be drunk				quiring the use of a Still (Scot-			
on the premises	5	10	3	land only)	0	10	6
Sellers of Strong-beer only, not				Retailers of Spirits, according to			
being Brewers	3	6	1½	the Rent of the Premises,			
Beer Retailers, according to {	1	2	0½	from 2l. 4s. 1d. to	11	0	6
the rent of the premises . . {	or			Retailers of Sweets	1	2	0½
{	3	6	1½	Manufacturers of Tobacco and			
Retailers of Beer, Cider, and				Snuff, according to the quantity			
Perry, to be drunk on the pre-				made . . . . . from 5l. 5s. to	31	10	0
mises (England only)	3	6	1½	Dealers in Tobacco and Snuff . .	0	5	3
Ditto, not to be drunk on the				Vinegar-makers	5	5	0
premises (England only) . . .	1	2	0½	Dealers in Foreign Wine, not			
Retailers of Cider and Perry				having Licences for retailing			
only (England only)	1	2	0½	Spirits and Beer.	10	10	0
Dealers in Coffee, Tea, &c. . .	0	11	6½	Ditto, having a Licence for re-			
Glass Makers, for every glass-				tailing Beer, but not Spirits .	4	8	2½
house	21	0	0	Ditto, having Licences to retail			
Maltsters, according to the quan-				Beer and Spirits.	2	4	1
tity made. . . from 2s. 7½d. to	4	14	6	Passage Vessels, on board of which			
Paper Makers.	4	4	0	Exciseable Liquors are sold .	1	1	0

II. An Account of the Articles subject to the Excise Duties in Ireland, in 1843, specifying the Rates of Duty on each, and the Nett Produce of the Duties.

Articles.	Rates of Duty.	Nett Produce of Duty in Ireland.
		£.
Auctions . . . . . {	Estates, Houses, &c. . 6d. in the £, and 5 per cent.	
	Furniture, &c. . . . . 10d. ditto ditto . .	12,186
	Sheep's Wool . . . . 2d. ditto ditto . . .	
	First Sale of Foreign } ¼ per cent. ditto . . .	
	Produce . . . . . }	
Game Certificates . .	. . . . 3l. 3s. per annum	11,721
	Flint . . . . 2d. per lb. and 5 per cent. . .	
	Crown. . . . . 3l. 13s. 6d. per cwt. ditto. .	
Glass . . . . . . {	German Sheet . . . . 3l. 13s. 6d. ditto ditto. .	5,748
	Plate . . . . 3l. 0s. 0d. ditto ditto. .	
	Common Bottles . . . 7s. 0d. ditto ditto. .	
Licences	Nearly the same as in Britain	90,810
Malt . . . . {	From Barley . . . . 2s. 7d. per bus. & 5 per cent.	175,891
	From Bear or Bigg . . 2s. 0d. ditto ditto. .	
Paper	All kinds . . . . . . 1½d. per lb. ditto. .	29,765
Spirits	Home-made . . . . . 2s. 8d. per gallon	942,887
Vinegar	. . . . 2d. per gallon, and 5 per cent.	453
	Total	£1,269,461

It has been objected to the excise duties that they "greatly raise the cost of subsistence to the labouring classes;" but a glance at the foregoing tables shows that this assertion has no solid foundation. Of the above sum of 12,634,850l., produced in Great Britain in 1843, the duties on spirits, malt, and licences produced no less than 9,428,220l. In fact, the only excise duty that can be

said to fall on a necessary is that on soap, which produced in 1843, in Great Britain (for this duty does not
extend to Ireland), 808,683*l.*; and taking the population in
that year at 19,000,000, it is plain that the soap-tax does
not, at an average, impose a burden of 10¼*d.* a-year on each
individual. If we estimate its annual pressure, on a labouring family of five persons, at 2*s.* 6*d.* or 3*s.*, we shall not be
within, but rather beyond, the mark.

Malt and Beer.—The duty on malt has been for a lengthened period the most productive of the excise duties. It was
first imposed in England in 1697, and in Scotland in 1713;
but it was not introduced into Ireland till 1785. Malt liquor
having early become the favourite beverage of the people of
England, it might have been supposed that the consumption
of malt would have increased according to the increase of the
population; such, however, has not been the case; and it is
a curious fact that the consumption of malt in England and
Wales varied but little from the first imposition of the duty
down to 1830, though the population had, in the interval, increased from about 5,135,000 to 13,840,751. This singular
result may safely be ascribed to a variety of causes, of which
the increase in the duties on malt and on beer (which last
was substantially a duty on the malt used in breweries) had,
no doubt, a very considerable influence. We doubt, however, whether the stationary consumption of malt, during the
greater part of the 18th century, was owing so much to this
as to other causes. In corroboration of this surmise we may
observe that, though the duty on malt continued stationary
at about 6¾*d.* a-bushel down to 1760, and at about 9¼*d.*
from that period down to 1779, and the beer-duty also continued stationary from 1697 to 1750,* the consumption did
not sensibly vary, during all this lengthened period, notwithstanding the considerable increase of wealth and population.
Probably, therefore, the stationary consumption of malt,
down to the close of the American war, is principally as-

* Hamilton's ' Principles of Taxation,' p. 8.

cribable to the great change that had taken place since the
beginning of the century in the tastes and habits of the
middle and upper classes, through the introduction of tea
and coffee. Perhaps, also, something is to be ascribed to
the increased consumption of spirits by the lower classes;
though there can be no doubt that this increase has been
exaggerated.

But whatever may have been the former influence of the
duty, the oppressive extent to which it was latterly carried,
coupled with the increased price of barley and the increased
amount of the beer-duty, had the most powerful effect in
checking the consumption of malt and beer. After various
previous additions the duty on malt was raised in 1804 to
4s. 5¾d. per bushel, or 35s. 10d. a-quarter, the beer-duties
being then also raised to 10s. per barrel; and as a quarter
of malt produced about three barrels of beer, it follows that
the duty on malt used in breweries really amounted at that
period to about 65s. 10d. a-quarter! The duty continued
at this exorbitant rate till 1816; and it is an extraordinary
fact, that during the twelve years ending with 1816 the consumption of malt amounted at an average to only 23,197,754
bushels a-year, being 993,550 bushels *less* than its average
annual consumption during the twelve years ending with
1720, notwithstanding the prodigious increase of wealth and
population in the interval! The tax had, in truth, been
completely overdone; and besides hindering the consumption of malt and malt liquors, it had the mischievous effect
of vitiating the public taste and stimulating the consumption of ardent spirits, especially of those made from raw
grain. In 1816, however, the duty on malt was reduced to
2s. 5d. a-bushel; and since 1823 it has amounted to 2s. 7d.
a-bushel, or 20s. 8d. a-quarter: and the beer-duty having
been abolished in 1830, this has been (with the exception of
that on hops) the only duty with which malt liquor has since
been affected.

We do not think, notwithstanding its influence over agriculture, that the existing malt-duty is open to any good

objection. It is neither excessive in amount, nor oppressive or troublesome in the mode of charge. The increase in the consumption of malt since 1830 shows that the duty no longer prevents the people from obtaining increased supplies of their favourite beverage. And as it falls on what is rather a luxury than a necessary, is collected with little difficulty and expense, and yields a large revenue, it would seem to be a decidedly good tax.

It is needless to say that the malt-tax, like other taxes on commodities, falls wholly on the consumers. Still, however, it must be admitted that it is, indirectly at least, if not directly, especially injurious to the agriculturists. Barley is a crop that is peculiarly suitable to light lands, and may be introduced with the greatest advantage, in an improved rotation, after green crops. But it is obvious that, by imposing a duty of 20s. 8d. a-quarter on malt, the produce into which barley is almost wholly converted, the demand for the latter is materially diminished; and the farmer is, in consequence, prevented from sowing barley, when, but for this circumstance, it might be more suitable than any other variety of corn. It is not easy to estimate the injury which this indirect influence of the malt-tax inflicts upon agriculture, but the fact of its inflicting an injury is indubitable. Suppose such a high duty were laid on bread as should lessen the demand for wheat a half, would any one presume to say that it was not especially injurious to agriculture? Or, supposing a high duty were laid on calicoes or broad cloths, is it not clear that it would be a serious injury to the manufactures affected by it?

In fact, a duty of 3½d. per square yard was imposed previously to 1831 on all printed cottons, which, like the duty on malt, fell directly on the consumer; but it was, notwithstanding, shown that it was indirectly most injurious to the producer, that it narrowed the market for his goods, and tended in no ordinary degree to paralyze his energies. In consequence of these well-founded representations the duty on printed cottons, which produced above 600,000l. a-year nett revenue, was repealed in 1830 ; and the subsequent increase of the trade has sufficiently justified the policy of the measure.

The case of the malt duty is precisely analogous, and most part of the statements that were made to show the pernicious influence of the duty on printed cottons over the manufacture might, *mutatis mutandis,* be applied to illustrate the influence of the malt duty over agriculture. We cannot, however, afford to lose the revenue derived from the latter, so that it were idle to talk of its repeal. Its diminution even would be most unwise. Indeed it is now only 2s. 8d. a-quarter above what Smith proposed to raise it to in 1776, in the event of the duty on beer being abolished ;* and we are disposed to regard it as one of those duties which, in case any considerable increase of revenue were required, might be most advantageously raised. At present however there is, luckily, no necessity for its increase ; but certainly there are very many duties that should be reduced or repealed previously to that on malt. We do not mean by this to forget or undervalue its indirect influence over agriculture ; but where is the tax, fitted to produce between *four* and *five* millions a-year, against which some weighty objections may not be urged? Its peculiar pressure on the land gives the agriculturists a legitimate claim, though all payments on account of tithe were abolished, to have a certain fixed duty imposed on foreign corn, in the event of the present sliding-scale being abandoned. It would be unjust, seeing that the tax, by narrowing the demand for barley, and obliging the farmers to adopt imperfect rotations, is especially inimical to their interests, to expose them, without any corresponding protection, to the competition of foreigners : perhaps it might require a fixed duty of 1s. 6d. or 2s. a-quarter to countervail the unfavourable circumstances now alluded to.

The acts imposing the malt-duty, and directing how it should be assessed and collected, were formerly exceedingly

* Wealth of Nations, p. 402.

numerous, complex, and contradictory; so much so, indeed, that it was hardly possible for the most expert trader, however honest, to avoid subjecting himself to penalties. These defects have been, however, to a great extent obviated by consolidating and simplifying the law: still, however, the malt act is very lengthened, and might perhaps be advantageously shortened and otherwise improved.

The beer-duty, besides being, when added to the malt-duty, oppressively heavy, was glaringly partial and unjust. It affected only the beer brewed by public brewers or for sale, that brewed for private use being exempted from its operation; and in consequence of this exemption the duty fell wholly on the lower and middle classes, who do not brew any beer, while the nobility and gentry, who brew their own beer, escaped it altogether! That such a distinction should have been made and submitted to for any considerable period may appear not a little surprising. Originally, however, the practice of private brewing was comparatively general; and the beer-duty, being at first confined within moderate limits and slowly increased, the force of habit reconciled the parliament and the country to its inequality and oppressiveness. But the public attention having been at length forcibly attracted to the subject, and the effect of the exorbitant duties on malt and beer, in increasing the consumption of ardent spirits, clearly pointed out,* the beer-duty was repealed, as already stated, in 1830. This measure does honour to the administration of the Duke of Wellington; which is also entitled to the credit of having put an end to the old licensing system, and established, for the first time, a comparatively free-trade in beer.

The *auction-duties*, which were first imposed in 1777, consist of duties proportioned to its value, charged on certain descriptions of property when sold by auction. They amount to 7*d*. per pound on the value of estates, houses, annuities, shares in public companies, ships, funds, and

* See ' Edinburgh Review,' No. 98, Art. iv.

some other articles ; and to 1*s.* per pound on the value of household furniture, books, horses, carriages, and all other goods and chattels. The exemptions are, however, very numerous, comprising various descriptions of movable property, with all sorts of property sold by order of the Courts of Chancery and Exchequer, or for behoof of creditors, or under distress for rent, &c. These duties were strongly, and, we think, justly, objected to by the Commissioners of Excise Inquiry. As it is admitted on all hands that the exposure of property to sale by auction affords the readiest means of ascertaining its value, it seems unreasonable, by imposing duties on auctions, to prevent resort being had to them in the disposal of property. Certainly, however, the duties materially lessen the number of auctions; and very many, perhaps we might say the greater number, of the estates put up to auction, are merely exposed in the view of ascertaining their value, being, to avoid the duty, bought in by the exposers, and then sold by private bargain. But it is not easy to see why, if a duty is to be laid on the transfer of fixed property, it should not be made to press equally on it whatever be the mode of its transfer, or why it should be made to fall heaviest on what has been transferred by auction. We, therefore, are inclined to approve of the suggestion made to the Commissioners of Excise Inquiry, and sanctioned by them, for commuting the duties on the sale of estates and other fixed property by auction for a small *ad valorem* duty upon all transfers of such property conveyed by deed or written instrument, without regard to the mode in which the transfer has been brought about. And were such commutation effected, the duty on sales of other property might be advantageously relinquished; for, while it is of no great importance to the revenue, it presses, from the number of exemptions, severely and unjustly on certain individuals.

Duties on property sold by public sale have been resorted to in most countries; but Spain, which has an unenviable pre-eminence in all that is bad, is the only country that has attempted to raise a revenue by taxing all transfers of property, whether by public or private sale. The *alcavala*, or duty on sales, originally established in 1341, consisted at first of an *ad valorem* tax of 10, increased afterwards to 14, per cent., charged on all commodities, whether raw or manufactured, as often as they were sold or exchanged, being always rated according to their selling price ! And this monstrous impost, which was of itself sufficient to annihilate commerce and industry, was permitted to shed its baleful influence over the far greater portion of the kingdom down to its invasion by Napoleon. This tenacity in clinging to so ruinous a tax is the more surprising, seeing that its destructive influence was repeatedly noticed in the Cortes; and was, at a later period, set in the most striking light by Ulloa,* Ustariz,† Campomanes,‡ and other able writers. Catalonia and Arragon purchased from Philip V. an exemption from the alcavala and *millones* (duties on butchers' meat and other articles of provision), by consenting to the imposition in their stead of a tax on the rent of lands and houses, and on profits and the wages of labour; and notwithstanding the extremely onerous nature of this tax, Mr. Townsend § and other intelligent individuals who visited Spain in the latter part of the last and the beginning of the present century, ascribe the comparatively flourishing state of industry in Catalonia and Arragon to their exemption from the alcavala.

But even the latter was not the worst tax to which the Spaniards were subject. This distinction is due to the *bolla*, characterized by Mr. Townsend as the most mischievous engine ever set on foot by fiscal rapacity, anxious to grasp at revenue without caring whether the source whence it flowed was destroyed. The bolla was a tax of 15 per cent. on the value of all manufactured goods! And to ensure its collection the weaver had to give notice previously to commencing his work to the proper officer, who

---

* Rétablissement des Manufactures, &c., de l'Espagne, Part I., 29.

† Theory and Practice of Commerce (Eng. Trans.), ii., 236, &c.

‡ Educacion Popular, passim.   § Travels in Spain, iii., 327.

came and marked the web, and when he had finished his work he had to give another notice and receive another official visit before he could remove the web from the loom! Even this tax maintained its ground till after the middle of last century, when it was abolished by Campomanes.*

The ruin of Spain has been commonly ascribed to the banishment of the Moors and the emigrations to America. But had the policy of the government been otherwise sufficiently liberal, had the freedom of industry and commerce been established, and the revenue been raised by means of moderate and well-contrived taxes, the losses occasioned by the expatriation of the Moors (which have been greatly exaggerated) would have been speedily obliterated, and the emigration to the New World would have been as little felt in Spain as in England. The truth is, that the Inquisition and the censorship of the press, established in 1502, assisted by vicious taxes, have reduced Spain to her present state of degradation. The former, by enchaining the faculties of the · mind, and stifling all useful inquiry and discussion, perpetuated every abuse; while the latter paralysed the productive energies of the people, and all but extinguished the spirit of industry and the desire of improvement.

Paper.—Previously to 1836 the duty on paper amounted to 3*d.* per lb. on the best, and to 1½*d.* per lb. on the secondary descriptions, provided the latter " were wholly made of tarred ropes, without the tar being previously extracted." The mischievous influence of such a duty is too obvious to require being pointed out. The higher rate of duty, which affected all sorts of paper used for printing and writing, varied from about 20 per cent. *ad valorem* on the finest, to about 150 per cent. on the coarser descriptions; and consequently operated, by raising the price of books and narrowing their sale, as a serious discouragement to literature. The tax on inferior or wrapping paper was also very heavy; while, by preventing it from being made, except from one sort of

* Townsend, i., 148.

material, the price of the latter was raised to an unnatural
elevation, and all improvement in the manufacture well nigh
obstructed. Happily, however, this preposterous system was
abandoned in 1836, when the duty on all sorts of paper was
reduced to $1\frac{1}{2}d.$ per lb., leave being at the same time given
to make them of any description of article. If the duty
is to be kept up (and we see no good reason for its repeal),
it is now probably as moderate and as fairly assessed as can
well be desired. As there is no longer any possibility of
evading a portion of the duty by passing off a superior for a
lower paper, and no attention is paid by the Excise to the
raw material, the vexatious surveillance formerly exercised
by the officers has been almost entirely got rid of; and
greater scope having been given to enterprise and exertion,
a considerable improvement has been effected in the quality
of paper since the adoption of the new plan; at the same
time that its price has been very materially reduced.

The laying of a duty on paper entails a peculiar grievance on the authors and publishers of books; by making
them pay a tax on their works previously to their being
brought to market, and before it can be ascertained whether they will sell. It is true, that where the whole impression of a book is sold off at the publication price, the
duty on paper, and the *five* copies which the author has to
give to public libraries, may be only a moderate deduction
from his profits; but this is not the case in *one* instance
out of *five*. More than half the books published, and
three-fourths of the pamphlets, do not pay the expense of
publication; and in every such case the duties have to be
paid out of the capital of the authors or publishers. This
is rather unfair. If a quantity of tea or wine, or anything
else, be imported, the importer is not called upon to pay
any duty unless he sell it for consumption; and if it become unsaleable, or be damaged and have to be destroyed,
it contributes nothing to the revenue. But the unlucky
author of an unsaleable book pays the duty on paper in
advance; and cannot claim its restitution even after his

anticipations of fame and fortune are found to be wholly
visionary; and his work, instead of finding its way into
libraries and drawing-rooms, is packed off to the trunk-
maker's and the butterman's! The *furor scribendi* is such,
however, that this treatment, though it may add somewhat
to the price of successful books, has no influence in checking
publication; the confidence of authors in their success being
sufficiently strong to make them overlook or disregard the
duty as well as the chances of failure.

Glass.—We are disposed to think that the duties on glass
are the most questionable of those at present under the
management of the Excise. Considering, indeed, the vast
importance of this beautiful fabric, and the many necessary,
convenient, and ornamental purposes to which it is, and to
which it may be, applied, it were much to be wished that it
could be exempted from taxation. But if the public exigencies make its taxation indispensable, the duties should, at
all events, be kept within reasonable limits, and imposed in
the way least likely to be injurious. It would seem, however,
as if these considerations had been wholly lost sight of in
the taxing of glass, the duties on it being objectionable
alike from their magnitude and the mode of their assessment. After successive augmentations they were raised in
1813 to 98*s.* a-cwt. on flint and plate glass! And despite
the great increase of wealth and population in the interim,
the consumption of both these sorts of glass was less in that
year than it had been in 1794, when the duty was 32*s.* 2¼*d.*
a-cwt. The progress of the manufacture and the variations
of the duties since 1813 are exhibited in the tables in the
Appendix.

We do not know whether it be possible materially to vary
the mode in which the duties are assessed, without opening
a still wider door to fraud than that which now exists. But
at present they not only augment the price of a most indispensable article by their entire amount, but they farther
augment it, and deteriorate its quality, by fettering the

operations of the manufacturers, and preventing them from making experiments and improvements, and introducing new processes. In this respect the duties are especially injurious ; being, in truth, the only cause that some important departments of the manufacture have hardly been attempted in this country, and that in others we are behind the Bohemians, and other foreigners who have no natural facilities for its successful prosecution. Indeed every one acquainted with the facts will be forward to admit that the Commissioners of Excise Inquiry were fully justified in expressing their conviction that *" no tax can combine more objections, or be more at variance with all sound principles of taxation, than this duty on glass."*

It is difficult to believe that there can be any cause other than the high price of plate glass occasioned by the duty, for the quantity of it used in the fitting-up of the houses of the middle and more opulent classes in this country being so much below what is used by the same classes in most parts of the continent. The taste for plate glass is, however, gradually gaining strength ; and were the duty abolished, the fair presumption is that it would be used to an incomparably greater extent in mirrors, in the glazing of prints, the windows of shops and houses, &c. The high price of glass is also the principal cause of the limited number of hot-houses and conservatories, which are luxuries from whose enjoyment all but the rich are debarred. But the pleasure and the advantages of these are such that there can be no manner of doubt, were the cost of glass sufficiently reduced, they would be infinitely more numerous than at present.

At the same time we are ready to admit that the interests of the revenue are the paramount consideration, and that it is the bounden duty of government to take care they are not compromised. But government is equally bound to provide that the necessary amount of revenue be raised in the way least adverse to the public interests ; and if the glass duties cannot be spared, and any mode were suggested in which the sum realised by them might be realised with far less trouble and cost to the public, it should, of course, be adopted. And it appears pretty evident that this might be done by commuting them for an addition of 50 per cent. to the duties on windows in houses of 10*l.* a-year and upwards. Even with this addition the window-duty would not be so high as in 1832, before its reduction; and those well acquainted with the subject are persuaded that the greater cheapness of glass would more than compensate most householders for this increase. And besides providing for the indefinite extension and improvement of the manufacture, and for a great addition to the comforts and enjoyments of the bulk of the population, the measure would save the heavy expense attending the collection of the glass duties, without adding anything to the cost of collecting the window duties, inasmuch as the officers employed to collect the latter at present could collect them with equal facility were they doubled or trebled. It is probably true that the commutation now proposed would not be popular; but we are not disposed to lay much stress on that circumstance. Popularity is rarely a proof of the goodness of any measure, and least of all, perhaps, of the goodness of a tax.*

The duty on glass was originally imposed by the Act 6 and 7 Will. and Mary, cap. 18. It was, however, repealed within four years by the 10 and 11 Will. III. cap. 18; because, as stated in the Act, while the duties were of small advantage to the crown, they lessened the duty on coals, hindered the employment of the poor, and endangered the loss of a manufacture beneficial to the kingdom. It is to be regretted that these conclusive reasons for the repeal of the tax were not sufficient to prevent its being revived, in 1745, by the 19 Geo. II. cap. 12. At first, indeed, the renewed du-

---

* In the course of last session (1844) the duty on flint glass of 2*d.* per lb. was reduced to ¾*d.* per do., being the amount of the duty on bottle glass. This equalisation had become necessary from the difficulty of distinguishing between them, and the practical inconveniences that were consequently occasioned. But in other respects the alteration is immaterial. The glass duties should not, in fact, be tampered with, but suppressed.

ties were comparatively moderate, but the immense additions
subsequently made to them, and the interference which their
assessment occasions with the manufacture, have made them
especially objectionable.

Soap.—The duties on soap, originally imposed by the 10
Anne, cap. 12, have also been much objected to, though probably without sufficient reason. Formerly, indeed, they were
quite exorbitant. The direct duty charged on hard soap,
which is by far the most extensively used, amounted, previously to 1833, to 3*d.* per lb., or 28*s.* per cwt., while the price
of soap duty paid rarely exceeded 6*d.* per lb., or 56*s.* per cwt.,
so that the duty was fully 100 per cent.! But besides this
enormous duty, the substances of which soap is made, viz. tallow, barilla, and turpentine, or resin, were respectively charged
with duties of 3*s.* 4*d.,* 2*s.,* and 4*s.* 4*d.* a cwt.; and taking
these indireet taxes into account, it may be truly stated that
soap was taxed from 120 to 130 per cent. *ad valorem!* The
imposition of so exorbitant a duty on an article indispensable
to the prosecution of many branches of manufacture, and to
the comfort and cleanliness of all orders of persons, was in
the last degree inexpedient. During the five years ending
with 1832, the consumption of duty-paid soap was nearly
stationary; though there can be little doubt, from the increase of manufactures and population during that period,
that it would have been considerably extended, but for
the increase of smuggling. This practice was facilitated by
the exemption of Ireland from the duty; for it not unfrequently happened that the soap made in this country, and
sent to Ireland under a drawback, was again clandestinely
introduced into Great Britain. It is obvious that nothing
but the effectual reduction of the duty could have put a stop
to the smuggling and fraud that were then so generally
practised; so long as a profit of 120 or 130 per cent. might
be made by breaking the law, so long was it sure to be
broken, despite the multiplication of penalties and the utmost
activity and vigilance of the officers. In 1833, however, the

duty on hard soap was reduced from 3*d.* to 1½*d.*; on soft, from 1¾*d.* to 1*d.* per lb., and the duties on the articles which enter into the composition of soap being then also materially reduced, the temptation to smuggle was diminished in a corresponding degree. The increased consumption that has followed the reduction of duty, has hindered the revenue from declining more than one-fourth part, or 25 per cent.; so that the advantages resulting from the check given to smuggling, and the influence of the reduced price of the article, in facilitating manufacturing industry, and in promoting habits of cleanliness, have been obtained without any very considerable fiscal sacrifice.

The entire repeal of the soap duty would be a popular measure; but, seeing that a large amount of revenue must be raised, and that those taxes only are productive which affect all classes of the community, the expediency of such a measure may be doubted. Instead of proposing its repeal, the better plan, perhaps, would be to extend it to Ireland. It is not easy to see on what grounds the exemption of one part of the United Kingdom from a duty of this sort imposed on another part, is to be justified. It will be impossible to get rid of smuggling so long as this distinction exists. Were the duty extended to Ireland, the necessity for granting drawbacks on the soap exported to it, and of laying countervailing duties on that imported from it, would, of course, fall to the ground. And we feel pretty confident that, though the rate of duty were reduced from 1½*d.* to 1*d.* per lb., its productiveness would not, under such circumstances, be materially impaired even in England. Some new regulations should also be made in regard to the allowances on account of the duties made to calico-printers and other manufacturers. At present they give rise to a great deal of fraud.

Licence Duties are partly and principally under the management of the Commissioners of Excise, but partly also under that of the Commissioners of Stamps and Taxes. They consist, as the name implies, of sums charged

for licences to carry on certain branches of industry, and
to exercise certain professions; being levied upon bankers,
brewers, distillers, maltsters, glass-makers, paper makers,
soap-makers, tobacco and snuff manufacturers, &c.; on
dealers in beer, spirits, wine, coffee and tea, gold and silver
plate, &c.; and on pawnbrokers, auctioneers, appraisers, &c.
While, however, nothing is easier than to enact that those
who carry on certain businesses or professions shall pay a
licence duty, few things are more difficult than to assess it on
a fair principle.   If the same duties be laid on those engaged
in different businesses or professions without reference to their
extent, it is abundantly obvious that they must either be peculiarly injurious to those who carry on business on a small
scale, or whose services are in little demand,—or peculiarly
advantageous to those who carry it on upon a large scale, or
who are in great request; for if, on the one hand, the prices
of the commodities produced or services rendered by the
former be raised to indemnify them for the tax, such rise will
more than indemnify the latter; while, on the other hand,
if the price of commodities and services be not raised (as
would certainly be the case in·every nineteen out of twenty
instances*), a burden would be imposed on petty manufacturers and tradesmen, which would not be felt by those who
carry on business on an extensive scale.   It is therefore
indispensable, if we would impose licence duties on a fair
principle, that reference should be had to the amount of business carried on by the party.   And in the cases of brewers,
distillers, paper-makers, and generally of those engaged in
businesses of which the extent is easily ascertained, there is
little difficulty in assessing the tax; for, the magnitude of the
business carried on by individuals being known, it may be assumed as a criterion of their capacity to bear it, and it should
be taxed accordingly.   No doubt it is, strictly speaking, true
that the extent of the business carried on by an individual or

* The superior class of manufacturers would, in fact, have no motive to
raise their prices, and consequently it would not be in the power of the others
to raise theirs.

company is no sure index of his or their profits. But we have already seen the futility of all attempts to assess taxes proportionally to real profits; so that taxes falling upon them must either be abandoned or assessed upon some assumed basis, such as the magnitude of the business whence they arise, which may, at an average, approach sufficiently near the truth for practical purposes.

Some of the existing licence duties are charged on those engaged in businesses the extent of which cannot be known. Bankers, for example, are burdened with a licence duty of 30*l.* each, though the business carried on by a first-rate house in the metropolis may be a hundred times more extensive and profitable than that carried on by a banker in a small country town. Auctioneers, too, are indiscriminately obliged to take out a licence charged with a duty of 5*l.* 5*s.*, though some of them be making large incomes by their profession, while others, especially those in remote parts of the country, perhaps hardly make enough to pay the duty. It is, indeed, quite impossible to assess such duties in any given proportion to the incomes of the contributors; and they consequently are liable to all the objections made to capitation taxes imposed according to the rank, station, or profession of the party, without reference to his means or ability to bear them. Such taxes may not be much objected to so long as they are confined, as at present, within narrow limits; but they are too contradictory of the plainest principles ever to become prominent sources of income.

It has sometimes been proposed to charge, in imitation of the French, licence duties on manufacturers and shopkeepers proportioned to the value of the buildings or works in which they carry on their business. But this value is no index of the value of the produce manufactured, or of the business transacted. Manufacturers who employ their industry upon bulky and not very valuable products, often require extensive and costly buildings and workshops, though the capital employed in the business, and the amount of profit, may be very much less than that of others who carry on their business in

less valuable premises.   In like manner, a shop in a fashionable part of the town may cost 500*l.* a-year, while a similar
shop in an inferior situation may cost only 250*l.*, and yet it
may, and frequently does happen that the profit realised by
the occupier of the cheaper exceeds that made by the occupier of the dearer shop.   It is really, therefore, quite nugatory to propose assessing licence duties on such inapplicable
bases.   They should be applied only to those businesses the
extent of which may be easily ascertained; and when so
limited, they appear to be as unobjectionable as most
taxes.

A licence duty of 4*l.* on all persons travelling through
the country as hawkers and pedlars, and of 4*l.* on every horse
or other animal used by them, was imposed in 1697, and is
still kept up.   It is believed, however, that this duty was
orginally contrived and has been continued, rather to conciliate the shopkeepers, by whom itinerant dealers are regarded
as a sort of interlopers, than with a view to the acquisition of
revenue.   In this latter respect, indeed, the duty is of little
importance, having, in 1842, produced only 28,844*l.*   But
whatever may be thought of the duty at present, when well-
furnished shops are to be found in most parts of the country,
and it is everywhere intersected by good roads, it might, when
first established, have been justly objected to.   There were
then many extensive districts in the remoter parts of the kingdom without either towns or shops, while, from the badness
of the roads, it was often no easy matter to visit those at no
great distance; so that the farmers and others resident in such
districts were in a great measure dependent for supplies of
various articles on the visits of the itinerant dealers.   But
the licence duties, by diminishing the number of the latter,
must also have diminished their competition with each other,
and would, consequently, enable them to get somewhat higher
prices for the goods than if the trade had been free.   At
present, however, the facility of getting to shops, and the
competition among the shopkeepers, go far to render the
intervention of hawkers and pedlars unnecessary.   And as

their business affords peculiar facilities for the practice of various sorts of frauds, we incline to think that as a measure of police it may be as well, perhaps, to retain a small duty by way of registration. The existing law should, however, be revised : it is full of anomalies, and affords opportunities, which are sometimes made use of, for perpetrating acts of a most oppressive and unjust description.

About the middle of last century Sir Matthew Decker, one of the best-informed merchants of his day, is supposed to have made a proposal,* which attracted a good deal of notice at the time, for repealing all the taxes then subsisting, and replacing them by licence duties, charged on the consumers of certain articles. But there are innumerable objections to such a project, some of which have been pointed out by Smith. It is sufficient here to observe, that if the licence duty to be paid by individuals who have expensive establishments were to be the fair equivalent of the various sums which are now directly and indirectly drawn from them, it would be so large that it would frequently be difficult for them to make, and, speaking generally, impossible for the officers to enforce its payment. As respects the inferior and labouring classes, it would be still worse. The taxes on the tea, sugar, tobacco, beer, and other articles which they make use of, being paid by degrees as the articles are wanted, are but little felt, or at least thought of by them; but were the daily and imperceptible payments that are thus spread over a twelvemonth consolidated into a single sum, and an equivalent duty demanded for a licence to consume, it would appear most oppressive; the chances, indeed, are ten to one that no adequate provision would be made to meet so large an outgoing; and we run no risk in affirming that it would not be paid in one case out of fifty ; and that no government which attempted to levy such a tax

* See the Essay on the Causes of the Decline of Foreign Trade. 4to., London, 1744. It is doubtful, however, whether Decker be really the author of this work ; and the probability seems to be that it was written by a Mr. Richardson. See Literature of Political Economy, p. 329.

would exist for six months. And even if the scheme were
practicable, it would be most unjust. At present a man pays
according to his consumption; whereas, if licence duties were
substituted for those on different articles, the prodigal and
the parsimonious, the temperate and the intemperate, would
be charged alike. But it is needless to dwell on such a
project. We may be assured that it is only by taxing commodities in general demand, and by identifying, as it were,
the tax with the cost of the article, that the bulk of the
population can ever be made to contribute largely to the
support of government.

Licence duties, or *Droits des Patentes,* are carried to a
much greater extent in France than in England. They were
imposed for the first time in 1791, and were intended to replace the old contributions raised under the names of *Ju-
randes, Maîtrises,* &c. Proprietors and occupiers of land are
exempted from this species of taxes, which fall exclusively on
the other classes. The legislation with respect to the *Droits
des Patentes* is exceedingly complex, and gives rise to a great
deal of litigation and dissatisfaction. The contributors are
divided into five different classes; the distribution depending
partly on the nature of the business in which they are engaged, partly on the population of the place in which it is
carried on, partly on the extent and value of the premises, &c.
It is needless after what has been stated above to enter into
any farther details to show the unequal pressure of these
duties. This inequality is, indeed, admitted by the French
authorities, and the tax exists only because it is established,
and because of the difficulty of providing a substitute. It
produced, in 1842, including the *Centimes Additionels,*
35,434,500 fr., or 1,417,380*l.*

Hops.—An excise duty was imposed on all hops grown in
Britain for four years, by the 9 Anne, cap. 12, which was
made perpetual by the 1 Geo. I. cap. 12. The duty was
originally fixed at 1*d.* per lb., at which rate it continued
down to 1780, when it was raised to 1½*d.* It was subse-

quently increased in 1782, 1783, and other years, till in 1804 it amounted to $2\frac{1}{2}d.$ per lb. ; but it was reduced in 1806 to 2$d.$, at which rate it still continues. Contrary to what might at first perhaps be expected, this duty is economically and efficiently collected, and is not supposed to interfere injuriously with the cultivation. Hops, being an exceedingly variable crop, the duty varies accordingly. In 1825, for example, it produced only 42,337$l.$ 12$s.$ 8$d.$, whereas in the following year it produced 476,895$l.$ 14$s.$ 7$d.$! In 1843 the duty produced a nett revenue of 308,366$l.$, there being at the same time 43,157 acres appropriated to the hop cultivation. The duty does not extend to Ireland.

The hop plant is a native of Britain; but its culture was originally introduced from Flanders in the reign of Henry VIII. Hops are first mentioned in the Statute Book in 1552, in the Act 5 & 6 Edw. VI. c. 5; and it would appear from an Act passed in 1603 (1 Jac. I. c. 18), that they were at that time extensively cultivated. Walter Blithe, in his *Improver Improved*, published in 1649 (3rd edit. 1653, p. 240), has a chapter upon improvement by plantations of hops, in which he observes that " hops were then grown to be a national commodity ; but that it was not many years since the famous city of London petitioned the parliament of England against two nuisances ; and these were, Newcastle coals, in regard to their stench, &c., and hops, in regard they would *spoil the taste of drink,* and endanger the people : and had the parliament been no wiser than they, we had been in a measure pined, and in a great measure starved, which is just answerable to the principles of those men who cry down all devices, or ingenious discoveries, as projects, and thereby stifle and choke improvement."

Bricks.—The duty on bricks, the article most recently subjected to the excise, was imposed in 1784, by the Act 24 Geo. III. c. 24. It was originally fixed at the rate of 2$s.$ 6$d.$ per 1000 on common bricks, but was increased at different periods between 1794 and 1806 to 5$s.$ 10$d.$ per

ditto, at which rate it still continues. The larger and finer
descriptions of bricks are charged with higher rates of duty.
A duty on tiles, imposed at the same time as that on bricks,
was repealed in 1833.

Bricks being the principal material used in London and in
most parts of England in the building of houses, immense
quantities are annually produced in that part of the United
Kingdom. And notwithstanding the influence of the duty,
their consumption in England nearly doubled during the
twenty years ending with 1840; the number that paid duty
in 1821 having been 899,178,510, whereas in 1840 it
amounted to 1,677,811,134. Inasmuch, however, as stone,
which is principally used for building in many parts of the
country, is exempted from any duty, the duty on bricks
is partial and unequal in its pressure. Had the house-tax
not been repealed the duty might have been advantageously
commuted for a small addition to it. The brick duty does
not extend to Ireland.

The above, with the exception of the duties on spirits
and post-horses, which will be brought under review in subsequent parts of this work, are the only excise duties at
present subsisting that seem to require any particular notice.
But though no longer existing amongst us, the duties on
salt, leather, and candles, especially the first, occupy a prominent place in the history of taxation in this and other
countries, and are eminently deserving of attention.

Salt.—The circumstance of salt being an article universally
in demand, and all but indispensable to subsistence, has probably led to its being almost everywhere burdened with
duties, and made a source of revenue. In some cases the
salt-mines or brine-springs whence the salt is obtained are
monopolized by government, and the produce sold at a
comparatively high price, while in others it is subjected, like
most taxed articles, to excise or customs duties, or both.

A duty on salt (*vectigal salis*) was established in ancient
Rome, anno U. C. 547, by the consuls C. Claudius Nero

and M. Livius, the latter of whom received from this circumstance the surname of *Salinator*.* At a later period
the Republic appropriated to itself the entire sale of salt,
which was partly produced in works carried on by slaves on
the public account (*mancipes salinarum*), and partly also, as it
would seem, by private parties who sold their produce to the
revenue officers and farmers of the public salt works. This
duty does not appear to have been deemed oppressive, or to
have been much objected to. Dureau de la Malle says,
*il étoit fixe, modéré, perçu à la fabrication, et ne gênait ni
l'agriculture ni les contribuables.*†

If this be a fair account of the duty on salt in ancient
Rome, it may be safely affirmed that it had but little in
common with the salt duties in most modern states. The
gabelle, or salt duty, was early established in France, into
which indeed it had been introduced by the Romans; but as
different provinces of that kingdom formerly enjoyed different privileges, the rate of duty varied accordingly. It is
stated by Necker that while the consumption of salt in the
provinces, subject to the *grande gabelle,* or high duty on salt,
amounted to only about $9\frac{1}{6}$ lb., its consumption in the *provinces rédimées* and the *provinces franches* (those which had
purchased an exemption from the tax, and those in which it
had never been imposed) amounted to about 18 lbs.!‡ This
well-authenticated statement shows that the duty must have
operated most injuriously in the highly taxed provinces; and
that it might have been considerably reduced without materially affecting the revenue. Its magnitude was not, however, its worst feature. From its being assessed on some provinces and not on others, it obliged their frontiers to be
guarded with as much jealousy as if they had been so many
independent states. And yet, despite the formidable obstacles thrown in its way, smuggling was carried on to such an
extent that, previously to the Revolution, from 3,000 to

* Liv. lib. xxix. cap. 37.
† Economie Politique des Romains, ii. 464; see also Burman, De Vectiga-
libus Pop. Rom., p. 90, 4to. ed.
‡ De l'Administration des Finances, ii. 12.

4,000 persons were annually sent to prison and the galleys
for offences against the salt laws! * Indeed every one in any
degree conversant with French history knows that the glaring
inequality of the gabelle, and the suffering it occasioned,
powerfully contributed to bring about that gigantic convulsion which destroyed it and so many other abuses and institutions.

But despite the painful recollections with which it was
associated, the vast expenditure occasioned by the wars in
which he was perpetually engaged, obliged Napoleon, in
1806, to impose a duty of 20 fr. per metrical quintal (100
kilogrammes) on salt. This duty was raised in 1813 to 40
fr., but was soon after reduced to 28 fr. 50 cents., at which
rate it still continues. From its pressing equally on all
parts of the kingdom, and not being so high as to give any
great stimulus to smuggling, the defects of the duty are
such only as are inseparable from it, and it is said to
be objected to more by the proprietors of salt-works than
by the contributors. It produced in 1842 a revenue of
65,904,000 fr. (2,636,160*l.*). At present the consumption of
duty-paid salt amounts, at an average of the kingdom, to
about 16 lbs. per head of the population, being about 2 lbs.
under Necker's estimate of the consumption of the provinces
exempted from the gabelle.†

Duties on salt occupy a prominent place in the fiscal
codes of Austria and Prussia. According to Tegoborski,
they are equivalent in France to a tax of 38 kreutzers per
head of the population, and in Austria and Prussia to 34·84
kr. and 32·23 kr. per ditto.‡

A duty on salt, at the rate of 3*s.* 4*d.* per bushel, was introduced into England in 1694, its management being intrusted to a peculiar set of commissioners. This duty produced, previously to its repeal in 1729, a gross revenue of
about 470,000*l.* a-year; but the drawbacks and other de-

* Young's 'Travels in France,' 598.
† Audiffret, 'Système Financier de la France,' ii. 168.
‡ Des Finances et du Crédit Public de l'Autriche, ii. 268.

ductions, and the expenses of collection, reduced its nett produce to less than 200,000*l*. But though a highly popular measure the country did not long enjoy the advantages anticipated from the suppression of the duty; for within two years the same minister, Sir Robert Walpole, by whom it had been repealed, proposed its revival! This inconsistency may, however, be easily explained. Walpole, though well aware of the many objections to which the tax was justly liable, was about this period peculiarly anxious to conciliate the support of the landed interest to his government; and in furtherance of this object chose rather to propose the revival of the salt duty than to add another shilling to the land-tax, which was then assessed at the low rate of 1*s*. per pound. The renewed duty began in 1732.

At the accession of George III., in 1760, the duty amounted to 3*s*. 4*d*. a bushel. It was raised during the American war to 5*s*. per bushel, and continued at this rate down to 1798, when it was raised to 10*s*. This addition to the tax having occasioned many complaints and a great increase of smuggling, a Committee of the House of Commons was appointed, in 1801, to inquire into the operation of the salt laws. Having collected a mass of evidence, by which the pernicious influence of the duty was completely established, the Committee recommended that it should be commuted for some less objectionable tax, or, if possible, repealed; declaring their conviction " that the salt duties are in their consequences detrimental to the public in a degree far exceeding the payment of the tax itself." But instead of carrying out the recommendation of the Committee, Mr. Pitt added, in 1805, another 5*s*. a bushel to the duty, which was thus increased to 15*s*., at which rate it continued till its repeal in 1823. It produced, during the latter years of its existence (including Scotland, in which, however, the duty was much less than in England), a nett revenue of about 1,500,000*l*. a-year.

From 1805 downwards the influence of the salt-tax was alike powerful and ruinous. The natural cost of salt being

rather under 6*d*. a-bushel, the duty was above *thirty* times
the price of the article on which it was laid! And it is
needless to say that, with such an overwhelming temptation
to smuggle, the practice was carried on to an immense extent. In his ' Case of the Salt Duties,' published in 1817,
Sir Thomas Bernard states, that the consumption of salt in
England was then supposed to amount to about 150,000
tons a-year, of which only about a third part paid duty.
" The contributions of the public are divided between the
Crown and the thief; and while the Government collects the
tax on about 50,000 tons, the thief and the smuggler receive
a moderated duty on about 100,000 tons more; a circumstance inseparable from the excess and nature of the tax,
and not caused by the want of pains, penalties, and perjuries, which, though multiplied ten-fold, would still be inadequate to their object."*

And if to its influence in encouraging smuggling, we add
its influence in depressing the herring and other fisheries,
which never made any real progress till after its repeal,†
and in enhancing the cost and deteriorating the food of the
labouring classes, it will not perhaps be easy to specify
another tax among the many that have at various periods
been adopted in this country of which the operation was
in all respects so mischievous. It certainly took directly
and indirectly from four to five times the sum from the
pockets of the public which it brought into the coffers of the
treasury.

Much, undoubtedly, of the oppressiveness of the tax was
ascribable to the extravagant height to which it was carried
by the additions made to it in 1798 and 1805; and it is

---

* Case of the Salt Duties, p. 29.

† Duty-free salt was allowed to be supplied for the fisheries, but the difficulties in the way of getting it were such as rendered this privilege little better
than nominal. In the latter years of the duty instances were every now and
then occurring, during the fishing season, of whole cargoes of herring becoming putrid and being thrown into the sea, from the inability of the fishermen to
find sureties or bail for the requisite supply of salt, conformably to the excise
laws! Macdonald's ' Survey of the Hebrides,' p. 513.

probable that its produce previously to its repeal would have been but little below what it actually amounted to had it been continued at its old level of 5s. a-bushel. But, independently of its exorbitance, and the stimulus it gave to smuggling, the great expense of its collection, and the innumerable ways in which it interfered with industrious undertakings, and with the subsistence of the poor, made it in the last degree objectionable. Hence, though various taxes which produced a greater amount of revenue have been repealed since 1815, the abolition of the salt-tax is believed to have been followed by the greatest public benefit.

We may be excused, perhaps, before quitting this part of our subject, for shortly adverting to a singular assertion of the Marquis Audiffret, who states in his valuable work on the *Système Financier de la France* (i. 56), in vindication of the duties on salt in that kingdom, that "*depuis la remise entière du droit du sel dans la Grande Bretagne la consommation est restée à peu près ce quelle était sous le régime fiscal antérieur.*" The learned author has not mentioned whence he derived this information; but certainly we have seldom seen any statement wider of the mark. It may be affirmed, with the utmost confidence, that the consumption of *duty-paid* salt in England is fully *three* times as great at present, per head of the population, as in 1822. And though but little increase has taken place in the direct consumption of salt for agricultural purposes, the repeal of the duty has been of the greatest advantage to the fisheries, and to some important arts and manufactures. The quantity of herrings taken and cured of late years has been more than 50 per cent. greater than the quantity taken and cured previously to 1830, notwithstanding the total abolition in that year of the bounty on which the very existence of the fisheries had previously been supposed to depend. Among other purposes to which salt has been applied since the abolition of the duty may be mentioned the preparation of artificial soda, which is now produced of so good a quality and at so cheap a rate that it has gone far to supersede the use of barilla and kelp: salt is

now also, we believe, begun to be extensively employed in the
manufacture of artificial manures, a business which will most
likely become of the greatest importance. But, without
laying any stress on these circumstances, the supposition
that the consumption of an article used by all classes of the
population should not have been increased, notwithstanding
its retail price has been reduced from about 18s. to 2s. 6d.
per bushel, is so very extravagant that, but for the circumstance of its having been referred to by Audiffret, and other
writers* of authority, as if it had been realized, we should
not have thought it worth notice.

Leather.—Next to that on salt, the duty formerly
charged on leather was, perhaps, the most objectionable of
the excise duties. It was imposed by the act 9 Anne, c. 11.
The duty amounted to 1½d. per lb. from its establishment
down to 1812, when it was raised to 3d., at which rate it
continued till 1822, when it was again reduced to its old
rate of 1½d. It was finally repealed in 1830.

The duty produced about 600,000l. a-year of nett revenue
previously to its reduction, and about 400,000l. subsequently
to that event. But instead of being reduced the duty should
have been wholly repealed in 1822. The retention of any
part of it made it necessary to keep up and enforce the
various regulations required for its collection, which were
more objected to by the manufacturers than the duty; while
a reduction of 1½d. per lb. in the cost of leather was too
trifling to be sensibly felt by the public, even if they had
received the entire advantage of this reduction. To have
secured this a corresponding deduction should, however, have
been made from the duty which was then laid on foreign
hides when imported; and this not being done, there can
be no doubt that the principal benefit of the reduction was
intercepted by the growers of cattle in this country, who
sold their hides at a proportionally increased price.† But,

* Tegoborski, ' Finances de l'Autriche,' ii. 284.

† This view of the matter is identical with that taken by Sir Robert Peel, in

apart from these considerations, could anything be more impolitic than to lay a duty on an article so indispensable to the labouring class, and to the prosecution of most branches of industry ; and to subject a most important and valuable manufacture, furnishing the raw material of many others, to a vexatious system of revenue laws, for the sake of a revenue of 400,000*l.*, or even 600,000*l.* a-year? Happily, however, these are now matters of history. The leather trade, relieved from every sort of trammel and restraint, has been vastly extended since 1830: and the customs duties on foreign hides being now merely nominal, their importation has rapidly increased, and the public have not merely profited by the abolition of the duty, but by the many improvements which it has allowed to be made in the tanning and dressing of leather.

Previously to the repeal of the leather tax, duty was paid on about 52,000,000 lbs. of leather. But we are well assured that the production of tanned and dressed leather is at present not under, if it be not above, 70,000,000 lbs. This quantity, supposing it to sell, at an average, for 1*s.* 6*d.* per lb., would be worth 5,250,000*l.* And, on this hypothesis, the total value of the articles into which leather is manufactured may fairly be estimated at fully 14,000,000*l.* a-year! If those who may suspect this estimate of exaggeration will reflect a little on the immense expenditure on shoes and harness only, exclusive of the other modes in which leather is employed, they will, perhaps, come to be of opinion that it is, if anything, rather below than above the mark.

In speaking of the leather manufacture, Dr. Campbell has the following observations :—" If we look abroad on the

submitting his financial statement to the House of Commons on the 11th of March, 1842:—"I do not know," said the Right Honourable Gentleman, " but that in respect to leather the reduction of that tax took place without public benefit. I fear that the full amount of the advantage did not go to the consumer. You did not adopt a measure you ought to have adopted with the reduction of the tax, a reduction of the duty on the importation of foreign hides. I fear that in this instance you reduced a duty which benefited monopolists."

instruments of husbandry, on the implements used in most
mechanic trades, on the structure of a multitude of engines
and machines; or if we contemplate at home the necessary
parts of our clothing—breeches, shoes, boots, gloves—or
the furniture of our houses, the books on our shelves, the
harness of our horses, and even the substance of our carriages; what do we see but instances of human industry exerted upon leather?   What an aptitude has this single material in a variety of circumstances for the relief of our
necessities, and supplying conveniences in every state and
stage of life?   Without it, or even without it in the plenty
we have it, to what difficulties should we be exposed!"*

Candles.—The duty on candles, imposed in 1710, by the
stat. 8 Anne, c. 9, was repealed in 1831.   For many years
previously to its repeal, the rate of duty amounted to 1*d.*
per lb. on tallow candles, and to 3½*d.* per lb. on those made
of wax.   But though the rate of duty could not be fairly
objected to, the tax itself was one of the worst that could
be devised.   Heavy penalties were laid on all parties,
however poor, who made any tallow or grease into candles,
unless they gave previous notice to the Excise, and declared
upon oath the quantity and description of candles they
meant to make!   It is obvious that such a duty could be
neither fairly assessed nor generally collected; and though
previously to its repeal it produced about 490,000*l.* a-year,
it certainly was far more productive of smuggling, perjury,
and oppression.

The duties on armorial bearings, carriages, horses and
horse-dealers, dogs, game certificates, servants, and windows,
are called, for what reason it is not easy to imagine, the
" assessed taxes."   They are under the management of the
Commissioners of Stamps and Taxes; but as they have no
connexion with the stamp duties, and belong to the class of

* Political State of Great Britain, vol. ii. p. 176.

inland duties, they may perhaps be as properly noticed here as anywhere else.

The assessed taxes produced, in 1843, the sum of 3,225,919*l.*, of which nearly a half was derived from the window duty. We have already seen that a tax on houses is in all respects preferable to a tax on windows; and that if either was to be abandoned, the latter should have been repealed in preference to the former. The existing window tax is, however, as reasonable as can well be desired. Houses with fewer than eight windows are exempted from its operation, and houses with that number pay only 15*s.* 6*d.* The duty increases with the increasing number of windows, till, on the largest houses, it attains a maximum rate of 46*l.* 10*s.* 3*d.* Windows in farm-houses under 200*l.* a-year are exempted from the duty. In 1843 this tax produced 1,545,281*l.**

The window duties were preceded by and may, indeed, be regarded as a substitute for hearth-money, or the old duty on hearths or fire-places. This last is of great antiquity. As early as the Conquest mention is made of *fumage* or *fuage,* vulgarly called smoke-farthings, which were paid by custom to the king for every chimney in the house. It would appear, however, that this custom had gradually fallen into disuse; and it was not till the reign of Charles II. that the hearth-tax was established as a regular source of income. The stat. 13 & 14 Car. II., cap. 10, enacted that a tax of 2*s.* should be charged upon every hearth in all houses paying to church and poor ; and subsequent statutes authorised the officers engaged in its collection to enter houses to ascertain the number of fire-places. This invasion of domestic privacy, and not its amount, made this a very unpopular tax. And, therefore, it was declared at the Revolution by stat. 1 William and Mary, cap. 10, that "hearth-money was not only a great oppression to the poorer sort, but a badge of slavery upon the whole people, exposing every man's house to be entered into and searched

* Exclusive of the 10 per cent. additional imposed by the 3 Victoria, c. 17.

at pleasure, by persons unknown to him; and, therefore, to erect a lasting monument of their majesties' goodness in every house in the kingdom, the duty of hearth-money was taken away and abolished." But, as Blackstone says, " the prospect of this monument of goodness was somewhat darkened," when in six years after taxes were laid on houses and windows by the statute 7 Will. III. cap. 18. The window has, in truth, no advantage of any kind over the hearth tax, except that it may in most cases be assessed without its being necessary to enter the house. In other respects the taxes are nearly upon a level; neither one or other affording any criterion by which to estimate the value of houses, or, consequently, the amount of tax they might fairly bear.

The tax on horses formerly extended to those employed in husbandry, which were charged with duties varying from 3s. to 17s. 6d. each. Happily, however, the latter were exempted from the tax in 1822 and 1823. The duty on them was objectionable, inasmuch as it not only tended directly to raise the price of corn by taxing the instruments of production, but to do the same thing indirectly by obstructing the progress of agriculture. At present there seems to be nothing to find fault with in the duty on horses. Probably, indeed, the rates on some of the classes might be advantageously increased. In 1826, when those employed in husbandry were charged, the duty was assessed on 1,161,430 horses; whereas in 1842 it was assessed only on 315,855 horses.

A duty on private carriages was imposed for the first time in 1747 by the Act 20 Geo. II. cap. 10. The rate of duty, which has since undergone many modifications, amounts at present to 6l. on a four-wheeled carriage, when only one is kept, and 6l. 10s. each when two are kept, and so on, increasing with the number kept. The fact that there are only about 28,000 private four-wheeled carriages in Great Britain (exclusive of pony carriages), goes far to show how idle it is to imagine that any very great amount of revenue can ever be realized by means of taxes falling on luxuries used only by the upper classes.

The duties on dogs and game certificates call for little re-mark. Dogs used in the care of sheep and cattle are ex-empted from the duty; and being unexceptionable in prin-ciple, the tax on other dogs and on game licences should be carried to the highest point of productiveness; that is, the duties should be elevated or depressed to the point at which they will yield the greatest amount of revenue.

The duties on all descriptions of servants, including wait-ers in taverns, produced, in 1843, about 220,000*l.* The duty amounts to 2*l.* 4*s.* on a person keeping one servant, in-creasing up to 3*l.* 16*s.* 6*d.* each servant, on persons keeping eleven servants and upwards.

The tax on hair-powder, imposed in 1797, produces little more than 4,000*l.* a-year, and is not worth keeping up. It is interesting only from its affording, as already stated, one of the most striking examples of a change of fashion induced by taxation; the habit of wearing hair-powder, which, pre-viously to the tax, was very general, having been completely rooted out by its introduction.

It is obvious from these statements that the assessed taxes are at present as moderate as can be desired; and whatever unpopularity may attach to them, does not originate in their magnitude, but in the circumstance of their requiring a direct money payment to be made to the collectors. We have previously endeavoured to show why the contributors are so generally averse to such payments; and the superiority in this respect of excise and customs duties, in which the tax being identified with the cost of the article is forgotten by the purchasers. But, apart from their unpopularity, the assessed taxes are as little objectionable as any duties of the kind can possibly be. And in our view of the matter, it would be good policy to augment them, by reviving the house-tax, and increasing the window-duty, so that a reve-nue might be raised to enable the duties on glass, bricks, cotton wool, &c., to be wholly repealed. The industry of the country and the well-being of all classes would be pro-moted by such commutation.

Duty on Plate.—In order partly to prevent fraud, and partly for the purpose of collecting a revenue, the manufacture of plate is placed under certain regulations. Those who carry it on are obliged to take out a licence, renewable annually, which costs from 2*l.* 6*s.* to 5*l.* 15*s.* Assay offices are established in different places; and any one selling any article previously to its having been assayed and marked forfeits 50*l.* No plate is passed at the assay offices, unless it be of the fineness of the old standard, or 11 oz. and 2 dwts., or of the new standard of 11 oz. and 10 dwts. Gold plate, with the exception of watch-cases, pays a duty of 17*s.* per ounce, and silver plate a duty of 1*s.* 6*d.* per ounce; but watch-cases, chains, tippings, mountings, collars, bottle tickets, teaspoons, &c., are exempted. The offence of counterfeiting, or the transference from one piece of plate to another of, the marks, stamps, &c., impressed on plate by the assayers, was formerly felony without the benefit of clergy; but is now punishable by transportation or imprisonment.

Besides being imposed on articles of luxury and ostentation, the duties on plate have been supposed to be advantageous by their serving as a guarantee for the genuineness of the articles on which they are imposed. It has, however, been alleged that the marks of the assayers are so easily counterfeited that the duty has an opposite effect; and that by making the buyers confide in them, it not unfrequently procures a ready sale at full prices for articles that are very much alloyed. There may probably be some truth in this statement; though on the whole the duty certainly helps to prevent the public from being cheated. Those who wish for perfect security should resort only to shops of established character and respectability. About 1,050,000 oz. silver plate, and 7,000 oz. gold, are retained for home consumption in the United Kingdom. In 1843 the duty produced 63,224*l.* This duty is also under the management of the Board of Stamps and Taxes.

Tolls, Port Dues, &c.—We briefly noticed in the Introduction to this work the modes that have been successively adopted for the construction and repair of the public roads ; and as nothing, perhaps, contributes so much to the improvement of a country as good roads, their formation and repair are objects of primary importance.   The funds for these objects are now usually provided, at least as far as respects the great lines, by tolls levied on the goods, carriages, horses, &c., passing along the roads; and if the tolls be kept within due limits, and the produce be judiciously and economically laid out, there is nothing to object to in their payment.   "When," says Dr. Smith, "the carriages which pass over a highway or a bridge, and the lighters which sail upon a navigable canal, pay toll in proportion to their weight or their tonnage, they pay for the maintenance of those public works exactly in proportion to the wear and tear which they occasion of them.   It seems scarcely possible to invent a more equitable way of maintaining such works.   This tax or toll, too, though it is advanced by the carrier, is finally paid by the consumer, to whom it must always be charged in the price of the goods.   As the expense of carriage, however, is very much reduced by means of such public works, the goods, notwithstanding the toll, come cheaper to the consumer than they could otherwise have done; their price not being so much raised by the toll, as it is lowered by the cheapness of the carriage.   The person who finally pays this tax, therefore, gains by the application more than he loses by the payment of it.   His payment is exactly in proportion to his gain. It is in reality no more than a part of that gain which he is obliged to give up in order to get the rest.   It seems impossible to imagine a more equitable method of raising a tax.

" When the toll upon carriages of luxury, upon coaches, post chaises, &c., is made somewhat higher in proportion to their weight than upon carriages of necessary use, such as carts, waggons, &c., the indolence and vanity of the rich are made to contribute, in a very easy manner, to the relief of the

poor, by rendering cheaper the transportation of goods to all
the different parts of the country."*

But, if tolls were imposed, not to furnish a fund for con-
structing and repairing the roads, but to yield a revenue to
government, their influence would be widely different. They
would then form a species of internal customs that would be
a very great incumbrance on trade; and if they were charged
according to the bulk and weight of the goods, which seem
to be the only indexes that can be resorted to in determining
the amount of tolls, they would become most unequal and
partial in their operation; and would fall with most oppressive
severity on the raw produce of the soil, coal, manure, and
other bulky articles of comparatively small value; while they
would have a slight and, indeed, almost imperceptible influence over most species of manufactured goods.

In backward and thinly-peopled districts, where it might
be impossible either to construct or keep up roads by means
of tolls, it may notwithstanding be expedient, with a view to
the general interests of the empire, that roads should be constructed; and in such cases their cost should be defrayed
partly and principally by the public, but partly also by a
small tax on the lands and houses of the districts in which
they are situated. It is obvious that the roads in the Highlands could not have been made, and, after being made,
could not have been kept up, by the produce of any tolls it
would have been practicable to levy. Indeed the imposition
of tolls on the roads in unfrequented districts is, in most
cases, inexpedient; and, if assessed, they should always be
at a very low rate. The excessive multiplication of tolls
in Wales, and the oppression thence arising, were among
the prominent causes of the late disturbances in the principality.

The above remarks apply with little variation to the
charges on shipping, for lights, harbour dues, &c. Everybody knows that these are of the greatest consequence to the
security of shipping and the dispatch of navigation, provided

* Wealth of Nations, p. 326.

the charges on their account be confined within moderate limits. But if they pass these their influence is very different: they then tempt the navigator to quit secure but expensive for more dangerous but cheaper channels. *Avara manus portus claudit; et cum digitos contrahit, navium simul vela concludit: meritò enim illa mercatores cuncti refugiunt quæ sibi dispendia esse cognoscunt.**

Exclusive of tolls, duties are charged on travelling either by public carriages or by private carriages drawn by post-horses. The duty on stage-carriages consists of a licence duty of 5*l*. a-year, and of a *mileage*, or duty of so much per mile travelled over, according to the number of passengers the carriage is licensed to carry, rising from 1*d*. per mile for four persons to 4*d*. per mile for twenty-one. This duty, and the duty of five per cent. on all sums received by railway companies for the conveyance of passengers, produced, in 1842, 444,214*l*. 11*s*. 4*d*. nett revenue. The duty on post-horses is very heavy, being 1½*d*. per horse, or 3*d*. per pair per mile travelled, and there is besides a licence duty of 7*s*. 6*d*. on every person letting a horse for hire, and of 5*l*. on every four-wheeled carriage, and of 3*l*. on every two-wheeled ditto. The post-horse duty produced, in 1842, 179,457*l*., inclusive of licences. Hackney-coaches are charged with a licence duty of 5*l*., and with a further payment of 10*s*. per week: both duties produced, in 1842, 54,872*l*.

It seems very difficult to vindicate the policy of these duties. Unlike the revenue derived from tolls, no part of their produce is appropriated to the construction and repair of the roads. And, notwithstanding it is admitted on all hands that whatever facilitates the intercourse between different parts of the country is of the greatest advantage, these duties make it more expensive, and consequently more limited than it otherwise would be. Taxes so opposed to the plainest principles and most desirable results should be got rid of as soon as practicable.

The duty on sea-borne coal, though charged at the ports

* Cassiod., lib. vii., cap. 9.

of importation, was properly a home or inland duty. It was originally imposed in the reign of William III., and was continued down to 1831, when it was finally repealed. After being long stationary at 5s. per chaldron, it was increased during the late war to 9s. 4d. per chaldron, but was reduced in 1824 to 6s. Scotland enjoyed for a considerable period an exemption from this tax, which fell principally on the metropolis and the southern parts of England, which are almost wholly dependent on water-borne coal.

This tax was in the highest degree partial and oppressive; partial because it only affected those parts of the empire to which coals had to be carried by sea; and oppressive because it added full 50 per cent. to the price paid to the coal-owner for an important necessary of life and the most efficient instrument of manufacturing industry. But it is needless to dwell on the demerits of a tax so contradictory of all principle, and so mischievous in its operation. Indeed, as Smith has justly stated, " if a bounty could in any case be reasonable, it might perhaps be so upon the transportation of coals from those parts of the country in which they abound to those in which they are wanted." *

It is to be regretted that when the coal-tax was repealed in 1831, a local duty on the coal brought by sea to London should have been retained to defray the cost of certain improvements in that city. It is more than doubtful whether a farther reduction in the price of coal would not be a more desirable improvement than any the duty is kept up to effect.†

* Wealth of Nations, p. 395.

† The repeal of the duty on sea-borne coal was preceded, and perhaps promoted, by a pamphlet by the author of this work entitled 'Observations on the Duty on Sea-borne Coal and on the Peculiar Duties and Charges on Coal in the Port of London,' 8vo., 1830.

CHAPTER VII.

STAMP AND LEGACY DUTIES.

SECT. I.—STAMP-DUTIES.

THESE duties form the third great branch of revenue in the United Kingdom, being the next most important after the Customs and Excise. They are imposed on written or printed instruments; and derive their name from the paper or other material being commonly impressed with a stamp showing the amount of the duty paid.

Many stamp-duties have no connexion with one another, beyond that of the mode in which the duty is levied, and have nothing in common in their policy or effect. Among others they include duties on newspapers; on policies of assurance; on appointments to offices of various kinds; on the grants of dignities and marks of distinction (the least objectionable of all taxes); on the certificates and licences which are required to the exercise of certain professions or trades, as those of attorney, appraiser, pawnbroker, and issuer of bank-notes. But the most important are the stamp-duties on the different kinds of conveyances and leases, mortgages, bonds, and settlements, and on the deeds and written instruments by which contracts are made or authenticated, and the duties (which are classed among the stamp-duties) on legacies and successions of certain kinds from a testator or from a person dying intestate.

The stamp-duties on " the instruments of conveyance, contract, obligation, and security for money," are, in effect, taxes on the sale and transfer of property, and on the authentication of the evidence of other contracts, and (as the law

T

in some cases makes writing essential to the validity of a contract) on the contracts themselves.

Taxes on the sale and transfer of property would be more objectionable than they are if the doctrine of Smith were true, that they fall wholly on the seller, and are paid out of the wreck of his fortune: "Taxes upon the sale of land," he observes, "fall altogether upon the seller. The seller is almost always under the necessity of selling, and must therefore take such a price as he can get. The buyer is scarcely ever under the necessity of buying; he will, therefore, only give such a price as he likes. He considers what the land will cost him in tax and price together. The more he is obliged to pay in the way of tax, the less he will be disposed to give in the way of price. Such taxes, therefore, fall almost always upon a necessitous person, and must, therefore, be frequently very cruel and oppressive."— (p. 389.)

But in the sales of fixed as of other property, there is a competition among buyers as well as among sellers. There are those who wish to buy estates as well as those who wish to sell them—money seeking an investment as well as land seeking a purchaser. A grocer must sell the tea and sugar in his shop, and no one needs buy either of him; but would it, therefore, be correct to say that he paid the duties on these articles? Notwithstanding the assent it has so generally received, the assertion of Smith would not be in any degree correct but for the circumstance of there being some kinds of property, or investment, such as funded property and the stocks of some of the great corporations, exempted wholly or in part from the duties on sales.* But despite the disturbing influence of these untaxed investments, and the occasional occurrence of "forced sales," a large proportion of the tax on the sale of lands certainly falls on the purchasers. In considering the expediency of sales, of which there are many for the purpose of division or convenience, the probable nett

* A transfer of Bank Stock or South-Sea Stock is subject to a duty only of 7s. 9d., a transfer of East India Stock to a duty of 30s.

produce is as closely weighed by the owners as the probable
return by intended purchasers, and any burthen on the
transfer keeps land as well as buyers out of the market.

The only good objection to taxes on the transfer of land
is that they obstruct transactions useful to the community.

It is an admitted principle, that every facility should be
given to the conveyance and exchange of all kinds of property, inasmuch as that is the most likely means to make
it find its way into the hands of those who will employ it
most advantageously. "Why," asks M. Say, "does an individual wish to sell his land? It is because he has another
employment in view in which his funds will be more productive. Why does another wish to purchase this same
land? it is to employ a capital which brings him too little,
which was unemployed, or the use of which he thinks susceptible of improvement. This exchange will increase the
general income, since it increases the income of these parties.
But if the charges are so exorbitant as to prevent the exchange, they are an obstacle to this increase of the general
income."*

The influence of the stamp-duty on conveyances in this
country has not, however, been sufficient materially to im-
pede transfers; and if it were imposed on fair principles,
a very considerable revenue might be raised by it without
complaint, or, at all events, without much legitimate cause
for complaint.

A tax on the transfer of property should bear a uniform
proportion to the value of the property transferred; and
the burden which it imposes should be, in part at least,
compensated by assessing the tax so as to facilitate and
authenticate the transactions on which it is charged, and to
render them less hazardous to the parties concerned. The
mode of levying this tax resorted to in many countries
of Europe, where it is imposed on registration, under a
system adapted to facilitate the proofs of transfer, and to

* Ricardo, Principles, &c., p. 167, 3rd edit.; and Say, Traité d'Economie
Politique, tome ii., p. 351.

guard against fraudulent conveyances, seems to secure these
advantages, and to be the best hitherto suggested.

In England, however, nothing of this kind is done or
attempted. The stamps are merely bought at a stationer's,
and instead of affording any security against fraud, or
facility to fair transactions, they multiply the chances of
invalidity and expense. The construction of the acts imposing the duties is in many cases extremely difficult; and
to obviate the mistakes thence arising, it is in most instances permitted to have improperly stamped instruments
re-stamped on payment of a moderate penalty. But this
indulgence goes but a very short way to remedy the evils to
which the obscurity of the law gives rise. There is not (as
there should be) any officer at the Stamp-Office, or elsewhere, competent to determine what are or what are not the
proper stamps to employ. This important information—so
important to the ends of justice and to the avoidance of
litigation—can be learned only when instruments are produced as matters of evidence in courts of justice. But if a
mistake has been committed, it is then too late to rectify it;
and if the court decide, which it sometimes does, after long
argument and consideration, that the instrument is improperly stamped, it is rejected. Many instruments which
have been stamped under the advice of experienced lawyers
have, when offered in evidence, met this fate because of the
insufficiency of the stamp; the whole expense of the litigation in the course of which the evidence is tendered being
thus often thrown on parties who never meditated or imagined
they were committing a fraud on the revenue.

In Chitty's Treatise on the Stamp Laws, published in
1841, there are references to no fewer than 616 cases in
regard to stamps to be found in the printed reports, and the
number has since greatly increased and is continually increasing, without, it is said, much conducing to the certainty
of the law! The stamp-duties, therefore, in their present
form, wholly want that compensating quality which has
often been ascribed to them (and with which they might be

endowed), of giving increased security to transactions. On the contrary, one would think they had been intended to serve as decoys with which to entrap parties, and force them into the courts: the difficulty which they create of determining what is and what is not a proper stamp, is itself a most prolific source of uncertainty, and consequently of litigation and expense.

The stamp-duties press also in their present form with undue severity on small transactions: their inequality is generally, indeed, admitted, but the *degree* of inequality will not be fairly appreciated without looking beyond the mere inequality of the *ad valorem* duties to the actual business of a transfer of property on a sale.

Of the instruments for conveyance, contract, and security, some are charged with *ad valorem* duties, professedly bearing some proportion to the expressed price or amount of the subject matter, as conveyances by way of sale, mortgages, bonds, settlements of money, or funded property, leases, and others of less importance. Other instruments are specially charged without an *ad valorem* scale, and (subject to some few exemptions) all deeds not specially charged are subject to a stamp-duty of 1*l*. 15*s*., with an additional charge of 1*l*. 5*s*. for every entire number of 1080 words beyond the first like number.

In cases where an attempt is made to impose *ad valorem* stamp-duties, the mode in which it has been executed is frequently very imperfect. Of the stamps on conveyances, the lowest which attaches where the purchase-money does not amount to 20*l*. is 10*s*.; where the purchase-money amounts to 20*l*. and not to 50*l*., 1*l*.; where 50*l*. and not amounting to 150*l*., 1*l*. 10*s*.; and there are twenty-three other enumerated stamps rising in amount by unequal steps, the highest being 1000*l*., where the purchase-money is 100,000*l*., beyond which, however high the purchase-money may rise, the tax does not increase. The general idea on which the scale was founded appears to have been to impose a tax of one per cent. at an average; but from the notion that it would be troublesome to provide separate stamps for every amount, or for comparatively near amounts, of purchase-money, the tax on some purchases is much above, and on others much below the average. The tax on a purchase where the price is 1000*l.* is 12*l.*, and no greater duty attaches where the price is 1999*l.* 19*s.* 11¾*d.*; but if it be increased to 2000*l.*, the duty is more than double, viz., 25*l.*, a difference of ¼*d.* in the price making a difference of 13*l.* in the tax! So it is in many other cases. The duty too on the smallest transactions is disproportionally high; and because it is presumed that those above 100,000*l.* are not of every-day occurrence, they are disregarded.

This is obviously a very rude and unfair application of the law of average. What consolation is it to A, who has paid 12*l.* on a conveyance stamp on a purchase of the value of 1000*l.*, that B has paid no more on a purchase of 1500*l.*, or C on one of 1999*l.*? The former might not object to the tax, provided all purchasers were equally affected by it; but it is plain to him, and to every one else, that he has been unjustly treated in the mode of its assessment.

At the same time we attach no weight to the statements made in the House of Commons and elsewhere, by those who have adduced instances of the irregularity apparent in the scale of conveyance stamps as evidence of the deliberate injustice of the wealthy classes by whom the business of legislation is said to be monopolized. There are no grounds whatever for believing that the "wealthy classes" had anything to do in the matter, or that the inequality arose from any worse motives than the desire to save the Stamp-Office the trouble, inconsiderable as it would be, of keeping a greater variety of stamps; and the undue neglect of the numerous cases of harshness on the one hand, and of partiality on the other, to which the application in charging duties by average scales, with wide intervals, necessarily gives rise. In truth and reality, however, the injustice of the duties is felt most in the case of those stamps to which the *ad valorem* principle is not applied.

In the case of the smallest conveyance of freehold land in possession, the law of England formerly required a double conveyance by lease and release, a fictitious possession under the lease being a substitute for the livery of seisin or feudal investiture. This absurdity is removed by a recent statute, the 4th Victoria, "*for rendering a Release as effectual for the conveyance of freehold estates as a Lease and Release by the same parties;*" but this Act expressly provides that the stamp-duty which would have been paid on the two instruments must still be paid on the one.* In the case of a 20*l.* purchase of freehold the stamp on the lease was the same as on the release, so that the duty was and still is 2*l.*, or 10 per cent. on the value; while in the 200,000*l.* or 300,000*l.* purchase (as on all conveyances of 150*l.* and upwards) the stamp is only 1*l.* 15*s.*, a fraction of the value too inconsiderable to deserve notice.

It often happens also in conveyances of properties of small amount, that besides this double (or doubly-stamped) conveyance, other deeds are required, as assignments or surrenders of terms and covenants for the production of title-deeds; and it is of importance to observe that the stamps on these deeds are the same, whether the purchase is 20*l.* or 200,000*l.* In the smaller purchases this expense prevents many purchasers availing themselves of whatever security or advantage may be derived from these deeds. But still the actual expense of the stamps on purchases of small amount is often very formidable, and in all cases very much heavier in proportion to the purchase-money than on large transactions.

As those contracts for the repayment of money which are subjected to stamp-duties, as bonds or mortgages, form a part only, and probably not the largest part of contracts of this kind (a practical exemption from duty being enjoyed by the rest), it is probable that Adam Smith's position is true in its application to these duties, that they really fall on the bor-

* The Act of last session, " for facilitating the transfer of property," which appears to have been intended to supersede the 4th Victoria, contains the like provision.

rower, by whom they are in practice paid.   But if all contracts of this kind were taxed, there is no reason to suppose
that the tax should be wholly borne by either of the contracting parties—the borrowers or lenders—between both
of which classes there is the same competition as in the case
of sales.

The stamp-duties on bonds or mortgages, so far as securities for large sums are concerned, are not so high as to
form any serious obstruction to the transactions on which
they fall.

The inequality of these duties is, however, more glaring
than that of the duties on conveyances by way of sale,
and they would, indeed, appear to be studiously unfair.
On any mortgage or bond for a sum under 50*l.* the stamp
is 1*l.*; for a sum exceeding 50*l.* and not exceeding 100*l.*,
1*l.* 10*s.*; for a sum exceeding 100*l.* and not exceeding 200*l.*,
2*l.*; for 200*l.* and not exceeding 300*l.*, 3*l.*; for 300*l.* and
not exceeding 500*l.*, 4*l.*   After this there are several strides
in the scale : on a sum exceeding 15,000*l.* and not exceeding 20,000*l.* the stamp is 20*l.*, and for any sum exceeding
20,000*l.*, however large, the stamp is 25*l.* only.   The *ad
valorem* stamp on a 50*l.* mortgage or bond (to say nothing
of smaller sums) is 2*l.* per cent., while on 20,000*l.* it is only
1-10th per cent., and on 100,000*l.* (an amount by no means
uncommon in mortgages), 1-40th per cent.   The rate of the
ad valorem duty, therefore, is 80 times as great on the security for 50*l.* as on that for 100,000*l.* !

In the case of mortgages, the observations on the pressure
of the duties on the incidental deeds which usually accompany the transfer of property, apply with the same force as
in the case of conveyances on a sale, for many of these deeds
frequently accompany mortgages for moderate sums, and
aggravate the inequality of the scale.

The scale of duties on leases, besides the apparent disregard (amounting in truth to contempt) for the lower class
of contributors, is most objectionable, as discouraging these

contracts, the importance of which all statesmen are now ready to admit. The duty where the yearly rent does not amount to 20*l*. is 1*l*., and where 20*l*. and not 100*l*., 1*l*. 10*s*.; the maximum duty, being that charged on a rent of 1000*l*. and upwards, is 10*l*. The counterpart or duplicate of the lease of the lowest class is charged with the same duty as the lease; while the counterpart of all other leases is charged with 1*l*. 10*s*. The duty, therefore, on a lease and counterpart at 10*l*. rent is 2*l*. or 20*l*. per cent. on the rental; whereas the duty on a rent of 1000*l*. a-year is 11*l*. 10*s*., or little more than 1*l*. per cent., and on 2000*l*. a-year little more than ½ per cent.

It is admitted, we believe, that there would be no great difficulty in charging the *ad valorem* duties in exact proportion to the price; and, at all events, there can be no difficulty whatever in lessening the intervals of the scale, and making the duties attach fairly to the higher transactions. And such being the case, it will be curious to see how long the present system will be permitted to continue.

The unequal operation of the duty on those deeds which are " not specially charged," that is, on those on which the fixed duty of 1*l*. 15*s*. is indiscriminately imposed, may be in part collected from the previous observations on conveyances and mortgages. But the inequality is severely felt in many other cases. The value of the contracts which are evidenced by deeds differs as much as the value of estates which are the subject of conveyance. All that can be said in favour of uniformity in the tax on deeds is, that the value of the contracts to which they relate could not generally be ascertained with facility or certainty. But where a tax of fixed amount is imposed on subjects so unequal, it is the duty of the legislature to take care that it be not so heavy as to be oppressive to the lowest and most numerous class of tax-payers.

Heavy taxes on instruments of contract are open to objections similar to those which were successfully urged by

Bentham against taxes on legal proceedings. They do not, indeed, prevent a man who has been injured from seeking legal redress, but they prevent the perpetuation of the evidence by which alone redress can be obtained, and sometimes load him with the expense of a fruitless litigation. They are taxes on those who have to bring themselves within the pale of the law ; and many of them, like taxes on law proceedings, fall on the tax-payer at the moment of his greatest need.

The head of settlements in the stamp-duty schedule is more remarkable for what it omits than for what it includes. The only subject matters of settlement charged by the schedule are "definite and certain sums of money," and "definite and certain" amounts of the Government funds, or Bank, East India, or South Sea stock.

On these the scale of duties is about the same as on mortgages, the highest being 25*l.* where the sum or value is 20,000*l.* or upwards, but the lowest stamp is out of all proportion to this, being 1*l.* 15*s.* on all sums or values below 1000*l.*

All other kinds of personal property and all landed property are exempted from any special tax on donation *inter vivos* or settlement, except that the deeds by which such donations or settlements are made are subject to the duties (before mentioned) on deeds not specially charged.

The settlement of landed property is undoubtedly, however, one of the fairest subjects for taxation. The same considerations which show the policy of facilitating transfers on sale, show the propriety of taxing the settlement of land. The objects of a settlement are to withdraw land from commerce, and (sometimes also) to protect it from the claims of creditors; to retain it in the family of the owner in spite of their extravagance or incapacity; and to make it pass to the children in spite of the debts and incumbrances of the usufructuary possessor. The owner of property may, on the occasion of his marriage, settle it on his wife and family, retaining full power, if he please, of directing the mode of

division among them; and it is thenceforth free from the
consequences of his subsequent debts, even though credit be
given him on the supposition that he is still the real proprietor of the estate, of which, of course, he often continues
so ostensibly. Whether the policy of the law which enables
a man to procure this immunity for his family be or be not
expedient, needs not here be discussed. It is, at all events,
of a very questionable character; and it can scarcely be
denied that a settlement by act *inter vivos* is one of those
dealings with property, or luxuries of the rich, on which a
high duty may be most justly levied.

Another circumstance connected with settlements of estates
deserves special notice in reference to a system of taxation.
It is not now necessary to the validity of such settlements in
England that they be in anywise registered. And such is the
law, that if the absolute owner of land settle it on the occasion
of his marriage, and subsequently sell it for a full price to a
person wholly ignorant of the previous settlement (and it is
only by accident that it can be known to any one but its
author), the purchaser may be evicted by the wife or children! These cases occasionally occur, and that they are
not more frequent is not owing to any effort of the legislature to prevent them. As a settlement on marriage
is generally unaccompanied by any change of possession, as
in the case of sale, or by any delivery of the deeds, as in the
case of mortgage, the making provision for the registration
of settlements would appear to be one of the most obvious
duties of the legislature, whatever may be done in the case
of other instruments.

The only tenable ground on which the exemption of settlements of land from taxation may be at present defended
is the impossibility of ascertaining the value of the property
on the face of the instrument, by which alone the sufficiency
of stamps is now determined. But if registration were
indispensable to the validity of a settlement, there would be
no difficulty on this head. It would be sufficient probably
to provide that the settler should make a declaration in re-

gard to value, and should be subject to surcharge in case of fraudulent misstatement. The duty should be paid not on the deed, but on the registration.

To recapitulate the improvements which the stamp-duties on the instruments of conveyance, contract, and security, require, they appear to be, 1, a simplification of the acts imposing the duties, so as to lessen the chances of litigation from the use of improper stamps; 2, a just adaptation of the principle of *ad valorem* duties to the stamps on conveyances, mortgages, and leases, by imposing an equal percentage on the consideration, money, debt, or rent (however high or low the amount); 3, a considerable reduction of the duty which is now indiscriminately charged on all deeds not specially charged, and other deeds where the value of the contract or matter cannot be ascertained; and 4, the imposition of such a duty on settlements as might, besides compensating for whatever loss might be sustained by the other reductions, yield an additional revenue.

A step in the way of improvement has been made by a recent Act, 7 & 8 Vict. c. 21, by which the stamps on short agreements have been reduced from 20*s.* to 2*s.* 6*d.*

Stamp-duties on the voluntary sale of commodities fall, like other taxes on them, wholly on the consumer; for, unless such were the case, the commodities would not be offered for sale subsequently to the imposition of the duties. Thus, the duties on cards, dice, and newspapers are paid by those who buy them. Such duties differ in no respect, so far as regards their incidence, from the excise-duties laid on commodities.

The duty on advertisements is sometimes paid by one party and sometimes by another. Where advertising is necessary to the prosecution of a business, such, for example, as that of a publisher, the duty adds proportionally to the cost of the works he sells, and is, of course, paid by the public. Generally, however, it acts unequally, and sometimes oppressively. Can anything be more anomalous or unjust than to impose the same duty on a notice of the publication of a sixpenny pamphlet, or of a servant wanting a place, as on that of the sale of a valuable estate? Inasmuch, however, as it would be quite impracticable to assess a duty of this sort on an *ad valorem* principle, the injustice cannot be obviated so long as it is kept up. It were, therefore, to be wished, as well with a view to the getting rid of its inequality, as for permitting the free circulation of information important to all classes, that the advertisement duty were repealed. It is now, however, much less heavy than formerly; having been reduced, in 1833, from 3s. 6d. to 1s. 6d. per advertisement. In 1843 it produced 127,832l.

Perhaps the duty on fire-insurance is the most objectionable of the existing stamp-duties. It amounts to 3s. per cent. on all property insured; whereas the premium paid to insurance-offices for common risks is only 1s. 6d. per cent., or half the duty; so that, if a person wish to insure 1000l. on a dwelling-house, shop, warehouse, or other commonly hazardous property, he pays 15s. to an insurance-office as an indemnification for the risk, and 30s. to government for leave to enter into the transaction! So exorbitant a duty cannot be too severely condemned. It discourages that providence and foresight, the encouragement of which should be an object with all prudent governments; and it is the cause that much property is not insured, and that what is insured is not sufficiently covered. Every individual, in fact, who insures any commonly hazardous property, is obliged to pay three times as much as the risk is really worth. Under such circumstances the wonder certainly is, not that a great deal of property is uninsured, but that such is not the case with a great deal more. Seeing the vast importance of insurance, it may well be doubted whether it should be charged with any duty, however light. But were the duty fixed at 1s. or 9d. per cent., or at two-thirds or half the premium, its influence in repressing insurance would not be very sensible, and the increase of business occasioned by such reduction of the duty would be so great, that it may be fairly presumed the reduced duty would in a few years yield nearly as large a revenue as is derived from the present exorbitant duty.

But despite the obstructions which its magnitude throws in the way of insurance, it appears from the official accounts that the duty received on policies of insurance against fire amounted, for the United Kingdom, in 1843, to 987,339*l.*, which, if the duty were universally 3*s.* per cent., would show that the property insured amounted to the prodigious sum of 658,226,000*l.*; but, as several of the risks are unusually hazardous, the property insured (for which duty is paid) is not so great as might be inferred from this statement, and does not, perhaps, exceed 500,000,000*l.*; a sum which, vast as it is, would very probably in a few years be doubled, or more, were the duty reduced to 1*s.* per cent. Insurances on farm-stock, barn-yards, &c., are exempted from the duty, and do not, therefore, appear in the above estimate of insured property.

The tax upon policies of marine insurance varies according to the amount of the premium. During the late war this tax was raised to a very high rate; and as this was the only country in which, at that period, insurances could be effected, it produced a large amount of revenue. But after the peace, insurances even on British ships began, in consequence of the magnitude of the duty, to be effected in Holland, Hamburgh, and elsewhere. To prevent the loss of an important branch of business, and of the revenue arising therefrom, Lord Althorp took, in 1834, fifty per cent. from the duties; and instead of being reduced, their produce was increased by this effectual diminution. The tax, however, was still too high; and the revenue of late years has been again decreasing. But the judicious reductions that were effected in the duties by the Act of last session (7 and 8 Victoria, c. 21), especially in those on the inferior risks, will most probably occasion a revival of the business, and a less sacrifice of revenue than might have been anticipated.

The tax on receipts, or acquittances for money, was introduced into this country in 1795. It is charged according
to an *ad valorem* scale, which, however, is not fairly applied,
the duty pressing with much greater severity on small than
on large sums. Previously to 1833 all receipts for sums
between 2*l.* (at which point the tax commenced) and under
5*l.* were charged with a duty of 2*d.*; but in that year receipts for sums below 5*l.* were exempted from the duty,
which is at present 3*d.* on sums of 5*l.* and under 10*l.*, and
6*d.* on sums of 10*l.* and under 20*l.*, &c.

Latterly it has, we understand, been proposed to repeal the existing receipt duty, and replace it by a uniform
duty of 1*d.* charged indiscriminately on all receipts. But
there can, we apprehend, be little doubt that a project of
this sort would occasion a considerable loss of revenue,
without being productive of any compensating advantage.
Probably, however, it might answer were it limited to
receipts for sums under 10*l.* Most persons who have to pay
bills of 10*l.* and upwards, require a stamped receipt as
evidence of the payment; but stamped receipts for sums
below 10*l.* are very frequently dispensed with, though if
they were made to apply to all sums under that amount
and above 1*l.*, and limited to 1*d.*, it is pretty certain they
would be used to an incomparably greater extent than at
present.

It has also been proposed to subject all checks drawn on
bankers to a uniform stamp-duty of 1*d.* or 2*d.*; and this,
perhaps, is a less exceptionable project than the former.
But the imposition of an equal duty on the transfer of sums
of every magnitude is essentially unfair, though from its
limited amount its unfairness might not be much felt or
objected to. Apart, however, from these considerations, it
may be doubted whether the revenue to be derived from
such taxes would compensate for the trouble and inconvenience they would entail on the public.

Stamp-duties were first levied in Holland. Most of the

accustomed methods of taxation having been resorted to, the
republic, in order to provide additional funds for carrying on
her contest with the Spanish monarchy, offered a considerable reward to any one who should devise the best new tax.
Among many other taxes, that of the *vectigal chartæ*, or
stamp-duty, was suggested ; and having been approved of,
it was introduced by an ordinance issued in 1624, setting
forth its necessity, and the benefits which it was supposed
would result from its imposition. *   Since that period stamp-
duties have become almost universal, and now form a very
prominent branch of the revenue of almost every country ;
affording a striking example of the justice of Smith's caustic
remark, that " there is no art which one government sooner
learns of another than that of draining money from the
pockets of the people." They, however, deserved to be
copied ; being, when imposed on fair principles, and not
carried to too great a height, a most legitimate source of
revenue.

Stamp-duties were introduced into England in 1671, by
a statute entitled " An Act for laying Impositions on Proceedings at Law." The duties were at first granted for nine
years only, and were afterwards continued for three years
more, when they were allowed to expire. They were again
revived in 1693, and have since been gradually and greatly
increased.

SECTION II.——LEGACY-DUTIES,

Or duties on the transfer of property from the dead to the
living, are now a very common species of tax. The *vicesima
hereditatum*, or twentieth penny of inheritances, imposed by
Augustus on the Romans, is the earliest example of a tax on
successions. Dion Cassius (lib. lv.) informs us that this duty
was laid on all successions, legacies, and donations in case
of death, except upon those to the nearest relations and to
the poor. Pliny has given some of the reasons for this exception; in speaking of the *vicesima*, he calls it *tributum*

* Beckman's ' History of Inventions,' vol. i., p. 379, Eng. Trans.

tolerabile et facile hæredibus duntaxat extraneis, domesticis grave. And a little after he adds, *Itaque illis* (that is strangers) *irrogatum, his* (that is near relations) *remissum, videlicet, quod manifestum erat, quanto cum dolore laturi, seu potius non laturi homines essent, distringi aliquid et abradi bonis, quæ sanguine, gentilitate, sacrorum denique societate meruissent, quæque nunquam ut aliena et speranda, sed ut sua semperque possessa, ac deinceps proximo cuique transmittenda, cepissent.* (*Panegyricus,* cap. 37.) In addition to these reasons for exempting the successions of near relations from the *vicesima,* it has been said that the death of a father is seldom attended with any increase, and frequently with a considerable diminution, of revenue to such of his children as live in the same house with him ; and that when this is the case, the burdening of his inheritance with a tax must plainly be a galling and cruel aggravation of their loss. But, on the other hand, it not unfrequently happens that the death of masters of families places fortunes at the disposal of their children or other descendants ; and, on the whole, there seems to be no good ground, provided the duty be moderate, for exempting them from its influence. Those on whom an unexpected or remote inheritance devolves are glad to accept it on any condition ; and uniformly pay such duties as may be laid on it with greater good will than any other impost whatever.

The principal objection to taxes on successions, or on the transfer of property from the dead to the living, depends, it is said, on the circumstance of their falling wholly on capital, without probably occasioning any effort to replace it, either by increased exertion or economy. " If," says Mr. Ricardo, " a legacy of 1000*l.* be subject to a tax of 100*l.*, the legatee considers his legacy as only 900*l.*, and feels no particular motive to save the 100*l.* of duty from his expenditure ; whereas, had he received the 1000*l.*, and been required to pay the 100*l.* by means of a tax on income, on wine, on horses, or on servants, he would probably have diminished, or rather not increased, his expenditure by that sum, and the capital of the country would have been unimpaired."* It might, however, be exceedingly inexpedient to impose or increase any one of the taxes suggested by Mr. Ricardo; and, provided the tax on successions be kept within due limits, we doubt whether the considerations he has stated be entitled to much weight. The slender influence of the tax over the legatee is, perhaps, correctly stated by Mr. Ricardo; but then it is to be borne in mind that the individual who leaves property is aware that it will be subjected to the tax, and he, consequently, has an additional motive to save and amass in order that his heirs may not be prejudiced by its payment. And this circumstance, and the fact of the tax being imposed when the contributors are receiving money or other property, and, consequently, when it is most convenient for them to pay it, appears to be a sufficient answer to the objections against it.

The taxes on successions and legacies in Great Britain are of three kinds: some species of property being subject only to one of these taxes; some to two; while some are altogether exempt.

The first of these taxes, or that commonly called the probate duty, is imposed on the whole mass of the personal property, including leaseholds for years, of every person who has not died intestate, and which may be recoverable under the authority of the probate, or other analogous instrument.

The second, or the duty on letters of administration, is a corresponding tax on the whole mass of the personal property, including leaseholds, of a person dying intestate, recoverable under the letters of administration.

From such one of these taxes as applies to the case no part of the personal property of the deceased, within the jurisdiction of the court by which the probate or administration is granted, is exempted.

The third, or legacy duty, is imposed not only on legacies, but on the residue of the personal property of a testator, or

* Principles of Political Economy, 1st edit., p. 191.

person dying intestate, which may become divisible among his next of kin. It also falls (which the probate and administration duties do not) on the produce of the sale of land directed by will to be sold,* on moneys charged by will, on real estate, whether as gross sums or as annuities.

The duties on probates and administrations do not in any case attach on real or heritable property, or to any interest in it, not being a leasehold interest; and real and heritable property is also exempted from the legacy duty, except under special circumstances. Where the will directs a sale of real estate, or directs money to be raised out of real estate, or charges it with legacies or annuities, the produce of the sale, or the estate itself, if it remain unsold—the money directed to be raised, and the legacies or annuities, as the case may be, are subject to the legacy duty. But no estate or interest in land, given without a charge or direction for conversion, is subject to the tax. Thus, if a testator give his real estate to his children, or to others, in shares, they escape; but if he direct that it be sold for the purpose of a division of the proceeds among them, they become subject to the tax: indeed they must, in the case now supposed, pay it, though they should agree among themselves to divide the land without a sale.†

The probate and administration duties are imposed without reference to the parties to whom the beneficial residue under the will or intestacy may be found to belong. They are proportioned only (so far as they are proportioned at all) to the gross mass of the personal property on which they attach. But, unluckily, these duties are not imposed accord-

* Debts owing to the deceased by persons resident abroad, and other personal property abroad, are not subject to the *probate or administration* duties, as they are not recoverable under our probate or administration. But all the personal property, wherever situate, of a British subject domiciled in Great Britain, is subject to the legacy duty.

† This difference, which seems so very capricious, was made on the strength of the argument, by which the general tax on successions to real estate was defeated; viz., that a tax on land devised or descended would entail the inconvenience of a sale or mortgage; for this objection could not apply where the testator had himself directed the land to be sold or charged.

ing to the same rate in all cases ; and the scales really seem
to be framed on the contradictory principle of imposing the
lower rates on the higher amounts.

In the case of probates, the duty on a property of the
value of 300*l*., and under 450*l*., is 8*l*.; of 450*l*., and under
600*l*., 11*l*.; of 600*l*., and under 800*l*., 15*l*.; of 800*l*., and
under 1000*l*., 22*l*.; of 1000*l*., and under 1500*l*., 30*l*.; of
1500*l*., and under 2000*l*., 40*l*. The scale, so far, is an
approximation to the rate of 2*l*. per cent. on the highest
amounts which the probate will cover. But in the case of
estates of larger amounts this rate is departed from, and
lower rates are charged. According to the rate at which
an estate sworn under 1000*l*. is charged, the duty on an
estate sworn under 20,000*l*. should be 440*l*.; but it is only
310*l*., being little more than 1½ per cent. According to the
rate before-mentioned on 1000*l*. the duties on estates sworn
under 100,000*l*., and under 1,000,000*l*., should be respectively 2200*l*. and 22,000*l*., but they are in fact only 1350*l*.
and 13,500*l*. On a million the duty is 15,000*l*., beyond
which there is no increase, however great the estate may
happen to be. The cases of estates above a million are no
doubt rare; but when they do occur, as is sometimes the
case, what good reason can be assigned for exempting them
from a rateable increase of charge?

The scale of duties on letters of administration is higher
than the scale of duties on probates, in the proportion of
about three to two; and displays throughout the same partiality towards the higher amounts of property. Thus the
duty on property sworn under 2000*l*., being 60*l*., is 3 per
cent.; whereas, the duty on property sworn under 100,000*l*.,
being only 2025*l*., is very little more than 2 per cent. A
million is charged with 22,500*l*.; beyond which (as in the
case of the probate duties) there is no increase of charge.

These duties present a strange collection of anomalies.
The difference between the scale of duties on probates and
letters of administration is not easily justified. The intestacy
of the head of a family is an evil to his successors which it

might be well to prevent, if there were any practicable means of doing so. But there is no reason to punish the widow and children for the neglect or ignorance of the husband or father, except on the principle extracted by Butler from the morality of the Greek Tragedy,—

> " That other men may tremble and take warning,
> How such a fatal progeny they 're born in."

It may be supposed, perhaps, that the imposition of the higher rates of duty on administrations may tend to discourage the suppression or destruction of wills; but it is scarcely reasonable to impose a sweeping tax of this kind to discourage criminal acts, which must be of very rare occurrence; and the temptation to which (where it really exists) can be but little affected by the increased rate of duty.

For the higher rates of charge payable in the case both of probates and administrations, on moderate than on large fortunes, there is neither defence nor palliation. We have previously shown how unjust it would be to impose a higher rate of duty on the income or property of the rich than is laid on that of their less opulent brethren; but to reverse the injustice by burdening the successions of the latter with a higher rate of duty than is charged on the successions devolving on the others, is a still more flagrant and monstrous abuse. An offensive anomaly of this sort should not be permitted to disgrace our fiscal code. It may, some day or other, become a precedent of dangerous import. There should be no favouritism in taxation; and, above all, no favour should ever be shown to the wealthy at the expense of the less affluent portions of the community.

A practical hardship is involved in the mode of paying the probate and administration duties, not undeserving the public notice. The duty is to be paid within a short limited time after the decease of the testator or intestate individual—not on the amount of the *clear* personal property, but of all the personal property of the deceased, including all debts owing to him, " but without deducting or allowing anything on account of the debts due and owing from the de-

ceased." (55 Geo. III., c. 184, § 38.)   The duty paid in
excess, in respect of the debts owing from the deceased, is to
be returned, if claimed within three years, or within such further time as the Lords of the Treasury may, under the circumstances, consider reasonable.   But, in the case (and there
must be many such) of a small tradesman, whose debts and
credits nearly balance, and are (say) about 2000*l*., it is
surely a wanton and most oppressive misapplication of a tax
on successions to make his family provisionally disburse 60*l*.
for the privilege of winding up his affairs !   And we incline
to think that the reader will agree with us, that the hardship
of so extraordinary a proceeding is but little alleviated by
the provision of the law which lays it down, that in the event
of an executor or administrator not having money sufficient
of his own or of the deceased to pay the duty, the Commissioners of Stamps *may* give him credit, taking (despite the
usury laws) 10 per cent. interest for the indulgence if the
duty be not paid within six months, or a less period !

The legacy duty is not open to some of the objections
which apply to the duties on probates and administrations.
It is imposed according to certain rates which (except in
their connexion with probates and administrations) are not
unreasonable on legacies and the clear residues of the estates
of testators or intestates, and of those moneys charged on
and arising out of land already noticed.   The duty in the
case of a child, or the descendant of a child of a father,
mother, or other lineal ancestor of the deceased is 1 per cent.;
on a brother or sister, or the descendant of a brother or sister,
3 per cent.; uncle or aunt, or their descendants, 5 per cent.;
great-uncle or great-aunt, or their descendants, 6 per cent.;
and on all persons more distantly related, or strangers in
blood, 10 per cent.   The husband or wife of the deceased is
wholly exempted, and legacies and shares under 20*l*.* are
not subject to the charge.

* There seems no particular reason for this exemption, except where the
legatee is within the nearest degrees.

The legacy duty is not paid in advance, but only when the legacy or share of residue itself is actually paid or retained ; and it therefore does not press, as the probate and administration duties occasionally do, on insolvent estates.

The grand objection to the legacy duty, as well as to the duties on probates and administrations, is its too limited range. It is not equal and universal, but unequal and partial. In fact it wholly falls, except in the instances previously referred to (which are comparatively few), on personal property ; the pressure of the duty on the latter being materially aggravated by the pressure of the other duties. Thus, in the case of a person who dies intestate possessed of personal property which ultimately leaves a residue exceeding 1500*l.* and not above 2000*l.*, his children have to pay a tax of 60*l.* for probate duty (with a risk of being called to disburse more in the first place), and 1 per cent. more for legacy when the residue is ascertained, making a total charge varying from 4 to 5 per cent. on the beneficial succession. But though the proprietor of an estate of 20,000*l.* a-year die intestate, his family succeed without contributing one farthing to these or to any equivalent duty !

Need we wonder that so unequal a tax should have excited much dissatisfaction? It has, it is true, been attempted to palliate its partiality by allegations as to the comparatively greater expense of the stamps required for the conveyance of landed property ; but it has been shown, over and over again, that, after making every allowance for the comparative weight of the burdens now referred to, the advantage on the side of landed and other real property is still very great, and that justice to the holders of personal property requires, either that the probate and legacy duties should be abolished, or that they should be equally assessed on all descriptions of property.

The circumstance of landed property being held under a settlement, and not passing by devise, should not be allowed to exempt it from the tax. Of what consequence is it to the public whether the succession to an estate or

other property be determined by a deed of settlement entered
into a century ago, or by a will only a year old, or by gift?
The capacity of the property to bear taxes cannot be affected
by such considerations; and, therefore, if the tax be imposed
at all, it should certainly be made to affect every sort of property when it descends, *mortis causa,* or in the way of gift,
from one individual to another, without reference to the
conditions of descent.

This, indeed, was the principle on which Mr. Pitt proposed to proceed when the probate and legacy duties were
originally introduced in 1796. Instead, however, of including the duties on real and those on personal property
in the same bill, it was judged better to introduce two bills;
and it reflects but little credit on the parliament of that day
that, while the bill for assessing personal property was passed
with but little difficulty, the bill for assessing the same
duties on real property encountered a violent opposition,
and had ultimately to be abandoned.

It would, however, be easy, provided it were wished
to effect so desirable an object, to obviate the partiality and
abuses inherent in the existing duties on legacies, probates,
and administrations. To do this, it would only be necessary
to suppress (or reduce to a merely nominal rate*) the duties
on probates and administrations; and to replace them and
the present legacy duty by a new duty, calculated to produce the same or a greater amount of revenue, that should
equally affect *all* legacies, or beneficial successions, whatever
their nature or amount.

The only objection to the proposal for imposing the legacy
duty on real estates, on which any stress can be fairly laid,
is the difficulty to which heirs and devisees might be exposed
in raising the amount required for payment of the tax as
compared with the advantage to the state. A heavy per
centage imposed on the saleable value of a real estate would,
it is alleged, require on the part of the owner a sale or mort-

---

* There may be a convenience in compelling, by a slight tax, all wills to be
brought under the notice of the officers of the revenue.

gage for the purpose of procuring the means of immediate payment, the expense of which would form a serious addition to the direct burden of the tax. In the case of the descent of an estate to an heir not within the favoured degrees of relationship, if a tax equivalent to the administration duty and legacy duty together were imposed, it would amount to between 12 and 13 per cent., and would in many cases absorb between four and five years' clear rental of the land. But precisely the same objections apply in the case of annuities which are subject to the legacy-duty; and special provision is made for obviating them in the legacy-duty acts by spreading the payment over a certain number of years. This provision, with the required modifications, might be applied to land. Neither should the amount of the duty be so great as the aggregate of the present duties; for, by extending the duty to land and other fixed property, the taxable matter would be so much augmented, that the produce of the tax would be materially increased even though the rates of duty were considerably diminished.

It would, therefore, seem that nothing could well be easier than to place the duties on legacies or successions on an unexceptionable footing. Their defects, like those that attach to some of the customs-duties, are not of their essence, but originate entirely in the partial and unjust mode in which they have been imposed. But were they imposed, as they might be without any difficulty, fairly and equally on all sorts of property, there would be nothing to object in them, even though they were made to produce a very considerably greater amount of revenue. We subjoin an

ACCOUNT of the NETT PRODUCE of the REVENUE from STAMPS aud LEGACIES in the United Kingdom in 1843, distinguishing the Revenue separately received on account of the different items in England, Scotland, and Ireland.*

	ENGLAND.	SCOTLAND.	IRELAND.	UNITED KINGDOM.
	£.　　s.　d.	£.　　s.　d.	£.　　s.　d.	£.　　s.　d.
Deeds and other instruments not included under any of the following heads	1,371,447 19　8¾	98,044　4　4	153,065　4　7¾	1,622,557　8　8¼
Probates of Wills and Letters of Administration . . . . . }	802,461　2　0	42,269　2　6	62,781　3　11	907,511　8　5
Bills of Exchange	379,064 18　8¼	81,168 19　7	96,833 16 10	557,067 15　1¼
Bankers' Notes	9,759 15　0	5,929　5　0	·　　·	15,689　0　0
Composition for Duties on Bills and Notes of the Banks of England and Ireland and Country Bankers . . . . . }	84,444　6　0	·　　·	16,470　8　6	100,914 14　6
Receipts	139,587 11　2¼	14,604 10　0	20,563　2　9	174,755　3 11¼
Fire Insurances	878,806　5　1	62,223 18　6	46,308 13　2	987,338 16　9
Marine ditto	223,695　7　9	28,879 10　0	954　3　9	253,529　1　6
Licences and Certificates	189,697 12　3	23,281 17　0	·　　·	212,979　9　3
Newspapers and Papers for Advertisements . . . . . . }	219,154 16　8	24,836 18 11	20,385 10　1½	264,377　5　8¼
Stamps for Patent Medicines . .	25,406　6　4¼	235 15　0	·　　·	25,642　1　4¼
Gold and Silver Plate	58,917 13　6¼	2,705　6　0	1,601　6　9¼	63,224　6　4
Cards	7,437 13　0	·　　·	·　　·	7,437 13　0
Dice	336　0　0	·　　·	·　　·	336　0　0
Advertisements	105,172 16　3	13,668 13　6	8,990　5　2	127,831 14 11
Legacies	1,109,930　5　8	86,876 11 11	38,809　5　8¼	1,235,616　3　3¼
Attorneys' Indentures and Admissions . . . . }	·　　·	·　　·	12,683　2　6	12,683　2　6
Barristers' and Students' Admissions . . . . }	·　　·	·　　·	3,540　0　0	3,540　0　0
Totals	5,605,320　9　2¼	484,724 12　3	482,986　3 10¼	6,573,031　5　4

* NOTE.—We have excluded from this account the duties on Stage and Hackney Carriages, which indeed it is absurd to include under the same head with Stamps and Legacies.

CHAPTER VIII.

DUTIES ON THE POSTAGE OF LETTERS.

THE conveyance of letters by post is one of the few industrious undertakings which are better managed by government than by individuals. It is indispensable to the satisfactory working of the post-office that it should be conducted with the greatest regularity and precision, and that all the departments should be made subservient to each other, and conducted on the same plan. It is plain that such results could not be obtained in any extensive country otherwise than by the agency of government; and the interference of the latter is also required to make arrangements for the safe and speedy conveyance of letters to and through foreign countries.

The organization of the post-office supplies one of the most striking examples of the advantages resulting from the division and combination of employments. " Nearly the same exertions that are necessary to send a single letter from Falmouth to New York will send 50,000. If every man were to effect the transmission of his own correspondence, the whole life of an eminent merchant might be passed in travelling without his being able to deliver all the letters which the post-office forwards for him in a single evening. The labour of a few individuals, devoted exclusively to the forwarding of letters, produces results which all the exertions of all the inhabitants of Europe could not effect, each person acting independently."*

The institution of posts may be traced to a very remote antiquity. It is, indeed, all but indispensable to the government of an extensive country that it should have means for the safe, regular, and speedy conveyance of public despatches from and to the capital and the different provinces. And it

---

* Senior on ' Political Economy,' Encyclopædia Metropolitana.

was in this view that posts were established among the principal nations of antiquity, and that they were originally introduced into modern Europe, in 1477, by Louis XI. of France.* In no long time, however, private individuals were allowed to avail themselves of the post to forward letters and despatches; and governments, by imposing higher duties or rates of postage on the letters and parcels conveyed by it than are sufficient to defray the expense of the establishment, have rendered the post-office productive of a considerable revenue. Nor, while the rates of postage are so moderate as not materially to affect the facility of correspondence, is there, perhaps, a less objectionable tax. "There cannot," says Blackstone, "be devised a more eligible method than this of raising money upon the subject; for therein both the government and the people find a mutual benefit. The government acquires a large revenue, and the people do their business with greater ease, expedition, and cheapness, than they would be able to do if no such tax (and of course no such office) existed."†

The post-office was not established in England till the 17th century. Post-masters, indeed, existed in more ancient times; but their business was confined to the furnishing of post-horses to persons who were desirous of travelling expeditiously, and to the despatching of extraordinary packets upon special occasions. In 1635 Charles I. erected a letter-office for England and Scotland; but this extended only to a few of the principal roads; the times of carriage were uncertain; and the post-masters on each road were required to furnish horses for the conveyance of the letters at the rate of $2\frac{1}{2}d.$ a-mile. This establishment did not succeed; and, at the breaking out of the civil war, great difficulty was experienced in the forwarding of letters. At length the post-office, or establishment for the weekly con-

---

* See Bergier, ' Histoire des Grands Chemins,' i., 198; Bouchaud, 'Recherches sur la Police des Romains,' &c., p. 136 ; ' Encyclopédie Francaise,' Art. ' Postes,' &c.

† Com., book i. c. 8.

veyance of letters to all parts of the kingdom, was instituted in 1649, by Edward Prideaux, attorney-general for the Commonwealth; the immediate consequence of which was a saving to the public of 7000*l.* a-year on account of postmasters. In 1657 the post-office was established nearly on its present footing, and the rates of postage that were then fixed were continued till the reign of Queen Anne.*

From the establishment of the post-office by Cromwell, down to 1784, mails were conveyed either on horseback, or in carts made for the purpose; and, instead of being the most expeditious and safest conveyance, the post had become, at the latter period, one of the slowest and most easily robbed of any in the country. In 1784 it was usual for the diligences between London and Bath to accomplish the journey in seventeen hours, while the post took forty hours; and on other roads the comparative rate of travelling of the post and stage coaches was in about the same proportion. In consequence of this difference in point of despatch a very great number of letters were sent by other conveyances than the mail; the law to the contrary being easily defeated by giving them the form of small parcels.

Under these circumstances it occurred to Mr. John Palmer, of Bath, afterwards Comptroller-general of the Post-office, that a very great improvement might be made in the conveyance of letters, in respect of economy, as well as of speed and safety, by contracting with the proprietors of stage-coaches for the carriage of the mail; the latter being bound to perform the journey in a specified time, and to take a guard with the mail for its protection. Mr. Palmer's plan encountered much opposition, but was at length carried into effect with the most advantageous results. The use of mail-coaches speedily extended to most parts of the empire; and while letters and parcels were conveyed in less than half the time that had been required under the old system, the coaches by which they were conveyed afforded, by their regularity and speed, a most desirable mode of conveyance for travellers. Mr. Palmer was the author of several other im-

* Black. Com., book i. c. 8.

provements in the economy of the post-office ; nor is there any individual to whom this department owes so much.*

Within the last few years, however, the construction of railways between most of the great towns of the empire has gone far to supersede the use of mail-coaches on the principal lines of road, and has added prodigiously to the facilities of correspondence and travelling. The journey from London to Liverpool, which had been accomplished by the mail in about twenty or twenty-two hours, is now accomplished, by railway, in nine or ten hours! and on other roads in the same proportion. The principal expense of the post-office consists, however, not so much in the conveyance of letters from place to place (though that amounts to a very large sum), as in their collection and subsequent distribution after they have been conveyed to their destination. This necessitates the establishment of a vast number of subordinate offices in the remote parts of the kingdom, many of which do not defray their expenses. This is particularly the case in Ireland, and in the Highlands of Scotland.

Previously to the introduction of the new system of a uniform penny rate of postage in 1839, under the provisions of the Act 2 & 3 Vict. cap. 52, rates of postage, increasing progressively according to the distance, were charged on all letters (not privileged) conveyed by post from place to place in the United Kingdom. The rates charged in Great Britain (with which the Irish rates were nearly identical) were, for a single letter,—

											d.
From any post-office in Great Britain to any place not exceeding 8 miles from such office.			.	.	.	.	.	.	.		2
For any distance above 8 miles, and not exceeding 15 miles				.	.	.	.	.			4
15	,,	20	,,	.	.	.	.	.			5
20	,,	30	,,	.	.	.	.	.			6
30	,,	50	,,	.	.	.	.	.			7
50	,,	80	,,	.	.	.	.	.			8
80	,,	120	,,	.	.	.	.	.			9
120	,,	170	,,	.	.	.	.	.			10
170	,,	230	,,	.	.	.	.	.			11
230	,,	300	,,	.	.	.	.	.			12

And so in proportion; the postage increasing progressively 1d. for a single letter for every 100 miles.

---

* Macpherson's ' Annals of Com.,' anno 1784.

Letters containing one enclosure charged with two single rates. Letters containing more than one enclosure, and not exceeding one ounce, charged with three single rates. Letters exceeding one ounce, whatever the contents might be, were charged with four single rates; and for every quarter of an ounce above that weight an additional single rate was chargeable.

On comparing the number of non-privileged letters conveyed by the general post with the gross amount of postage, it appears that of late years they had paid an average rate of about 7d. or 7$\frac{1}{2}d$. each.

Exclusive, however, of these rates of postage, letters posted in London and other large towns for delivery in such towns, were charged 2d. each in London, and 1d. each in the other towns in which such local posts were established.

In addition, too, to the letters on which postage was charged, all the principal officers of government, and the members of both houses of parliament, enjoyed (either to a greater or less extent) the privilege of " franking," or of sending and receiving letters by the post free of postage, and this privilege was very extensively exercised.

The gross produce, deducting overcharges, of the post-office revenue of Great Britain, exclusive of Ireland, in the undermentioned years, has been—

Years.	Duty.	Years.	Duty.	Years.	Duty.	Years.	Duty.
	£.		£.		£.		£.
1722	201,804	1810	1,675,076	1835	2,107,677	1840	1,249,248
1755	210,663	1814	2,005,987	1837	2,103,994	1841	1,369,134
1775	345,321	1820	1,993,885	1838	2,116,798	1842	1,449,162
1793	745,238	1825	2,160,390	1839	2,162,915	1843	1,519,745
1800	1,083,950	1830	2,053,720				

The progress of the Scotch branch of the post-office revenue has been quite extraordinary. In 1698, Sir Robert Sinclair of Stevenson had a grant from William III. of its entire produce, with an extra allowance of 300l. a year, on condition of his keeping up the post; but, after trial, he abandoned the undertaking as disadvantageous. In 1709, the Scotch post-office revenue was under 2000l.; whereas its amount in 1838 was 223,491l. gross, and 211,543l. nett;

having increased more than a hundredfold in little more than a century! In 1781, the Glasgow post-office produced only 4341*l.* 4*s.* 9*d.*, while in 1839 it produced 47,527*l.**

The expenses of collecting the post-office revenue amounted, under the old system, to from 24 to 30 per cent. on the gross receipt.

The increase of the post-office revenue, as evinced by the above statements, has been very remarkable. It is mostly, no doubt, to be ascribed to the increase of population, the diffusion of education, and the growing intercourse among all classes of the community; though a good deal must also be ascribed to the efforts made in the early part of the reign of George III. to suppress some of the grosser abuses that had grown out of the privilege of franking, and still more to the additions that were repeatedly made to the rates of postage. Unfortunately, however, the latter were, in the end, carried far beyond their proper limits, imposing a heavy burden on the public, without any corresponding advantage to the revenue. This is obvious from the fact of the post-office revenue having continued stationary for the twenty years ending with 1839; though, from the great increase of population and commerce during that period, it is obvious, had the rates of postage not been so high as to force recourse to other channels, the revenue must have rapidly increased from the termination of the war downwards. When the rates of postage are moderate, the greater despatch and security of their conveyance by post, prevent any considerable number of letters being sent through other channels. But when the rates become oppressive; when, for example, a postage (as under the late system) of 11*d.* is charged on the conveyance of a single letter between London and York, of 13*d.* between London and Edinburgh, and so on, a serious interruption is given to that facility of intercourse which is so important, at the same time that a very large proportion of

* Stark's Picture of Edinburgh, p. 144; Cleland's Statistics of Glasgow; Finance Book for 1838 and 1839, &c.

the correspondence which is carried on is unavoidably forced
into private channels. It was, no doubt, attempted to prevent the transfer of letters from the post, by forbidding, under
heavy penalties, their conveyance by private parties. But,
as might have been anticipated, this prohibition could not be
enforced, and had little or no effect. Considering, indeed,
the facilities which have long existed for the transmission of
letters in parcels between different parts of the country, and
the oppressive rates of postage, the wonder is, not that the
post-office revenue was nearly stationary previously to 1839,
but that it did not fall off. Although, however, the rates of
postage then existing, amounting, as already stated, to an
average charge of about $7d.$ or $7\frac{1}{2}d.$ on all single letters conveyed by the general post, were very decidedly too high, it
did not therefore follow that an invariable charge of $1d.$,
whether a letter were conveyed 1 mile or 1000 miles, or
singly or with 10,000 others, was the precise charge that
should have been imposed! But, notwithstanding this was
rushing blindfold from one extreme, or rather absurdity, to
another, and endangering a large amount of revenue without
any equivalent advantage, the project, brought forward by
Mr. Rowland Hill, for a uniform penny postage, to be paid
in advance, was eagerly adopted. It must be admitted, too,
that it had various recommendations in its favour. Being
calculated to obviate trouble and save expense to the public,
it could not fail to be generally acceptable (what reduction
of taxation is not?), especially to mercantile men and others
having an extensive correspondence. No doubt, however,
the scheme was far more indebted for its popularity to the
oppressiveness of the old rates of postage, than to any in-
trinsic merits of its own. Had these rates been properly reduced in 1837 or 1838, that is, had the postage of letters of
$\frac{1}{2}$ oz. weight passing between Scotland and Ireland and London been reduced to $4d.$ or $6d.$, and other letters in proportion, and mercantile circulars, advertisements, and notices of
sales, &c. been allowed to pass under covers open at the ends
at $1d.$ or $2d.$ each, we venture to say that the clamour for a

uniform penny postage would never have made any way. But government, though hostile to the project, took no step calculated to stop the agitation in its favour. They neither reduced the old rates of postage, nor attempted to give any increased facilities for the conveyance of letters by post. And it happened in this, as it all but invariably happens on similar occasions, that those who decline making reasonable and necessary concessions at the outset, are, in the end, compelled to concede a great deal more than would at first have been satisfactory. Such, at all events, was the case in this instance. The clamour for a uniform penny rate became too powerful to be resisted; and parliament, whether it were so inclined or not, was obliged to lend its sanction to the measure. The act 2 & 3 Victoria, cap. 52, for regulating the duty on postage, did not indeed enact that the charge for conveying letters of a given weight should, in all cases, be reduced to 1*d*.; but it was introduced for the avowed purpose of enabling the Treasury to take the necessary steps to bring the change about with the least inconvenience to all parties. In this view it gave the Treasury power to alter and reduce the rates of postage, without reference to the distance which letters may be conveyed, according to the weight of the letters, and not to the number or description of their enclosures: it also gave them power to adopt such regulations as they might think expedient in regard to stamped covers or envelopes; to suspend parliamentary franking, &c.

In virtue of the powers so conveyed, regulations were issued (rendered permanent by the act 3 & 4 Vict. c. 96), by which all inland letters, without regard to the number of enclosures or the distance conveyed, provided they be paid when posted or despatched, are—

If not exceeding ½ oz. weight, charged 1*d*.; 1 oz. 2*d*.; 2 oz. 4*d*.; 3 oz. 6*d*.; and so on, 2*d*. being added for every additional ounce up to 16 oz., beyond which, with the following exceptions, no packet, whether subject to postage or not, is received :—

1. Parliamentary petitions and addresses to her Majesty.
2. Parliamentary proceedings.
3. Letters and packets addressed to or received from places beyond sea.

4. Letters and packets to and from public departments.

5. Deeds, if sent open, or in covers open at the sides. They may be tied with string and sealed, in order to prevent inspection of the contents, but they must be open at the sides, that it may be seen that they are entitled to the privilege.

6. Bankers' parcels, despatched from London, and specially delivered at the General Post-Office, under certain regulations.

With these exceptions, all packets above the weight of 16 oz. will be immediately forwarded to the Dead Letter Office.

All letters not paid when they are posted or despatched are charged *double the above rates*.

All parliamentary and official franking has been put an end to; but members of either house of parliament are entitled to receive petitions and addresses to her Majesty, and petitions to parliament, free of charge, provided such petitions and addresses be sent in covers open at the ends, and do not exceed 32 oz. weight.

The punctual delivery of letters may be insured by getting them *registered* when posted. A fee of 1*s.* is charged for the registration of each letter over and above the rate of postage to which it may be liable.

To facilitate the working of the plan, government furnish adhesive stamps of 1*d.*, &c. each, which being pasted on letters, they are of course delivered to those to whom they are addressed free of any further charge for postage; and it also furnishes stamped envelopes at the low rate of 24 for 2*s.* 3*d.*, the 3*d.* being for the paper and manufacture. Hence, as any quantity of stamps or of stamped envelopes may, in most parts of the country, be procured beforehand, the necessity that must otherwise have existed of paying the postage at the moment when letters are posted, has been pretty generally obviated.

Such are the more prominent features of the new system; and no doubt it has the recommendations of simplicity (if we may apply such a phrase to a uniform charge for services costing widely different sums) and cheapness in its favour, and has greatly facilitated correspondence. But it may, notwithstanding, be easily shown that its adoption was most unwise. It is, no doubt, very convenient for merchants, bankers, middlemen, retail dealers, and indeed for most persons, to get letters for 1*d.* that previously cost them 7*d.* or 7½*d.*; but their satisfaction is not the only thing to be attended to in forming a fair estimate of the measure. The public exigencies require that a sum of above fifty millions a-year should be raised, one

x 2

way or other ; and so long as we are pressed by an unreasoning necessity of this sort, it is not much to say in favour of the
repeal or diminution of any tax, that those on whom it fell
with the greatest severity are delighted with the reduction.
Sugar has, in England, become a necessary of life ; and its
consumption, to say the least, is quite as indispensable to the
bulk of the people, and especially to the labouring classes, as
the writing of letters.   But would it, therefore, be a wise
measure to repeal the duty on sugar, or to reduce it to 1*s*.
a cwt. ?   It has been alleged, indeed, that taxes on the transmission of letters are objectionable on principle, and should
therefore be repealed, independently altogether of financial
considerations!   But it is easier to make an allegation of this
sort than to prove it.   All taxes, however imposed, if they be
carried (as was the case with the old rates of postage) beyond
their proper limits, are objectionable; but provided these be
not exceeded, we have yet to learn why a tax on a letter
should be more objectionable than a tax on the paper on
which it is written, on the food of the writer, or on fifty other
things.

It was contended, when the plan was under discussion, that
there would be no loss of revenue, and that the increase of
correspondence growing out of the reduction of the postage
would be so vast as fully to balance the reduced rate of
charge!   But though there has been a great increase in the
number of posted letters, principally occasioned by their
being withdrawn from the private channels in which they
were previously conveyed, it has fallen far short of this.
Notwithstanding all that has been said about the *cacoethes
scribendi*, letter-writing is generally looked upon as a duty
rather than a pleasure ; and it does not follow, when the
expense of postage is reduced, that the occasions for writing
letters are proportionally increased.

The total gross receipt of the Post-office revenue of the
United Kingdom, deducting overcharges and returned
letters, amounted in 1838 (before the late changes began)
to 2,346,278*l*., while the expenses of the establishment for

the same year amounted to 686,768*l.*, leaving a nett revenue of 1,659,510*l.* In 1843, however, three years after the new system had been in full operation, the gross receipt of the Post-office revenue amounted to only 1,535,215*l.*, while the expenses of the establishment for the same year amounted to 980,650*l.*, leaving a nett revenue of only 554,565*l.*, being no less than 1,104,945*l.* under its amount in 1838. This, however, is not all. Of the Post-office revenue in 1838, 45,156*l.* consisted of postage paid by public offices, which, being a mere charge by one government department against others, must be deducted in order to learn the nett available revenue produced by the Post-office. Owing, however, to the abolition of franking, the postage charged against government departments is now greatly increased, and in 1843 amounted to no less than 116,503*l.* Hence it will be found, on deducting these sums, that in 1838 the Post-office produced to government, over and above all charges, a clear available income of 1,614,354*l.*, which in 1843 was sunk to 438,062*l.*, being a nett diminution of 1,176,292*l.*! The subjoined account sets these important particulars in the clearest point of view (see p. 310).

It is plain, therefore, that the adoption of the new Post-office system has occasioned a sacrifice of above 1,100,000*l.* a-year of revenue. And though it be true that a sacrifice of this amount might not, under other circumstances, have been of much consequence, it is to be borne in mind that it was incurred when the revenue was already inadequate to meet the expenditure, and when, consequently, the deficiency had to be otherwise provided for, though probably in some more onerous way. We should not, however, have thought the loss of revenue, nor even the quackery of a uniform penny rate, a valid objection to the new plan, had there been no means other than its adoption of getting rid of the inconveniences attached to the old system. But such was not the case. All its defects might have been effectually obviated without any, or with but a very inconsiderable loss of revenue. Had franking been abolished, and the old rates

An Account showing the GROSS and NETT POST-OFFICE REVENUE, and the Cost and Management, for the United Kingdom, for each of the Years ending 5th January, 1839, 1840, 1841, 1842, 1843, and 1844, excluding from the Account, whether of Gross Revenue or Cost of Management, any Advances that may have been made by the English to the Irish Post-Office, and Advances to the Money-Order Office. (Parl. Papers, No. 207, Session 1844.)

Year ending	Gross Revenue.*	Cost of Management. †	Nett Revenue.	Postage charged on the Government Departments.	Nett Revenue, exclusive of Charges on Government Departments.
	£. s. d.	£. s. d.	£. s. d.	£. s. d.	£. s. d.
5th January, 1839	2,346,278 0 9½	686,768 3 6¾	1,659,509 17 2¾	45,156 0 11	1,614,353 16 3¾
,, 1840 ‡	2,390,763 10 1½	756,999 7 4	1,633,764 2 9½	44,277 13 4	1,589,486 9 5½
,, 1841	1,342,604 5 2	858,677 0 5¼	483,927 4 8¾	90,761 3 2	393,166 1 6¾
,, 1842	1,495,540 9 0¾	938,168 19 7½	557,371 9 5¼	113,255 15 10	444,115 13 7¼
,, 1843	1,578,145 16 7½	977,504 10 3	600,641 6 4½	122,161 8 9	478,479 17 7½
,, 1844	1,535,215 8 4¼	980,650 7 5¾	554,565 0 10½	116,503 1 0	438,061 19 10½

* Namely, the gross receipts, after deducting the returns for "refused letters," &c.

† Includes, over and above what are properly the expenses of collection, all payments out of the revenue, in its progress to the Exchequer, amounting to about 10,000*l.* a-year in pensions to the Duke of Marlborough and others, except advances to the Money-Order Office.

‡ This year includes one month of the fourpenny rate.

of postage so reduced that the average charge might have been about 2½*d*. or 3*d*. a letter, the revenue would not probably have lost anything, while every really advantageous object effected by the present system would have been secured. Indeed, we see no good reason why the present rates of postage should not, and very many why they should, be doubled, or increased to 2*d*. for a letter weighing ½ oz., 4*d*. for one weighing 1 oz., and so on. We are well convinced that, were this done, and the troublesome practice of forcing the prepayment of letters abandoned, the revenue would be nearly doubled, with little or no inconvenience to the public.

The increase of the Post-office revenue, while this system is maintained, will redound nothing to its credit; this being a necessary result of the increasing population, wealth, commerce, and education of the country. The revenue would increase quite as fast under any reasonably well contrived system; all taxes on articles in general use are sure, provided they be not excessive, to increase with every increase of population and wealth.

The abolition of franking, which, however, is in nowise connected with a penny rate of postage, is by far the least exceptionable of the late alterations. Franked letters were in most instances addressed to those who could best afford to pay the expense of postage; and who in this way escaped a burden that fell with its full weight on their less opulent and less known neighbours.*

CHAPTER IX.

LOTTERIES, &c.

Most modern governments have endeavoured to raise a revenue by licensing lotteries; and they were authorised in this country from the Revolution down to 1823. The

---

* See for farther details the article Postage and Post-Office, in ' Commercial Dictionary.'

overweening confidence placed by every individual in his
own good fortune has insured their success, notwithstanding the certain loss they must, at an average, occasion to
those who are adventurous enough to embark in them.
" The world," says Dr. Smith, "never saw, and never will
see, a perfectly fair lottery, or one in which the whole gain
compensated the whole loss. In the state lotteries the tickets
are really not worth the price which is paid by the original
subscribers, and yet they are commonly sold in the market
for 20, 30, and sometimes 40 per cent. advance.   The
vain hope of gaining some of the great prizes is the sole
cause of this demand. The soberest people scarcely look
upon it as a folly to pay a small sum for the chance of
gaining ten or twenty thousand pounds, though they know
that even that small sum is perhaps 20 or 30 per cent.
more than the chance is worth. In a lottery in which no
prize exceeded twenty pounds, though in other respects it
approached much nearer to a perfectly fair one than the
common state lotteries, there would not be the same demand for tickets. In order to have a better chance for
some of the great prizes, some people purchase several
tickets, and others small shares in a still greater number.
There is not, however, a more certain proposition in mathe-
matics than that, the more tickets you adventure upon, the
more likely you are to be a loser. Adventure upon all the
tickets in the lottery, and you lose for certain; and the
greater the number of your tickets, the nearer you approach
to this certainty."*

But the loss of money by those who embark in the lottery is an inferior consideration. The real evil of the system consists in its tendency to diffuse a gambling spirit;
and to stimulate persons to attempt to relieve themselves
from their difficulties by adventuring in the lottery rather
than by an increase of exertion or economy. It is obvious
that an institution productive of such effects is directly

* Wealth of Nations, p. 48.

opposed to the growth of all those qualities in the people, the promotion of which should be a principal object of every wise government. During the continuance of the lottery system, the gaining of a prize by an individual belonging to a country village was about the most serious evil that could befall it, inasmuch as it invariably gave a shock to industry, and spread a taste for gambling among the inhabitants. A curious instance of this was mentioned in a debate in the House of Commons on the lottery in 1819. A village in which a benefit-club, for the support of aged and infirm persons, had been established, had the misfortune to have a lottery adventurer in it, who gained a prize of 3000*l.* In consequence of this unlucky circumstance the benefit-club was immediately suppressed, and a lottery-club established in its stead. And, not satisfied with this, many persons carried almost all their furniture, and some even their bed-clothes, to the pawnbroker's, to get a little money to throw away on lottery-tickets!

In 1808 the lottery system was carefully inquired into, and its numerous abuses set in a striking point of view by a Committee of the House of Commons, who conclude their Report by expressing their decided opinion, " That the pecuniary advantage derived from a State lottery is much greater in appearance than in reality. When we take into consideration the increase of poor-rates arising from the number of families driven by speculations in the lottery, whether fortunate or otherwise, to seek parochial relief; the diminished consumption of excisable articles during the drawings, and other circumstances; they may well be considered to operate as a large deduction from the gross sums paid into the Exchequer by the contractors. On the other hand, the sum raised upon the people is much greater in proportion to the amount received by the State, than in any other branch of revenue.

" No mode of raising money appears to your Committee so burthensome, so pernicious, and so unproductive; no species of adventure is known where the chances are so great against the adventurer; none where the infatuation is more powerful, lasting, and destructive.

" In the lower classes of society the persons engaged, whether successful or unfortunate, are, generally speaking, either immediately or ultimately tempted to their ruin; and there is scarcely any condition of life so destitute and abandoned, that its distresses have not been aggravated by this allurement to gaming, held forth by the State."

The lottery never produced any considerable amount of revenue; and it really seems astonishing that a system productive of such pernicious results should have been so long and so generally tolerated. It is to be hoped that it may never again make a figure in the budget of this country.

In England all private gaming-houses have been prohibited for a lengthened period; in other countries, however, they are sometimes licensed by government, and yield a considerable revenue. The question, which of these is the preferable mode of dealing with gaming-houses, is one of considerable delicacy. It is objected to their being licensed, that it has a tendency to disseminate a spirit of gambling among the middle and lower ranks; and it is, on the other hand, contended that, though suppressed in law, they exist in fact, and that their proscription, by putting them under the control of desperate and profligate characters, and securing them from the inspection of the police and the public, renders them infinitely more noxious than they would be were they legalized. It must be owned that this is a case of considerable difficulty. But, on the whole, we should be inclined to think that, though our system may be more injurious to those who resort to gaming-houses, it is preferable to the other, as well for the stigma which it attaches to gambling, as for its tendency to prevent its making any great progress among the great mass of the people. This opinion would also seem to be gaining ground on the Continent. Previously to 1837 the French government realized a considerable revenue by licensing gaming-houses; the licences were then, however, withdrawn, and the gaming-houses of Paris, like those of London, may now, on being discovered by the police, be suppressed as a nuisance.*

* We borrow the following account of the gains of the late legalized gaming-houses in Paris from the *Siècle :*—

" The original lease was from 1819 to 1836, but was continued for one year more. On the 31st December, 1837, when the licence was at an end, there were seven houses open in Paris, containing together seventeen tables; nine of which were for roulette, six for trente-un, and two for creps. A separate account of the gains and losses of each table was settled every month, making 204 settlements in each year. Of these 204 settlements for 1837, only seventeen showed losses. The following are the results :—

HOUSES.	TABLES.	PRODUCE.	
		f.	c.
No. 129, Palais Royal .	1 Roulette	1,734,618	81
	2 Trente-un		
No. 113, Palais Royal .	2 Roulettes	329,963	58
No. 36, Palais Royal .	2 Roulettes	2,254,405	45
	1 Trente-un		
No. 154, Palais Royal .	1 Trente-un for gold	1,677,661	20
	1 Trente-un for silver		
	1 Roulette		
	1 Roulette	398,118	16
Rue Marivaux . . .	1 Trente-un	622,218	61
	1 Creps		
	1 Trente-un		
Frascati	1 Roulette	2,271,595	80
	1 Creps		
		9,288,581	51
Deduct for losses of the seventeen monthly settlements .		809,486	40
Balance of gain		8,479,095	11

This gain divided into the several quarters of the year shows the following results :—

	fr.	c.
First quarter.	2,621,911	75
Second quarter	1,870,419	61
Third quarter	1,715,465	16
Fourth quarter	2,271,598	59
	8,479,095	11

The table which produced the greatest monthly gain in the year was one for trente-un, which in February yielded a profit of 162,837fr. 79c. This was during the carnival, when, from the excitement of the season, the extent of play is always the greatest. None of the tables in the Palais Royal showed a loss in any one month except that for trente-un, at which only gold was staked. Consequently, the system of gambling is the more mischievous and fatal the lower the stakes allowed to be played for. The table at which only gold was

CHAPTER X.

CIRCUMSTANCES WHICH DETERMINE THE EXTENT TO WHICH
TAXES SHOULD BE LAID ON COMMODITIES—CAUSES OF
SMUGGLING—MEANS BY WHICH IT MAY BE PREVENTED.

THE capacity of a tax on a commodity to raise a revenue
depends, *first*, on the nature and extent of the demand for
the commodity; and, *second*, on the facility with which it
may be prevented from being smuggled. Every tax, by
raising the price of the commodity on which it is laid, has
a tendency to bring it within the command of a smaller
number of purchasers, and to lessen its consumption. Dr.
Swift has shrewdly remarked that, in the arithmetic of the customs, two and two do not always make four, but sometimes
only one. An individual who might be able and disposed
to pay a duty of 1s. a-bottle on wine might neither have the
means nor the inclination to pay 2s. or 3s.; and, instead of
being augmented, the revenue might be diminished by such
increase of duty. And hence, whenever the duties on commodities are raised beyond a certain limit—a limit, however, which it is impossible to define, and which necessarily
varies according to the nature of the taxed commodities,
and the varying tastes and circumstances of society—their

taken made a return of loss for five months out of the twelve. The trente-un
table of the Cercle made six returns of loss out of the twelve.

BALANCE SHEET OF THE ACCOUNT FOR 1837.

Amount of gains . . . . 8,479,095fr. 11c.
        Deductions.
Licence-rent . . . . . 6,055,100⎫
Expenses of management . 350,000⎬ 7,430,100fr. 0c.
Interest of caution-money . 25,000⎭

Nett profit . . . . 1,048,995fr. 11c.

Of this profit, the city of Paris received 786,746fr. 33c., and the farmer of the
games 262,248fr. 78c. The city also received out of the licence-rent 555,100fr.,
which, added to its portion of the gains, made an income from this lamentable
source of no less than 1,341,846fr. 33c."

effect is to depress consumption to such an extent as to render them less productive than if they were lower.

Variations in the amount of the duties affecting commodities have the same effect on their price, and consequently on their consumption, as corresponding variations in the cost of their production. But it is clear that any reduction in the price of commodities whose natural cost is very considerable, and which can, therefore, be used only by the rich, will not have so powerful an influence in increasing consumption as a corresponding reduction in the price of cheaply-produced commodities in general demand. A fall of 50 per cent. in the price of coaches would not add greatly to the demand for them; for, notwithstanding this reduction, they would still be luxuries which none but the rich could afford to use; whereas a fall of 50 per cent. in the price of spirits, beer, tea, sugar, or any article in general request, would extend the demand for it in a much greater ratio. The reason is, that the middle and poorer classes, especially the latter, form by far the most numerous portion of society; and as such commodities are even now extensively used by them, a fall of 50 per cent. in their price would bring them fully within their command, and would add prodigiously to their consumption. The truth of this observation is strikingly exemplified in the case of cotton goods. At the accession of George III., in 1760, their price, owing to the difficulty of their production, was extremely high, and the value of those annually brought to market did not exceed 200,000*l*. But, thanks to the genius and inventions of Hargreaves, Watt, Arkwright, Crompton, and others, the price of cottons has been so far sunk as to bring them within reach of the poorest individuals; and yet such has been the increase of demand, that, notwithstanding the extraordinary reduction in their price, the value of the cottons annually manufactured in Great Britain, and either disposed of at home or sent abroad, amounts, according to the best estimates, to the immense sum of THIRTY-FOUR MILLIONS! No doubt, however, had cottons been loaded with high duties, and that reduction in their price which has been brought about by the improvement of machinery been brought about by a reduction of such duties, the effect would have been the same. The demand would have equally increased; and the greater consumption of low-taxed articles would have rendered the reduced duties more productive than the higher. Similar effects have uniformly followed from similar causes; low duties on commodities in general demand being invariably found to be more productive than when they are carried to a great height, and more productive than high duties on commodities used only by the rich.

Besides diminishing the revenue by diminishing consumption, oppressively high duties diminish it by originating and encouraging the practice of smuggling. The risk of being detected in the smuggling of commodities, under any system of fiscal regulations, may always be valued at a certain rate; and whenever the duties exceed this rate, smuggling will be practised. Thus, if the duty on an article imported from abroad be 10, and the risk of smuggling 10 or 12 per cent., it is clear that none will be clandestinely imported; but if, while the risk continues the same, the duty be raised to 15 or 20 per cent., smuggling will immediately begin, and will most probably be carried to such an extent as to make the high duty less productive than the lower. Now there are plainly but two ways of checking this practice; either the temptation to smuggle must be diminished by lowering the duties,* or the difficulties in the way of smuggling, or its risk, must be increased. The first is obviously the most natural and effectual mode of accomplishing the object in view; but the second has been most generally resorted to, even in cases where the duties were quite excessive. Governments have usually consulted the officers employed in the collection of the revenue respecting the best modes of rendering taxes effectual; though their

* " Le vrai remède à la fraude est de ne donner aucun intérêt de frauder."
—*Turgot, Œuvres*, iv. 227,

interests, prejudices, and peculiar habits obviously tend to disqualify them from forming a sound opinion on such a subject. With few exceptions they seem to think that were they to recommend a reduction of duties as a means of repressing smuggling and increasing revenue, they would be virtually acknowledging their own incapacity to detect and defeat illicit practices: and, instead of ascribing the prevalence of smuggling to its true causes, they have, therefore, very generally ascribed it to some defect in the laws, or in the mode of their administration, and have proposed repressing it by new regulations, and by increasing the number and severity of the penalties affecting the smuggler. These attempts have, as was to be expected, proved, in the great majority of cases, signally unsuccessful. No doubt it is highly proper that every practicable effort should be made, by improving the efficacy of the revenue laws and the mode of carrying them into effect, to obstruct smuggling, and to ensure the collection of the duties. But it has invariably been found that no vigilance on the part of the officers, and no severity of punishment, can prevent the illicit supply of such commodities as are either prohibited or loaded with oppressive duties. Assuredly we have no wish to defend the practice of smuggling, or to apologise for the crimes and outrages to which it inevitably leads; but how much soever it may be condemned, it is still true that it owes its origin to oppressive taxes and vicious regulations, and that it will flourish so long as these are maintained.

" To pretend," says Dr. Smith, " to have any scruple about buying smuggled goods, though a manifest encouragement to the violation of the revenue laws, and to the perjury which almost always attends it, would, in most countries, be regarded as one of those pedantic pieces of hypocrisy which instead of gaining credit with anybody, serve only to expose the person who affects to practise them to the suspicion of being a greater knave than most of his neighbours. By this indulgence of the public, the smuggler is often encouraged to continue a trade which he is thus taught to consider as in some measure innocent ; and when the severity of the revenue laws is ready to fall upon him, he is frequently disposed to defend with violence what he has been accustomed to regard as his just property ; and, from being at first, perhaps, rather imprudent than criminal, he at last too often becomes one of the hardiest and most determined violators of the laws of society." *

It is idle to imagine that the bulk of society should consider the smugglers who supply them with cheap silks, brandy, Geneva, and tobacco as guilty of any very heinous offence. They are disposed to conclude that those who dig the pitfall, and not those who stumble into it, that the makers and not the breakers of bad laws, are really responsible for all the mischiefs that may ensue. To create, by means of high duties, an overwhelming temptation to indulge in crime, and then to punish men for indulging in it, is, indeed, a proceeding obviously subversive of every principle of justice. It revolts the feelings of the people, and makes them take an interest in the worst characters —for such smugglers generally are,—espouse their cause, and avenge their wrongs. A punishment not proportioned to the offence, and which does not carry the sanction of public opinion along with it, can never be productive of any good effect. The true way to suppress smuggling is to render it unprofitable—to diminish the temptation to engage in it; and this is not to be done by embodying armies of revenue officers, multiplying oaths and penalties, and making our coasts the scene of ferocious and bloody contests, and our courts of perjury and chicanery, but simply by repealing prohibitions and reducing the duties on smuggled commodities. We must seek in this, and in this only, for an effectual check to smuggling. Whenever the profits of the fair trader become nearly equal to those of the smuggler, the latter is forced to abandon his hazardous profession. But so long as prohibitions and oppressively high duties are kept up, or, which is really the

* P. 407. See also Montesquieu, ' Esprit des Loix,' liv. xiii. cap. 8.

same thing, so long as a high bounty is held out to encourage the adventurous, the needy, and the profligate to enter on this career, we may be assured that legions of excise and customs officers, backed by the utmost severity of the revenue laws, will be insufficient to hinder them.

Excessive duties defeat their object, not only by tempting the producers and dealers to evade them, but by enabling them to offer such high bribes to the inferior officers as it is very difficult for persons in their situation to resist, and against which no system of checks can ever effectually guard. In the plan hitherto pursued it is common to encourage the officers to suppress smuggling by giving them extra rewards for detecting frauds and making seizures. These are supposed to be the best means of securing their integrity and stimulating their activity. But it is obvious that, when part of the emoluments of the inferior officers is derived from fines and seizures, it is for their interest that there should be frauds to discover and seizures to make. And though the system may increase their vigilance in watching the proceedings of the smugglers, it will not stimulate them to attack the sources of smuggling. It is not by rat-catchers that the breed of rats will ever be exterminated.

The oaths that have been so generally imposed on traders and revenue officers are miserably inefficient for securing the fair collection of high duties. When the oath of a trader or manufacturer is taken, government must either trust entirely to it, or they must accompany it with a system of checks to detect those who might be tempted to make a false oath. Now, in the *first* place, it is clear that, if the oath be alone trusted to, it gives those who swear falsely a very great advantage over those who do not, and thus really operates as an incentive to, and premium on, perjury. But supposing, in the second place, that the oath is accompanied with checks, these either are or are not perfect. If, on the one hand, they are perfect, the oath is unnecessary; and if, on the other hand, they are imperfect, they afford no security against false swearing and the corruption of the offi-

Y

cers; for should a trader or manufacturer be detected in making a false oath to avoid a tax, it becomes absolutely necessary for him, if he have any regard for character, to endeavour to bribe the officer to connive at the fraud he has committed. The odium and disgrace attached to the taking of a false oath, or the emitting a false declaration, being infinitely greater than that which is attached to mere smuggling, the temptations that will be held out to the officer to make him conceal or overlook the crime will be proportionally great: and hence it is that the intermixture of oaths or declarations, and checks, opens a new source of corruption that is different from, and more powerful than, the desire to evade duties, and which seldom fails to paralyse the best contrived system of regulations.*

Too high duties on any description of commodities will occasion smuggling; but it is chiefly caused by their being laid on commodities in general demand whose natural or necessary price is not very considerable. It is commonly said, when a proposal is made for laying a heavy duty on a low-priced article, that its lowness of price fits it to bear such a duty, and that, notwithstanding its imposition, it may still be brought to market at a sufficiently moderate rate. But the encouragement to smuggling depends more on the proportion which the duty bears to the price of the commodity than on the circumstance of its being absolutely high or low. To illustrate this, let us suppose that taxed commodity, as soap, costs, exclusive of duty, 10d. a-pound. If a duty of 1d. a-pound were laid on it, the inducement to smuggle would be equal to 10 per cent. of the value of the article; and if the duty were 2d., the inducement would be 20 per cent., and so on. Now let us suppose that the cost of producing the soap, or its natural price, falls to 5d., a duty of 1d. a-pound would then make an inducement to smuggle of 20 per cent. of its value, and a duty of 2d. would be an inducement of no less than 40 per cent. And hence it is obvious that, in order to prevent smuggling,

---

* Hamilton's 'Principles of Taxation,' p. 22.

a system should be adopted, precisely the reverse of that which is generally followed in the imposition of taxes. Instead of making duties vary inversely as the price of commodities, that is, instead of raising them when the cost of producing the articles on which they are laid is diminished, and reducing them when it is increased, they should be made to vary directly as this cost,—rising when it rises, and falling when it falls. Disproportionally heavy taxes are the great cause of smuggling; and they have the further and most injurious effect of preventing its being corrected by its natural and proper punishment—the confiscation of the commodities. Recourse is, in consequence, had to extraordinary pains and penalties, and all proportion of punishment being done away, "*des gens*," says Montesquieu, "*qu'on ne saurait regarder comme des hommes méchants, sont punis comme des scélérats; ce qui est la chose du monde la plus contraire à l'esprit du gouvernement modéré.*" *

If, however, there should be any commodity in extensive demand, which, from the greatness of its bulk, as compared with its value, or from its susceptibility of being impressed with a stamp, or any other cause, is not easily smuggled, such commodity (provided it be in other respects advisable) may be charged with a comparatively high duty. But as a general rule, and in the absence of the peculiarities now referred to, it cannot be doubted that, in order to prevent fraud, the duties should always be proportioned to the cost of the articles on which they are laid.

It would be useless to enter in this place into any lengthened details to prove the truth of what has been said above in respect to smuggling. Unluckily the entire financial and commercial history of the country abounds with instances in point, many of which must be familiar to every reader. The prohibition of foreign products, or the imposition of heavy duties on foreign or native products, does not take away the taste for them. On the contrary, it would seem as if the

* Esprit des Loix, liv. xiii., cap. 8.

desire to obtain prohibited or over-taxed articles acquired
new strength from the obstacles opposed to its gratification.

> " Per damna, per cædes, ab ipso
> Ducit opes animumque ferro."

The prohibition of foreign silks that existed previously to
1826 did not hinder their importation in immense quantities.
The vigilance and integrity of the custom-house officer were
no match for the ingenuity, daring, and *douceurs* of the
smuggler ; and at the very moment when the most strenuous
efforts were made to exclude them, the silks of France and
Hindostan were openly displayed in Almack's, in the drawing-rooms of St. James's, and in the House of Commons, in
mockery of the impotent legislation by which it was attempted
to shut them out.   There is, in truth, great room for doubting whether the exchange of the subsisting *ad valorem* duty,
for the old system of prohibition, has been productive of any
material increase in the imports of foreign silks.   The repeal of the latter was certainly a most judicious measure ;
but the duty being unfortunately fixed at too high a limit
has continued to give an overwhelming stimulus to smuggling.   The expense of the clandestine importation of silks
from France may be roughly estimated at about 15 per cent.
ad valorem ; and as the duty on silks is double that amount,
or 30 per cent., we need not wonder that it should be estimated, according to the best attainable information, that
from a third to a half of the total quantity of imported silks
escapes the duty.   Indeed every one is aware that their
clandestine importation has been, and perhaps still is,
carried on to a great extent, within the port of London,
and in the custom-house itself, by the corruption and con-
nivance of the officers !   And we may be assured that this
is not a solitary instance ; and that the corruption of the
officers is one of the inevitable consequences of the over-tax
system.

The enormous duties that were imposed previously to 1823
on home-made Scotch and Irish spirits produced, as will be
afterwards seen, an extent of smuggling and demoralization

of which it is not easy for those who have not attended to such matters to form an idea. At present, however, the duties on tobacco, brandy, hollands, and silk goods, are the grand incentives to smuggling. The coast-guard, the expense of which exceeds 530,000*l*. a-year, is kept up for little other purpose than to hinder the clandestine importation of these articles. But notwithstanding its efforts, immense quantities of them find their way into the country without being subjected to any duty. And how should it be otherwise? The price of tobacco, brandy, and hollands in the contiguous continental ports may, at an average, be taken, the first at from 4*d.* to 6*d.* per lb., and the two latter at about 4*s.* a-gallon: and as the duty on tobacco is 3*s.* 2*d.* per lb., and on brandy and hollands 22*s.* 10*d.* a-gallon, need we be surprised to learn that, allowing for the expenses of smuggling, if one cargo out of three be safely landed, the business is as profitable as it is adventurous and exciting? A trade that would otherwise have been productive of the most advantageous results has thus, through fiscal rapacity, been perverted into a prolific source of vice and crime. The excess of duty has tempted great numbers of people to despise and trample on the law; it has rendered smuggling, though probably the most direct road to the gallows, a favourite occupation; and made the smuggler, even when soiled with the blood of some revenue officer, an object of public sympathy and support.

It may, however, be right to state that it must not be imagined that the mere diminution of an oppressive duty on any article will put down the smuggling to which the duty may have given rise. The diminution may not be sufficiently great; and if so, it will have but little influence. Thus, taking as above the cost of smuggling French and other foreign silks into England at 15 per cent. *ad valorem*, a reduction of the present duty from 30 to 25 or even 20 per cent. would, it is plain, do little or nothing to prevent their clandestine importation. In reducing duties, either for the prevention of smuggling or the increase of consumption, the reduction must be effectual to its end ; that is, in the former case, it must be such as to bring the duty nearly to the level of the cost of smuggling, and in the latter it must be such as to bring the article within the command of a decidedly larger class of consumers. A reduction of 5s. or 6s. from the subsisting duty of 22s. 10d. a-gallon on foreign brandy and hollands would be of no use, and would not have any sensible influence either in lessening smuggling or increasing consumption. But a reduction of 10s., 12s., or 13s. a-gallon would do both ; though of the sums now stated the last would be the most effectual and best fitted to attain its object.

These considerations show the degree of weight that should be attached to the statements of those who endeavour to excuse or apologise for the continuance of exorbitant duties, by showing that they have sometimes been reduced without any material increase taking place in the consumption of the articles on which they are laid, or any material diminution of smuggling. In exemplification of this, it has been stated that though the duty on tobacco was reduced in 1825 from 4s. to 3s. per lb., the consumption was not increased in anything like the same proportion ; and that, notwithstanding the rapid growth of population, a period of ten years elapsed before the tobacco revenue rose to its former level. But no one acquainted with the facts could have anticipated any other result. Taking the cost of tobacco at an average at 6d. per lb. (which is considerably beyond the mark), the duty previously to and since the reduction has been respectively 800 and 600 per cent. *ad valorem !* And it is needless to say that the least of these duties holds out an overwhelming temptation to smuggling and fraud. The truth is that the reduction of duty in 1825 was an ill-advised measure ; and there is no reason to conclude that the farther reduction of the present duty of 3s. 2d. per pound to 2s. would be much wiser, or that, while it sacrificed revenue, it would be at all sufficient to suppress illicit practices. It is idle, therefore, by referring to instances of this sort to endeavour to make it be believed that an adequate diminution of taxation is not followed by a corresponding increase of consumption, Had the duty on coffee, instead of being reduced in 1808 from 1*s*. 8*d*. per lb. to 7*d*., been reduced only to 1*s*. 3*d*. (the proportion in which the tobacco duty was reduced), the effect would have been all but imperceptible; and instead of the consumption being immediately increased from about 1,000,000 lbs. to 9,000,000 lbs., the presumption is it would not have been increased to 1,500,000 lbs. In taxation, as in everything else, unless the means be adequate to the desired ends, the result will be nothing. If you offer a premium of 8 to 1 on smuggling, do you imagine you will abate the nuisance you have called into existence by reducing the premium to 6 to 1 or 4 to 1? It will be found in every case in which a reduction of duty is not followed by a more than corresponding increase of consumption, that the article continues to be overtaxed, or that the duty left upon it continues either to exceed the cost of smuggling, or to place it beyond the reach of those who might otherwise become its consumers. We are bold to say that no instance can be found in the financial history of this or of any other country of the adequate reduction of the duty on an over-taxed article not being followed by a cessation of smuggling and a great increase of consumption.

There seem to be pretty good grounds for thinking that were the duty on tobacco reduced to 1*s*. per lb., such a check would be given to smuggling and fraud, that in no very lengthened period the revenue might lose but little by the measure. But any less reduction than this would serve no good purpose; and all things considered, it would seem that the question of the tobacco duty may be conveniently postponed. There are other duties the reduction of which is of incomparably greater importance. Except, indeed, in the encouragement it gives to smuggling, there is nothing to object to in the tobacco duty. It is assessed on a " filthy " luxury. And if (of which, however, there is not the smallest

chance) smuggling could be put down without its reduction,
it would certainly be about the very last duty in the tariff
that should be diminished.

The smuggling of prohibited and over-taxed articles, and
the corruption of the officers, are not, however, the only evils
to which the protective and over-tax system is sure to lead.
It also occasions the fraudulent manufacture of spurious articles, and their substitution for those that are genuine.   This
species of fraud is always carried on to a greater or less
extent when any. article in extensive use is loaded with
oppressive duties.   A paper by Addison, in the 'Tatler,'
No. 131, does justice to the ingenuity of the home producers
of wine, who were originally called into existence by the
high duties laid on foreign wines in the reign of William III.
"There is," says the accomplished essayist, " in this city
a certain fraternity of chemical operators, who work under-
ground in holes, caverns, and dark retirements, to conceal
their mysteries from the eyes and observation of mankind.
These subterraneous philosophers are daily employed in the
transmutation of liquors; and, by the power of magical
drugs and incantations, raise under the streets of London the
choicest products of the hills and valleys of France.   They
can squeeze Bordeaux out of the sloe, and draw champagne from an apple.   Virgil, in that remarkable pro-
phecy,—

Incultisque rubens pendebit sentibus uva—*Ecl.* iv. lin. 29,—

seems to have hinted at this art, which can turn a plantation
of northern hedges into a vineyard.   These adepts are known
among one another by the name of wine-brewers, and, I am
afraid, do great injury not only to her Majesty's customs, but
to the bodies of many of her good subjects."
    But, despite the wit of Addison and the more formidable
prosecutions of the Excise, this fraternity continues to be as
vigorous and flourishing as ever, and the belief is, that from
a third part to a half of the champagne and sherry (or

rather of the trash called by these names) sold in London is the produce of the home presses !

The adulteration of the inferior qualities of tea, which are burdened with an enormous duty of above 200 per cent. *ad valorem*, is also extensively carried on; chiccory is largely substituted for coffee; from 10,000 to 12,000 tons of potato-flour and other adventitious matters are believed to be annually disposed of as sugar;* and those who buy brandy and hollands, on the assurance and in the belief that they have come from Cognac and Schiedam, most frequently, perhaps, purchase the produce of the British distillers and rectifiers ! The adulteration of tobacco, especially of snuff, is also carried on to a very great extent; and it appears to be the general opinion of those best acquainted with the trade that the revenue derived from tobacco suffers more from this practice than from its clandestine introduction, notwithstanding the great extent to which the latter has been carried. Duties on commodities cannot, in fact, be carried beyond certain reasonable limits; and when any attempt is made to push them beyond their natural bounds, their increase, instead of increasing revenue, invariably produces only an increase of smuggling and fraud.

Spain may be referred to in illustration of what is now stated. The manufactures of the Peninsula being in the most backward state imaginable, there is a proportionally great demand for foreign goods. The latter, however, being mostly prohibited or loaded with oppressive duties, are almost wholly supplied by the smuggler. The severities occasionally inflicted on the latter, instead of abating, seem really to have increased, the evil of smuggling. The contraband trade has long been a favourite occupation, and has been eagerly followed by the adventurous, the necessitous, and the desperate. For a lengthened period from 100,000 to 150,000 individuals have been pretty constantly engaged in this occupation; that is, they have been engaged in

* It is a curious fact that potato-starch when treated with sulphuric acid becomes sugar. A manufacture of such sugar is now carried on at Stratford.

trampling on the laws, obstructing their officers, and committing acts of violence and blood.

And, strange to say, notwithstanding the ruinous influence of this wretched system was long since exposed by Ulloa, Campomanes, and other distinguished Spaniards, and by Mr. Townsend and other foreigners who had visited the country, and notwithstanding all the vicissitudes Spain has undergone during the last half century, her old anti-commercial policy still continues to maintain its ascendancy. The existing tariff is divided into classes; and in addition to innumerable prohibitions, and exorbitant duties on many articles of the first importance, the numerous forms to be observed at the custom-house, and the delays in entering any article, constitute of themselves a considerable premium on smuggling. It is stated that at present about 3000 actions are annually instituted against *contrabandistas* and others engaged in illicit trade, which terminate in the ruin of a vast number of families; at the same time that the courts of law are filled with perjury, and the country with bloody conflicts. And yet these atrocities secure no one object government has in view. Native manufactures are not improved, and the customs revenue is all but annihilated.

Notwithstanding their being absolutely prohibited, English and French cotton goods may, at this moment, be bought in every shop in Madrid, and generally throughout Spain; the former at from 20 to 30 per cent. above their price in Gibraltar, where they are about as cheap as in Manchester; and the latter at from 20 to 30 per cent. above their price in Bayonne, which is nearly identical with their price in Rouen! While Cadiz was a free port, about 6000 persons are said to have been employed in it twisting cigars, which, as soon as finished, were forthwith smuggled into the interior. Three-fourths, in fact, of the foreign trade of Spain is in the hands of the *contrabandistas*, and is carried on in defiance of the law. And where such is the case, need we wonder at the low state of industry, or at the prevalence of those ferocious and sanguinary habits that disgrace the Spanish character.

CHAPTER XI.

COMPARATIVE PRODUCTIVENESS OF HIGH AND LOW TAXES.

THE statements and reasonings in the previous chapter are sufficient to establish the superior productiveness of taxes on commodities when confined within moderate limits. But the subject deserves to be treated at greater length: and as the history of taxation, both in this and other countries, furnishes various, conclusive, and well-established proofs of this important principle, we shall take leave to bring a few of them under the notice of the reader. They will consist indifferently either of instances in which a reduction of duty has been followed by an increase of revenue; or of instances in which an increase of duties has been followed by a diminution of revenue.

The reductions made in the duties on tea in 1745 and 1784 strikingly evince the superior productiveness of low duties on articles in general demand. Previously to 1745 tea was charged with an excise duty of no less than 4*s.* per lb., and with a customs duty of 14 per cent. *ad valorem:* and it appears that, at an average of the five years ending Midsummer, 1745, the teas entered for consumption amounted to 768,520 lbs. a-year, yielding an average excise and customs revenue of 175,222*l.* a-year. But though the taste for tea was then comparatively little diffused, it was well known that its clandestine importation was extensively carried on, and that its real was much greater than its apparent consumption. To check this illegitimate traffic, which enriched the smuggler at the expense of the revenue and of the fair trader, a bill was carried through parliament in 1745, in pursuance of the recommendation of a Committee of the House of Commons, by which the excise duty on tea was reduced from 4*s.* to 1*s.* per lb. and 25 per cent. *ad* *valorem:* and as the price of the teas sold at the Company's sales was then about 4*s.* per lb., the 25 per cent. was, in fact, equivalent to 1*s.* per lb., making the new excise duty 2*s.* per lb., being a reduction of 50 per cent. This measure, which had in a great degree the merit of originality, was eminently successful. In the year immediately after the reduction of the duty, the entries of tea for consumption amounted to about 1,800,000 lbs., being nearly three times as much as they had amounted to in the last year of the high duties; and the increase in the second and third years of the new system was also most striking. But to set the operation of this well-considered measure in the clearest point of view, we subjoin

An Account of the Quantities of TEA entered for Consumption, and of the Produce of the Excise and Customs Duties thereon during each of the Five Years preceding and subsequent to Midsummer, 1745, when the Excise Duty on Tea was reduced from 4*s.* to 2*s.* per lb.

Years.	Quantities.	Duties.		Years.	Quantities.	Duties.
	lbs.	£.	*s.*		*lbs.*	£.
1741	880,700	200,799	0	1746	1,800,000	230,400
1742	836,200	190,653	10	1747	2,000,000	256,000
1743	797,200	181,761	10	1748*	2,600,000	358,800
1744	708,500	161,538	0	1749	2,700,000	372,600
1745	620,000	141,360	0	1750†	2,700,000	372,600
Totals . .	3,842,600	876,112	0	Totals . .	11,800,000	1,590,400
Average of 5 Years }	768,520	175,222	8	Average of 5 Years }	2,360,000	318,080 ‡

* In 1748, 5 per cent. was added to the customs duty on dry goods; but its influence on tea was next to imperceptible.

† In 1752 the entries increased to 3,000,000 lbs.

‡ This measure was principally carried by the exertions and through the influence of Sir S. T. Janssen, alderman and representative of the city of London. The above account is abstracted from a statement by Janssen in Postlethwaite's Dictionary, art. ' Tea,' in which the operation of the measure is shown more in detail. We borrow from this statement the following paragraphs:—

"This experimental trial upon the article of ' tea' was the first of the kind, of any material consequence, which was ever made to prove, that the lowering of a high duty upon an article of consumption hath considerably advanced the produce of the public revenue upon such article, by occasioning the surprising general increase of its consumption.

" It shows, That a foreign commodity, even of a luxurious nature, may be-

But notwithstanding this unanswerable demonstration of the superior productiveness of low duties, they were again increased in 1759 ; and fluctuated, between that epoch and 1784, from about 65 to 120 per cent. *ad valorem*. The effects which followed this inordinate extension of the duties are equally instructive with those which followed their reduction. The revenue was not increased in anything like a corresponding proportion; and as the use of tea had become general, smuggling was carried to an infinitely greater extent than at any former period. In the *nine* years preceding 1780, above 118 million lbs. of tea were exported from China to Europe in ships belonging to the continent, and about 50 million lbs. in ships belonging to England. But from the best information attainable it appears that the real consumption was almost exactly the reverse of the quantities imported; and that, while the consumption of the British dominions amounted to above 13 million lbs. a-year, the consumption of the continent did not exceed five and a half millions. If this statement be nearly correct, it follows that an annual supply of about *eight* million lbs. must have

come a general article of consumption, and be rendered fashionable and habitual amongst all ranks and degrees of people, in consequence of reducing a high duty thereon to a moderate one, and thereby augment the revenue, in proportion to the general augmentation of the consumption of such foreign commodity.

" It indicates the next degree to a demonstration, that duties upon commodities may be strained to so high a pitch as to cause a general diminution in their consumption, and consequently to occasion a proportionable diminution in the public revenue which used to arise from the high duty. It excites the unfair trader to act in concert with the smuggler, and the latter to hazard his life to reap the advantage which so great a temptation lays before him. It induces the consumer to enter into a close connexion with the smuggler, in order to come at the commodity which fashion and pride have made necessary to him, since his pocket cannot otherwise reach it.

" It proves that the price of teas has fallen so very considerably, in consequence of the government adopting this plan, that the custom of tea-drinking has since become universal throughout the kingdom, amongst all degrees of people; that the smuggling of this article is greatly abated, and that a surprising increase in the consumption of sugar has ensued, to the great improvement of the sugar colonies, as well as the great increase of the revenue by the duty on sugar; and all these consequences have naturally attended an increase in the consumption of teas, chiefly and principally owing to the lowering the high duty thereon."

been clandestinely imported into this country, in defiance
of the revenue laws. But this was not the worst effect
of the high duties ; for many of the retail dealers who
purchased tea at the East India Company's sales, being in
a great measure beaten out of the market, were, that they
might put themselves in a condition to stand the competition
of the smugglers, tempted to adulterate their teas, by mixing
them with sloe and ash leaves.* At length, in 1784, ministers, after having in vain tried every other resource for
the suppression of smuggling, resolved to follow the precedent of 1745, and reduced the duty on tea from 119 to
12½ per cent. This measure was as successful as the former. Smuggling and the practice of adulteration were immediately put an end to. The following statement shows
that the *quantity* of tea sold by the East India Company
was about *trebled* in the course of the *two* years immediately
following the reduction.

In 1781 the quantity of tea sold at the East India Com-
pany's sales amounted to				.	.	.	5,023,419 lbs.
1782	.	.	.	.	.	.	.	6,283,664 „
1783	.	.	.	.	.	.	.	5,857,883 „
1784 (duties reduced)			.	.	.	.	.	10,148,257 „
1785	.	.	.	.	.	.	.	16,307,433 „
1786	.	.	.	.	.	.	.	15,093,952 „
1787	.	.	.	.	.	.	.	16,692,426 „ †

While the quantity of tea sold at the Company's sales
was thus rapidly augmenting in consequence of the reduction of the duty, the quantity of tea imported into the
continent from China, which had, in 1784, amounted to
19,027,300 lbs., declined with still greater rapidity, and, in
1791, was reduced to only 2,291,500 lbs.‡

The duties on tea, at an average of the five or six years
preceding 1784, produced about 700,000*l.* a-year. And,
on their being reduced to 12½ per cent., an additional duty,
estimated to produce 600,000*l.*, was laid on windows, as a

---

* Macpherson's ' Commerce with India,' p. 208. Milburn's ' Oriental
Commerce,' vol. ii., p. 540.

† Macpherson's ' Commerce with India,' p. 416.

‡ Ibid., p. 210.

commutation tax, to compensate for the deficiency which it was supposed would take place in the revenue derived from tea. But instead of the duties falling off in the proportion of 119 to 12¼, or from 700,000*l*. to 73,000*l*., they only fell off, in consequence of the increased consumption, in the proportion of about *two* to *one*, or from 700,000*l*. to 340,000*l*. The commutation act has been always regarded as one of the most successful financial measures of Mr. Pitt's administration. The plan was generally understood at the time to have been suggested by Mr. Richardson, accountant-general of the East India Company; but the popularity of the measure was so great as to induce several other individuals to claim this honour, and even to occasion some hot disputes on the subject in the House of Commons. In point of fact, however, the merit of originally suggesting the plan neither belonged to Mr. Richardson nor to any of those who then claimed it; and such of our readers as will take the trouble to look into a pamphlet ascribed to Sir Matthew Decker ('Serious Considerations on the Present High Duties'), published in 1743, will find that the measure adopted in 1784 had been strenuously recommended forty years before.

But the principle of the commutation act, and the striking advantage that had resulted from the reduction of the duty, were soon lost sight of. In 1795 the duty was increased to 25 per cent.; and after successive augmentations in 1797, 1798, 1800, and 1803, it was raised, in 1806, to 96 per cent. *ad valorem*, at which it continued till 1819, when it was raised to 100 per cent. on teas above 2*s*. per lb. We have exhibited the influence of these duties on consumption in the 'Commercial Dictionary' (Art. TEA), to which we beg to refer the reader; for as their influence was mixed up with that of the Company's monopoly, it would lead us into inquiries unsuitable to this work were we to attempt to exhibit in this place the operation of the duties only.

We regret to have to add that, despite our previous experience, the tea-duties are, at this moment, excessive in amount, and their assessment grossly partial and unfair. When the tea-trade was thrown open by the abolition of the Company's monopoly in 1834, the following duties were imposed on teas when entered for consumption, viz. : —

	s.	d.
Bohea	1	6 per lb.
Congou, twankay, hyson skin, orange pekoe, and campoi	2	2 „
Souchong, flowery pekoe, hyson, young hyson, gunpowder, imperial, and other teas not enumerated .	3	0 „

Inasmuch, however, as the prices of bohea and congou in bond rarely exceed, the former $9d$. or $1s$., and the latter from $1s$. to $1s$. $10d$. per lb., the above duties were obviously quite excessive; and when it is further considered that these descriptions of tea are largely consumed by the lower and middle classes, and are in fact necessaries rather than luxuries, the duties will appear to have been as impolitic and oppressive as they were wholly disproportioned to the cost of the articles on which they were imposed. Had the duties on bohea been reduced to $10d$., and on congou to $1s$. per lb., they would have been, if anything, still too high; but the above rates of duty were so exorbitant that they could not fail to reduce the consumption—directly, by the enormous additions they made to the price of tea; and indirectly, by the encouragement they gave to adulteration.

The above scale of duties was not, however, long in operation. Though the qualities and prices of some sorts of tea differ very widely, as much so as the qualities and prices of some sorts of wine, the proximate varieties are not easily distinguishable; and it was alleged that practically it was found to be impossible to discriminate between the teas on which different rates of duty were to be paid; and that teas admitted at one port at the low duty of $1s$. $6d$. were charged at other ports with the higher duties of $2s$. $2d$. and $3s$. per lb. It is impossible to doubt that there was some considerable foundation for these statements; but the best-informed parties believed them to be much exaggerated, and were of opinion that, by confining the importation of teas to two or three principal ports, and employing officers well acquainted with their qualities, a classified scale of duties might have been enforced with sufficient fairness. It was only, indeed, in the substitution of congou for bohea that any considerable frauds either could or were alleged to take place; and if they could not otherwise have been got rid of, the better plan would have been to have admitted congou, or all black teas, at the same duty as bohea, or at 10*d.* or 1*s.* per lb. And had this been done, and the duties on other descriptions of tea been allowed to remain as before, the grievance complained of would have been sufficiently redressed, and a very great boon conferred on the public.

This course was not, however, adopted. Government, influenced partly by a wish to get rid of the clamour and outcry raised by the importers against the discriminating duties, and partly, perhaps, by a doubt whether they could be fairly collected, consented to their abolition. This was effected by the statute 5 and 6 William IV. cap. 32, which enacted, that from the 1st of July, 1836, a duty of no less than 2*s.* 1*d.* per lb. should be charged on all teas entered for consumption in the United Kingdom. But while we admit that the necessity of the case, or the impossibility of fairly assessing discriminating duties, may have justified the repeal of the discriminating duties, and the imposition of a single duty in their stead, we contend that nothing can justify the magnitude of this single duty, which is, beyond all question, the most objectionable in our tariff.

It has, we are aware, been alleged that the duty of 2*s.* 1*d.* per lb. is not really so bad as it looks; that it is a mistake to suppose that the lower classes use inferior teas; and that the reduction of the duty on them would not materially increase their consumption! But those who make such statements either know nothing of the facts of the case, or reckon on the ignorance of those to whom they address themselves. It appears from the official returns, that in 1816-17 and 1817-18, the price of bohea sold at the Company's sales was about 2*s.* 6*d.*, so that it must have

z

cost the buyer, duty included, about 5*s.* per lb.; and in
these years the consumption amounted, at an average, to
1,784,000 lbs. a-year.   But in 1830-31 and 1831-32, when
the price of tea to the buyer was reduced to 3*s.* 4*d.* per lb.
(1*s.* 8*d.* price, and 1*s.* 8*d.* duty), the consumption rose to
6,285,000 lbs.; showing, beyond all dispute, that a fall of
1*s.* 8*d.* in the price of bohea had *more than trebled* its consumption !   And though St. Augustine has said that *Nullum*
mendacium tam impudens est ut teste careat, we hardly think
any one will venture to affirm, in the teeth of an experiment
like this, that bohea is not used by the poorer classes; or
that the demand for it would not be very greatly extended
by a reduction of 1*s.* 1*d.* or 1*s.* 3*d.* per lb. in its price.

Taking the average price of bohea in bond in London at
10*d.* or 1*s.* per lb., a duty of the same amount would, of
course, be equal to the *ad valorem* duty of 100 per cent.
under the Company's regime, which is certainly high for a
duty on a necessary consumed by the poor.   But even with
a duty of this amount, bohea might be retailed at 2*s.* 6*d.*
per lb.; and at this price there can be no manner of doubt
the consumption would amount to eight or ten millions of
pounds.   The reduction of the duty on congou to 1*s.* per lb.
would, also, be of the greatest importance to the lower and
middle classes; and the powerful stimulus it would give to
consumption, and consequently, also, to the demand for
sugar, which is indispensable to the use of tea, makes it all
but certain, that in no very lengthened period the revenue
would, instead of losing, gain by the change.

But supposing that the revenue were to lose at the outset
some 500,000*l.* or 600,000*l.* a-year by the proposed reduction; is the getting rid of the injustice of the present tax, and
the effectual encouragement of the trade with China, not
worth even a greater sacrifice?   Taking the price of bohea
and low congou in bond in London at 1*s.* per lb. (and it is
frequently less), the duty of 2*s.* 1*d.*, with which they are at
present charged, is equivalent to an *ad valorem* one of more
than *two hundred* per cent.; whereas, taking the price of the

hyson and other superior teas consumed by the rich at from
3s. to 4s. per lb., the duty on them does not exceed from
50 to 66 per cent. *ad valorem,* that is, it does not amount to
more than from $\frac{1}{4}$ to $\frac{1}{6}$ part of the duty laid on the teas consumed by the poor!   Surely, however, this is neither an age
nor a country in which an anomaly of this sort can be safely
maintained.   The public necessities require that the tea,
sugar, and other necessaries of the poor should be taxed ;
but the obvious principles of justice, also, require that the
duties on them should be, if not lower, at all events no
higher than those laid on the necessaries or luxuries of the
rich.   The existing tea duties contradict this plain principle,
and are at once unjust and exorbitant.   The duty on bohea
and the lower congous should not, in fact, exceed 4d. or 6d.
per lb. ; and we trust that at no distant period means may
be found of reducing it to that amount.

Without an effectual reduction of the duties on tea, the
anticipations so generally entertained of an immense increase
of the trade with China, will, most likely, be wholly disappointed.   However desirous, the Chinese cannot possibly
buy our manufactured or other goods unless they can at the
same time sell some of their peculiar products.   The exportation of silver must raise its price, and will not, probably,
be of long continuance.   And, tea excepted, the Chinese
seem to possess few articles of merchandise suitable for our
markets that we may not import at a cheaper rate from
others.   But unless we reduce the duty on it in some such
way as has been previously suggested, it is, we are afraid,
idle to look for any considerable increase of its consumption,
or, consequently, of the trade with the Celestial Empire.

If the temporary loss of revenue which would, most probably, follow the adoption of the necessary measures in relation to the duties on tea, be more than can conveniently
be afforded, it might be supplied by adding 5s. a-quarter to
the malt duty; for this, though not an unobjectionable
measure, would be incomparably less so than the keeping up
of the present duties on tea.

Previously to 1732, the duty on coffee amounted to 2*s.* a-pound; but an act was then passed, in compliance with the solicitations of the West India planters, reducing the duty to 1*s.* 6*d.* a-pound; at which it stood for many years, producing, at an average, about 10,000*l.* a-year. In consequence, however, of the prevalence of smuggling, caused by the too great magnitude of the duty, the revenue declined, in 1783, to 2869*l.* 10*s.* 10½*d.* And, it having been found impossible otherwise to check the practice of clandestine importation, the duty was reduced, in 1784, to 6*d.* The consequences of this wise and salutary measure were most beneficial. Instead of being reduced, the revenue was immediately raised to near *three* times its previous amount, or to 7200*l.* 15*s.* 9*d.*, showing that the consumption of legally imported coffee must have increased in about *a ninefold proportion;* a conclusive proof, as Mr. Bryan Edwards has observed, of the effect of heavy taxation in defeating its own object.*

The history of the coffee trade abounds with similar and still more striking examples of the superior productiveness of low duties. In 1807 the duty was 1*s.* 8*d.* a-pound; and the quantity entered for home consumption amounted to 1,170,164 lbs., yielding a revenue of 161,245*l.* 11*s.* 4*d.* In 1808 the duty was reduced from 1*s.* 8*d.* to 7*d.*; and in 1809 no fewer than 9,251,847 lbs. were entered for home consumption, yielding, notwithstanding the reduction of duty, a revenue of 245,856*l.* 8*s.* 4*d.* The duty having been raised in 1819 from 7*d.* to 1*s.* a-pound, the quantity entered for home consumption in 1820 fell to 6,869,286 lbs., yielding a revenue of 340,223*l.* 6*s.* 7*d.* In 1824, however, the duty being again reduced from 1*s.* to 6*d.*, the quantity entered for home consumption in 1825 was 10,766,112 lbs. In 1830 it had increased to 21,840,520 lbs., producing a nett revenue of 558,544*l.*; and in 1842 the consumption amounted to 28,519,646 lbs., and the revenue to 768,886*l.* And it is worthy of especial observation that this extraordinary increase

* 'History of the West Indies,' vol. ii., p. 340, 8vo. ed.

in the consumption of coffee has taken place, not only without any diminution, but with a very material increase, in the consumption of tea.

The history of the duties on spirits furnishes equally conclusive evidence of the superior productiveness of reasonable duties, and of the loss of revenue, smuggling, and other pernicious consequences that inevitably follow every attempt to carry them beyond their natural limits. There can, indeed, be no better subjects for taxation than spirituous and fermented liquors. They are essentially luxuries; and while moderate duties on them are, in consequence of their being very generally used, exceedingly productive, the increase of price which they occasion has a tendency to lessen their consumption by the poor, to whom, when taken in excess, they are exceedingly pernicious. Few governments, however, have been satisfied with imposing moderate duties on spirits; but partly in the view of increasing the revenue, and partly in the view of placing them beyond the reach of the lower classes, have almost invariably loaded them with such oppressively high duties as have entirely defeated both objects. The imposition of duties does not lessen the appetite for spirits; and as no vigilance of the officers or severity of the laws has been found sufficient to secure a monopoly of the market to the legal distillers, the real effect of the high duties has been to throw the supply of a large proportion of the demand into the hands of the illicit distiller, and to superadd the atrocities of the smuggler to the idleness and dissipation of the drunkard.

During the latter part of the reign of George I., and the earlier part of that of George II., gin-drinking was exceedingly prevalent; and the cheapness of ardent spirits, and the multiplication of public-houses, were denounced from the pulpit, and in the presentments of grand juries, as pregnant with the most destructive consequences to the health and morals of the community. At length ministers determined to make a vigorous effort to put a stop to the further

use of spirituous liquors, except as a cordial or medicine.
For this purpose an act was passed in 1736, the history
and effects of which deserve to be studied by all who are
clamorous for an increase of the duties on spirits.   Its preamble is to this effect :—" Whereas the drinking of spirituous liquors, or strong water, is become very common, especially among people of lower and inferior rank, the constant
and excessive use of which tends greatly to the destruction
of their health, rendering them unfit for useful labour and
business, debauching their morals, and inciting them to per-
petrate all vices; and the ill consequences of the excessive
use of such liquors are not confined to the present generation,
but extend to future ages, and tend to the destruction and
ruin of this kingdom."   The enactments were such as might
be expected to follow a preamble of this sort.   They were
not intended to repress the vice of gin-drinking, but to root
it out altogether.   To accomplish this, a duty of 20*s.* a-
gallon was laid on spirits, and a licence duty of 50*l.* a-year
on retailers, at the same time that their sale in any less
quantity than *two* gallons was prohibited.   Extraordinary
encouragements were also held out to informers, and a fine
of 100*l.* was ordered to be rigorously exacted from unlicensed dealers, and from every one who, were it even
through inadvertency, should vend the smallest quantity
of spirits which had not paid the full duty.   Here was
an act which might, one should think, have satisfied the
bitterest enemy of gin.   But instead of the anticipated effects,
it produced those directly opposite.   Respectable dealers
withdrew from a trade proscribed by the legislature; so that
the spirit business fell almost entirely into the hands of
the lowest and most profligate characters, who, as they had
nothing to lose, were not deterred by penalties from breaking
through all the provisions of the law.   The populace having
in this, as in all similar cases, espoused the cause of the
smugglers and unlicensed dealers, the officers of the revenue
were openly assaulted in the streets of London and other
great towns; informers were hunted down like wild beasts;

and drunkenness, disorder, and crimes increased with a frightful rapidity. " Within two years of the passing of the act," says Tindal, "it had become odious and contemptible, and policy as well as humanity forced the commissioners of excise to mitigate its penalties."*

The same historian mentions (vol. viii. p. 390), that during the two years in question no fewer than 12,000 persons were convicted of offences connected with the sale of spirits. But no exertion on the part of the revenue officers and magistrates could stem the torrent of smuggling. According to a statement made by the Earl of Cholmondeley, in the House of Lords,† it appears, that at the very moment when the sale of spirits was declared to be illegal, and every possible exertion made to suppress it, upwards of seven millions of gallons were annually consumed in London, and other parts immediately adjacent ! Under such circumstances government had but one course to follow—to give up the unequal struggle. In 1742 the high prohibitory duties were accordingly repealed, and such moderate duties imposed in their stead as were calculated to increase the revenue, by increasing the consumption of legally distilled spirits. The bill for this purpose was vehemently opposed in the House of Lords by most of the bishops, and many other peers, who exhausted all their rhetoric in depicting the mischievous consequences that would result from a toleration of the vicious practice of gin-drinking. To these declamations it was unanswerably replied, that it was impossible to put down the practice by prohibitory enactments; and that the attempts to do so had been productive of far more mischief than had ever resulted, or could be expected to result, from the greatest abuse of spirits. The consequences of the change were highly beneficial. An instant stop was put to smuggling; and if the vice of drunkenness was not materially diminished, it has never been stated that it was increased.

* ' Continuation of Rapin,' vol. viii., p. 358, ed. 1759.
† Timberland's ' Debates in the House of Lords,' vol. viii., p. 388.

But it is unnecessary to go back to the reign of George II. for proofs of the impotency of high duties to take away the taste for spirits, or to lessen their consumption. The occurrences that took place during the reign of George III. are equally decisive in regard to this question.

Perhaps no country has suffered more from the abuse of duties on spirits than Ireland. If heavy taxes, enforced by severe fiscal regulations, could make a people sober and industrious, the Irish would have been the most so of any. To make the possessors of property join heartily in suppressing illicit distillation, the novel expedient was resorted to in Ireland, of imposing a heavy fine on every parish, townland, manorland, or lordship, in which an unlicensed still was found; while the unfortunate wretches found working it were subjected to transportation for seven years. But instead of putting down illicit distillation, these unheard-of severities rendered it universal, and filled the country with bloodshed, and even rebellion. "The Irish system," says the Rev. Mr. Chichester, in his valuable pamphlet on the Distillery Laws, published in 1818, "seems to have been formed in order to perpetuate smuggling and anarchy. It has culled the evils of both savage and civilised life, and rejected all the advantages which they contain. The calamities of civilised warfare are, in general, inferior to those produced by the Irish distillery laws; and I doubt whether any nation of modern Europe, which is not in a state of actual revolution, can furnish instances of legal cruelty commensurate to those which I have represented." *

These statements are borne out to the fullest extent by the official details in the Reports of the Revenue Commissioners. In 1811, say the Commissioners (Fifth Report, p. 19), when the duty on spirits was 2s. 6d. a-gallon, duty was paid in Ireland on 6,500,361 gallons (Irish measure); whereas, in 1822, when the duty was 5s. 6d., only 2,950,647 gallons were brought to the charge. According to the

* Pp. 92—107.

commissioners the annual consumption of spirits in Ireland was at this very period not less than ten millions of gallons; and, as scarcely three millions paid duty, it followed that seven millions were illegally supplied; and " taking one million of gallons as the quantity fraudulently furnished for consumption by the licensed distillers, the produce of the unlicensed stills may be estimated at six millions of gallons." —(Ib. p. 8.) Now, it is material to keep in mind, that this vast amount of smuggling was carried on in defiance of the above barbarous statutes, and of the utmost exertions of the police and military to prevent it; the only result being the exasperation of the populace, and the perpetration of revolting atrocities both by them and the military. " In Ireland," say the commissioners, " it will appear, from the evidence annexed to this Report, that parts of the country have been absolutely disorganised, and placed in opposition not only to the civil authority, but to the military force of the government. The profits to be obtained from the evasion of the law have been such as to encourage numerous individuals to persevere in these desperate pursuits, notwithstanding the risk of property and life with which they have been attended."

To put an end to such evils, the commissioners recommended that the duty on spirits should be reduced from 5s. 7¼d. to 2s. 4¾d. (the imperial gallon); and government having wisely consented to act upon this recommendation, the duties were reduced accordingly, in 1823.   The following official account (p. 346), which exhibits the consumption, and the rates of duty on corn-made spirits from 1791 down to 1843 both inclusive, exhibits the salutary effects of this reduction : and it also shows the powerful operation of the previous and subsequent changes of the duty.

Sir Robert Peel is reported to have said, in his financial statement on the 11th of March, 1842, that the consequences that followed the reduction of the duty on coffee, in 1808, from 1s. 8d. to 7d. per lb. (see p. 340) furnish by far the most favourable illustration of the principle of the superior

An ACCOUNT of the QUANTITIES of CORN SPIRITS made in IRELAND, which have paid the Duties of Excise for Home Consumption: stating the Rate of Duty paid, and also the Nett Amount of Revenue received, in each Year since the Year 1790.

Years.	No. of Gallons.	Rate per Imperial Gallon.	Nett Amount of Revenue. £.	s.	d.
1791	3,416,766	1*s*. 1¼*d*.	187,495	5	6
1792	3,343,578	,,	183,479	1	7
1793	3,833,763	,,	210,378	0	6
1794	4,153,785	,,	227,911	15	3
1795	3,612,083	1*s*. 5¼*d*.	254,846	0	0
1796	3,787,771	,,	267,241	0	3
1797	4,694,254	,,	331,196	16	3
1798	4,173,439	1*s*. 11*d*.	392,601	17	6
1799	3,553,594	2*s*. 4¼*d*.	417,865	3	1
1800	275,013	,,	32,047	14	7
1801	,,	,,	,,		
1802	4,715,098	2*s*. 10¼*d*.	674,575	11	10
1803	4,343,095	2*s*. 10¼*d*.—3*s*. 6¾*d*.	671,622	11	11
1804	3,543,599	3*s*. 6¾*d*.—4*s*. 1*d*.	680,083	9	8
1805	3,686,233	4*s*. 1*d*.	658,222	6	5
1806	3,858,107	,,	725,367	3	0
1807	5,597,204	,,	1,141,149	3	9
1808	3,575,430	,,	834,064	12	3
1809	71,628	,,	19,505	14	11
1810	4,630,675	4*s*. 1*d*.—2*s*. 6½*d*.	617,252	5	9
1811	6,378,479	2*s*. 6½*d*.	812,597	1	11
1812	4,009,301	2*s*. 6½*d*.—5*s*. 1¼*d*.	942,880	12	7
1813	1,809,849	5*s*. 1¼*d*.—5*s*. 7¼*d*.	498,757	3	2
1814	5,392,458	5*s*. 7¼*d*.	1,454,359	9	10
1815	4,323,844	5*s*. 7¼*d*.—6*s*. 1½*d*.	1,312,908	15	0
1816	3,557,200	6*s*. 1½*d*.—5*s*. 7¼*d*.	1,037,185	14	0
1817	3,586,932	5*s*. 7¼*d*.	1,014,268	1	2
1818	4,284,347	,,	1,164,534	18	1
1819	3,676,516	,,	1,032,091	2	0
1820	3,299,650	,,	907,284	9	3
1821	3,311,462	,,	903,141	13	3
1822	2,910,483	,,	801,987	18	8
1823	3,590,376	5*s*. 7¼*d*.—2*s*. 4¾*d*.	619,271	0	3
1824	6,690,315	2*s*. 4¾*d*.	795,163	8	4
1825	9,262,744	,,	1,107,449	15	7
1826	6,834,867	2*s*. 10*d*.	963,172	13	1
1827	8,260,664	,,	1,155,783	15	1
1828	9,937,903	,,	1,404,646	6	8
1829	9,212,224	,,	1,304,655	1	8
1830	9,004,539	2*s*. 10*d*.—3*s*.—3*s*. 4*d*.	1,409,128	3	7
1831	8,710,672	3*s*. 4*d*.	1,451,580	7	0
1832	8,657,756	,,	1,442,845	9	0
1833	8,168,596	,,	1,360,769	6	8
1834	9,708,462	3*s*. 4*d*.—2*s*. 4*d*.	1,368,952	3	2
1835	11,381,223	2*s*. 4*d*.	1,327,805	14	8
1836	12,248,772	,,	1,428,744	2	0
1837	11,255,635	,,	1,310,765	13	9
1838	12,296,342	,,	1,434,331	16	4
1839	10,815,709	,,	1,261,741	17	6
1840	7,401,051	2*s*. 4*d*.—2*s*. 8*d*.	935,652	19	4
1841	6,485,443	2*s*. 8*d*.	864,105	10	2
1842	5,290,650	2*s*. 8*d*.—3*s*. 8*d*.	904,780	0	8
1843	5,546,483	3*s*. 8*d*.—2*s*. 8*d*.	852,306	16	10

productiveness of low duties. Perhaps, however, the reader may be disposed to think that the reduction of the duty on spirits in Ireland in 1824, now brought under his notice, is but little, if at all, less conclusive in favour of the principle referred to. In the instance of coffee there was little smuggling or adulteration (for chiccory had not then been heard of) to provide against; and it was next to certain that to whatever extent consumption might be increased, through the reduction of the duty, the revenue would be proportionally indemnified. But in the instance of the spirit duties this was not the case. The consumption had not declined, but had been diverted into illegitimate channels; and it was clear that all the ingenuity and resources of the smuggler would be brought into the field, and be exerted to preserve the trade he had long carried on, and to defeat and evade the duty. And yet, despite these adverse circumstances, a reduction of duty from 5s. 7¼d. to 2s. 4¾d. per imperial gallon, being at the rate of about 50 per cent., was immediately followed by an increase of the legitimate consumption of spirits from about 3½ to above 9 millions of gallons, and by the revenue increasing, from between 600,000l. and 800,000l., to above a million sterling! In 1826 a small addition was made to the duty, raising it to 2s. 10d. the imperial gallon; and in 1828 the revenue rose to above 1,400,000l.! It is not easy to imagine a more unanswerable demonstration of the greater productiveness of moderate duties.

It has been objected to this measure that it was injurious in a moral point of view, by occasioning an increased consumption of spirits. But the statements already made show the groundlessness of this allegation. The reduction of the duties substituted legal for illegal distillation, and freed the country from the perjuries and other atrocities that grew out of the previous system; but it would be wholly erroneous to say that it increased drunkenness. It has been already seen that the commissioners, who had the best means of obtaining accurate information, estimated the consumption of spirits in Ireland, in 1823, at ten millions of gallons; and when greatest, in 1838, thirteen years after, when the population had been largely increased, the consumption was only 12,296,342 gallons. No doubt, therefore, the measure deserves to be considered as having been, in every point of view, most successful. The table shows that the increase of duty, from 2s. 10d. to 3s. 4d., in 1830, perceptibly diminished the quantity of spirits brought to the charge; and as it was found to give a considerable stimulus to smuggling, which had previously been nearly extinct, it was again reduced, in 1835, to 2s. 4d. The extraordinary diminution in the consumption of spirits, since 1839, though in some degree, perhaps, ascribable to the addition of 4d. a gallon made to the duty in 1840, is principally owing to the great exertions of Father Matthew, and the spread of temperance societies; and notwithstanding the loss of revenue it has occasioned, the change has certainly been of much public advantage; and provided it be maintained, few things could have occurred seemingly better fitted to improve the physical as well as the moral condition of the people. The ill-advised addition of 1s. a gallon made to the duty in 1842 was repealed in 1843; for while it gave a powerful stimulus to clandestine distillation, it is abundantly certain it would not have added anything to the revenue, or given any additional stimulus to the temperance movement.

The experience of Scotland is hardly less conclusive in regard to the advantage of low duties on spirits than that of Ireland; exorbitant duties having produced nearly the same effects in the former as in the latter. Mr. John Hay Forbes, formerly sheriff-depute of Perthshire, now a lord of session, stated in evidence before the commissioners, that, according to the best information he could obtain, the quantity of illegally distilled spirits annually produced in the Highlands could not amount to less than two millions of gallons. In corroboration of this he stated that, in 1821, only 298,138 gallons were brought to the charge in the Highlands; and of these, 254,000 gallons were permitted to the Lowlands, leaving only 44,000 gallons for the consumption of the whole country; a supply which, we are well assured, would hardly be sufficient for the demand of two moderately populous parishes. In a letter of Captain Munro, of Teaninich, to the commissioners, it is stated that, "at Tain, where there are upwards of twenty licensed public-houses, not one gallon had been permitted from the legal distilleries for upwards of twelve months," though a small quantity of smuggled whisky had been purchased at the excise sales, to give a colour of legality to the trade. The same gentleman thus expresses himself in another part of his letter :—" The moral effects of this baneful trade of smuggling on the lower classes are most conspicuous, and increasing in an alarming degree, as evidenced by the multiplicity of crimes, and by a degree of insubordination formerly little known in this part of the country. In several districts, such as Strathconon, Strathcarron, &c., the excise officers are now often deforced, and dare not attempt to do their duty; and smuggled whisky is often carried to market by smugglers escorted by armed men, in defiance of the laws. In short, the Irish system is making progress in the Highlands of Scotland."

To arrest the progress of demoralisation, government, pursuant to the judicious advice of the commissioners, reduced the duties on Scotch to the same level as those on Irish whisky; and the consequences were equally signal and salutary. The subjoined statement shows the effect of the various changes in the rates of duty from 1799 down to the present time (see p. 350).

This table sets the advantage of the reduction of the duty in 1823 in the clearest point of view; the consumption of duty-paid spirits having more than doubled in the course of two years, at the same time that illicit distillation was all but suppressed. The addition of 6d. to the duty in 1830 gave a check to the consumption from which it did not speedily recover, and revived, though happily to no great extent, the dormant energies of the smuggler. The influ-

An Account of the Quantities of Corn Spirits made in Scotland, which have paid the Duties of Excise for Home Consumption; stating the Rate of Duty paid, and also the Nett Amount of Revenue received, in each Year since the Year 1798.

Years.	Number of Gallons.	Rate per Gallon. In the Lowlands.	Rate per Gallon. In the Highlands.	Nett Amount of Revenue. £.	s.	d.
1799	1,670,388	64*l.* 16*s.* 4*d.* per gall. of still content, and 1*s.* 1½*d.* per gallon of spirits made.	7*l.* 16*s.* 0¼*d.* per gall. of still content, and 1*s.* 4¼*d.* per gallon of spirits made.	255,085	18	0
1800	775,750	64*l.* 16*s.* 4*d.* per gall. of still content.	7*l.* 16*s.* 0¼*d.* per gall. of still content.	82,868	17	5
1801	,,	,,	,,	,,		
1802	1,158,558	3*s.* 10½*d.* per gall. of spirits.	3*s.* 4¼*d.* per gallon of spirits.	217,866	0	0
1803	2,022,409	,,	,,	370,086	1	5
1804	1,889,757	5*s.* 9¾*d.*	5*s.* 0½*d.*	499,002	3	3
1805	1,625,987	,,	,,	421,896	16	2
1806	1,812,237	,,	,,	461,835	11	6
1807	2,653,478	5*s.* 8¾*d.*	5*s.* 0½*d.*—4*s.* 11¼*d.*	783,547	8	2
1808	2,683,342	,,	4*s.* 11¼*d.*	778,029	17	10
1809	,,	,,	,,	,,		
1810	,,	,,	,,	,,		
1811	1,581,524	5*s.* 8¾*d.*—8*s.* 0½*d.*	4*s.* 11¼*d.*—6*s.* 7½*d.*	444,834	11	5
1812	1,318,115	8*s.* 0½*d.*	6*s.* 7½*d.*	586,427	0	8
1813	,,	,,	,,	,,		
1814	1,474,187	,,	,,	578,741	0	1
		Lowlands and Highlands.				
1815	1,591,148	9*s.* 4½. per gallon of spirits.		741,926	14	1
1816	918,859	,,		420,481	15	8
1817	1,906,950	6*s.* 2½*d.*		598,786	15	5
1818	2,066,988	,,		662,383	0	2
1819	2,125,150	,,		658,334	11	0
1820	1,863,987	,,		575,880	2	4
1821	2,385,495	,,		737,347	3	1
1822	2,225,124	,,		686,369	15	11
1823	2,303,286	6*s.* 2*d.*—2*s.* 4¾*d.*		556,843	18	5
1824	4,350,301	2*s.* 4¾*d.*		524,137	9	9
1825	5,981,549	,,		717,872	1	4
1826	3,988,788	2*s.* 10*d.*		563,256	16	9
1827	4,752,199	,,		672,450	6	6
1828	5,716,180	,,		809,559	4	10
1829	5,777,280	,,		818,172	4	2
1830	6,007,631	2*s.* 10*d.*—3*s.*—3*s.* 4*d.*		939,258	6	0
1831	5,700,689	3*s.* 4*d.*		950,041	4	3
1832	5,405,439	,,		900,906	10	0
1833	5,988,556	,,		998,051	3	3
1834	6,045,043	,,		1,007,505	10	0
1835	6,018,932	,,		1,002,305	0	10
1836	6,620,826	,,		1,103,450	3	4
1837	6,124,035	,,		1,020,569	18	10
1838	6,259,711	,,		1,043,180	18	4
1839	6,188,582	,,		1,031,213	10	0
1840	6,180,138	3*s.* 4*d.*—3*s.* 8*d.*		1,087,749	2	11
1841	5,989,905	3*s.* 8*d.*		1,098,118	1	11
1842	5,595,186	,,		1,025,743	13	7
1843	5,593,798	,,		1,025,506	1	6

ence of the 4*d*. unwisely added to the duty in 1840 is also most perceptible.

Previously to the reduction of the duty on Irish and Scotch spirits, in 1823, the duty on English spirits amounted to 11*s*. 8½*d*. a-gallon. This high duty, and the restrictions under which the trade was placed, were productive of the worst effects. They went far to enable the distillers to fix the price of spirits, "and consequently" (we quote the words of the commissioners) "to raise it much beyond that which was sufficient to repay, with a profit, the cost of the manufacture and the duty advanced to the Crown." And, in proof of this, the commissioners mention that, in November, 1823, "when corn spirits might be purchased in Scotland for about 2*s*. 3*d*. a-gallon, raw spirits could not be purchased in England for less than 4*s*. 6*d*. ready money, and 4*s*. 9*d*. credit, omitting in both cases the duty." In consequence of this state of things, the adulteration of spirits was carried on to a great extent in England; and the large profits made by the smuggler occasioned their clandestine importation in considerable quantities from Scotland and Ireland. To obviate these inconveniences, and at the same time to neutralise the powerful additional stimulus that the reduction of the duties in Scotland and Ireland would have given to smuggling, had the duties in England been continued at their former amount, the latter were reduced, in 1826, to 7*s*. a-gallon; facilities being at the same time given to the importation of spirits from the other parts of the empire; and, in consequence of these measures, the quantity of spirits brought to the charge was about doubled. In a fiscal point of view the success of the measure was too obvious and decided to admit of dispute; but it has, like the preceding measures in Ireland and Scotland, been complained of for the encouragement it is said to have given to the vice of gin-drinking. But there is really no foundation for this allegation. At the period (1823) when the consumption of home-made spirits appeared, from the excise returns, to

An ACCOUNT of the QUANTITIES of CORN SPIRITS made in ENGLAND, which have paid the Duties of Excise for Home Consumption; stating the Rate of Duty paid, and also the Nett Amount of Revenue received in each Year since the Year 1790.

Years.	No. of Gallons.	Rate per Gallon.	Nett Amount of Revenue.		
			£.	s.	d.
1791	4,072,735	3s. 4¾d.	653,168	11	1
1792	4,544,618	,,	771,415	16	4
1793	4,244,447	,,	720,305	1	3
1794	4,594,793	3s. 4¾d.—3s. 10¾d.	828,488	14	9
1795	4,711,640	3s. 10¾d.—4s. 4½d.	973,765	7	1
1796	300,627	4s. 4½d.	54,713	12	2
1797	2,808,948	4s. 4½d.—4s. 10¼d.	672,440	19	9
1798	3,630,872	4s. 10¼d.	881,188	15	1
1799	4,114,936	,,	998,334	15	9
1800	4,335,550	4s. 10¼d.—5s. 4¼d.	1,014,430	19	8
1801	99,744	5s. 4¼d.	27,809	7	2
1802	3,464,380	,,	937,311	3	6
1803	5,353,309	5s. 4¼d.—8s. 0½d.	1,460,738	19	4
1804	3,678,679	8s. 0½d.	1,493,168	18	2
1805	4,927,475	,,	2,040,061	17	7
1806	4,091,637	,,	1,688,140	4	2
1807	4,741,939	,,	1,935,593	0	10
1808	5,384,394	,,	2,210,042	0	7
1809	630,340	,,	263,439	4	2
1810		,,			
1811	112,868	8s. 0½d.—10s. 2¾d.	47,040	12	7
1812	3,622,970	10s. 2¾d.	1,873,207	7	2
1813	162,191	,,	83,016	3	8
1814	4,053,706	,,	2,086,268	18	4
1815	5,468,987	,,	2,840,591	16	0
1816	4,745,484	,,	2,447,136	19	11
1817	4,133,663	,,	2,132,320	16	9
1818	5,259,662	,,	2,681,131	3	5
1819	4,146,505	10s. 2¾d.—11s. 8¼d.	2,218,007	7	9
1820	4,284,798	11s. 8¼d.	2,510,822	6	6
1821	4,125,616	,,	2,419,280	18	6
1822	4,694,055	,,	2,749,372	5	3
1823	3,803,312	,,	2,222,273	8	5
1824	4,392,611	,,	2,567,378	3	6
1825	3,655,232	,,	2,055,027	4	5
1826	7,407,204	7s.	2,592,521	13	1
1827	6,671,562	,,	2,335,046	15	9
1828	7,759,687	,,	2,715,890	9	0
1829	7,700,766	,,	2,695,268	2	0
1830	7,732,101	7s.—7s. 6d.	2,857,147	19	0
1831	7,434,047	7s. 6d.	2,787,767	12	6
1832	7,281,900	,,	2,730,712	10	0
1833	7,717,303	,,	2,893,988	12	6
1834	7,644,301	,,	2,866,608	11	4
1835	7,315,053	,,	2,743,124	15	1
1836	7,875,702	,,	2,953,388	5	0
1837	7,133,869	,,	2,674,899	16	9
1838	7,930,490	,,	2,973,908	5	0
1839	8,186,552	,,	3,069,952	6	0
1840	8,278,148	7s. 6d.—7s. 10d.	3,183,865	1	0
1841	8,166,985	7s. 10d.	3,198,548	6	9
1842	7,956,054	,,	3,116,121	3	0
1843	7,719,458	,,	3,023,444	17	8

amount to about three millions and a half gallons, the commissioners of revenue inquiry estimated it, taking the smuggled spirits into account, at between five and six millions ditto! and it appears from the foregoing account (p. 352), that it amounted for the year ended the 5th of January, 1844, to 7,719,458 gallons, producing 3,023,445*l.* of revenue; so that making allowance for the increase of population since 1823, and for the check given to adulteration and smuggling, and considering also that the consumption of foreign spirits was not greater in 1843 than in 1823, it may be safely affirmed that the practice of spirit drinking has not increased in England during the last twenty years. No doubt, however, it is still much too prevalent, and a great deal of money is wasted by the poor on gin which had far better be expended on other things. But how much soever we may deplore the prevalence of gin-drinking, the evil is not one that can be cured, or even mitigated, by increasing the duties on spirits. Such increase would substitute illegitimate for legitimate channels of supply; it would injure the public revenue and diffuse among the populace the predatory and ferocious habits that mark the character of the smuggler; and it would do all this without lessening in any degree the vice of drunkenness.

But though we cannot lessen the consumption of gin by increasing the duties thereon, we may lessen it by making the necessary reductions on other things. A taste for tea is not very compatible with a taste for gin; and the reduction of the duties on tea to a reasonable amount, would, by encouraging its consumption, be one of the best means of discouraging the consumption of gin, and consequently of promoting the progress of temperance and the well-being of the lower classes. And as this change, however advantageous, would merely be from one taxed article to another, the interests of the revenue would not suffer by its taking place.

The history of the duties on foreign spirits (brandy and geneva) affords an additional illustration of the pernicious influence of oppressive duties. At an average of the four years ending with 1782, when the duties on brandy and geneva amounted to 9s. per wine gallon on proof spirits, and to 18s. per do. on such as were of greater strength, 740,604 gallons (643,112 brandy, and 97,492 geneva) were annually entered for consumption. But it appears, from a statement in the First Report of the Revenue Commission in 1783, that the Commissioners of Excise estimated that in the preceding *three* years upwards of 13,000,000 gallons of foreign spirits had been clandestinely imported.* This estimate may, perhaps, have been exaggerated; but that smuggling was then carried on to an unprecedented extent, is a fact which no one has ever attempted to dispute. Mr. Pitt, who was fully aware of the magnitude of the evil, determined upon its suppression, and in that view reduced the duty to 5s. a-gallon. The event more than answered his expectations; the entries for consumption having amounted, in 1789 and 1790, to 2,114,025 gallons a-year, at an average. In 1791 the duty was raised to 5s. 10d. per gallon; the quantities entered for consumption in that year and in 1792 being respectively 1,949,418 and 1,984,822 gallons.

During the war that soon after broke out with France the duties were increased till, at length, they amounted, in 1814, to 18s. 10d. per wine gallon (equal to 22s. 6d. per imperial gallon), at which rate they continued till 1840, when 4d. per gallon being added to them, they have since been 22s. 10d. a-gallon!

During the war the trade was liable to so many interruptions from other causes than the variations in the rate of duty, that no proper estimate can be formed of the peculiar influence of the latter; but since the peace the mischievous influence of the exorbitant height to which it has been carried has been obvious to every one.

At an average of the four years ending with 1792, when the duty was 6s. 6d. per imperial gallon, the entries for con-

* Hamilton's Principles of Taxation, pp. 273, 275.

sumption (in Great Britain) amounted to 1,733,816 imperial gallons a-year. And as the population has nearly doubled since 1790, had the consumption continued at its old level, as compared with the consumers, it should at present have amounted to about 3,460,000 gallons. But, in point of fact, it only amounted, during the three years ending with 1842, to 1,134,061 gallons, being less than one-third part, as compared with the population, of what it amounted to when the duty was 6s. 6d. a-gallon.

But in this, as in all similar cases, the real is much greater than the apparent consumption. The cost of brandy and geneva varies in the contiguous continental ports from 3s. to 5s. a-gallon; and it is needless to say, that under such circumstances smuggling and adulteration are very extensively practised. Round the coasts of Kent and Sussex the fishermen and country-people are more than half smugglers; and ferocious contests not unfrequently take place between them and the coast-guard. And while, on the one hand, the revenue is defrauded by the clandestine introduction of foreign spirits, it is, on the other, equally defrauded by the sale of counterfeits, passed off as genuine Cognac and Schiedam.

Under these circumstances can any one doubt that the reduction of the duty on foreign spirits to 10s. or 12s. a-gallon (for any less reduction would be of no use) would be a most advantageous measure? The precedent of 1786, when Mr. Pitt trebled the legitimate consumption of foreign spirits and added considerably to the revenue by taking 50 per cent. from the duties, is in all respects applicable to the existing state of things. It may be supposed, perhaps, that were the consumption of brandy and geneva to increase, that of British spirits would be proportionally diminished; so that the revenue would lose on the one hand by the reduction of the duties what it gained on the other. Such, however, could not be the case. The duties on British spirits are, in England, 7s. 10d.; in Scotland, 3s. 8d.; and in Ireland, 2s. 8d. per gallon respectively; making it plain that to whatever extent they might be superseded by spirits charged with a duty of 10s. or 12s. per gallon, the revenue would be largely benefited.   There is not, however, any real ground for supposing that the proposed change would sensibly affect the consumption of British spirits.   The latter would be used after the reduction of the duty on foreign spirits, as they are used at this moment, by the bulk of the lower classes, the consumption of foreign spirits being principally confined to those of a superior grade.   The reduction of the duty on foreign spirits in 1786 was not followed by any falling off in the consumption of British spirits; and though the consumption of coffee was increased more than six-fold by the reduction of the duty in 1808, that increase, gigantic as it was, had no effect whatever on the consumption of tea. And what reason is there for thinking that the increased consumption of foreign spirits should have a different effect? The reduction of the duty to 10s. or 12s. a-gallon would make an end of that smuggling and adulteration which is now so extensively carried on ; and would, in this way, add materially to the revenue and to the well-being of the population.

But the question with regard to the reduction of the duty on foreign spirits is not to be looked at only in a fiscal point of view.   Their reduction to a reasonable amount would be of very great importance to the commercial interests of the country.   Our trade with France has increased during the last ten years more rapidly than almost any other branch of our commerce; and nothing would be so likely to extend it as the reduction of the duties in question.   Brandy is one of the principal equivalents France has to offer for foreign commodities ; and those who exclude it, or load it with oppressive duties, lay, by so doing, their trade with her under serious difficulties.   We are apt enough to find fault with the commercial policy of France, which, indeed, is in many respects highly objectionable.   In truth and reality, however, she is more liberal to us than we are to her; and for some years past the value of the exports from England to France has very materially exceeded that of the imports.   But, whatever policy France may adopt, more than enough has been said to show that our interests would be most materially promoted by the effectual reduction of the present exorbitant duties on foreign spirits. Such a measure would suppress a widely extended system of smuggling and fraud; would increase the revenue; and would add very considerably to our trade.

It is a curious fact that notwithstanding the immense increase of population and wealth since 1790, the consumption of wine has remained nearly stationary. This singular result has been ascribed to the change of habits, and the increase of temperance among the middle and upper classes. But though this has, no doubt, had considerable influence, we incline to think that the great increase in the numbers of those who drink wine would more than countervail the change of habit; and that the falling off in the consumption as compared with the population is to be ascribed to the increase of the duties, and to the extensive adulteration to which wine is subject (see *ante,* p. 328). We have previously noticed the sudden and rapid increase in the consumption of French wines occasioned by the reduction of the duty, in 1825, from 13*s.* 9*d.* to 7*s.* 6*d.* per imperial gallon (*ante,* p. 168). And the gradually increasing consumption of Marsala, which now exceeds 400,000 gallons a-year, shows the powerful influence of cheapness in creating a demand even for an indifferent wine. But to show how much the consumption of wine is promoted by moderate duties, it is only necessary to state that the reduction in 1825 was not confined to French wines; but that it was universal, and that it amounted to about 50 per cent., the duty on Portuguese, Spanish, and Sicilian wines being reduced from 9*s.* 1*d.* to 4*s.* 10*d.* per imperial gallon, and that on Rhenish from 11*s.* 3*d.* to 4*s.* 10*d.* Now observe the influence of this effectual reduction. At an average of the four years ending with 1824, the consumption amounted to 4.792,259 gallons a-year; whereas at an average of the four years beginning with 1826 (being those after the reduction),

the consumption amounted to 6,566,208 gallons a-year, or
to 1,773,949 gallons more than during the high duties.   In
consequence of the increase of consumption the loss to the
revenue occasioned by the reduction in 1825 was but inconsiderable.   But circumstances are at present materially different; and it is not so easy a matter, keeping, as government is bound to do, the interests of the revenue in view, to
deal with the existing duties.   Being only 5s. 9d. per imperial gallon, or rather less than 1s. per bottle, they cannot
be objected to when charged on the. superior qualities.
They are not oppressive except when applied to the inferior
qualities; and from the difficulty of fairly assessing *ad
valorem* duties on wine (p. 173), it is no easy matter to obviate this defect.   A reduction of the present duty to the
low rate of 3s. per gallon, would occasion a serious loss of
revenue without being of any material advantage.   Such
reduction would not amount to 6d. a-bottle, and would consequently be all but imperceptible in as far as regards the
finer and higher priced wines; and even as regards those
of an inferior quality it may be doubted whether its influence
would be very considerable.   Unless, therefore, means
should be discovered for obviating the difficulties in the way
of assessing an *ad valorem* duty on wine, there would probably be but little advantage in disturbing the subsisting
arrangement.

From the reign of William III. down to 1831, French
wines were burdened with duties which were never less than
33⅓ per cent. higher than those laid on other wines.   During
its continuance this was the most unjustifiable and mischievous regulation in our commercial code.   It was directly
injurious by forcing the consumption of an inferior in preference to a superior wine; and it was still more injurious
by its offensive character, and by its provoking and justify-
ing the retaliatory measures adopted by the French against
our trade.   The abolition of this miserable remnant of a
short-sighted, vindictive policy was one of the wisest of the
commercial measures of this century.

The history of other countries abounds with equally conclusive examples of the superior productiveness of moderate
duties.   In 1775 M. Turgot deducted a *half* from the
customs and other duties chargeable on the fish sold in the
Paris market ; but, notwithstanding this reduction, the
amount of the duties collected was not diminished.   The
demand for fish must therefore have been doubled, in consequence of the inhabitants being enabled to supply themselves at a comparatively cheap rate.*

In 1813, when sugar imported into the French empire
paid a duty of one franc sixty cents. the *livre* or pound,
the imports amounted to about fourteen millions of pounds,
which, as France, and the countries then incorporated with
her, contained about forty-two millions of inhabitants, gives
the *third* part of a pound weight to each.   In 1814 this
exorbitant duty was reduced to about a *fifth* part, or to
thirty cents. the pound; and though the population of
France had then been reduced from forty-two to about
twenty-eight millions, the average annual importations of
1814 and 1815 amounted to forty-four millions of pounds,
being upwards of $1\frac{1}{2}$ lb. to each individual, or about *five*
times as much as the consumption had amounted to under
the high duty.   In consequence of this increase of consumption the low duty yielded nearly as large a revenue as the
high duty.†

Ustariz gives a variety of details respecting the disastrous
effects which certain taxes have had on industry in Spain,
and the advantages resulting from the repeal and modification of others, some of which we have previously noticed.
Among other instances, he tells us that Valencia, though
barren of grain and flocks, and not equal in extent to two-
thirds of Arragon, paid a much larger revenue to the royal
treasury.   This, he says, was owing to the comparatively
flourishing state of commerce and manufactures in Valencia ;

* Say, ' Traité d'Economie Politique,' tome ii., p. 339.   Lord Kames, in
his ' Sketches of the History of Man,' states that these duties amounted to forty-
eight per cent. *ad valorem.* Vol. i. p. 486, 4to. edit.

† ' Richesse des Nations,' par Garnier, v., p. 304, 2de éd.

and he then adds,—" This increase and improvement in manufactures and commerce is ascribed to the equitable and kind treatment the weavers receive in that province, and to his majesty's goodness in reducing the excessive taxes which were charged upon flesh meat and other provisions ; and his taking off wholly that which was laid on bread in ancient times; as also the imposts known by the name of ancient duties and generalities. These duties were partly replaced by others, but in such a manner that they were rendered much lighter, the people in general eased, and the royal revenue improved."*

The case of Ireland during the latter years of the late war affords evidence, which is of itself more than sufficient though there were none else to which to appeal, to demonstrate the impotency of taxation when carried beyond a certain extent to produce revenue. We have previously seen that the too great additions made to the duty on spirits in Ireland, occasioned a serious diminution and not an increase of revenue; and similar results followed the excessive additions made to the customs duties on spirits, wines, tobacco, and other articles imported into that country. But without tiring the reader by entering into details, it is sufficient to direct his attention to the following account of the nett revenue of Ireland in 1807, 1817, &c. :—

REVENUE of IRELAND paid into the Exchequer in British Currency, excluding the trifling articles of Quit-rents and Fees, in

	1807	1817	1818	1819	1820	1821
Customs	1,976,961	1,483,805	1,635,470	1,514,259	1,202,380	1,437,653
Excise	1,765,466	1,687,941	1,833,473	1,705,328	1,564,651	1,632,640
Assessed Taxes .		442,708	342,615	280,150	264,570	308,223
Stamps	564,424	520,266	509,039	482,469	407,403	400,827
Post-Office . . .	71,390	57,230	46,153	53,538	59,077	65,538
Total . . .	4,378,241	4,191,950	4,366,750	4,035,744	3,498,081	3,844,881

But in the interval between 1807 and 1816 taxes were

* ' Theory and Practice of Commerce,' vol. ii. p. 310. Eng. Trans.

imposed in Ireland which it was estimated would produce as follows :—

Taxes imposed in 1808						£363,000
,,	,,	1809	.	.	.	. 600,000
,,	,,	1810	.	.	.	No budget.
,,	,,	1811	.	.	.	. 338,000
,,	,,	1812	.	.	.	. 229,000
,,	,,	1813	.	.	.	. 595,000
,,	,,	1814	.	.	.	. 521,000
,,	,,	1815	.	.	.	. 730,000
	Total		.	.	.	£3,376,000

Now, if we deduct from this sum taxes estimated to produce about 360,000*l.* a-year remitted at the end of the war, it follows, had the estimates on which the taxes were imposed been good for anything, that the nett revenue of Ireland should have been about three millions greater in 1817 and the subsequent years than in 1807. But the above account shows that instead of being increased, the revenue had been diminished in the interval between 1807 and 1817 ; and, consequently, that the new taxes, which it was said would produce above 3,000,000*l.* a-year, had not, in fact, produced a solitary sixpence. They diminished consumption, and threw the greater part of the supply of taxed articles into the hands of smugglers, but they were unable to divert a single farthing from the pockets of the people into the Treasury.

Now, look at the other side of the picture : the duty on spirits, which amounted in 1817 to 5*s.* 7½*d.*, was, in 1843, only 2*s.* 8*d.* per gallon; the assessed taxes, which produced, in 1817, 442,708*l.*, have since been wholly repealed ; the rates of postage have been reduced from (probably) about 4*d.* or 5*d.* to 1*d.* ; and some important reductions have been made in the customs duties : and yet, despite these reductions, despite the efforts of Father Matthew, which have materially affected the duty on spirits, and despite the pernicious agitation which disturbs, distracts, and impoverishes the country, the nett revenue of Ireland amounted in 1843 to 4,097,385*l.*! Can more be required to establish the immeasurable superiority in every point of view of moderate over oppressive taxes?

CHAPTER XII.

INFLUENCE OF VARIATIONS IN THE VALUE OF MONEY
ON TAXATION.

THE rate of taxation is affected by variations in the value of money, increasing when its value rises, and diminishing when it falls.

Hume has observed, in his ' Essay on Money,' that " In every kingdom into which money begins to flow in greater abundance than formerly, everything takes a new face; labour and industry gain life, the merchant becomes more enterprising, the manufacturer more diligent and skilful, and even the farmer follows his plough with greater alacrity and attention. But when gold and silver are diminishing, the workman has not the same employment from the manufacturer and merchant, though he pays the same price for everything in the market. The farmer cannot dispose of his corn and cattle, though he must pay the same rent to the landlord. The poverty, beggary, and sloth that must ensue are easily foreseen."

Hume appears to have supposed that the stimulus he has so well described, given by an influx of money to industry, originated in the circumstance of the additional money coming first into the hands of capitalists, and enabling them to extend their businesses and employ more work-people. But though this would undoubtedly have some considerable influence, we incline to think that the philosophical historian has overlooked the mode in which an increase in the quantity and a fall in the value of money principally contribute to excite industry and enterprise. Such fall proportionally diminishes the taxes, and other fixed money-payments borne by the industrious classes. The prices of commodities vary with variations in the value of money, while taxes, rents, mortgages,

and other pecuniary burdens continue stationary. The latter
are rated or specified in certain amounts of money ; those to
whom they are due being obliged to receive the stipulated
amounts in payment, though the value of money should have
fallen 10, 20, or even 50 per cent. since the date of the contract
or engagement in which the payments originate; those by
whom they are due being on their part bound to pay the same
amounts though there had been a corresponding rise in the
value of money.* Hence the powerful influence of variations
in its value over the different classes of society. When it
declines, the debtor portion of society, or those who have
fixed money-payments to make, are proportionally benefited at the expense of the creditor portion, or those who have
such payments to receive, and conversely when it rises.
Fundholders, annuitants, landholders during the currency of
the leases of their estates, mortgagees, &c., suffer according
to the diminution in the value of the currency; for though
their money-incomes and claims continue nominally the same,
their value is really reduced, and they no longer have their
former command over necessaries and conveniences. But
the farmer, while he pays the same rent to his landlord, the
same taxes to government, and, perhaps, the same composition for tithe, sells his produce for a price increased proportionally to the reduced value of money. In like manner the
merchant, manufacturer, and tradesman pay the same duties
on their goods, the same port and market dues, the same tolls,
the same rent for shops and warehouses, the same rate of interest for capital borrowed, while they all obtain increased
prices for whatever they have to sell. In other words, the
condition of farmers, manufacturers, and tradesmen of all descriptions is improved at the expense of their landlords and
creditors, and of the fundholders, and other receivers of taxes,
whose incomes are either temporarily or permanently re-

---

* In antiquity, when the weight and fineness of coins were liable to frequent
changes, it was not unusual to stipulate that *valor monetæ considerandus atque
inspiciendus est a tempore contractus, non autem a tempore solutionis.* But such
stipulations are now unknown.

duced through the fall in the value of money. The greater the fall the more advantageous for them, and conversely.

Now, when we consider the endless variety of fixed or stationary pecuniary payments in such a country as this, including not only the sums paid as interest on the public debt, but most of the other outgoings of government which do not speedily accommodate themselves to the altered value of money, with the rents payable for farms and houses let on lease, or under equivalent agreements, fees, duties, the interest of mortgages, and other stationary loans, the sums payable to private annuitants and to clergymen, the fees of lawyers, physicians, &c., it is obvious that the total of such payments must amount to a vast sum. No doubt it sometimes, and, indeed, not unfrequently happens, that individuals belong to both classes, or that they have fixed payments to receive as well as to make, and that, therefore, neither the gain to the one party, nor the loss to the other, from fluctuations in the value of money, is so great as might be at first supposed. Still, however, there is no room for doubting that the greater proportion by far of fixed payments is made to the classes not engaged in business, or in industrious undertakings, by those who are. And hence the signal advantage conferred by any considerable fall in the value of money on the latter, that is, on those whose well-being is commonly, though improperly, supposed to be identical with that of the public. Such fall, by lightening the burden of taxation and all the fixed charges affecting them, increases universally the productiveness of industry and the rate of profit; and it is hardly necessary to add, that this increased profit operates as a spur to production; that it quickens all the operations of trade, and occasions an increased demand for labour.

The opposite effects follow, of course, when, instead of falling, the currency becomes more valuable. Taxes and fixed charges being then augmented in an equal degree, the profits of those by whom they are principally borne are proportionally reduced; industry is depressed; and the situation of the productive classes changed for the worse.

Hence it is always indispensable, if we would form a fair estimate of the pressure of taxation at different periods, to learn, in the first place, whether money has been of the same value at the periods to be compared; and if not, how much it has varied. A large nominal amount of taxation may not, provided money have a low value, be a greater burden than a comparatively small nominal amount of taxation, where money has a high value.

In illustration of this statement we may observe, that at an average of the three years ending with 1816, the depreciation of the currency as compared with gold, amounted to 20 per cent., having in 1814 exceeded 25 per cent. Now, as the average nett revenue of the United Kingdom amounted during the same period of three years to 68,536,521*l.* a-year, it follows, allowing for the depreciation of the currency, that it did not then really exceed 54,829,217*l.* estimated in our present money, being only about 3,000,000*l.* a-year greater than the revenue in 1840, 1841, and 1842. And it has been argued, that if to the advantages accruing to the productive portion of the community during the latter years of the war, from the diminution of taxation occasioned by the depreciation, we add the advantages they derived from the diminution of rent, interest, and other fixed payments, it will be found that the burdens they had to bear at the period referred to were really less than those they have since had to sustain, notwithstanding the repeal of so many taxes.

But though the rise in the value of the currency subsequently to 1815 added most materially to the burdens laid on the productive classes, it certainly has not done this to anything like the extent implied in this statement. Had population and industry remained about stationary since 1815, we do not know that those who contend that the payments on account of taxes and fixed burdens now to be made by the industrious classes do not differ materially from those they had to make in that year, would be very wide of the mark. But everybody knows that, instead of being stationary, the population, wealth, and productive capacities of the United

Kingdom have increased prodigiously since 1815; so that, supposing the real amount of the public burdens and fixed charges to have varied but little since the above epoch, it must now, from the greater field over which it is spread, and the greater ability to bear it, be proportionally less felt. The same amount of taxation that would entail great privations on an individual worth only 300*l.* a-year would be comparatively little felt by him were his income increased to 400*l.* or 450*l.* And we incline to think that the increase of the public income since the conclusion of the revolutionary war with France has been in something like this proportion.

Although, however, there cannot, as it appears to us, be any doubt that a fall in the value of money, though injurious to large classes, is, on the whole, advantageous to a country, we hope it will not be thence inferred that we are disposed to approve in any degree of an intentional reduction of its value. Money being the standard or measure of value, it is of the utmost importance that it should vary as little as possible. Governments are bound to do all in their power to give effect to the legitimate contracts and engagements of individuals; and it would be the grossest injustice were they to attempt, by raising or lowering the value of money, to benefit certain classes at the expense of others. Whatever might be gained, on the one hand, by a depreciation of the currency would, there is every reason to think, be more than lost, on the other, by the flagrant breach of faith by which it would be accompanied. Public and private credit would, for a while, be destroyed; and a large amount of capital would be transferred to other countries as to places of security. It is needless to attempt to apologize for a measure of this sort by saying, that it is necessary to lighten the pressure of a taxation too great for the resources of the country. Were such really the case, the proper plan would be to make an equivalent deduction from the public debt; for this would accomplish the object in view without affecting the creditors of private individuals, and defrauding every one who had lent money or sold goods on credit of a portion of his just claims. "When it becomes

necessary for a state to declare itself bankrupt, in the same
manner as when it becomes necessary for an individual to do
so, a fair, open, and avowed bankruptcy is always the measure which is both least dishonourable to the debtor, and
least hurtful to the creditor.   The honour of a state is surely
very poorly provided for, when, in order to cover the disgrace of a real bankruptcy, it has recourse to a juggling
trick of this kind, so easily seen through and at the same
time so extremely pernicious."*

It has sometimes been alleged that the rise in the value of
the currency in the interval between 1814, when the depreciation was greatest, and 1821, when it ceased, was really much
greater than is indicated by the difference during that period
between the values of paper and gold; inasmuch as it is contended that the value of gold was itself raised by the return to
specie payments.   We doubt, however, whether this opinion
have any good foundation.   The quantity of the precious
metals distributed among the various nations of the earth is
too vast to have been sensibly affected by the drain occasioned
by the resumption of cash payments in this country; and it is
probable that the facilities given for the employment of bills,
and other substitutes for money, by the nearly simultaneous
cessation of hostilities on the continent, more than countervailed
the increased demand for specie in Great Britain.   The remarkable fall that has taken place in the prices of corn and
most other articles since the peace has frequently been referred
to as affording a conclusive proof of a general rise in the
value of money.   We believe, however, that it is impossible
to specify a single article that has fallen in price since 1815,
of which the fall may not be satisfactorily accounted for by
changes in the channels of its supply, or in the cost of its
production, or both.   It is to the increased facilities given to
commercial intercourse, and the wonderful improvements and
discoveries in the arts, and not to any increase in the value of

* Wealth of Nations, p. 423.

gold, that we are really indebted for the reduction in the price of commodities since 1816.

In so far, indeed, as the prices of commodities in this country were raised by the depreciation of the currency during the latter years of the war, in the same degree were they reduced when the currency recovered its value, and cash payments were resumed.   But there are really no grounds for thinking that the measure had any effect beyond what is now stated, or that it sensibly affected the value of gold, or raised the standard of the currency.

We have elsewhere given a pretty detailed account of the circumstances which led to the suspension of cash payments by the Bank of England in 1797 ; * and at present it is only necessary to observe that these were wholly of an accidental character ; and that though eventually the suspension led to an over-issue of bank paper, and the depreciation of the currency, it was not introduced because it was supposed or imagined it would have any such results.   The error (and it has produced the most mischievous consequences) consisted in not reverting to specie payments immediately after the crisis of 1797 had passed away.   Seeing, however, that the standard had been virtually abandoned in 1797, and that the currency had been depreciated from 1800 down to 1819, and especially from 1809 to 1816, it is perhaps to be regretted that the standard was not diminished in 1815, or 1816, by raising the mint price of gold from 3*l.* 17*s.* 10½*d.* to 4*l.* 10*s.*, or 4*l.* 15*s.* an ounce.   Great injustice was certainly done to those who had lent money to the state, or to individuals, previously to 1800, by the subsequent depreciation; though, as a large proportion of the debts or credits originally belonging to them must have changed hands during the depreciation, at a proportional discount, the farther injustice that would have been done to these parties, by reducing the standard in 1815 or 1816 to the extent already mentioned, would not have been nearly so great as might at first be supposed; at the same time that it would have prevented the injury which the

* Wealth of Nations, Note on Money, p. 496.

rise in the value of the currency between 1816 and 1821 did to the country, by making the loans and engagements entered into during the period of the depreciation be made good in an undepreciated currency. The truth is, however, that the restoration of the value of the currency was in a great degree accidental; and that no proper opportunity was given for inquiring whether, on the whole, it would be better to continue the depreciation, or to revert to the old standard. The large importations of foreign corn, subsequent to the opening of the Dutch ports in 1814, by occasioning a heavy fall in its price, produced an unprecedented degree of distress, first among the agriculturists, and latterly amongst the country bankers. In 1814, 1815, and 1816 no fewer than 240 private banking companies either became altogether bankrupt or at least stopped payments; and the reduction that was thus occasioned in the quantity of bank paper in circulation raised its value so rapidly that in October, 1816, the depreciation was reduced to 1*l.* 8*s.* 7*d.* per cent. In 1817 and 1818 the average depreciation of paper did not exceed 2*l.* 13*s.* 2*d.* per cent. In the early part of 1819 it rose to about 6*l.* per cent; but it very soon declined, and in 1820 and 1821 paper was nearly on a level with gold.

It will, therefore, be observed that when the resolution to revert to specie payments at the old standard was taken in 1819, the currency had, owing to circumstances beyond the reach of legislative control, been for three years nearly at par. Rents, as well as prices, had been generally reduced; a vast number of annuity bonds had been cancelled; and much of the revulsion and mischief which every sudden increase in the value of money is sure to occasion had been got over. Had the question in regard to the restoration of the standard been agitated between 1810 and 1815, a different decision would, perhaps, have been come to. But when the matter was decided the currency had nearly recovered its value; so that the object of Parliament was not merely to restore the old standard, which it had pledged itself to do, but also to shut the door against a fresh depreciation, and to prevent the value of paper, which for about three years had been nearly on a par with gold, from being again degraded.

But even if it could be shown that the Act of 1819 (Sir Robert Peel's Act) was inexpedient at the time when it was passed, that would add little or nothing to the plea of those who are now clamouring for its repeal or modification. All the objections which it was possible to make to the degradation of the standard in 1819, must apply with tenfold force to every scheme for degrading it in 1845; while, on the other hand, all the arguments that could have been urged in favour of the measure in 1819 are now comparatively worthless. The restored standard has been maintained for twenty-six years, and ninety-nine out of every hundred existing contracts have been entered into with reference to it. To tamper with it now would be unmixed folly. We should again witness the most pernicious subversion of private fortunes. Debtors would be enriched at the expense of their creditors; the ignorant and the unwary would be the prey of the cunning and the crafty; and capitalists would be eager to leave a country where, owing to the bad faith of government, it was impossible to make loans except at the risk of getting repaid in a depreciated currency. "Whatever, therefore," to avail ourselves of the just and forcible expressions of Mr. Harris, "may be the fate of future times, and whatever the exigencies of affairs may require, it is to be hoped that that most awkward, clandestine, and most direful method of cancelling debts by debasing the standard of money, will be the last that shall be thought of."*

With the exception of the change occasioned by the discovery of the American mines, the value of the precious metals appears to have varied but little from the earliest times. It is, however, supposed by many, and apparently on pretty good grounds, that the value of gold (which is the standard of our currency) is again about to undergo a further,

* Harris on Money and Coins, Part II., p. 108.

and, perhaps, even a greater change than was brought about in the 16th century and the first half of the 17th, by the importation of bullion from the New World. The late increase in the quantity of gold obtained from the washings and mines of Asiatic Russia is altogether unprecedented; and if it should continue for a few years longer, it can hardly fail to occasion a fall in its value as compared with silver and with everything else. It appears from the official accounts that the total produce of the washings in Siberia in 1830 amounted to rather less than 6 poods; whereas it has since gone on increasing with such extraordinary rapidity that in 1842 it amounted to 631 poods. The total produce of all the Russian mines and washings in that year being 971 poods, equivalent to 42,571 lbs. troy, or (at 46*l.* 14*s.* 6*d.* per lb. troy) to 1,989,129*l.* sterling! And the fair presumption would seem to be that this extraordinary supply will not only be maintained, but that it will continue to increase. At all events the produce of the washings and mines amounted in 1843 to no fewer than 1342 poods, or 2,749,135*l.* 9*s.* 3*d.* sterling, being an increase of more than a third on the produce of the previous year. And it is material to observe that these returns comprise only the gold on which duty is paid to the Russian Government; and considering the magnitude of the duty, which varies from 20 to 25 per cent., and the consequent temptation to fraud and smuggling on the part of the officers, as well as of the producers, we may be well assured that the produce must have been a good deal greater than is stated in the returns. We have heard this excess variously estimated; but taking it at a fifth part, which we incline to think may be pretty near the mark, the total produce in 1843 will be 3,298,962*l.* 11*s.* 1*d.*

It may be supposed, perhaps, seeing the vast surface over which it has to be spread, that even this additional supply, great as it obviously is, will not have any very marked effect upon the value of gold, at least for a lengthened period. This, however, will depend in a considerable degree on the continuance of tranquillity. Gold is used as coin and in the

2 B 2

arts; but there is little ground for supposing that the quantity of it used in the latter will be materially increased unless its value fall. It is probable, were Europe involved in war, that the hoarding of the precious metals that would then take place would absorb a large proportion of the increased supply of gold; but so long as peace is preserved it seems probable that, owing to the increasing use of substitutes for coin, and the various methods for economizing its use that are everywhere being adopted, the quantity of bullion converted into coin will not be very rapidly increased. It is true that the increase of population and of civilization going on in Europe, America, and Australia adds proportionally to the field for the employment of the precious metals, and tends in so far to hinder their increase from sinking their value. Still, however, we are well convinced that, should the production of gold in Russia continue for any considerable number of years to be as great as in 1843, it will have a marked influence over its value: and, should such be the case, it will also have a marked, and, as we have seen, a highly beneficial influence over the condition of the productive classes in this and most other countries.

Changes in the value of money, after taxes have been laid on commodities, not only vary the pressure of taxation, but vary, also, the profits of those engaged in different businesses, and the distribution of capital and industry. Were no taxes laid on commodities, when any alteration took place in the value of money they would all sustain an equal rise or an equal fall. So that if the value of bread, or any other article, varied from this cause 5, or 10, or 20 per cent., all other articles would vary to the same extent, and in the same way. But this is not the case when certain commodities are taxed: for, with respect to a taxed commodity, it is clear, inasmuch as the nominal amount of the tax continues the same, that only that portion of its price which is independent of the tax will vary with variations in the value of money. Suppose, by way of illustration, that a quantity of butchers' meat and a quantity of tea sell for the same sum, or for 100*l.*; and suppose, farther, that money falls 10 per cent. in value; it is evident that the price of butchers' meat, which is not affected by any tax, will immediately rise to 110*l.*; but as, at least, half the price of tea consists of a tax, the nominal magnitude of which is not affected by the change in the value of money, the depreciation will affect only that portion of the price of tea which is over and above the tax; so that, while the butchers' meat rose to 110*l.*, tea will only rise to 105*l.*

A rise in the value of the currency would have a precisely opposite effect. The money price of an untaxed article would then be reduced proportionally to the whole increase in the value of money; whereas that part only of the price of taxed articles that is exclusive of the tax would fall when money rose in value.

In these cases a change is made, not only in the pressure of taxation generally, but in its particular pressure on certain classes of producers; and a change being, in consequence, effected in their profits, capital is withdrawn from certain employments to be vested in others. Suppose, to exemplify this statement, that profits are at the same, or near the same level, taking all things into account, in different businesses: if, on the one hand, the value of money fall, the burden of taxation being proportionally diminished, the profits of all who are engaged in the production of taxed commodities will be evidently raised above the common level; while, on the other hand, if the value of money rise, the profits of those who produce taxed commodities will be as evidently sunk below the same level. It consequently follows that all fluctuations in the value of money, whatever may be their direction, if they be at all considerable, necessarily occasion at the time a good deal of derangement in commercial plans and speculations, and a stagnation in some businesses with a corresponding excitement in others. But the distinguishing circumstance is that, in the end, when money rises in value, the profits of the industrious classes are diminished, and that when it falls they are increased. Hence the advantage, in a national point of view, when it is brought about by natural causes, or by an increased facility of production, of a fall in the value of the precious metals.

But, as already seen, no advantage of this sort can be derived through the interference of the Legislature. The rights and properties of all classes of its subjects being alike entitled to protection, no change of this description can ever originate with, or be countenanced by, a just government. However disguised, it must, in fact, be a robbery of one class or other: and it is not merely the duty of governments resolutely to oppose all attempts to change the value of money, but it also is the bounden duty of those by whom the issue of paper, or of other substitutes for coin, is authorized or tolerated, to take effectual means for maintaining the value of such paper or other articles constantly on a par with that of gold. No supposed advantage should ever tempt governments to palter with this principle, or to countenance any tampering, whether direct or indirect, with the currency. There is never any real distinction between what is just and what is useful. Nor is the use of light weights more disgraceful to an individual than the use of depreciated coin or paper is to a government.

CHAPTER XIII.

REAL AND COMPARATIVE WEIGHT AND INFLUENCE OF TAXATION IN DIFFERENT COUNTRIES.

Real different from Nominal amount of Taxation; how former is to be ascertained—Difficulty of finding any Standard by which to compare the Pressure of Taxation in different Countries—Probable Results of a comparatively high Rate of Taxation—Case of Holland—Illustrations of the high Rate of Taxation in England—Means by which the Pressure on the National Resources may be lightened.

It would seem, from the silence that has prevailed on the subject, as if it had been all but invariably taken for granted that wherever publicity is given to financial details, the exact amount of the taxation borne by a country might be learned by a mere inspection of the public accounts. We, however, are inclined to think that this supposed facility has been a consequence principally of the subject having, notwithstanding its importance, been strangely overlooked ; for a little inquiry would have sufficed to show that there are few things more difficult to learn than the exact amount of the public burdens borne by any considerable country. In making this statement we do not refer to any want of clearness or comprehensiveness in the public accounts : for, however distinctly they may be made out, it will, we apprehend, be found that they are far from supplying means by which to form a just or fair estimate of the magnitude of the national burdens.

The total gross revenue of the United Kingdom for public purposes, raised by taxation, including crown lands, amounted, in 1843, to 56,709,832*l.* But it is probable that a part of this sum will be speedily remitted, so that we may, perhaps, estimate its ordinary amount at about 54,000,000*l.* And it may be supposed that if we add to this the taxation for local purposes, the sum will be the amount of the national burdens. This, however, would be a most erroneous conclusion; and we shall endeavour briefly to state why it would be so.

Clearly to understand this subject, it must be borne in mind that society consists of, and may be divided into, two great classes : those who subsist wholly or principally on incomes derived from their own property, or from private resources ; and those who subsist wholly or principally on incomes derived from the state or from taxes. It is true that these two classes are mixed up in various ways—individuals deriving their principal revenues from private sources being sometimes, also, sharers in the produce of taxation, and conversely. But supposing these discrepancies on the one side and the other to be balanced or adjusted, it is plain that whatever may be the nett revenue, or income free of all sorts of charges, which public functionaries of every description, and public creditors, derive from the state, it must be wholly paid by the other class, and will be identical (supposing the revenue and expenditure equal) with the amount of taxation.

It is easy, however, to see that the amount of taxation estimated in this way will be materially less than its amount as given in the official accounts. The latter, in fact, make all payments and receipts greater than they really are. The interest and other charges on the public debt amount at present to about 29,000,000*l.* a-year; but not less, perhaps, than a fourth part of this sum is drawn back by means of taxes; so that the sum really paid to the public creditor does not exceed 21,750,000*l.*; and so in other cases. A public functionary, for example, gets a salary of 1000*l.* a-year; but if one-fourth part of this sum be drawn back by taxes, his real salary or cost to the country is only 750*l.* Were all taxes superseded by an income-tax, the operose practice which is necessary at present of paying government annuitants and persons in the public service certain sums, and then drawing back portions of these sums by taxes on consumption, might be avoided, and their dividends or salaries proportionally reduced; and were such the case the public revenue and expenditure would each appear to be reduced by the amount of the deductions so made.

We may observe, in farther illustration of this statement, that the cost of keeping up a regiment (and the same principle holds as to all other public establishments) is to be measured by the cost of the various articles, supposing them to be exempted from duty, required for the supply of the officers and soldiers. But these articles being used by other parties than public servants, it is necessary to subject them to duties; and, therefore, the pay of the troops is increased, so that they may be able to provide themselves with the necessary quantity of taxed articles. It is obvious, however, that this increase of pay entails no sacrifice on government; for, being intercepted by the duties, it finds its way back to the coffers of the Treasury, and is again reissued to be again restored to them.

Hence it is indispensable, in attempting to form anything like a fair estimate of the national burdens, to deduct from their apparent amount all that portion of the taxes which is paid by public functionaries, and by those subsisting on the dividends or interest of money lent to government. The balance of taxation remaining after this sum is deducted forms the burden really borne by the public. If A. owe B. on one account 100*l.*, and B. owe A. on another 20*l.* or 30*l.*, it is plain that the sum really due by A. to B. amounts to only 70*l.* or 80*l.* ; and such is precisely the Case with the public. The state owes certain sums to certain parties; but these parties have, by means of taxes, to pay certain sums to the state ; so that the sum really paid by the latter amounts only to the balance or difference between the two.

It would, however, be exceedingly difficult, or rather, perhaps, impracticable, to make anything like a fair estimate of what the balance in question may amount to in this or any other country. Much obviously depends on the nature of taxation. In countries like England, where by far the largest portion of the revenue is derived from taxes on consumption, the sums received from the public functionaries, creditors, and dependents on government, will, of course, be very much larger than in countries where the public revenue is mainly derived from land-taxes, or such like sources.

The inexpediency of attempting to raise any considerable revenue by means of income-taxes, has been sufficiently shown in previous parts of this work. But, without adverting to its other effects, if the rate of the present income-tax were increased, and corresponding abatements made from the duties on tea, sugar, tobacco, and such like articles, it is plain (unless a reduction were simultaneously made in their pay) that the condition of soldiers, sailors, and all government servants with salaries of less than 150*l.* a-year, would be materially improved; for, if their pay were not diminished, it would buy a greater quantity of the articles on which it has been expended, in consequence of their falling in price from the reduction or repeal of the duties; and, for the same reason, such a measure would be highly advantageous to the large body of funded proprietors who have incomes under 150*l*. But we may take leave to add that it is more than doubtful whether the supposed change would be advantageous to any one else. It would certainly lessen the means of capitalists to employ labour, and increase the temptation to carry capital abroad: and it has not yet been shown how a measure productive of such results should be otherwise than injurious to the labouring classes.

But taking the taxation of the United Kingdom as it now stands, we shall not, perhaps, be far wrong if we estimate the real magnitude of the national burdens at about 25 per cent. under their nominal amount given in the official and other accounts. And supposing the latter to average, including local taxes,* about sixty-four millions, the real burden will, on this hypothesis, be about forty-eight millions.

The previous statements show the kind of deductions which it is necessary to make from the budget of every country, in order to arrive at the true amount of the burdens it has to sustain. And as these deductions vary in different countries with the varying nature of their taxes, and other circumstances, which do not admit of being precisely determined, it follows that we can have no really accurate information respecting the absolute amount of the taxation to which they are subject. But supposing this to be known, or to be approximated to with sufficient precision for practical purposes, there would still be extreme difficulty in determining the degree in which different countries are taxed, as compared with their ability to bear taxes.

The amount of population has sometimes been supposed to be an index of capacity to support taxes; but were this the case, it would follow that Ireland, which has a population of

---

* We exclude tithes from this estimate, as they will most probably, at no distant period, wholly fall on rent.

above *eight* millions, could afford to pay three times the amount of the taxes paid by Scotland, which has a population of but little more than *two and a half* millions. So far, however, from this being the case, the revenue of Ireland hardly equals that of Scotland; and yet there is no reason for thinking that the pressure of taxation is felt more severely in the latter than in the former.

Others have suggested that the amount of the capital belonging to different countries may be taken as a test by which to measure the comparative weight of their burdens. But this would also lead to the most erroneous results; it being plain that a small capital where profits are high may be more productive than a large one where they are low. The market-rate of interest, which is generally proportional to the customary rate of profit, is usually about twice as great in the United States as in England. *One* million of capital employed in America must therefore be about as productive, that is, it must yield about as large an annual income, as *two* millions employed in this country. And hence, if taxation, as compared with the amount of capital, were the same in both countries, it would, as compared with the profits or revenue derived from that capital, be about twice as heavy in England as in America.

Taxes being a portion of the incomes of individuals transferred to the State, it has been said that, if we ascertain the aggregate income of any two or more countries, and the number of their inhabitants, we may thence deduce the average incomes of individuals in each; and that it will be easy, by comparing the latter with the amount of the taxes falling on individuals, to learn the sum, and the proportion of their incomes, which they have respectively to contribute to the public revenue. This criterion is, however, but little better than the others. It is quite impracticable to form anything like a correct estimate of the total or aggregate income of any extensive country; and though this difficulty were got over, and the income, population, and taxation of any two countries were known, it might be all but impossible to say which was

most, and which was least heavily taxed. The same amount
of income yields a very different supply of necessaries and conveniences in different countries; and, supposing other things to
be equal, the well-being of individuals obviously depends, not
on the amount of their money-incomes, but on the amount of
necessaries and conveniences for which those incomes will exchange. Hence, supposing the average incomes of the people
of two countries amount, before their taxes are paid, to 20*l.*
a-head; and that the taxes payable in the one amount to 4*l.*,
and in the other to 5*l.* a-head; we should not be able to
say, without farther examination, whether taxation was really
heavier in the latter than in the former; for its pressure is to be
measured, not so much by what it takes, as by what it leaves;
and if the 15*l.* of income remaining to the inhabitants of the
one gave them a larger command over necessaries and conveniences than the 16*l.* remaining to those of the other, we apprehend it would be correct to say that of the two they were
the least heavily taxed.

Experience shows, speaking generally, that the inhabitants of cold or temperate, and not very fertile countries,
are more laborious than those of countries which are comparatively hot and fruitful. In the latter the wants of the
inhabitants are more easily supplied; and the motives to
industry being fewer or less urgent, it is prosecuted with
less ardour. But if the motives to industry were strength-
ened in such countries by an increase of taxation, it could
not, if kept within reasonable bounds, sensibly deteriorate,
while it might, and most probably would, materially improve the condition of the population. Thus, if it were
possible, by any system of training, to make the inhabitants
of modern Italy nearly as industrious as the English, they
might, it is obvious, afford to pay a much larger share
of the produce of their labour in taxes, their necessities,
owing to the mildness of the climate, being so much more
limited.

The tastes or fashions, as well as the wants of people,
have also a great deal to do in determining their capacity

to bear taxes. Where a taste for holidays, shows and pro-
cessions, and the *dolce far niente*, is widely diffused, the
people are generally deficient in industry, and having little
surplus produce to dispose of, can contribute but little to the
treasury. But where, on the other hand, they care little for
holiday pastimes, and prefer regaling themselves with wine,
beer, spirits, or such like stimulants, government may, by
taxing these, raise a very large sum in the least objectionable way. A Neapolitan lazzarone contributes nothing,
whereas an English gin-drinker, or tobacco-smoker, contributes a great deal to the revenue. We do not mean by this
to give any opinion as to the comparative merit or demerit of
different tastes; though it is abundantly obvious that if the
prevailing taste of our people should undergo any material
change, and the consumption of beer, spirits, and tobacco
be gradually abandoned, it might be difficult to supply the
deficiency it would occasion in the revenue without resorting
to direct taxation. It is doubtful, however, whether the population would gain anything by lessening their consumption of luxuries. No doubt if they lessened their consumption of gin and tobacco to make equivalent additions to their
consumption of tea and coffee, the change would be greatly
for their advantage. But without some such commutation,
and if they merely restricted their expenditure upon luxuries,
that they might exist or meet the increasing difficulties of
their situation, their position would certainly be changed for
the worse. A population which consumes but few luxuries
is always in a very perilous situation; being confined to necessaries, it can make few or no retrenchments in bad years,
so that if dearth in such cases be not accompanied with all
the horrors of famine, it must drive the poor in crowds to the
workhouse. But a population which is habitually supplied
with luxuries can, by relinquishing or diminishing their use,
provide a resource in bad years, and can withstand their pressure with comparatively little difficulty. Those, therefore,
who are so very fond of inveighing against the luxury, waste,
and dissipation of the lower classes, take generally, we are

inclined to think, a narrow and prejudiced view of the subject. Their expenditure is certainly, in very many cases, far from being the best; but still it is better that they should drink beer and smoke tobacco than that they should lose these tastes without acquiring others in their stead. Such persons contribute largely to the public revenue, and they have besides room to retrench in periods of adversity; whereas those whose consumption is limited to necessaries, contribute little or nothing to the wants of the public, and in bad years must either starve or live on alms.

The facility of transferring capital and skilled labour from one country to another, is also an important consideration in estimating the pressure of taxation. A rich and industrious people, provided they were surrounded by Bishop Berkeley's wall of brass, might permanently support a comparatively heavy load of taxes without a murmur. But, in the actual state of the world, with a facility of intercourse between different countries greater than that which formerly existed between contiguous provinces of the same country, the unequal magnitude of taxation may lead to important practical consequences. For though the taxes a people have to sustain should not really, when compared with their ability to bear them, be so heavy as those borne by their neighbours, yet if their absolute amount be materially greater, capital and skilled labour will gradually find their way to the latter. It must not, therefore, be supposed that because taxation bears in two or more countries the same proportion to the wealth or ability of the contributors, that it will have the same influence; for, if the rates of duty, or the number of duties, be greater in one than in others, individuals in the higher taxed country will see that if they emigrate to the others, and still more if they can contrive to carry their capital or property along with them, they will escape a large portion of the taxes they have at present to pay; for they will in such a case have the fortunes of a rich with the taxation of a poor country. It is true that a great deal always depends, in cases of this sort, on the condition of the country where taxation is comparatively low ; on the temptations which in other respects it holds out to residence ; on its language ; the nature and tone of its society ; the presumed stability of its government ; its proximity, and an endless variety of considerations.   The situation of a country with comparatively low taxes may be otherwise such as to deter either foreigners or foreign capital seeking a residence or investment in it ; whereas a country may have so many other attractions that a very little difference in respect of taxation might occasion a great influx of strangers and of wealth.

The doubts entertained with respect to the stability of the existing order of things in France, and the bad faith of the Americans, have powerfully contributed to hinder the efflux of capital from this country.   Were the same confidence placed by our capitalists in the permanence of the constitutional system established in France, that is placed in the permanence of our own system, there can be no doubt that a much greater amount of British capital would have found its way to the former ; that funded property in France would have borne about the same price that it bears in England ; and that the manufactures of Rouen and the trade of Havre would have been far more extensive.   But any feeling of insecurity is a most formidable obstacle to the investment of capital, and is more than sufficient to countervail a host of advantages. This has been strikingly evinced in the instance of the United States.   The uncertainty that attaches to most sorts of public investments in the Union, from the badness of the banking system, and the want of principle so glaringly manifested by several of the subordinate legislatures, have all but wholly checked the transfer of capital to America, notwithstanding the high rate of profit it realizes in the States, and the identity of language, and other circumstances calculated to draw it to them.

But these, however powerful in their operation, are but contingent and accidental circumstances ; and, *cæteris paribus,* it is quite as natural that capital should leave a country where profits are low to seek employment in one where they are high, as that water should flow from a high to a low level. And though local and peculiar circumstances may countervail for a longer or a shorter period the influence of a low rate of profit in sending capital abroad, the latter always exists, and is sure, whenever an opportunity offers, to manifest itself. There is in fact no instance of a country being burdened with comparatively high rates of taxation in which this effect has not been experienced, or from which there has not been an efflux of people and of wealth.

A reduced rate of profit and inadequate wages seem to be necessary consequences of a high rate of taxation. The amount of the latter forms of course an equivalent deduction from the produce of industry; and the greater that deduction the less necessarily remains to be divided among the parties employed in production. Suppose that a capitalist and the labourers in his employment produce in a given period 100,000 quarters of wheat, or 100,000 yards of cloth, of which a fifth part, or 20,000, go to replace the capital wasted in the production : the remaining 80,000 quarters or 80,000 yards would, supposing there were no taxes, be divided between the capitalist and his work-people, 20,000 probably going as profit to the one, and 60,000 as wages to the other ; and whatever quantity might go to each, it is plain there would be no one else to share in the gross amount. But instead of taxation being unknown, it usually forms a large deduction from the produce of industry ; being seldom perhaps less than 8 or 10, and sometimes as much as 25 or 30 per cent. of that produce. Suppose now that in the case before us taxation abstracts directly and indirectly a fourth part, or 25 per cent., of the produce of industry, that is, of the 80,000 quarters, or 80,000 yards, remaining after the capital wasted in their production has been replaced; in such case the gross income of the capitalist and his labourers will be reduced from 80,000 to 60,000, the profit or income of the capitalist being probably reduced from 20,000 to 10,000, and the wages or income of the labourers from 60,000 to 50,000.

At all events it is clear that in whatever way the deduction on account of taxation may affect the different parties, it must be subtracted from the produce they have conjointly raised; and that in whatever degree its amount may be increased such increase must fall on the one party or the other, or both. The presumption is, for the reasons already stated, that an increase of taxation will in most cases affect in the end profits to a greater extent than it affects wages; but it generally, also, if it be carried to any very considerable height, makes a serious inroad on the latter, and compels the labourer to economize.

It is no doubt true, as has been fully shown in previous parts of this work, that if not very sudden and oppressive, an increase of taxation is most commonly defrayed wholly or in part by a proportionally increased degree of economy, industry, and invention. This, however, is nowise inconsistent with the principles now stated. However great the produce of industry, a high rate of taxation necessarily abstracts a large portion of that produce; and though the condition of those engaged in industrious undertakings in a highly taxed country, may not be worse than when it was less heavily taxed, and may even be very materially improved, every one sees that it would be still better were taxation reduced. The increased ability to bear the burden is forgotten, and the attention is exclusively fixed on the burden itself. Its influence, and the inconveniences thence arising, are exaggerated; and all classes become desirous to escape its pressure, or to throw it on others.

It is also true that the increased industry and invention which may at the time more than neutralize an increase of taxation, is apt at a future period to be exerted under less advantageous circumstances. Those improved processes, and more economical methods of carrying on industrious undertakings, occasioned by the increase of taxation, gradually make their way to other countries where the burdens falling on the industrious classes are less heavy; and while they improve the condition of those among whom they are thus introduced, they of course enable them to become more formidable antagonists of the more highly taxed producers in the markets common to both. The temptation to convey away capital and skilled labour from highly taxed countries is thus also progressively augmented; so that the fair inference seems to be that a heavy rate of taxation, though, if it have been judiciously imposed, it may, for a lengthened period, act as a powerful stimulus to industry and invention in the country subject to its influence, may not improbably in the end occasion its decline and fall.

The case of Holland seems to confirm in a very striking manner the truth of what has now been stated. Notwithstanding the laudable economy of her rulers, the vast expense the republic incurred in her struggle to emancipate herself from the blind and brutal despotism of Old Spain, and in her contests with Cromwell, Charles II., and Louis XIV., led to the contraction of an immense public debt, the interest and other charges on which, with the current expenses of the government, obliged her to lay heavy taxes on the most indispensable necessaries. Among others, high duties were laid on foreign corn when imported, on flour and meal when ground at the mill, and on bread when it came from the oven. Taxation affected every source of production and every channel of expenditure; and so oppressive did it become, that it was supposed to double the price of bread consumed in the towns, and it was a common saying in Amsterdam, that every dish of fish brought to table was paid for once to the fisherman and six times to the State! For awhile, however, or during their increase, and for some considerable time thereafter, these enormous taxes appear to have had little or no influence in retarding the progress of the republic; her commerce, fisheries, and manufactures having continued to increase down to the invasion of her territories by Louis XIV. in 1672. But from this epoch, or perhaps a little previously, their pernicious operation began gradually to become more and more obvious; and subsequently to the Treaty of Utrecht, in 1713, it became a subject of frequent discussion, and engaged the serious attention of her principal merchants and statesmen. Wages having been raised so as to enable the labourers to subsist, the weight of taxation fell principally on the capitalists. Profits being in consequence reduced below their level in the surrounding countries, the United Provinces gradually lost their ascendancy; their fisheries and manufactures were undermined; and their capitalists chose in the end rather to transfer their stocks to the foreigner than to employ them at home. The well-informed author of the ' Richesse de la Hollande,' says in reference to this subject, " *L'augmentation successive des impôts, que les payements des intérêts et les remboursements ont rendu indispensables, a détruit une grande partie de l'industrie, a diminué le commerce, a diminué ou fort altéré l'état florissant où étoit autrefois la population, en resserrant chez le peuple les moyens de subsistence.*"* The same distinguished authority tells us in another place, that in 1778 the Hollanders had about 1,500,000,000 livres (62,000,000*l.* sterling) in the public funds of France and England. And if any further proof of what has now been stated should be required, we might refer to the interesting ' Memoir on the Means of Amending and Redressing the Commerce of the Republic,' drawn up from information communicated by the best informed merchants, and published by order of the Stadtholder, William IV., Prince of Orange, in 1751. The various causes that originally promoted, and which subsequently depressed the trade and industry of Holland, are skilfully developed in this Memoir. And its authors place " At the head of all the causes that have co-operated to the prejudice and discouragement of trade, the oppressive taxes by which, under different denominations, it has been burdened. It can only be attributed to these taxes, that the trade of this country has been diverted out of its channel, and transferred to our neighbours; and that it must daily be still more and more alienated and shut out from us, unless the progress thereof be stopped by some quick and effectual remedy. Nor is it difficult to see from these contemplations on the

* Richesse de la Hollande, 4to. ed., ii. 179.

state of our trade, that the same can be effected by no other means than a diminution of all duties." *

But, as every one knows, this "quick and effectual remedy" was not applied; and though the prudence and economy of the Dutch, and the possession of Java, have enabled them to preserve a large amount of wealth with a respectable share of the commerce of the world, their pecuniary and mercantile preponderance are now matters of rather remote history. Notwithstanding their partial bankruptcies, the Dutch continue to be burdened with an amount of debt and taxes that would crush any less industrious and frugal people.

It would, however, be unphilosophical to conclude, because such has been the pernicious influence of the too great increase of debts and taxes in Holland, that such also will be their influence in England and elsewhere. The fate of nations depends on a vast variety of contingent and accidental circumstances, which it is, for the most part, impossible to estimate with any degree of precision, or even to foresee. These circumstances may on the one hand, by increasing the productive capacities, the commerce and riches of a country, enable her to support a heavy load of taxes with comparatively little difficulty; or they may, on the other hand, have a directly opposite effect, and by crippling her means and resources, proportionally increase the severity of their pressure. Hence the folly of laying much stress on theoretical conclusions in regard to the future influence of taxation over the fortunes of any great country. The discovery of improved processes and new inventions in the arts, changes in the channels of commerce, and in the value of money, the overthrow of old and the establishment of new forms of government, the occurrence of wars, and a thousand other events which it is impossible to conjecture, may vastly increase or proportionally diminish the power of countries to bear taxes, at the same time that they may add to or lessen their magnitude.

But whatever may be the fate of a country subject to a

* Memoir, p. 27. Eng. ed., Lond. 1751.

high rate of taxation, it seems impossible to doubt that it operates as a clog on her progress ; and that *cæteris paribus* it is a source of impoverishment and weakness.   We have seen the extreme difficulty of forming anything like a correct estimate of the comparative pressure of taxation in different countries ; but, unluckily, the severity of its pressure in England is but too apparent.   It has been sufficiently shown in the course of this chapter that the real amount of our public and local burdens (exclusive, however, of the influence of the duties imposed either wholly or partly for the sake of protection) may be taken at about forty-eight millions.   Now, as the rental of the whole landed property of Great Britain is certainly under forty millions, it follows, that though Government were proprietors of every acre of land in this island, the revenue thence arising would be wholly insufficient to meet the public outgoings ; and that it would be necessary to seize, in addition, upon the greater portion of the rent of Ireland !

The serious inroad made by taxation on the produce of the land and labour of the country, may be further illustrated by comparing it with the produce either of agricultural or manufacturing industry.   Without pretending to minute accuracy, which on such subjects is unattainable, the quantity and value of the corn annually grown in England may probably be estimated as under :—

	£.
Wheat, 14,000,000 quarters at 50s. . . .	35,000,000
Barley, 5,000,000 do. at 30s. . . .	7,500,000
Oats, peas, and beans, 12,000,000 do. at 25s. . .	16,000,000
	£58,500,000

We incline to think that this estimate is near the mark, and that at all events it is not underrated.   And supposing it to be about accurate, it shows that the value of the share of the produce of the land and labour of the United Kingdom taken as taxes is considerably more than the total value of all the wheat and barley annually produced in England !

It is, perhaps, unnecessary to say more in illustration of

the magnitude of our taxation. We may, however, shortly compare it with the cotton manufacture. Everybody is aware of the extent and importance of the latter. The great towns of Manchester, Glasgow, Bolton, Oldham, Preston, Blackburn, Bury, and a host of others, are principally dependent on this great branch of industry. But the total annual value of its produce in woven fabrics and yarn, including the raw material, cannot with any show of probability be estimated at above 34,000,000*l.* or 35,000,000*l.* a-year, so that it is obvious that though the produce and value of the cotton manufacture were increased forty per cent., and then wholly appropriated by Government, it would hardly suffice to defray the public expenditure!

Though moderate in the extreme compared with most of those that have been put forth on this subject, these statements are yet sufficient to show that taxation is very heavy in this country, and that it abstracts a large proportion of the produce of our land and labour. And such being the case it is not possible, generally speaking, in the existing state of industry, that profits should be otherwise than low, or that the average and ordinary rate of wages should be such as to afford the labouring classes the means of commanding a liberal supply of necessaries and conveniences. The increase of taxation may have been, and perhaps was unavoidable; but however urgent the necessity for its increase, and however much it may have stimulated industry and invention, it has become a heavy burden on the productive capacities of the nation, and may occasion in the end the most serious results. These it is true are contingent only; and it is to be hoped that the course of events may be such as to give new vigour to the productive classes, and to enable them to sustain, without difficulty, the present or even an additional weight of taxation. But at the same time it is not to be disguised that the evil is one of a very marked character; and that till it be materially mitigated, it will furnish matter for perennial agitation and discontent, and be a formidable obstacle to our

progress. Considering the degree in which the population is
dependent on our ascendancy in manufactures, it is not easy
to form any notion of the extent of disorder and wretchedness
that would most likely grow out of their decline.

These statements are sufficient to demonstrate, not the expediency merely, but the necessity, if we would guard against
the most tremendous evils, of adopting every just and practicable means for lessening the weight of taxation and relieving the pressure on the national resources. It is needless,
however, to expect that this can be done by means of reductions in the public expenditure. Some petty savings may,
perhaps, be effected in a few departments; but so long as we
make adequate provision for the security and good government of the different parts of the empire, there is not so much
as the shadow of a ground for supposing that our expenditure
can be sensibly reduced. On the contrary, the probability
is, that it will have to be enlarged. At all events, it is the
merest delusion to look to savings from expense as any
resource against the evils with which we may be assailed.
A country like England, with colonies and dependencies in
every part of the world, must have always on foot a very
formidable force. Without the ability and the determination to maintain, at all hazards, every iota of her rights,
no nation can be really independent, or exist otherwise than
by sufferance. Treaties, conventions, and the sanctions of
public law are but little to be depended on. Like the paper
cannons of the Chinese, they are good only for holiday service.
The motto of the old Scottish kings, *Nemo me impune
lacesset,* embodies the only principle on which any stress can
be safely laid. Our free institutions, and all that we most
value, are, in truth, wholly supported by our bayonets and
our ships of war. To weaken the latter is to endanger the
former.

Happily, however, though we cannot materially lessen
our expenditure, we are not without great available resources.
Our people are as eminent as ever for energy, perseverance,
and industry; and though government may not be able

directly to reduce their burdens, the effect will be the same if it increase their ability to bear them. And can any one doubt that the productive capacities of the country would be largely augmented, and the pressure on the industrious classes materially diminished, by striking off the shackles that fetter and restrain the freedom of commerce? Notwithstanding the serious inroads that have been made upon the restrictive and protective system, it still continues to oppress and weigh down the national energies. Though scotched, the snake has not been killed. We have seen how deeply the country has been injured by the prohibitory duty on foreign sugar; and it is also seriously injured by the disproportioned amount of the duty on tea; by the discriminating duty in favour of timber from the American colonies; and by the existing corn-laws. The injurious influence of the latter has no doubt been stupidly and factiously exaggerated. Still, however, it is incontestible, that the sliding scale is productive of great loss and inconvenience; and we have seen that the substitution in its stead of a fixed duty of 5s. or 6s. a-quarter, to countervail the peculiar burdens falling on the land, would be a signal improvement.

We have further endeavoured to show, that much might be done to extend the trade, and to increase the ability of the country to bear taxes, by reducing the exorbitant duties on silks, wines, brandies, and other articles brought from France. Even under its present burdens, our trade with that country has increased more rapidly of late years than any other branch of our commerce; and considering the wealth, population, and proximity of France, and the endless variety of products she possesses suitable for our markets, the presumption is that we should have, under a reasonable system of duties, a far more extensive and advantageous trade with her than with any other nation. It does not, we allow, depend on us fully to open the trade with France; and, however we may act, if the French load our products with heavy or prohibitory duties, the trade will never arrive at anything like its natural and proper importance. But while we may gain we cannot certainly lose anything by the adoption of a more liberal system of policy. The existing duties on silks and brandies are quite as hostile to our interests as to those of the French, and are, in truth, good for nothing, unless it be to stifle all legitimate commerce, and to throw such as may still be carried on into the hands of smugglers.

We have previously seen that a good deal might also be done, though less perhaps than has sometimes been supposed, to promote industry by commuting some of the more objectionable of the existing taxes: such as that on glass for an increased duty on windows: and the soap-tax, the duty on bricks, and half the existing duty on tea, might be exchanged for a reasonable house-tax. A commutation of this sort would contribute to improve many important branches of industry and trade. And the increased excise and customs revenue that would result from this improvement would in no very lengthened period allow, most probably, of the repeal of other taxes.

It were absurd, with such an amount of direct and indirect taxation, and with such a vast manufacturing population, to imagine that the situation of this country presents nothing critical. But in so far as respects taxation we are sanguine enough to believe that, provided tranquillity be maintained, and the reforms be adopted which, we have seen, are so just, so necessary, and so easy of execution, its depressing influence will in no long time cease to be very sensibly felt; and that we shall, as heretofore, outgrow our burdens.

Unfavourable inferences have been sometimes drawn in relation to the state of the country, from the declining or slowly progressive consumption of some leading articles subjected to taxation. The little increase in the demand for sugar for several years past, the stationary state of the wine trade, and the decreased productiveness of the duties on foreign spirits, have been appealed to in proof of these inferences; and it is further affirmed that the increase in the consumption of malt is not such as might have been expected. But we doubt whether much stress can be fairly laid on these circumstances. The increase of population is, indeed, most rapid; and if no deterioration take place in the condition of the bulk of the people, a corresponding increase may be fairly anticipated in the consumption of most articles in general demand. We can hardly, however, look for the full development of this principle, except in those instances in which the duties are moderate; the unavoidable effect of oppressive or too high duties being either the diminution of consumption, or its conversion into illegitimate channels in which it cannot be observed. But it would be useless, after what has been previously stated, to enter further on these considerations. The limited use of foreign spirits is undoubtedly a consequence of exorbitant duties; while the stationary consumption of wine is perhaps the result of the duties being too high, of a change of habits, and of other influences: and we have seen that the stationary consumption of sugar, which appears to give most countenance to the opinion noticed above, has been owing to the increase in its cost occasioned by the monopoly of its supply.

But, however accounted for, the stationary consumption of the above and other articles deserves the most serious consideration. It is doubtful, perhaps, whether the condition of the labouring part of the population has not been deteriorated during the last five-and-twenty years; and, at all events, it is but too certain that their comforts and enjoyments have not been increased in anything like the same proportion as those of the classes above them. Inasmuch, however, as the labouring poor constitute the majority of the population, their condition is of the utmost importance, not only in regard to their own well-being, but also in regard to that of the other classes. The poverty and depressed condition of any very large class, especially if it be strongly contrasted with vast wealth, extravagance, and luxury on the part of others, is a most undesirable state of things, and one which can hardly fail to produce discontent, sedition, and disturbance of all kinds. Lord Bacon says, that " of all rebellions those of the belly are the worst." And he adds, " The first remedy or prevention is to remove, by all means possible, that material cause of sedition of which we speak, which is want or poverty in the estate." No one, indeed, can doubt that it is the bounden duty of the legislature to adopt every safe and practicable measure for eradicating or countervailing the causes of poverty among the mass of the people, and for adding to their comforts and enjoyments. But of these causes none seem to be more prolific of mischief than oppressive and ill-contrived taxes. And if we have succeeded in showing how the condition of the working people might be improved by the modification of existing duties, we shall, at the same time, have shown how the stability of our institutions, and that security which is so indispensable, may be best increased and perpetuated.

PART III.

FUNDING SYSTEM.

——

CHAPTER I.

ADVANTAGES AND DISADVANTAGES—RISE AND PROGRESS OF THE FUNDING SYSTEM.

THE expense of the government of civilised nations in time of peace does not often exceed, at least to any great extent, their ordinary revenue. It is otherwise, however, in time of war. When the independence and honour of a nation are at stake, proportional sacrifices must be made to maintain them; hostile aggression and insult must be opposed and avenged. But to do this requires extraordinary funds; and the question how they may be most advantageously provided is one of no ordinary importance.

It was the common practice of antiquity to make provision in times of peace for the necessities of war, and to hoard up treasures beforehand as the instruments either of conquest or of defence, without trusting to extraordinary imposts, much less to borrowing in times of disorder and confusion. The Athenians are said to have amassed upwards of 10,000 talents in the interval between the Persian and Peloponnesian wars, and the Lacedæmonians imitated their example.* A large treasure, part of which had been stored up from the age of Cyrus, fell into the hands of Alexander the Great on the

* Hume's Essays on the Balance of Trade and on Public Credit.

conquest of Susa and Ecbatana.* In the Roman commonwealth the *aurum vicesimarium*, or tax of the twentieth penny on the manumission of slaves, was accumulated, along with various sums taken from subjugated states, in the Temple of Saturn, as a sacred deposit to be used only in the utmost emergency. On leaving Italy, Pompey was weak enough, or careless enough, to leave this treasure behind him, which, in consequence, became the prey of his less scrupulous or more vigilant rival.† At a subsequent period Augustus, Tiberius, Vespasian, and all the more able emperors, were in the habit of accumulating treasure. Paulus Æmilius brought a large amount of gold and silver to Rome, which is, however, admitted to have been a part only of the wealth of the Kings of Macedon, Perseus having previously dissipated a considerable portion in his wars with the Romans. The practice, in fact, was universal in the ancient world; but in modern times it has been but little followed, except by the canton of Berne, Frederick the Great, and a few other princes. The circumstance of its policy having been strongly commended by Hume is perhaps the most that can be said in its favour. But he appears to have overlooked the important fact that those who amass treasure, withdraw, in so doing, a corresponding amount of capital from the great work of production; and that, consequently, it must, by diminishing the wealth and means of employment of the countries in which it is accumulated, render them less opulent and powerful. For this and other reasons the practice of hoarding is now generally admitted to have been founded on erroneous principles: and modern politicians and economists seem to be universally of opinion that war expenditure should either be entirely defrayed by a proportional increase of taxation, or partly in that way and partly by loans.

---

* Hume's Essays on the Balance of Trade and on Public Credit.

† Middleton's Life of Cicero, 4to. ed., ii., 104; Plin. Hist. Nat., lib. iii. cap. 3; and the famous passage in Lucan, lib. iii., lin. 115—158, &c.

The question which of these modes should be adopted has been long and vehemently discussed, and has given rise to the most contradictory statements. This, however, appears to have arisen more from the partisan spirit so generally displayed by those who have engaged in the discussion than from any real difficulty inherent in the subject. Neither party seems to have taken any very comprehensive view of the different bearings and incidences of the question. Proceeding on some general principle which, perhaps, was doubtful in itself, and which, at all events, did not admit, in such a matter, of being carried to an extreme, they have concluded either that the one or the other mode of providing for any extraordinary expenditure should be exclusively adopted. But it will be found that this is a question of balanced difficulties, and in which much depends on circumstances; that at one time an increase of taxation may be the preferable mode of raising the supplies, and that at another they should be raised by loan, or partly in the one way and partly in the other. On occasions when either plan may be adopted with tolerable facility and without danger to the government, or to industry, we are disposed to conclude, for the reasons that will be immediately stated, that an increase of taxation should be preferred. But this is a mode of meeting extraordinary expenses that can be advantageously resorted to only by a strong and well-established government, and when the situation of a country is such as fits it for bearing a sudden and considerable increase of taxation. If the government be weak, or if the country be already heavily burdened, as compared with its ability to bear taxes, loans would seem to be the best means for providing for an emergency.

Before proceeding to inquire into the merits of the funding or borrowing system, as a plan for providing for the extraordinary expenses of a state, we may shortly observe that in its infancy the nature and influence of the public debt were very generally misunderstood, and several unfounded theories were advanced respecting it which are not yet entirely relinquished. Bishop Berkeley pretty plainly insinuates that he considered " the public funds as a mine of gold."* Melon, the author of the ' Essai Politique sur le Commerce,' published in 1735, does not go quite so far as Berkeley; but he contends, and his opinion has had many supporters, that the debts of a nation are " debts of the right hand to the left;" and that, consequently, they have no tendency either to increase or diminish national wealth.† But the speculations of his predecessors were all thrown into the shade by those of Pinto, a Jew merchant resident in Holland, and author of an otherwise ingenious work, ' De la Circulation et du Crédit,' published in 1771, who undertook to demonstrate that public debts, far from being a burden, were so much added to the national wealth by the magical influence of credit! (p. 44, &c.) And, singular as it may seem, not a few individuals of eminence have expressed their belief in this ridiculous paradox. Truly did Hume say of such theories that they "might have passed for trials of wit among rhetoricians, like the panegyrics on folly and fever, on Busiris and Nero, had we not seen them patronised by great ministers and even by a whole party amongst us."‡ The fallacy of such notions is, indeed, so very obvious that it is not a little surprising they should ever have been entertained. It may be conceded to Melon, for it is unnecessary again to notice Pinto, that the *interest* of the public debt is a debt of the right hand to the left, or is so much money paid by one portion of society to another; but the question does not regard the interest, but the PRINCIPAL, for which the interest is paid. And as it was not made over by one

* Querist, No. 233.   † Essai, &c., p. 296, ed. 1736.
‡ Essay on Public Credit.

set of individuals to another, but to the government, by whom it has been spent as revenue, or annihilated, it follows that the income of the stockholders must now be wholly derived, by means of taxes, from the property and industry of others.

This doctrine has been stated, with his usual ability and clearness, by Mr. Justice Blackstone:—"By means," says he, "of our national debt, the quantity of property in the kingdom is greatly increased in idea, compared with former times; yet, if we coolly consider it, not at all increased in reality. We may boast of large fortunes and quantities of money in the funds; but where does this money exist? It exists only in name, in paper, in public faith, in parliamentary security; and that is undoubtedly sufficient for the creditors of the public to rely on. But then, what is the pledge which the public faith has pawned for the security of these debts? The land, the trade, and the personal industry of the subject; from which the money must arise that supplies the several taxes. In these, therefore, and in these only, does the property of the public creditors really and intrinsically exist: and, of course, the land, the trade, and the personal industry of individuals are diminished in their true value just so much as they are pledged to answer. If A's income amounts to 100*l.*, and he is so far indebted to B that he pays him 50*l.* a-year of interest, half the value of A's property is transferred to B, the creditor. The creditor's property exists in the demand which he has upon his debtor, and nowhere else; and the debtor is only a trustee to his creditor for half the value of his income. In short, the property of a creditor of the public consists in a certain portion of the national taxes; by how much, therefore, he is the richer, by so much the nation, which pays these taxes, is the poorer."*

It is not, however, meant, in laying these statements

* Commentaries, i. 327.

before the reader, to deny the policy of contracting debt. That depends on wholly different considerations; and supposing a war to be just and necessary, and that it has been ascertained that its expense may be best defrayed by means of loans, their expediency is no longer a question. It is further to be borne in mind, that as the taxes required to defray the interest of loans are seldom very oppressive, they not unfrequently exert a beneficial influence over industry; and through the stimulus they give to invention and economy usually replace (and sometimes more than replace) the interest. Neither is it to be doubted that there are several considerable indirect advantages connected with the existence of a public debt. The readiness with which portions of it may be transferred from one individual to another; the facilities which it consequently affords for investing the smallest as well as the largest savings, have certainly had a beneficial influence; and it is not easy, indeed, to see how some of our most important businesses, as those of banking and insurance, could be advantageously carried on, did the public debt not exist. Still, however, if we consider it apart from the urgent circumstances which make it be contracted, the disadvantages connected with the accumulation of a large public debt appear very much to outweigh its advantages. The heavy taxes which the payment of the interest involves lays a country under the most serious difficulties; by reducing the rate of profit, crippling the public energies, and stimulating the transfer of capital and skill to other countries, where taxes are less oppressive.

But, however important, these, after all, are matters of subordinate interest. The preservation of national independence and honour is in every case the paramount consideration; and no sacrifice, whether of treasure or of blood, should be deemed too great by which they may be maintained and transmitted entire to the remotest pos-

terity. Nothing can compensate for their loss or insecurity. And if loans be the only, or the best, means by
which, in cases of emergency, these great interests may be
preserved, they should, without hesitation, be resorted
to, whatever may be their ultimate influence.

Summum crede nefas, animam præferre pudori,
Et propter vitam vivendi perdere causas.

When, however, the necessity is not so urgent, or
when any extraordinary expense may be defrayed either
by means of loans, or by an equivalent increase of taxation, or partly in the one way, and partly in the other,
it is of the greatest importance to be able to decide,
on just grounds, which should be preferred.

If the facility with which money may be obtained
were the only circumstance to be attended to in comparing the borrowing system with the plan for raising
the supplies within the year by a corresponding increase
of taxation, the preference would, in every case, have to
be given to the former. The regularity with which the
stipulated interest is paid, the ease with which funded
property may be disposed of, and the hope which every
one's confidence in his own good fortune makes him entertain of profiting by fluctuations in its price, make
capitalists accommodate governments with loans in preference to individuals, and enable them to obtain the
largest supplies on the shortest notice and with very
little difficulty. The public, on their part, are equally
well pleased with this system. Instead of being called
upon to advance a large sum in taxes, they are only
taxed to pay the interest of that sum. A burden of this
limited extent, as it lays no individual under the necessity of making any considerable additional exertions, or
any considerable reduction of his expenditure, is generally
submitted to without a murmur. Such a mode of providing for the expenses of a war seems to divest it of
more than half its hardships; and we cease to feel sur-

prise that governments should universally resort to a system which, while it furnishes them with the largest supplies, is so very popular with their subjects.

But the merits of the funding system are not to be determined merely by the *facility* which it affords for raising supplies. That certainly is a consideration which is not to be overlooked; but there are others which are of still greater importance. The real effects of any financial operation can never be ascertained by looking only at those of which it is immediately productive. We must extend our observations to those which are more remote, and endeavour, if possible, to trace its permanent and ultimate influence. Now, if we do this, if we attend, not to the transitory only, but also to the lasting effects of the practice of funding, we shall find that the facility which it gives of raising the supplies is only on certain occasions an advantage, and that, on others, it may be a serious defect. It is nugatory to imagine that any scheme for defraying war expenditure can ever be proposed capable of protecting individuals from the losses and privations inseparable from national struggles and contests. Every people involved in war, however just and necessary the contest may be, must sooner or later experience the effect of the waste of capital, or of the means of future production, which it rarely fails to occasion. And it is clear that no scheme of finance can be bottomed on sound principles which disguises these necessary consequences of war, and deceives the public with regard to their real situation. This, however, is notoriously the case with the funding system. It is truly said to require no individual to make any extraordinary sacrifice at any particular period: and in this respect it bears a close resemblance to those most dangerous diseases which steal slowly and imperceptibly on the constitution, and do not discover their malignant symptoms until they have fastened on the vitals and vitiated the whole animal economy. There are no means whatever by which the profusion and waste occasioned by a war can be counteracted, except by the industry and economy of individuals; and to make these virtues be practised, individuals should be made fully sensible of the influence of war expenditure over their own private fortunes. The radical defect of the borrowing system consists in its deceiving the public on this point, and in its making no sudden encroachments on their comforts. Its approaches are gradual and almost unperceived. It requires only small immediate sacrifices; but it never relinquishes what it has once gained; while the necessity for fresh sacrifices, arising from their own ambition, injustice, and folly, as well as from those of their neighbours, continues as great as ever. Such a system is essentially delusive and treacherous. It occasions the imposition of tax after tax, hardly one of which is ever again repealed; so that before the public are awakened from their trance, and made aware of their actual condition, their property and industry are probably encumbered with a much larger permanent payment on account of the *interest* of the public debt than would have been required, had they submitted to it at once, to defray the expenses of the war.

It may perhaps be said, that supposing we are engaged in a war which costs twenty millions a-year, it is really the same thing, provided the rate of interest be five per cent., whether we pay the twenty millions at once, by a proportional increase of taxation, or borrow them, and pay the lenders an interminable annuity of one million a-year; for when interest is at five per cent., twenty millions in one payment, and an interminable annuity of one million, are of the same value. But it is precisely because these two modes of defraying war-expenditure have never been, and never will be, considered equally expensive by the public, that the funding system is most injurious. Suppose, for example, that the supplies are raised within the year, and that the share falling to an individual is 1000*l.* The wish to maintain himself in his former station, and to preserve his fortune unimpaired, would stimulate him, on being called upon for this sum, to discharge it, partly by increased exertion, and partly by a saving of expenditure, without suffering it to continue to encumber his property. But by the system of loans, he is called upon to pay only the interest of this 1000*l.*, or 50*l.* a-year; and instead of endeavouring to save the whole 1000*l.*, he is satisfied if he save the interest. The whole nation, acting in the same way, save only the interest of the loan, or *one* million, and allow the principal sum of *twenty* millions, which they would have either wholly or partly saved, had they been called upon to pay it at once, to remain as a mortgage on their property and industry. Men act thus, because they invariably reckon a war burdensome in proportion only to what they are at the moment called upon to pay for it in taxes, without reflecting on the probable duration of these taxes. It would be useless to attempt to convince most persons that a perpetual payment of 50*l.* a-year is as burdensome as a single payment of 1000*l.* Accidents or revolutions may occur to relieve our properties from the perpetual payment; and at all events, we look upon it as certain that the greater portion of it will have to be defrayed by posterity. Indeed, this very circumstance of its throwing a portion of the expense of every contest on posterity, is one of the recommendations of the funding system principally relied on by its advocates. But it is easy to see that this advantage is in great part illusory; and that the more the interests of posterity are protected, provided those of the present generation be not injured, the better. And this is what the practice of raising the supplies within the year would accomplish. Supposing, however, that it did not generate an additional spirit of industry and economy, still its adoption would do no

possible harm, either to the present or the future generation, but would have the same effect with respect to
them both as the system of loans : for it must obviously
be a matter of indifference to an individual, whose share
of the expenses of a war amounts to 1000*l.*, and also to
his heir, whether he pays it at once, and leaves the latter
1000*l.* less, or does not pay it, and leaves him 1000*l.*
more, subject to a constant charge of 50*l.* a-year. But
it is the peculiar advantage of the plan for raising the
supplies within the year, that while it entails no greater
burden on any individual than the system of borrowing,
and gives full liberty to every one who is so disposed,
to remove a part of that burden from his own shoulders
to those of his successors; it has a powerful tendency
to render the public less inclined to avail themselves of
this power, and more disposed to make immediate sacrifices, and to become more industrious and parsimonious.
It is an error to suppose that it protects the interests of
posterity, by laying any heavier burden on the existing
generation; it protects them only because it gives additional force to the accumulating principle, and because it
stimulates every individual to maintain himself in his
station, and to preserve his capital undiminished.

Here then is a distinguishing criterion of the two
systems. The funding system occasions only such an
additional degree of exertion and economy as may be
required to produce and save the interest of the capital
that has been borrowed; whereas the system of raising
the supplies within the year gives infinitely greater force
and activity to the spirit of exertion and economy,
and makes the public endeavour to produce and save
a sum equivalent, not to the interest only, but to the
principal of the loan. If, therefore, the question, with
regard to the merits of the two systems, were to be
decided by a comparison of their respective influence
over national wealth,—and this is admitted by Gentz,
the ablest defender of the funding system, to be *la*

*première considération, et celle qui doit toujours l'emporter
sur toutes les autres,*—there can be no manner of doubt
that the preference would have to be given to the plan
for raising the supplies within the year.

Not only, however, would this plan be a means of stimulating individuals to defray their share of the public
expenditure, by increased exertion and economy, but it
would also, by making them feel the full pressure of the
burdens it occasions, render them less disposed wantonly
to engage in expensive contests, and more inclined to
embrace the earliest opportunity of making peace on
fair and reasonable terms. It would teach governments
and their subjects to be more economical, and to conduct
public affairs in the least expensive way. To a nation
that defrayed all, or the greater part of the extraordinary expenses of war by a corresponding increase of
taxation, peace might be truly said to bring " healing
under her wings." As soon as the peculiar crisis had
ceased, the taxes that had been imposed to meet it
would also cease. Prices would fall back to their natural
level; and industry, relieved from the burdens of the
war, and improved by the stimulus it will most likely
have given to invention, would spring forward with fresh
energy. Had we always acted on this system, our taxes
would not at this moment have exceeded some eight or
ten millions a-year. And it is reasonable to suppose, had
such been the case, that profits and wages would have
been considerably greater, and that we should have been
more powerful, and more able to repel and avenge any
attacks on ourselves, as well as to interpose with better
effect in defence of our allies.

But how conclusive soever these statements and reasonings may appear, it is still true that the plan for
raising the supplies within the year is open to some very
weighty objections, and that its superiority to the funding system is not so decided as we might be at first dis-

posed to conclude. Among other objections to this plan it has been said, that it would be extremely oppressive on landlords and manufacturers, who are not generally possessed of large sums of ready money, to force them to make an immediate contribution of their entire share of the expenses of the war. Suppose, for example, that a manufacturer's share of the expenses of a war amounts to 1000*l*., and suppose further, that he can neither save this sum from his expenditure, nor withdraw it without great loss from his business, the advantage of the funding system consists, we are told, in relieving him from the necessity of making this payment, and in enabling him to carry on his business as before, subject only to a deduction of 50*l*. a-year, which he can easily spare from his profits. But a little consideration will serve to show that this advantage, though certainly considerable, has been a good deal overrated. If it be asked, how does the practice of funding relieve the manufacturer from the necessity of paying down 1000*l*.? the answer is, by government or its agents going into the money-market and borrowing 1000*l*. on his account, with the interest of which he is charged. And, such being the case, the presumption seems to be that, had this practice not prevailed, the manufacturer would have done that directly which he has done by deputy, that he would have gone into the market himself and borrowed the same sum. "That there are persons disposed to lend to individuals," says Mr. Ricardo, who has laid great stress on this argument, " is certain from the facility with which government raises its loans. Withdraw this great borrower from the market, and private borrowers will be readily accommodated. By wise regulations and good laws the greatest facilities might be afforded to individuals in such transactions. In the case of a loan A advances the money, and B pays the interest, and everything else remains as before. In the case of war-taxes, A would still advance the money, and B pay the interest, only with this difference, he would pay it directly to A; now he pays it to government, and government pays it to A."

We cannot, however, help thinking that Mr. Ricardo has, in this instance, pushed an argument that is true, within certain limits, to an extent that will not hold. When government goes into the money-market and contracts for a loan, it is true that it borrows for those who would otherwise have to borrow for themselves, but it does not negotiate a separate loan on account of each individual; it borrows for them in a mass; and by pledging the national credit for the entire loan, it is obtained on the best terms. By this means the loans, for behoof of those whose security is comparatively indifferent, are negotiated at a much lower rate of interest than if they had been managed directly by the parties; and the saving so effected is, of course, an advantage on the side of the funding system.

Undoubtedly, however, the grand argument against the plan for raising the supplies within the year, and in favour of the funding system, is to be found in its obviating the necessity of making any sudden and oppressive addition to the weight of taxation. It is impossible to say, à priori, in how great a degree taxes may be augmented without operating injuriously : but countries may be, and frequently are so situated that any immediate and considerable increase of taxation would produce a dangerous revulsion, and give such a shock to industry as could not easily be repaired. To fit a country for bearing a heavy load of taxes, they should, if possible, be gradually and slowly increased. We have already endeavoured to show that a moderate increase of taxation infuses a greater spirit of economy into the people, and becomes a spur to industry and invention. But a sudden and very great increase of taxation might have an opposite effect, and instead of producing an increase of invention and economy, might occasion the decline of both. It is obvious, therefore, that the policy of raising the supplies for a war by means of loans, or by an equivalent increase of taxation, cannot be decided on general principles, but depends on the peculiar circumstances of the country at the time. Whenever there is no risk of giving an injurious shock to industry, by making an equivalent increase of taxation, it would certainly seem, for the reasons already stated, that the preference should be given to the plan for raising the supplies within the year. And even though a loan should be required to obviate too great an increase of taxation, still the inconveniences attending the rapid accumulation of debt are so very great, that every practicable effort should be made to raise taxation to the highest limit to which it may be safely carried, and to make it defray a considerable part, at least, if not the whole, of the extraordinary expenditure. When the expenses of a war are brought directly home to individuals, it is abundantly certain, for the reasons already stated, that the wish to relieve themselves of this burden will be a more powerful motive to increased exertion and economy than the wish to relieve themselves of the interest of loans. The real effect of increased public expenditure on private parties is then made obvious; the deception caused by loans is avoided; and every one has a plain and distinct motive to exert himself to get rid of *his share* of the public expense; whereas by resorting to the plan of funding, the property and industry of all classes is mortgaged and incumbered, at the same time that each individual, looking only at the debt *en masse*, and ignorant of the extent of the burden affecting himself, never once dreams of its payment, or of saving a capital for the extinction of his own share.

The fact that two such able and ingenious inquirers as Hume and Smith should have entertained the strongest apprehensions of the mischievous influence of the public debt when it was hardly a tenth part of what it now amounts to, and that notwithstanding its vast increase in the interval the wealth and population of the country should have increased still more rapidly— has naturally enough generated a disposition to look with distrust on all such sinister auguries. It does not really, however, appear that Hume and Smith formed any false estimate of the influence of a large public debt, but only that they did not lay sufficient stress on the circumstances by which this influence might be (and by which, in the case of England, it has been) counteracted. None of them made sufficient allowance for the possible effects of new inventions, and improved methods of production, in enabling a country to support without difficulty additional taxes; and none of them, though in this respect Hume was the clearer-sighted of the two, was sufficiently alive to the powerful influence which an increase of taxation has in adding new strength to enterprise and economy. The stupendous inventions and discoveries of Watt, Arkwright, Crompton, Wedgwood, and others, have hitherto falsified all the predictions of those who anticipated national ruin and bankruptcy from the rapid increase of the public debt; but these inventions and discoveries might never have been made but for the stimulus given to the public energies by the increase of taxation that grew out of the funding system; and though they had been made, there is no reason to suppose that they would have been so rapidly introduced, or that they would have been so much perfected and improved in so short a period in the absence of this stimulus. It is impossible, perhaps, in estimating the progress of this country since 1760, to say how much is to be ascribed to the desire of rising in the world, and how much to the fear of being thrown down to a lower station by the increase of taxes. But it would not, we believe, be difficult to show that the latter has had the greater influence of the two.

But despite the powerful countervailing influences

now alluded to, there can, we apprehend, be little doubt
that we have carried the practice of funding to a vicious
excess; and that a much larger portion of the sums required to carry on the American war and the first half of
the late French war might and should have been raised
by taxation. Probably, indeed, the facility of defraying
any extraordinary expense by means of funding, and the
temptations which it consequently holds out to ministers
to resort to it rather than encounter the unfounded
clamour that would be occasioned by the imposition of
any considerable amount of taxes, is the greatest drawback on the practice. It is, in fact, almost sure to be
abused. " It would scarcely," says Hume, " be more
imprudent to give a prodigal son a credit in every
banking shop in London, than to empower a statesman
to draw bills in this manner upon posterity." *

The history of most modern nations confirms the
truth of this statement. The funding system has been
almost universally adopted, and it has uniformly been
abused; and how serviceable soever at first, has become,
in the course of time, generally injurious. It was carried to a great extent in Holland; and we have already
seen that it is to it, or rather to the excessive taxation
in time of peace which it occasioned, that the low rate
of profit in that republic, and the decline of her fisheries,
manufactures, and commerce, are to be ascribed. "Nous
avons remarqué que l'accroissement successif des impôts, et la nécessité de faire des emprunts, ont con-
couru, plus que toute autre cause, à faire décroître le
commerce de la Hollande. C'est là une suite inévi-
table surtout des emprunts, parce qu'une paix ne mor-
tifie pas les dettes de l'état. Tous les avantages d'une
guerre heureuse ne bonifient pas les désavantages que
l'état en souffre. Les peuples sont moins heureux,
et l'état s'est affoibli. C'est toujours là le résultat in-

* Essay on Public Credit.

évitable de l'usage des emprunts. C'est là peut-être l'un des fléaux de la guerre moderne, qui répand le plus des calamités, en ce qu'il affecte tous les peuples dans un détail infini et plusieurs générations. La politique qui dès nos jours a trouvé l'art de soutenir la guerre par l'usage du crédit, ne pourroit produire un art plus funeste à l'humanité." *

The funding system was introduced into France by Louis XIV., at the suggestion of Louvois, in opposition to the opinion of Colbert.† It was, as might have been anticipated from the irresponsible nature of the government, most shamefully abused; so much so that it produced, so early as 1715, a public bankruptcy. This experience, however, was very soon forgotten, and a fresh bankruptcy took place in 1769. But even this was not enough to open the eyes of the authorities to the necessity of a radical reform in the financial system of the

---

* La Richesse de la Hollande. Tom. ii., p. 201, ed. in 4to. Amst., 1778.

† We extract the following account of the way in which Colbert's efforts were defeated, from a valuable Memoir on the State of the French Finances, presented to the Duc d'Orléans, Regent of France, in 1717 :—

" M. de Louvois," says the author of the Memoir, " comme tout le monde le sçait, n'étoit pas faché de voir la guerre. Au commencement de celle qui fut entreprise en 1672, il fallut des secours extraordinaires.

" M. Colbert fit quelques traités des nouvelles impositions et des augmentations des droits; ce qui excita des plaintes dans le public, et des représentations même de la part des magistrats.

" M. de Louvois, instruit de ces difficultés, alla trouver un des premiers magistrats, le Premier Président du Parlement de Paris, homme d'un mérite distingué et d'une probité reconnue. Il lui dit qu'il rendroit un service essentiel au Roi, en lui remontrant qu'au lieu de ses traités (excises) extraordinaires que le parlement se faisoit tant de peine d'enrégistrer, et qui étoient si insupportables au peuple, il étoit bien plus simple et plus aisé de créer des rentes ; *qu'un million de rentes crées produiroit tout d'un coup vingt millions, et que ce seroit un petit objet par rapport aux revenus considérables dont jouissoit sa Majesté.* Ce magistrat suivit de bonne foi l'avis qui lui était donné. Le Roi ravi de cet expédient, qui lui venoit d'un homme si approuvé, dit à M. Colbert qu'il n'y avoit qu'à créer des rentes. M. Colbert, qui en prévoyoit les suites et les inconvéniens, voulut avant que de rendre l'Edit, se donner la satisfaction de parler au premier Président. Il lui fit sentir les conséquences du conseil qu'il avoit donné à bonne intention, et lui dit qu'il repondroit devant Dieu du préjudice qu'il causoit à l'état, et du mal qu'il faisoit au peuple."— (Forbonnais, *Recherches sur les Finances de la France*, tom. vi., p. 117.)

country.   The disgraceful abuses in the assessment and
collection of taxes, instead of being suppressed, were
permitted to gather new strength.   The baffled attempts
at reform by Turgot, and the writings of Necker, served
only to disclose the hopelessness and the magnitude of
the evil.   And the deficiencies of the revenue during the
American war being made good by fresh loans, the
bankruptcy and revolution of 1789 followed almost as a
matter of course.

But despite the dangerous nature of the borrowing
system, and its all but irresistible temptations to abuse, it
is not unfrequently a most valuable resource.   Thus, as
already seen, if a country engaged in war be so situated
that the imposition of the taxes required to carry it on
would give any serious shock to industry, loans should
certainly be negotiated, if not for the whole, at least for
a portion of the extraordinary expense.   Political considerations may also make recourse to loans indispensable.
An increase of taxation is always unpopular; and a
weak or insecure government might not have power to
levy any considerable additional amount of taxes, however able the country might be to bear such increase.
The rise of the funding system in Great Britain was
mainly ascribable to circumstances of the kind now mentioned.

With the exception of the trifling sum of 664,000*l.*,
the National Debt has been wholly contracted since the
Revolution, when the unsettled state of the government,
and the difficulty of imposing new taxes, compelled recourse to be had to loans.   Lord Bolingbroke, Dean
Swift, and other writers of their party, have, indeed,
alleged that the practice of funding was adopted, not
because it was the best, or rather the only, way of raising money at the æra in question, but in order to procure the support of the monied interest to the new government;—and some Jacobite writers have even gone so

far as to insinuate that William III. purposely involved us in debt and difficulties, that the Hollanders might have the better chance of surpassing us in manufactures and commerce!* It would be useless to waste the reader's time by any lengthened exposure of the falsehood of these imputations on the memory of our great deliverer. Every one in any degree acquainted with the state of Britain at the Revolution, must be aware that funding was the only means of raising supplies to which government could then resort; and that we are in a very high degree indebted to the aid which it afforded to the revolutionary leaders for the establishment of our free institutions, and, consequently, for the wealth and greatness to which we have since attained. Louis XIV., then in the zenith of his power, espoused the cause of the exiled family of Stuart, and exerted himself to replace them on the throne. It would not, under any circumstances, have been an easy task to make head against a monarch who was master of the greatest and best disciplined armies, and of the ablest generals and engineers, that had hitherto appeared in modern Europe. But the danger from without, though great and imminent, was inferior to the danger from within. James II. was master of almost all Ireland; and in Great Britain a numerous and powerful party was favourable to his pretensions. Such being the state of affairs, it would have been madness to have attempted, by imposing new taxes, to raise the sums required to defray the cost of the war it was necessary to wage for our independence and liberties. Had any such attempt been made, it would have given the Jacobites the means of traducing the new government, of inflaming popular discontents, and most probably of overturning the revolutionary establishment. The land-tax was the only considerable addition made to the revenue during the reign of William III.; and

* History of the National Debts and Taxes. Part i., p. 7.

a considerable part of its produce was required to make up the deficiency caused by the loss of the hearth-duty, which government had been obliged to abolish, and by the falling off in the duties of tonnage and poundage. It is clear, therefore, that the circumstances under which they were placed, the *res dura et regni novitas,* fully justified the revolutionary leaders in resorting to loans. Their doing so was not, in truth, a matter of choice, but of necessity. It is visionary to suppose that they could have raised a revenue equal to the exigency of the crisis in any other way. No doubt, on account of the supposed instability of the government, the terms on which loans were contracted during the reigns of William III., Anne, and George I., were most unfavourable. This, however, was but a trifling consideration, compared with the interests they were indispensable to secure. It was through their aid that our liberties were firmly established; the ambitious projects of Louis XIV. effectually crushed; and the political ascendancy of Great Britain placed on a solid foundation.

But, however necessary to a weak and precarious government, funding should never, for the reasons already stated, be made the principal support of a well-established government in a country capable of bearing a much larger amount of taxation; and hence the practice should either have been wholly abandoned at the accession of George II., or confined within comparatively narrow limits. Although, however, its insidious nature and dangerous tendency were very soon exposed by various members in the House of Commons, and by Hume and other able writers out of doors, the facilities which it afforded to successive administrations of meeting extraordinary expenses without imposing equivalent taxes, secured its ascendancy. Had ministers attended to the dictates of sound policy, they would have acted differently, and imposed, despite the clamours of the ignorant, such additional taxes as might have sufficed to defray a far more considerable portion of our outlays. But it is found in the affairs of nations as in those of individuals, and perhaps to a still greater extent in the former than in the latter, that the desire to secure some immediate though inconsiderable advantage is permitted to overbalance a very large amount of prospective inconvenience. The wish to conciliate public favour, to withhold from their opponents so fertile a topic of declamation and invective, as a sudden and considerable increase of taxation is always sure to afford, and in part also the real difficulty of carrying such a measure, tempted the ministers of George II. and George III. to persevere in the system of funding; and, in consequence, we are now subject to a much greater permanent burden, on account of the interest of the debt, than would suffice to defray the cost of the most expensive war.

These observations will, perhaps, be enough to enable a sufficiently fair estimate to be formed of the peculiar advantages and disadvantages of the plans we have been considering. The grand defects of the funding system consist in its making the loss occasioned by war-expenditure seem less than it really is, which prevents an adequate stimulus being given to industry and economy, and in its tempting, from the facility which it affords of raising supplies, governments and nations to embark in rash and perilous enterprises. The plan for raising the supplies within the year, by a corresponding increase of taxation, is free from these defects. The considerable increase of taxation that it occasions, goes far to preclude the chance of its being incurred, except on just and solid grounds; while by making every one directly furnish his share of the public outgoings, and apportioning what would otherwise be a national burden, which no one would feel any particular interest in discharging, among individuals, it infuses a more powerful spirit of industry, invention, and economy into all classes. On the other hand, however, the system of funding gives no sudden shock to industry. It habituates the public to bear their burdens; and by not calling upon them to do much at once, it, perhaps, enables them to do more in the end. Here, therefore, the advantage is on the side of the funding system. But if the situation of a country be such that taxes may, without occasioning any very great inconvenience, be imposed to meet any extraordinary expense, and if its government be powerful enough to impose such taxes, the last-mentioned advantage does not appear to be so very considerable as to countervail the many disadvantages incident to the practice of funding, and the contraction of a large public debt. We should not wish to speak with undue confidence on such a point; but there does not seem to be much doubt that an income-tax of 10 or 12 per cent. might have been levied during the American war: and, notwithstanding its inequality and the serious inconveniences by which it is attended, it may be doubted whether, had an income-tax of that amount been imposed in 1793, it would have been so injurious as the great additions that were then made to the customs and excise duties; while, by providing a large additional revenue, it would have obviated the necessity of funding largely, and on the most disadvantageous terms, at the commencement of the war.

The following table exhibits the progress of the National Debt from the Revolution downwards.

Account of the Principal (Funded and Unfunded), and Annual Charge of the Public Debt of the United Kingdom, at different Periods, from the Revolution downwards :*—

	Principal, Funded and Unfunded.	Interest and Management.
	£.	£.
Debt at the Revolution in 1689	664,263	39,855
Excess of Debt contracted during the reign of William III. above Debt paid off. . . .	15,730,439	1,271,087
Debt at the accession of Queen Anne in 1702 .	16,394,702	1,310,942
Debt contracted during the reign of Anne . .	37,750,661	2,040,416
Debt at the accession of George I. in 1714 . .	54,145,363	3,351,358
Debt paid off during the reign of George I. above Debt contracted	2,053,125	1,133,807
Debt at the accession of George II. in 1727 .	52,092,238	2,217,551
Debt contracted between the accession of George II. and the peace of Paris in 1763, three years after the accession of George III., above Debt paid off	86,773,192	2,634,500
Debt in 1763	138,865,430	4,852,051
Debt paid off from 1763 to 1775	10,281,795	380,480
Debt at commencement of the American war in 1775	128,583,635	4,471,571
Debt contracted during the American war . .	121,267,993	5,395,794
Debt after conclusion of the American war in 1786	249,851,628	9,867,365
Paid during peace from 1786 to 1793 . . .	5,411,322	243,277
Debt at commencement of French war in 1793 .	244,440,306	9,624,088
Debt contracted during French war	603,842,171	22,829,696
Debt at the Consolidation of the English and Irish Exchequers at the commencement of 1817 .	848,282,477	32,453,784
Debt cancelled from 1817 to 5th January, 1844	55,942,584	3,184,624
Debt on 5th January, 1844, and charge thereon during preceding year	792,339,893	29,269,160

This table would afford ample materials for a lengthened commentary. The rapid progress of the debt during periods of war compared with the little

* This Table has been principally compiled from Dr. Hamilton's work on the National Debt (3rd edit. p. 100), and from the Annual Finance Accounts. It may, perhaps, not be in all respects quite accurate; but we feel pretty confident that its errors are immaterial, and not such as sensibly to affect any inference that may be drawn from it.

progress made in paying it off during periods of peace, cannot fail to strike every one. And it is further to be observed that the reductions made in the principal of the debt have been chiefly effected through the very questionable practice of converting stock into life annuities; and that the reductions in the annual charge on account of the debt have been principally effected through the fall in the rate of interest since the peace having enabled government to offer to pay off certain classes of stockholders in the event of their not agreeing to a diminution of their claims. Had it not been for the extremely objectionable plan on which the greater portion of the debt has been funded, this resource would have been much more available; but notwithstanding its limited operation, it is to it, and not to the influence of sinking funds, or to the employment of surplus revenue to pay off debt, that we are principally indebted for the reductions that have been made in the amount of our engagements.

Seeing the vast magnitude of our present incumbrances, our readers will hardly suppose how small an immediate sacrifice would have sufficed to avert them. The capital of the debt has been swelled out beyond all reasonable bounds by the vicious practice of funding a larger amount of capital stock than the sums borrowed, and there have, also, been large deductions from the loans for prompt payment and bonuses of various descriptions. The funding system was probably more abused during the American war than in any other period of our history; but to show its operation it is not necessary to go further back than the late French war, which about trebled the debt. In showing how the expenses of that contest were, and how they might have been provided for, we shall not lay any stress on any doubtful or irritating topic. It is probably true that there was a good deal of extravagance and waste on our part in the way in which the struggle was carried on, at least during its earlier portion. But it is immaterial to our object, whether such were or were not the case. And taking it for granted that the war was just and necessary, and that there was no useless expenditure in carrying it on, we have to inquire how much it would have cost had the expenditure been defrayed by a corresponding increase of taxation, and how much it has cost by the adoption of the borrowing system.

At the commencement of the war, in 1793, the charge on account of the funded and unfunded debt amounted to 9,624,088*l*., which would have been gradually, though slowly, reduced by the falling in of annuities, &c. Now, it is obvious, that if we add to the charge on account of the public debt as it stood at the commencement of the war, the charges on account of the government of the country and of the war, we shall have the whole sum that, had it been raised within the year, would have defrayed the entire charge against the country without resorting to loans. And by comparing this sum with the revenue actually received, we shall get the deficiency which, not being provided for by taxes, was provided for by loans. The following table (p. 422) exhibits the results of these statements and comparisons.

The results of this table will probably be thought not a little curious. It shows that the total expenditure of the country on account of internal government, colonies, the war, and the debt contracted previously to 1793, and from 1793 to 1816, both inclusive, was only 151,327,007*l*. greater than the revenue actually derived from taxes during that period. It further appears that this deficit principally took place during the first ten years of the war; and that, but for the interest of the debt contracted to meet this deficit, the revenue in several of the latter years of the war would have considerably exceeded the expenditure. It is difficult to say what proportion of the expenditure of the first period might have been provided for by an increase of taxation, had a vigorous effort been made with that object. But, though we are inclined to dissent

TABLE showing the Total Charge on Account of the Unredeemed Public Debt due January 5, 1793, in that and every subsequent Year to the 5th of January, 1817; the Total Charges of the State exclusive of the Debt; the Total Charges of the State inclusive of the Debt contracted previously to 1793; the Amount of the Nett Revenue received by the Treasury in each Year from 1793 to 1816, both inclusive; and the Excess of Expenditure over Revenue, and of Revenue over Expenditure.*

Years ending 5th Jan.	1. Charge on Funded and Unfunded Debt, as it stood Jan. 5, 1793, and as it would have stood in the following Years had no Additions been afterwards made to it.			2. Total Charge on Account of War Expenditure, Internal Government, Colonies, &c.			3. Totals of No. 1 and 2, or Charge, as it would have been, had the Supplies been raised within the Year.			4. Total nett Revenue (exclusive of Loans) received by the Treasury.			5. Excess of Expenditure over Revenue.			6. Excess of Revenue over Expenditure.		
	£.	s.	d.	£.	s	d.	£.	s.	d.	£.	s.	d.	£.	s.	d.	£.	s.	d.
1793	9,624,088	8	5¼	7,670,108	5	2	17,294,196	13	7¼	19,258,814	6	4¼	....			1,964,617	12	9
1794	9,623,441	5	8¾	14,759,206	15	11½	24,382,648	1	8¼	19,845,705	10	4	4,536,942	11	4¼	....		
1795	9,622,237	8	2	19,702,489	2	11½	29,324,726	11	1½	20,193,074	4	6½	9,131,652	6	7	....		
1796	9,620,466	3	1	34,300,764	17	4	43,921,231	0	5	19,883,520	13	0¾	24,037,710	7	4¼	....		
1797	9,618,550	15	0	45,814,275	8	11¾	55,432,826	3	11¾	21,454,728	4	5¼	33,978,097	19	6½	....		
1798	9,614,818	10	11½	36,202,873	13	11½	45,817,692	4	11	23,126,940	7	1	22,690,751	17	10	....		
1799	9,613,055	15	4½	33,279,071	18	5¾	42,892,127	13	10¼	31,035,363	2	4¼	11,856,764	11	6	....		
1800	9,611,668	10	8¾	38,166,697	19	7½	47,778,366	10	4½	35,602,444	8	11¼	12,175,922	1	5¼	....		
1801	9,609,884	13	5	39,074,449	13	11½	48,684,334	7	4½	34,145,584	4	1	14,538,750	3	3½	....		
1802	9,607,659	0	8	40,690,486	9	6¾	50,298,145	10	2¾	34,113,146	18	4¾	16,184,998	11	10	....		
1803	9,606,509	16	8	29,610,471	2	3¼	39,216,980	18	11¼	36,368,149	14	5	2,848,831	4	6¼	....		
1804	9,581,270	13	1¾	28,289,364	9	0½	37,870,635	2	2	38,609,392	8	6	....			738,757	6	4
1805	9,580,272	3	1½	37,876,084	9	4½	47,456,356	12	6	46,176,492	19	8	1,279,863	12	10	....		
1806	9,548,920	6	3¼	44,765,873	0	10¾	54,314,793	7	2	50,897,706	5	10¼	3,417,087	1	3¾	....		
1807	9,538,508	1	7¼	45,485,499	7	0	55,024,007	8	7¼	55,796,086	8	2	....			772,078	19	6¾
1808	9,524,724	1	5½	43,970,956	9	8	53,495,680	11	1½	59,339,321	19	4¼	....			5,843,641	8	2¾
1809	9,104,238	8	7	49,821,335	7	0	58,925,573	15	7	62,498,191	9	7¾	....			3,572,617	14	0¾
1810	9,103,379	7	3	52,274,730	5	0½	61,378,109	12	3½	63,719,400	18	11	....			2,341,291	6	7½
1811	9,102,580	17	2½	52,551,395	4	3½	61,653,976	1	6	67,144,542	18	4¼	....			5,490,566	16	10¼
1812	9,101,931	10	11½	58,646,377	8	3½	67,748,308	19	2¾	65,173,545	12	8¾	2,574,763	6	6	....		
1813	9,101,399	7	7½	60,604,064	7	7½	69,705,463	15	3	65,037,850	1	7	4,667,613	13	8	....		
1814	9,100,154	8	1	77,406,919	8	6	86,507,073	16	7	68,748,363	6	3	17,758,710	10	4	....		
1815	9,098,917	16	4¼	76,227,766	18	10	85,326,684	15	2¼	71,134,503	2	2½	14,192,181	12	11¾	....		
1816	9,098,046	6	10¼	60,559,275	15	11½	69,657,322	2	9¾	72,210,512	15	7¼	....			2,553,090	12	9½
1817	9,090,000	0	0	31,907,673	8	4	40,997,673	8	4	62,264,546	12	2½	....			21,266,873	3	10½
	235,446,723	16	8¾	1059,658,211	8	1	1295,104,935	4	9¾	1143,777,928	13	0½	195,870,641	12	10½	44,543,635	1	1
							Deduct—Excess of Revenue						44,543,635	1	1			
							Excess of Expenditure over Revenue . .						151,327,006	11	9½			

* We inserted a similar Account in an article in the Edinburgh Review for October, 1823; but in that instance we were obliged to depend on statements which turned out to be, in many respects, erroneous, so that our conclusions were vitiated in a corresponding degree. But the above table may be safely depended upon: it was prepared (with the exception of the last year) from official sources for the Finance Committee, of which Sir Henry Parnell was chairman, and is given in his 'Financial Reform.' The line for the year ending 5th of January, 1817, has been added from the same sources, with the exception of the first item in it, which is an estimate only, but which cannot possibly involve any sensible error; none, in fact, that could affect the results deduced from it.

from those who think that it might have been wholly provided for in this way, there are not, we apprehend, any good reasons for doubting that the revenue raised by taxation might have been very materially increased. And had only half the deficiency been made good by additional taxes, it would, by proportionally diminishing the amount of the loans and enabling them to be negotiated on preferable terms, have been of singular advantage; and would, by lessening the necessity for further loans, have reduced the debt contracted during the war to less than half its actual amount.

We should, however, convey a false impression to our readers, if we led them to suppose that all the immense sums that were borrowed during the war, exclusive of the above sum of 151,327,007*l.*, were absolutely lost or wasted. Though the funding system encourages waste and profusion, it is not so bad as this. By not making the public provide the 4,536,943*l.* of deficient revenue in 1793, the 9,131,652*l.* deficient in 1794, &c., these sums were left in their hands to be employed as capital in producing additional wealth; and if we suppose they could have lived without these sums, we must, in fairly testing the operation of the system, also suppose that they accumulated them at compound interest during the whole period of the war; and compare their amount, when so accumulated, with the sums borrowed during the same period. But, for the same reasons on which it is supposed that the public saved the sums and their accumulations at compound interest, left in their hands by the operation of the funding system when the revenue was deficient, we must suppose that they lost the sums with their accumulations in those years in which, but for the funding system, the revenue would have exceeded the expenditure; so that the difference between these two sums when so accumulated will be the sum to be compared with the debt contracted. Now it appears that the balances of expenditure over income in column 5 of the previous table, when accumulated at 5 per cent. compound interest, amounted, on the 5th of January, 1817, to 435,881,999*l.* ; while the balances of revenue over expenditure, in column 6, calculated in the same way, amounted at the same period to 57,930,485*l.* ; and deducting the one of these sums from the other, we have 377,951,514*l.* for the amount of the capitals and their accumulations at compound interest which the adoption of the funding system left in the pockets of the public over what would have been taken from them, had the supplies been raised within the year by a corresponding increase of taxation.

It appears, however, from the subjoined statement (p. 445, deduced from the Parliamentary Paper No. 145, Sess. 1822), that in the interval between 1794 and 1816, both included, government borrowed in all 584,874,557*l.*, of which sum 188,522,350*l.* was transferred to the Commissioners of the Sinking Fund, leaving 396,352,207*l.* for the amount of the sums borrowed to defray the expenses of the late war, exclusive of an additional issue of 33,289,300*l.* of Exchequer Bills, making in all the sum of 429,641,507*l.*

But we have already seen that the entire amount of the sums which the adoption of the funding system left in the pockets of the public, over what would have been taken out of them, had the supplies been raised within the year, with their accumulations at 5 per cent. compound interest, amounted to 377,951,514*l.*; and this sum being deducted from the above sum of 429,641,507*l.*, raised by funding and issuing Exchequer Bills, leaves a balance of 51,689,993*l.* for the nett amount of the direct surplus expenditure occasioned by funding over what would have been expended had the supplies been raised within the year! We are not aware that any good objection can be made to these statements. They are all deduced from official returns: the calculations have been carefully checked, and the principle on which they are bottomed is most favourable for the funding system. And yet they show (or rather demonstrate) that, exclusive of its other mischievous influences,—of the profusion and contempt of economy, which are its immediate, and the interminable and heavy taxes which are its ultimate results,—it occasioned during the late war, by means of premiums on loans and otherwise, a special sacrifice of about *fifty-two* millions sterling! This experience should not be thrown away. We have already stated that it is more than doubtful whether funding could have been dispensed with during the earlier part of the war. But, no doubt, the amount of revenue from 1792 to 1803 might have been most materially augmented by resorting to house and income taxes; and the statement now made shows the immense sacrifice the public has had to sustain in the end for the temporary convenience afforded by carrying funding to the extreme to which it was then carried.

It is certainly true, as will be immediately shown, that the inconveniences naturally incident to the system have been enormously aggravated by the vicious method in which the loans contracted during the American and late French wars were funded. But loans, though effected in the best possible mode, should always be regarded as an extraordinary, or rather as a *dernier ressort*. The heir of an entailed estate who makes the issue of post-obit bonds an habitual source of revenue, is not really more short-sighted and improvident than ministers who resort to loans to supply such portions of the public expenditure as may be defrayed by taxation.

It may, perhaps, be said that however large the amount of our debt, it has been sufficiently shown in the course of these inquiries, that the increase of the taxes imposed to defray the interest, has operated as a powerful spur to industry and economy, and that the probability is that the capital of the country is not at this

moment materially different from what it would have
been had the American war and the late French war
never occurred. But though such, most probably, is
the case, we have also seen that the inconveniences
attending the magnitude of the debt are notwithstanding of a very formidable description. It has occasioned
the imposition of heavy taxes on many desirable articles
and even on income; and though it be true that our
means of paying these taxes have proportionally increased, we are, for the most part, alive only to the sacrifice, and forget altogether the increased ability to bear
it. We also, as already seen, contrast our taxes with
those of other countries, and in the event of the latter
being lower, individuals are tempted to become absentees; while the low rate of profit, which is either wholly
or in part a consequence of taxation, makes large
amounts of capital be employed in foreign investments.
The circumstances which have latterly counteracted this
tendency of capital to go abroad are not of a permanent,
but of an accidental and evanescent description (*ante*,
p. 383); and should they become less powerful, its efflux,
in large quantities, will doubtless recommence. This
is one of the greatest inconveniences attending the contraction of a large public debt, and the consequent
taxation which it occasions. Indeed the fair presumption is, that if our manufacturing superiority be at
any time seriously compromised by the competition of
foreigners, they will be found to have been trained,
and in great part supported, by English workmen and
English capital. It will also most probably be found,
should our taxes cease to be so productive as formerly, or should they not increase with the increasing
wealth and population of the country, that it is not
because the contributors cannot, but because they will
not pay them; because they find on looking around that
there are other countries open for their reception in
which taxation is less heavy, and to which, consequently,

DIFFERENT METHODS OF FUNDING.   427

they may be tempted, should our taxes not be reduced, to emigrate. And hence the importance of preventing, in as far as possible, the contraction of a large public debt, in the first instance, and of its substantial reduction if it should be contracted.

CHAPTER II.

DIFFERENT METHODS OF FUNDING.

In the infancy of the funding system, loans were most commonly raised in anticipation of the produce of certain taxes imposed for a limited number of years; it being supposed that the produce of these taxes for the term for which they were granted would be sufficient to discharge the debt. But these expectations were rarely realized; and as the public necessities required the taxes to be mortgaged again for new loans, often before their former term was expired, they were prolonged from time to time, and were at last, in almost every instance, rendered perpetual.

The statutory rate of interest at the commencement of the funding system, was six per cent., the reduction to five per cent. not having taken place till 1714. But, owing to the supposed insecurity of the revolutionary establishment, the rate of interest paid on loans to the public, previously to the accession of George II., was generally much higher than the legal rate. In 1692, an attempt was made to borrow a million upon annuities for ninety-nine years, for which ten per cent. was to be given for eight years, and seven per cent. afterwards, with the benefit of survivorship during the lives of the nominees of those who contributed; but so low was the credit of Government at that period, that only 881,000*l.* could be procured even on these extravagant terms. None of the loans negotiated during the wars in the

reign of William III. was effected at less than eight per
cent.; and the interest was, in many instances, as in the
one just mentioned, a good deal higher.   The sums borrowed during the reign of Queen Anne were also obtained on very expensive terms.

Since the reign of Queen Anne, very little money has
been borrowed either upon annuities for terms of years,
or upon those for lives.   The practice of granting perpetual annuities, or annuities redeemable only on payment of the principal, has long superseded every other.
And notwithstanding the objections that have been urged
against this practice, by Dr. Price and others, it appears
to be the best hitherto proposed.   To show the principle
on which the objections to it are founded, let us suppose
that an annuity is granted for a hundred years.   This
annuity, according to the principles on which such com-
putations are founded, is nearly equivalent to an annuity
for ever, its value at four per cent., being twenty-four
and a half years' purchase, and, therefore, only half a
year's purchase less than its value were it perpetual.
Supposing, therefore, that the public were able to borrow
at four per cent. on annuities for ever, it should not give
above 1s. 7d. per cent. more for money borrowed on
annuities terminable in a hundred years.   But admitting
that it might be obliged to give a quarter or even a half
per cent. more, those who advocate this system contend,
that the additional burdens that would thus be imposed
would hardly be sensible; and that the privations caused
by them would, in any view of the matter, be inconsiderable, compared with the advantages that would result
from the necessary and gradual annihilation of the debt.

" By such a method of raising money," says Dr. Price,
" the expense of one war would, in time, come to be
always discharged before a new war commenced; and it
would be impossible that a state should ever have upon
it, at one time, the expense of many wars; or any larger
debts than could be contracted within the limited period

of the annuities; and consequently it would enjoy the invaluable privilege of being rendered, in some degree, independent of the management of its finances by unskilful or unfaithful servants."[*]

But several important considerations have been left out of view in this statement. In the first place, a considerably larger payment on account of interest would be required, were loans made on such annuities, than Dr. Price supposes. It is true that an annuity for 100 years is really worth nearly as much as a perpetuity, and should, therefore, one should think, form nearly as desirable a security to the lender. But the decisions of mankind, with respect to money matters, are but rarely governed by purely mathematical principles. The trustees of public bodies, and all those individuals who buy into the funds in order to make family settlements, the prospective clauses of which frequently refer to remote posterity, would evidently feel disinclined to purchase into a fund whose value was continually diminishing; and such persons form a very large proportion of the holders of stock; and hence it is clear, that although the real value of an annuity for a long term of years may be about the same with that of a perpetual annuity, it will hardly ever find nearly the same number of purchasers. Even the subscribers to a new loan, who generally mean to sell their subscription as soon as possible, invariably prefer a perpetual annuity, redeemable by Parliament, to an irredeemable annuity for a long term of years, of about an equal amount. The value of the former being always the same, or very nearly the same, it makes a more convenient transferable stock than the former.

But, in the second place, though it were true that terminable annuities were as readily negotiable at their *true* value as interminable ones, we should not, therefore, be disposed to recommend their adoption. No government

---

[*] Observations on Reversionary Payments, 7th edit., i., 275.

should ever countenance any scheme of public finance, or
indeed any institution of any sort, that has any tendency
to weaken the providence and forethought of its subjects.
But such, we apprehend, would be the effect of the adoption of any scheme of funding on terminable annuities,
whether for a specified number of years, or for lives.
The purchaser of an annuity terminating with his life, is,
in almost every instance, desirous, not only of consuming
the interest of his capital, but also the capital itself; and
the same principle most commonly influences, though not,
perhaps, to the same extent, the greater number of the
purchasers of annuities terminable at specified and not
very distant periods; and if the granting of such annuities
were countenanced by Government, and they were established on a large scale, it seems natural to conclude that
the odium which now attaches to such investments would
be gradually weakened, and that numbers of individuals
would be tempted, by the immediate addition it would
make to their incomes, to vest their capitals either in
life annuities, or in annuities which they supposed would
most likely terminate nearly at the same period as their
lives.   A practice of this sort is suitable only to persons of slender means, and with no near connexions,
and were it confined to them there would be nothing to
object to in it: but if it should ever make any considerable progress among the bulk of the community, it
would be productive of the worst consequences, both
in a moral and economical point of view.   A person
whose income is derived from an annuity payable by the
State, can in a great measure dispense with that good
opinion of his neighbours, which is so essential to individuals engaged in professional or industrious employments; and if he be the holder of an annuity for life, or
for a term of years, and is anxious only to consume the
whole of his fortune without caring about those who
are to come after him, he ceases, in a great measure, to
feel any interest in the public welfare, and becomes

wholly selfish in the literal and degrading sense of the term.

Few things, therefore, would, we conceive, be more injurious than the establishment of any system in the management of the finances of a great nation, that might possibly tend to generate and spread those purely selfish and unsocial passions, which lead individuals to consider their own interests as everything, and those of others as nothing. No doubt a considerable time would most probably elapse in a country where the feelings of society are so much opposed to this selfish system as in England, before any change of circumstances could enable it to obtain any very considerable footing. But, though insensible at first, its influence might ultimately become alike extensive and powerful; and if so great a stimulus were given to it as would result from the conversion of any considerable part of the national debt into annuities terminable in periods of moderate duration, its introduction might be more rapid than it is perhaps very easy to imagine.

A large proportion of the present holders of funded property consists of individuals not engaged in business, who subsist either wholly or partly on the dividends, and leave the principal to their children or relations. But if the principal belonging to these persons were turned into a terminable annuity, it is plain that at its termination, they, or their heirs, would be left destitute, unless they had effected an insurance with some society, or accumulated, in some way or other, such a portion of their annuity as might suffice to yield a corresponding revenue when it terminated. But these are all operations that require an acquaintance with business, and a peculiar combination of circumstances, to enable them to be carried into effect; and it appears obvious that very many holders of funded property would, from thoughtlessness, want of opportunity, want of information, and a thousand other causes, either never think of the matter at all, or be induced indefinitely to postpone it. In this way the system would probably be introduced with greater rapidity than we might at first be led to suppose; and, as it obviously strikes at the very foundation of the principle of accumulation, and of all those habits which are most conducive to the interests of society, it should not certainly receive any countenance, whether direct or indirect, from Government.

For these reasons we incline to doubt the policy of the acts 48 Geo. III., 10 Geo. IV. c. 24, and 3 and 4 Will. IV. c. 14, which authorise the Commissioners of the National Debt to grant annuities for lives, or for terms of years, on receiving payment either in money or stock, according to rates specified in tables approved by the Treasury. At the outset government lost very large sums by this project, from their granting annuities on advanced lives at too low rates. This error has, however, been rectified, and the annuities are now sold at their fair value. On the 5th of January, 1844, the terminable annuities payable by government amounted to 3,924,723*l.*, being equivalent (according to Mr. Finlaison) to a perpetual annuity of 1,550,762*l.* Latterly the amount of terminable annuities has been declining, so that it may probably be presumed the system has attained its maximum. And though, speaking generally, the purchase of life annuities should be discouraged, there are a few cases in which they are a legitimate and advantageous resource; and should the system not make any greater way than it has done, it may not, in a practical point of view, be worth objecting to.

Annuities for lives have sometimes been granted upon schemes called Tontines, from Tonti, an Italian banker, by whom they were first proposed. In tontines, the benefit of survivorship is allowed. The subscribers usually appoint nominees, who are divided into classes according to their ages, a proportional annuity being assigned to each; and when any of the lives fail, the amount of the disengaged annuity is divided amongst the survivors so long as any remain, or until the annuity payable to each amounts to a large sum, according to the terms of the scheme.

More money should be raised upon an equal revenue appropriated to a tontine annuity, than upon annuities for separate lives; inasmuch as an annuity with a right of survivorship is worth more than an equal annuity for a single life. But, notwithstanding this circumstance, tontines seem to be about the very worst means that have been devised for raising money. They are, in fact, a species of lotteries; and besides having the same influence in leading people to convert their capital into revenue as annuities for lives, or annuities terminable at specified periods, they contribute powerfully to diffuse a taste for gambling. Life annuities are also, in almost every respect, more advantageous for the holders, inasmuch as they yield a constant and equal revenue from the outset; whereas, in tontines, an individual gets at first only a comparatively small revenue, and trusts chiefly to the chance, which, in most cases, must prove unfavourable, of out-living the other subscribers, and attaining to ease and opulence in old age.

In addition to these objections to tontines, it may be observed, that it is very difficult to establish them on sound principles, or according to the rules deduced from the theory of probabilities. The authors of such schemes are principally desirous of presenting them under the most attractive forms. The different classes of subscribers are not arranged with sufficient care, so that some individuals have an undue advantage over others. To establish a fair tontine, it would be indispensable to class together none but individuals of the same age, and who were placed under nearly the same circumstances; and to cnact, that the entire annuity of each class should always go to the last survivor. But it would be impossible to establish any extensive tontine upon such principles, that is, on principles that would render the chances of the subscribers equal, and fully worth the sum paid for them.*

A very large proportion of the old public debt of France was raised upon tontines; most of which were contracted for in the most improvident manner on the part of the public, and on the most unequal terms on the part of the subscribers. And the fact that, previously to the Revolution, a very large proportion of the people of France evinced the strongest desire to embark in these schemes, or to convert their capitals into life-annuities, dependent on contingencies, and that a spirit of gambling had been widely diffused amongst the lower and middle classes, is a practical proof of the correctness of the conclusions we have already drawn on general principles; and shows the extreme impolicy of establishing any system which may either teach individuals to disregard the interest of their heirs, or to trust to combinations of chances for the acquisition of that opulence, which, speaking generally, can only spring from industry and economy. Fortunately, however, this pernicious practice of borrowing upon tontines has been discontinued since the Revolution; and funding is now effected in France as in England, by granting interminable annuities redeemable at pleasure.

Tontines have been very seldom attempted in England: the last that was undertaken was in 1779, and proved a losing concern to the contractors.

Presuming, therefore, that the advantage of funding in perpetual annuities, redeemable at pleasure on payment of the principal, has been sufficiently established, we have next to inquire into the best method of constituting these annuities.

The credit of nations, like that of individuals, is liable to vary from the operation of many different causes;

* Lacroix, Traité Elémentaire des Probabilités, éd. 2nde, p. 235.

and, though their credit were uniform, they would necessarily experience more or less difficulty in obtaining supplies upon loan, according to variations in the amount of floating capital, and the facilities for its profitable employment in industrious undertakings. It is obviously impossible, therefore, that public loans can always be negotiated on the same terms; and, in point of fact, these are perpetually varying.

But it is plain that, in contracting for a loan, there are only two elements that can be varied—the principal and the interest. Suppose that it has been usual for individuals to make advances to Government on receiving 100*l.* of four per cent. stock for every 100*l.* advanced; and suppose further, that, from some cause or other, money can no longer be obtained on these terms. Under such circumstances, two courses are open, viz. (1), To give the lender a right to a greater amount of stock than the money he actually advances amounts to, and to allow him interest on such stock; or (2), To restrict the stock created, in the lender's favour, to the amount of the loan, and to make the required bonus by raising the rate of interest. The first of these plans is that which has been usually followed in this country; though it appears difficult to imagine that any preference was ever less deserved.

The system of funding to a greater extent than the money actually borrowed amounted to, began in the reign of Queen Anne; but it was not carried to any great extent till the war terminated by the treaty of Aix-la-Chapelle. About that time, however, the public debt began to be considered in the light of a permanent or irredeemable incumbrance; and it was, therefore, thought better to dispose of variable quantities of stock bearing a uniform rate of interest, according to the state of the market at the time, than to fund the same principal sums at different rates of interest. At first this practice was infinitely less objectionable than it has since become. The price of stocks, during the reigns of George I. and

George II., did not diverge materially from par; and until the rebellion of 1745, the three per cents had never fallen below 89.   But the same practice has been pursued ever since, even when the three per cents. have sold for little more than half their nominal value; and it consequently follows, were any considerable progress to be made now, or at any future period, in paying off the public debt, that the three per cents. would immediately rise to about par; and, unless the holders were to consent to accept a stock bearing a lower rate of interest, the public would have to pay 100*l*., when perhaps they only received 50*l*. or 60*l*. !

It must, however, be admitted that the plan of funding a large capital in a stock bearing a low interest, has some advantage, though of a very limited description, over the plan of funding a less capital in a stock bearing a high interest.   The fluctuations in the price of the former species of stock being more considerable than in the latter, it affords a better field for speculation: and the confidence placed by individuals in their own sagacity and good fortune, naturally disposes them to buy that species of stock which affords, what they conceive to be, the best opportunities for increasing their capital.   It has been most commonly supposed that it was exclusively in consequence of this principle that the late five per cent. stock always bore a lower relative value than the three per cents.; or, which is the same thing, that a given sum of money applied to purchase five per cents., always yielded a higher rate of interest than if it had been applied to purchase three per cents.   But although the circumstances previously mentioned must, undoubtedly, have had some influence in raising the value of the three per cents., as compared with any other species of stock yielding a higher interest, it will be afterwards seen that the discrepancy in question was mainly owing to an entirely different circumstance.

Mr. Ricardo seems to have inclined to the opinion

that the increased charge for interest, had the loans been made for an equivalent amount of stock, would have equalled, or perhaps exceeded, the advantage gained by the reduction of the principal.* There are really, however, no good or tenable grounds for this conclusion. If, indeed, the public debt is to be regarded in the light of a permanent burden; and if no efforts are ever to be made to lessen its amount, either by the operation of a really efficient sinking fund, or any other means; then, of course, the payment on account of interest is the only thing that needs be attended to, and the magnitude of the principal must be a matter of complete indifference. But even when considered in this point of view, it will be found that whatever relief may be gained in the payment of interest by funding a larger capital than the amount of the money borrowed, is only temporary and inconsiderable; and that it is sure to entail in the end an incomparably greater permanent burden on the country.

In the first place, though it be true, as has been previously stated, that four and five per cent. stocks have always borne a lower relative value in the market than three per cent. stock, it is not true that this lower value has been either wholly, or even principally, caused by the greater scope for speculation afforded by the three per cents. Those who held, or who speculated in five per cent. stock were aware that, in the event of its rising to par, as it should have done when the three per cents. rose to 60, it would be in the power of government to reduce the interest on it, an event which actually took place, and from the specific cause now assigned, in 1822. Hence it is plain that at least 1 per cent., or rather $1\frac{1}{2}$ per cent., of the dividends payable on five per cent. stock should only be considered in the light of a short annuity. Any given annuity derived from the five per cents. was not, therefore, really worth so much as an equal annuity derived from the three per cents.; nor did they, from

* Article Funding System, in Encyclopædia Britannica.

their liability to be reduced, when the three per cents.
were above 60, constitute so advantageous a fund in
which to make investments. This same principle held,
also, in the case of the four and three and a half per
cents.; their relative value being always somewhat depressed, as compared with the three per cents., occasioned by the greater risk of the dividend being reduced.

It is also, in the second place, abundantly obvious that
a small increase of interest must be sufficient to balance
the chance that funding in a stock at low interest gives of
increasing the stockholder's capital. The additional rate
of interest begins to accrue from the moment that the
loan is bargained for; whereas the chances of a rise of
the funds depend on the events and termination of the
war, on the state of the revenue and the country when it
is terminated, and a thousand other contingencies. The
great majority of those who subscribe to loans never
think of such remote contingencies, but look only to the
circumstances of the moment. Indeed, persons well versed
in such subjects have confidently affirmed that an addi-
tion of from $\frac{1}{4}$ to $\frac{1}{2}$ per cent. of interest to the rate actually bargained for, would have more than enabled Go-
vernment to fund all the loans contracted during the late
war, without any artificial increase of capital.

The grand recommendation of the plan of bargaining for loans, by offering such a rate of interest as may
be required to procure them at the time, without creating any fictitious capital, consists in the facility which it
affords of reducing the charge on their account during
peace. Under the system of increasing the interest on
loans, by funding a greater capital than is actually
received by Government, the country may be prevented
from profiting by the means which peace almost invariably brings along with it, of raising money at a less
cost. Thus, if a loan had been made during the late
war, and an equivalent amount of stock had been created,
bearing 5 or 6 per cent. interest, it would have been in

the power of Government, soon after the peace, to reduce
the charge, on account of this loan, to 4, and thereafter
to 3 or at most 3½ per cent., by offering to pay off the
principal, in the event of the holders refusing to agree to
the reduction. But under the system that has unluckily
been adopted, of funding a large fictitious capital at a
low rate of interest, the total charge for interest is rendered very near as high as it would have been, though no
fictitious capital had been created, while it has become
impossible to reduce it, without being previously in a condition to pay off the fictitiously increased capital at par.

The statements now made, and the inferences drawn
from them, are so obvious as hardly to require any con-
firmation. It may however be worth while to mention,
that they are not advanced on any speculative or doubtful hypothesis, but that they rest on the solid and unas-
sailable ground of fact and experiment. The additions
made during the reigns of William III. and Anne to the
principal of the public debt, over and above the sums
borrowed, were of comparatively trifling amount; and
hence Sir Robert Walpole, by availing himself of the
facility with which money was obtainable after the
treaty of Utrecht, was enabled materially to reduce the
annual charge on account of interest; which was still
farther reduced in 1727 and 1749 (see *post*).

But in spite of the practical and decisive proofs that
had thus been afforded of the advantage of funding a
smaller amount of capital in a stock bearing a high rate
of interest, in preference to funding a larger amount of
capital in a stock bearing a low rate of interest, the
latter plan has been almost uniformly followed since the
commencement of the American war; and we are, in consequence, compelled to pay, on the loans so contracted,
the same rate of interest during peace, that was sufficient
to cause the subscribers to come forward during the agitation and alarm incident to a protracted and doubtful

contest! We shall endeavour, in as few words as possible, to make our readers acquainted with the practical operation and real effect of this most improvident system.

In 1781 a loan of 12,000,000*l.* was negotiated; and for this sum Government gave 18,000,000*l.* of three per cent. stock; and 3,000,000*l.* of four per cent. stock. On the whole, therefore, 660,000*l.* of interest was paid for this loan, being rather more than 5½ per cent., and a fictitious capital was created in favour of the lenders of no less than *nine* millions! But it is obvious that, had this loan been negotiated without any increase of capital, at 5¾ or even 6 per cent., the charge on its account might have been reduced, in the course of half-a-dozen years, to 3 or 3½ per cent. on the 12,000,000*l.* actually borrowed; whereas, owing to the mode in which it was contracted, nothing could be deducted from the annual charge until after the prices of the three and four per cents. rose above par, without being previously prepared to offer the holders twenty-one millions for the twelve they had originally advanced! And as this has not yet occurred with the three per cents., we are still in 1845 burdened with a payment of about 5 per cent. on account of this loan!

Nothing, we are sorry to say, is more easy than to point out innumerable instances of this sort, in which the public interests have been sacrificed, not intentionally, indeed, but through ignorance, or a desire to grasp at an immediate advantage, in the most extraordinary manner. The very next loan negotiated by Lord North, in 1782, was for 13,500,000*l.*, for which Government gave 13,500,000*l.* three per cents., and 6,750,000*l.* four per cents., exclusive of an annuity of 17*s.* 6*d.* for every 100*l.* advanced, for 78 years. The country was, in this way, bound to pay an interest of 793,125*l.* a-year, inclusive of the annuity, being at the rate of 5*l.* 16*s.* 10*d.* per cent.; and it was rendered impossible to reduce this heavy charge at any future period, except under the contingency alluded to above, without previously consenting to sacrifice 6,750,000*l.*!

But it is unnecessary to go back to the American war for proofs of the extreme inexpediency of funding in this manner. Most of the loans negotiated during the late war were funded in the same way, and some of them on still more ruinous terms on the part of the public. Thus, according to the conditions on which a loan of 18,000,000*l.* was bargained for in 1795, a capital of 18,000,000*l.* three per cent. stock, and 6,000,000*l.* four per cents., exclusive of a long annuity of 9*s.* 6*d.* per cent., was assigned to the subscribers. But the terms of the loan of 17,000,000*l.*, negotiated in 1798, were still more extravagant; for every 100*l.* advanced entitled the lender to 200*l.* three per cent. stock, and an annuity of 4*s.* 11*d.* per cent. for 62¾ years; or, in other words, for every 100*l.* advanced, Government bound the country to pay an annual interest of 6 per cent., exclusive of the long annuity! We admit that this was a period of unusual difficulty; that the urgency of the crisis required that higher terms than ordinary should be offered to the subscribers; and no just objection could have been made to granting them whatever rate of interest might have been required to induce them to come forward. This, too, was in fact really done; but owing to the way in which it was done, by granting the subscribers three per cent. stock to *double* the amount of the money they advanced, the public was effectually prevented from so much as attempting to reduce the annual charge on account of this loan until the rate of interest for which new loans might be contracted should be under 3 per cent.! And we are now, in the thirtieth year of peace, paying 6 per cent. on this loan; whereas, had it been funded in a six and a quarter or six and a half per cent. stock, the interest might have been reduced, five-and-twenty years ago, to 4 or 4½ per cent., and would now have been reduced to 3¼ per cent., and in 1854 to 3 per cent. or to half its present amount. It is probable that those who negotiated the loan of 1798 never reflected on these things, and it is indeed most likely that they believed the interest they contracted to pay would be the minimum rate in all time to come; for otherwise it is hardly possible to imagine that they should have made the reduction of the interest contingent on what must then have appeared so very unlikely an event as the rise of the three per cents. to above par.

But no experience of the pernicious effects of this system, and no change of circumstances, were sufficient to induce our finance ministers to abandon it. Accordingly, when a loan of no less than 36,000,000*l.* was bargained for in 1815, it was stipulated that every subscriber of 100*l.* should be entitled to 174*l.* three per cent. stock, and 10*l.* four per cent. stock, yielding together an interest of 5*l.* 12*s.* 4*d.* per cent. The improvidence of this transaction is glaringly obvious. There can be no manner of doubt that an addition of ¼ or ½ per cent. to the interest would have procured this loan without any increase of principal; but supposing that 1 per cent. additional interest had been required, instead of being very probably subjected to a constant payment, in all time to come, of above 5*l.* for every 100*l.* advanced, we should have had 6*l.*, or 6*l.* 10*s.*, to pay for four or five years, and 3*l.*, or at most 3*l.* 10*s.*, afterwards.

This, we beg our readers to remark, is not in any respect hypothetical reasoning; for in the very same year in which the loan now referred to was negotiated, upwards of 18,000,000*l.* of Exchequer bills were funded at the rate of 117*l.* five per cent. stock for every 100*l.*, affording consequently an interest of 5*l.* 17*s.* per cent.; being only 4*s.* 8*d.* per cent.* more than was

---

* This, however, as Dr. Hamilton has observed, represents the difference of interest of an equal sum funded in the three and five per cents., as greater than it really is. In loans the public pay the whole interest for the year in which the

paid for the loan of that year, though the subscribers to the latter had 84*l.* of artificial capital created for every 100*l.* advanced, and the holders of Exchequer bills only 17*l.* But this is not all. In consequence of the measures adopted in 1822 for reducing the interest of the stock formed out of the five per cents., and those adopted in 1834 and the current year, the charge on account of the Exchequer bills funded in that stock in 1815 cannot now materially exceed 3 per cent.; and if, instead of raising the principal to 117*l.*, a six per cent. stock had been created, the charge would have been reduced in 1854 to precisely 3 per cent.

We have not entered into these details in the view of uselessly reflecting upon measures long since past, and which, however erroneous, can no longer be amended, but in the view of guarding against their repetition. The perpetual peace of the Abbé de St. Pierre is not very likely ever to be realised. We may lay our account with being again involved in war; and whether indispensable or not, there can be little doubt that loans will be then resorted to. But though nations be proverbially slow and reluctant learners, it is to be hoped that the experience we have had of the disadvantage of funding fictitious capitals in a stock bearing a low rate of interest, may be sufficient to hinder the practice being resorted to in future. It is the most improvident

loan is contracted, though it is paid by instalments, or, if otherwise, discount is allowed. When a loan is made in five per cent. stock, this advantage is fully equivalent to an additional capital of 50*s.* on every 100*l.* advanced, or to a constant payment of 2*s.* 6*d.* a-year. But as no such advantage is gained in the funding of bills, it follows that this sum ought to be deducted from the greater interest (4*s.* 8*d.* per cent.) paid on the capital funded in the five per cents.; so that it is plain that the payment of so small a sum as 2*s.* 2*d.* per cent of additional interest in the meantime, was all that was required, in the instance referred to in the text, to balance an artificial capital of 67*l.* (184*l.* — 117*l.*) on every 100*l.* advanced; and at the same time, to secure to the public the power of reducing the interest on the loan from 5½ per cent. to 3 or 3½ at the termination of the war! And yet our financiers refused to purchase such advantages at such a cost.

and ruinous that can be imagined; being productive of little or no immediate advantage, and of great and all but endless loss. We beg to subjoin an Account of Loans contracted in each Year from 1793 to 1816, both inclusive (see p. 445).

Many of those who have argued against the practice of funding have particularly deprecated borrowing from foreigners. Raynal contends that the bargaining for loans from foreigners is in effect selling to them one or more provinces; and he doubts whether it would not be more rational to deliver up the soil than to cultivate it for their use!* Blackstone,† Hume,‡ and Montesquieu,§ though they do not carry their objections to this ridiculous extreme, join, notwithstanding, in condemning this practice. But a more unprejudiced inquiry has shown the fallacy of these objections. If a loan be decided upon, and if it may be obtained from foreigners on more favourable terms than at home, it is certainly most advantageous to transact with them. It is to no purpose to contend that, as the money borrowed is spent in warlike operations, it yields no revenue, while the national income is burdened with the payment of the interest. Had the loan not been obtained from abroad, it must have been raised at home; and it is obvious that though a transaction of this sort may force an annual payment to be made to a foreign country, it saves at the same time a more than equivalent portion of the capital of the borrowing nation, and gives it the means of easily making the payment. The objection in question is therefore quite untenable; and in the event of a loan being determined upon, sound policy will always dictate that it be negotiated wherever it can be had on the lowest terms, whether at home or abroad.

* Histoire Philosophique, iv. 663, ed. 1788.   † Commentaries, i. 320.
‡ Essay on Public Credit.   § Esprit des Loix, liv. xxii. c. 17.

Account of Loans contracted in each Year from 1793 to 1816, both inclusive; of the Amount of all sorts of Stock created on account of these Loans; of the total Interest or Dividend payable on them; of the Portions of said Loans paid to the Commissioners of the Sinking Fund; of the Amount of all sorts of Stock purchased by said Commissioners; and of the Amount of the Dividends on said Stock.—(Compiled from the Parliamentary Paper No. 145, Sess. 1822.)

YEARS ending 1st February.	Amount of Loans contracted in each Year.	Amount of Stocks of all kinds created.	Total Annual Charge of Dividends and Annuities on such Stock.	Account of the Portions of the Loans paid to the Commissioners of Sinking Fund	Amount of all Funds or Stocks of every Description purchased by the Commissioners of Sinking Fund.	Amount of Dividend on Stock purchased by Commissioners.
	£.	£.	£.	£.	£.	£.
1794	4,500,000	6,250,000	187,500	1,630,615	2,174,405	65,232
1795	12,907,451	15,676,526	599,118	1,872,200	2,804,945	84,148
1796	42,090,646	55,539,031	2,132,369	2,143,596	3,083,455	97,574
1797	42,756,196	56,945,569	2,274,528	2,639,724	4,390,670	131,720
1798	14,620,000	29,019,300	935,579	3,361,753	6,716,153	201,485
1799	18,000,000	35,624,250	1,105,602	3,984,253	7,858,109	235,743
1800	12,500,000	21,875,000	656,250	4,288,209	7,221,338	216,640
1801	18,500,000	29,045,000	871,350	4,620,479	7,315,002	219,450
1802	34,410,450	55,954,312	1,775,530	5,117,723	8,091,454	249,594
1803	23,000,000	30,351,375	910,541	5,685,542	7,733,421	246,257
1804	10,000,000	16,000,000	512,083	6,018,179	10,527,243	315,817
1805	10,000,000	18,200,000	546,000	6,521,394	11,395,692	344,711
1806	21,526,700	39,543,126	1,140,632	7,181,482	12,234,064	367,022
1807	18,000,000	29,880,000	896,400	7,829,589	12,807,070	384,212
1808	12,200,000	18,373,200	577,060	8,9 8,674	14,171,467	425,142
1809	12,000,000	13,693,253	587,744	9,555,854	13,965,824	435,758
1810	19,532,100	22,173,645	947,312	10,170,105	14,352,771	453,923
1811	16,311,000	19,811,107	765,955	10,813,017	15,659,194	481,443
1812	24,000,000	29,244,712	1,191,736	11,543,881	18,147,245	544,417
1813	27,871,325	40,743,031	1,486,272	12,439,632	21,108,442	633,253
1814	58,763,100	93,731,523	3,230,600	14,181,006	24,120,867	723,626
1815	18,500,000	24,694,830	851,833	12,748,232	19,149,684	574,490
1816	45,135,589	70,888,403	2,577,820	11,902,051	20,280,098	608,403
1817	3,000,000	3,00 ,000	90,000	11,491,670	18,515,556	555,537
	520,124,557	776,257,193	26,849,814	176,648,860	283,824,109	8,595,597
Loans raised on account of Ireland in Great Britain	64,750,000	103,032,750	3,324,550	11,873,490	19,087,846	572,635
Total Sum raised	584,874,557	879,289,943	30,174,364	188,522,350	302,911,955	9,168,232
Deduct, Sums raised on account of Sinking Fund........	188,522,350	302,911,955	9,168,232			
Balance	396,352,207	576,377,988	21,006,132			

CHAPTER III.

REDUCTION OF THE NATIONAL DEBT.

Reduction of Interest in 1716, 1727, 1749, 1822, &c.—Sinking Fund—Assessment on Capital to Pay off Principal of Debt.

THE saving effected in the charge on account of the national debt in 1716 (referred to in the previous chapter); when the rate of interest on most funds was reduced to 5 per cent., by offering to pay off the fundholders unless they accepted this lower rate, amounted to 324,456*l*. a-year, the dividends being reduced from 1,598,602*l*. to 1,274,146*l*. A farther saving of about 340,000 a-year was effected in 1727, by reducing the interest on the greater portion of the debt from 5 to 4 per cent., and by other transactions with the South Sea Company.

In 1737 the *three* per cents. rose to the extraordinary height of 107, or to seven per cent. above par, being the highest elevation which they have hitherto reached. This rise afforded a very favourable opportunity for further reducing the interest payable on the debt, which was strongly recommended by Sir John Barnard, and other members of the House of Commons. But Sir Robert Walpole (for reasons of which no satisfactory explanation has been given) strongly opposed the measure; and when Barnard introduced a bill to carry the reduction into effect, he exerted his influence against it, and procured its rejection. In 1749, however, the reduction of the interest on the greater part of the debt, from four to three per cent., was effected by Mr. Pelham, with the assistance of Sir John Barnard; the consequent saving to the public being about 565,600*l.* a-year.*

There were no further reductions of the interest for a lengthened period, or till 1822. And the plan of funding usually adopted in the American and French wars having, as already seen, nearly tied up the hands of the public, prevented, to a great extent, government from profiting by the facility with which money might have been raised since the peace to effect a reduction of the dividends. Happily, however, the practice of funding increased capitals in a three per cent. stock, though general during these contests, was not universal; and the interest of all that portion of the debt that was funded in other stocks has been progressively reduced. The first reduction was made in 1822, and the last in the course of the present year (1844). The following table (p. 448) gives a view of the various reductions since 1822, and their results.

It appears from this table, that in October, 1854, when the three-and-a-quarter per cent. stock will be reduced to three per cent., there will have been a total reduction of 3,142,192*l.* effected, since 1822, in the interest of those portions of the debt funded in stocks bearing a higher rate of interest than three per cent. And if the entire debt contracted since the commencement of the seven years' war had been funded without any increase of capital in stocks bearing the interest really payable on the loans, the total reduction, instead of being little more than *three,* would have amounted to from *nine* to *ten* millions a-year!

Funding, like some of the most effective medicines, is a dangerous as well as a powerful resource, and requires to be skilfully administered. But our finance ministers can claim no credit for peculiar expertness or ability in

---

* Sinclair's History of the Public Revenue, 3rd ed., i. 506, &c.; Coxe's Sir Robert Walpole, ii. 406, &c., 8vo. ed.; Considerations on the Proposal for reducing the Interest of the National Debt (by Sir John Barnard), passim, &c.

RESULTS of the Conversions since 1822 of Stock bearing a High into Stock bearing a Lower Interest.

	CAPITAL.		INTEREST.	
	OLD.	NEW.	OLD.	NEW.
1822.	£.	£.	£.	£.
Navy Five per Cents. (less, paid off dissentients, 2,794,318l. .)	149,627,825	..	7,481,391	
Into New Four p. Cents. (with a bonus of five per cent., 7,481,393l.)	..	157,109,218	..	6,284,368
1826.				
Old Four per Cents. (less, paid off dissentients, 6,149,246l.) .	70,105,403	..	2,804,216	
Into Three-and-a-half per Cents. Reduced	..	70,105,403	..	2,453,619
1830.				
New Four per Cents. (less, paid off dissentients, 2,649,366l.) .	151,021,728	..	6,040,869	
Into New Three-and-a-Half per Cents . .	..	150,344,051	..	5,285,759
Into New Five per Cents.	..	474,374		
1834.				
Four per Cents., 1826	10,622,911	..	424,916	
Into New Three-and-a-Half per Cents. . .	..	10,622,911	..	371,800
1844.				
New Three-and-a-Half per Cents. . . .	157,329,286	..	5,506,525	
Into New Three-and-a-Fourth per Cents.* .	..	157,329,286	..	5,113,202
	538,707,153	545,985,243	22,257,917	19,508,748
Increase of Capital	..	7,278,090		
Decrease of Interest	..	..	..	2,749,169

* The interest on this stock is to be reduced to 3 per Cent. in October, 1854. It is not redeemable till after 10th of October, 1874 (7 Victoria, c. 4).

this respect. On the contrary, the previous statements show that we sustain ten times more injury from the unskilful and ruinous mode in which the business of funding has been conducted, than from those mischievous influences inherent in the system itself, which excited the fears of Hume and Smith. The opposition of Walpole to the reduction of the interest in 1737 occasioned a loss to the public of 6,787,200*l*. (565,600*l*. × 12 years). But this sinks into insignificance when compared with the immense and apparently interminable sacrifice of from *six* to *seven** millions a-year, entailed on the public through the ignorance and errors of succeeding ministries and parliaments.

The plan for the gradual extinction of the national debt, by consolidating the various surpluses of revenue arising from the reduction of interest and other sources into a sinking fund, to be constantly applied to purchase stock, was first proposed by Earl Stanhope, and adopted by Sir Robert Walpole, in 1716; and its advantages, from its being supposed to operate at compound interest, are very fully detailed in an elaborate 'Essay on the Public Debts of the Kingdom,' ascribed to Sir Nathanael Gould, M.P., published in 1726. The Act establishing the sinking fund declares that the various surpluses of which it consisted " shall be appropriated, reserved, and employed to and for the discharge of the principal and interest of such national debts and encumbrances as were incurred before the 25th December, 1716, and to and for no other use, intent, or purpose whatsoever." But, in despite of this clear and explicit enactment, the sinking fund was very soon perverted from its original destination. Several

* The difference between the reductions actually made in the charge on account of interest, and those which might have been made had no artificial capitals been effected.

disguised encroachments were made in the interval between 1727 and 1732, but the first open and avowed encroachment was made in 1733. In 1732 the land-tax had been reduced to 1s. in the pound; and in order to supply the deficiency of revenue that had been thus occasioned, half a million had been borrowed, and the interest charged to the salt-tax, which was now revived, after being abolished only two years before. In the following year it became necessary to raise an additional 500,000l., and Sir Robert Walpole moved that it be taken from the sinking fund; adding, that if this proposal were objected to, he should be obliged to increase the land-tax from 1s to 2s. in the pound. The motion was of course carried by a very great majority; and in 1735 and 1736 the entire produce of the fund was anticipated and mortgaged!

The authors of the ' History and Proceedings of the House of Lords,' in giving an account of this alienation, observe, " When any additional tax is imposed, the public feel the weight of the annual public expense. This puts them upon inquiring into the necessity of that expense; and when they can see no necessity for it they murmur, and those murmurs become dangerous to the minister. Whereas no man feels what is taken from the sinking fund, therefore no man inquires into the necessity of that expense which occasions its being plundered; and for this reason it will be always looked upon by ministers as a fund which they may squander with safety." *

Dr. Price laments this perversion in the most piteous terms : —" Thus," says he, " after an existence of a few years, expired the Sinking Fund—that sacred blessing, once the nation's only hope, prematurely and cruelly destroyed by its own parent. Could it have escaped the

---

* Vol. iv. p. 511. See also the striking paragraph in the ' Wealth of Nations,' p. 418.

hands of violence it would have made us the envy and terror of the world, by leaving us at this time not only *tax-free*, but in possession of a treasure, greater perhaps than ever was enjoyed by any kingdom."

But although Dr. Price was perfectly right in censuring Sir Robert Walpole for not imposing additional taxes to supply the deficiency in the disposable revenue, he was totally wrong in his estimate of the influence of a sinking fund. The truth is, that no sinking fund, even though it consist of clear surplus revenue, ever operates at compound interest. Suppose, to illustrate the mode of its working, that there is a million of surplus cash in the Treasury, and that it is formed into a sinking fund. In the first place, the commissioners for managing this fund would purchase a million's worth of stock, and would receive at the end of the year the dividend or interest on this stock, which had previously been paid to the public creditor. If this dividend were 5 per cent., or 50,000*l*., the commissioners would purchase additional stock with it; and would consequently have at the end of the *second* year 52,500*l*. to invest in a new purchase; at the end of the *third* year 55,125*l*., and so on. Now, this is what Sir Nathanael Gould, Dr. Price, and Mr. Pitt call paying off the public debt by a Sinking Fund operating at compound interest; but it is obvious that whatever diminution may be effected in the amount of the public debt in the way now stated, is brought about by appropriating a portion of *the produce of taxation* to its extinction. It is true that by employing any given sum to purchase stock, and then constantly applying the dividends upon the stock so purchased to the redemption of debt, its diminution will be effected in the same way that it would be were the original sum increasing, by an inherent energy of its own, at compound interest; but it is essential to know, that though the results be the same, the means are totally different. The debt is reduced because that portion

2 G 2

of the produce of the taxes required to pay the dividends or interest on the stock purchased by the Sinking Fund Commissioners, instead of being remitted to the contributors, continues to be taken from them, and applied to the purchase of fresh stock. It is the merest delusion to suppose that the debt either has been or ever can be reduced by the agency of an independent fund increasing at compound interest. To make capital increase in this way, it must be employed in some sort of productive industry; and the profits, instead of being consumed as income, must be regularly added to the principal, to form a new capital. It is unnecessary to say that no such sinking fund ever existed. Those that have been set on foot in this and other countries have all been supported either by loans or by the produce of taxes, and have never paid off a single shilling of debt by their own agency. We are not, however, to consider this notion of the wonder-working effects of sinking funds as only a mere harmless error; for there can be no question that it has, by making it be believed that the greatest amount of debt might be defrayed without loss to any one, been one of the principal causes of the ruinous extension of the funding system.

Delusive, however, as were his notions with respect to the effect of sinking funds operating at compound interest, the writings of Dr. Price gave them the greatest currency; and, coupled with some visionary calculations he had made respecting the number of *globes of gold* to which a penny laid out at compound interest at the birth of Jesus Christ would have amounted in 1772, completed the delusion. The most intelligent men in the country were induced to believe that the public debt might be diminished, notwithstanding the contraction of new loans, by the operation of a sinking fund; that " war, while such a scheme was going on, would increase its efficacy; and that any suspension of it then would be the madness of giving it a mortal stab *at the very time it was making the quickest progress towards the accomplishment of its end."* *

By way of showing that these conclusions, how extravagant soever they may appear, were really well founded, Price puts the following case:

"Let a state be supposed to run in debt 2,000,000*l.* a-year, for which it pays 4 per cent. interest; in seventy years a debt of 140,000,000*l.* would be incurred. But an appropriation of 400,000*l.* per annum, employed in the manner of a sinking fund, at compound interest, would, at the end of this term, leave the nation beforehand 6,000,000*l.*" †

If this were true, it follows that 2,000,000*l.* (and *cæteris paribus* any larger sum) might be annually borrowed at 4 per cent., of which 1,600,000*l.* might be annually expended without incurring any more debt than would be paid by the regular appropriation of the remaining 400,000*l.* Unluckily, however, the art of *hocus pocus* has not yet arrived at this state of perfection. Dr. Price has forgotten to state how the interest of his annual loan of 2,000,000*l.* is to be provided for. But, had there been a corresponding surplus revenue, the loan would have been unnecessary; and supposing consequently (as we must do), that new taxes are annually imposed to defray the interest, the gross amount of these taxes would, in twenty-five years, equal the loan itself; and in the last, or 70th year of its contraction they would amount to no less than 5,600,000*l.* (80,000*l.* interest for one year × 70), or to 3,600,000*l.* more than the amount of the loan! so that the debt, which is said to be reduced by the annual appropriation of the 400,000*l.* or one-fifth part of the loan, is wholly reduced by the new taxes. To prove that such is the case, suppose that only 1,600,000*l.* a-year has been borrowed and

* Price's Appeal to the Public on the subject of the National Debt, p. 17.

† Appeal, &c., p. 7.

expended, but that taxes have been annually imposed
sufficient to defray the interest of a loan of 2,000,000*l.*,
the debt would be discharged in precisely the same time.
It must, indeed, be evident, on the slightest consideration,
that neither the debts of individuals nor of states can
ever be diminished by the mere borrowing of money to
pay them off.   And had it not been for the mysterious
manner in which propositions like that now examined
were put forth, their fallacy must have struck every one.
Borrowing money to pay off debt, unless when it is
obtained at a lower rate of interest, never serves any
purpose other than to increase its amount and to en-
tangle and perplex the public accounts.   If any reduction
of debt be really effected while such borrowing is going
on, it will invariably be found, on examination, to have
been occasioned by an increase of revenue or a diminution of expenditure, or both.

The delusion occasioned by Price's writings,* though
very general, was not, however, universal.   During the
discussions on the Sinking Fund of 1786, a little tract was
published, entitled ' Considerations on the Annual Million Bill, and on the Real and Imaginary Properties of
a Sinking Fund,' in which the hollowness of Price's
theories is most ably exposed, and in which it is demonstrated that no debt can ever be paid off except by the
application of surplus revenue to that object.   But this
valuable tract appears to have made little or no impression.   The plans and calculations of Price, instead of
being allowed, like those of most projectors, to fall into
oblivion, were adopted by Mr. Pitt, and formed the basis
of his famous sinking fund.†

To constitute this fund, *one million per annum* was appropriated by Parliament, which was to be allowed to

* The influence of Price's writings was increased by his high character, his
earnestness and perfect integrity.

† It is not creditable to Mr. Pitt that, while he piqued himself upon the
Sinking Fund, he made no public acknowledgment of the obligations, in regard to it, he was under to Dr. Price.

accumulate at compound interest, by the addition of
the dividends on the stock which it purchased. In 1792
some farther additions were made to this fund; and it
was then also enacted, that besides providing for the interest of any loan that might henceforth be contracted,
additional taxes should be imposed to form a sinking
fund of *one* per cent. on the capital stock created by
such loan. As there was a considerable excess of revenue in the period from 1786 to 1793, the debt was
reduced by about 5½ millions, and this reduction was
ascribed to the effect of the sinking fund acting at compound interest, though it is plain it entirely resulted
from the application of surplus taxes to the purchase
of stock. Subsequently to the commencement of the
revolutionary war, the income of the country uniformly
fell greatly short of the expenditure, and the debt
rapidly increased. But though there was no *annual
million* in the Treasury to transfer to the Commissioners,
the juggle of the sinking fund was kept up. The loans
for the service of the year were uniformly increased, by
the whole amount of the sums placed at the disposal of
the Commissioners ; so that, for every shilling's worth
of stock transferred to them by this futile proceeding,
an equal or greater amount of new debt had to be contracted, exclusive of the loss incurred on account of
management !

And yet this worthless compound of delusion and absurdity was lauded by all parties. The opposition vied
with the ministry in celebrating its praises. The sinking fund was universally considered as the great bulwark
of the country; " as a means by which a vast treasure
was to be accumulated out of nothing !" And so lasting
and powerful was the delusion, that after fourteen years'
experience of its worse than absolute nullity, when a
new financial project was introduced in 1807, it contained a system of checks to prevent the evils likely to
result from allowing the sinking fund to accumulate

without any limit, and deluging the country with a flood
of wealth, by "a too prompt discharge of the public
debt!" We doubt whether the history of the world can
furnish another instance of so extraordinary an infatuation. Had the sinking fund involved any unintelligi-
ble dogmas,—had it addressed itself to popular feelings
and passions,—or had the notion of its efficacy originated
with the mob, the prevalence of the delusion would have
been less unaccountable. But it was from the first a
matter of calculation; it was projected by some of the
best informed persons in the country, who continued for
upwards of twenty years to believe that they were rapidly
diminishing the public debt by the agency of the sinking
fund, which was all the while kept on foot by fresh loans!
Dr. Hamilton, of Aberdeen, has the merit of having
dissipated this delusion—the grossest, certainly, by which
any civilised people have ever been blinded and de-
ceived. He showed * that the sinking fund, instead of
reducing the debt, had increased it: and he proved to
demonstration, that the excess of revenue above expenditure is the only real sinking fund by which the public
debt can be discharged. "The increase of revenue," he
observes, "or the diminution of expense, are the only
means by which this sinking fund can be enlarged, and
its operations rendered more effectual; and all schemes
for discharging the national debt, by sinking funds operating at *compound* interest, or in any other manner,
unless in so far as they are founded upon this principle,
are completely illusory."

"The extent of the sinking fund is artificial, and may
be brought, by a mere change in the arrangement of the
public accounts, to bear any proportion to the amount of
debt, without the slightest advantage, or any tendency
to promote its discharge. In time of war, we raise a

---

* In his work, entitled ' An Inquiry Concerning the Rise and Progress, the
Redemption and Present State, and the Management of the National Debt of
Great Britain and Ireland.' 1 vol. 8vo., 3rd edit. Edinburgh, 1818.

certain sum by taxes for the expense of the year, and
borrow what farther is wanted. If a sinking fund be
maintained, the sums appropriated are deducted from
what would have otherwise been expended on the war,
and a greater loan is required. We may throw into the
sinking fund any share of the revenue we please. We
have only to add as much to the loan, and we shall raise
a larger sum in the form of loan with the same facility,
by the effect of the sums thrown into the money market
for the stock purchased by the Commissioners. In time
of war, the sinking fund is nominal ; in time of peace, a
large sinking fund will discharge the debt more quickly;
but this amounts to no more than that a continuance of
the taxes which we paid in war, after peace is restored,
will be attended with a speedier reduction of debt, than
what would take place if a large part of these taxes were
repealed.

" A similar circumstance, held forth to ease the alarms
arising from the magnitude of the national debt, is the
progress already made in its discharge by the sinking
fund, and the large sum redeemed. We are told that
these operations have succeeded beyond expectation, and
that the whole debt existing in 1786, amounting to
238,000,000*l.*, is already paid off. This is altogether
fictitious and delusive. We may pay off as much debt
as we please at any time by borrowing; but the only real
alteration in the state of our finance is the difference between the debt contracted and the debt paid off; and
while the former of these exceeds the latter, our situation is growing worse to the extent of that difference.

" A private gentleman, whose estate is incumbered,
may, if he have any credit, pay off all his debt every
year, by borrowing from other hands; but if he spend
more than his free income, his embarrassments will continually increase, and his affairs are so much the worse
by being conducted in this manner, from the fees he pays
to his agents. The absurdity of supposing any advan-

tage derived from this annual discharge of his debts will appear still stronger, if we suppose him, instead of borrowing from other hands, only to renew the securities to the same creditors annually, paying a fee to the agents, and a *douceur* to the creditors themselves on the renewal. All these observations are equally applicable to the debt of a nation, conducted as ours is. It would not be impracticable, or very difficult, to redeem our whole debt in any year, if the measures we follow be redemption. It would only require a large loan every month, and the large sums we were thus enabled to pay would supply the funds for these loans. Our capitalists would be well pleased to promote these loans, as they would derive a bonus from each. Such a system would be ruinous in the extreme; and the system we follow is the same on a smaller scale, and is therefore only pernicious in a less degree."*

These statements are conclusive as to the folly of supposing that it is possible to make any reduction in the amount of the public debt, by the agency of a sinking fund kept on foot with borrowed money. But a sinking fund of this sort is a costly as well as a delusive juggle. It appears from the previous table (p. 445) that the loans contracted in each year from 1794 to 1816, both inclusive, amounted in all to 584,874,557*l.*, at an annual charge to the public of 30,174,364*l.* But the Commissioners of the Sinking Fund received 188,522,350*l.* of these loans, the annual charge on such portion being, of course, 9,726,090*l.*† It appears, however, from the table previously referred to, that the stock which the Commissioners purchased with this sum of 188,522,350*l.*, transferred to them out of the loans, only yielded an annual dividend of 9,168,232*l.* On the one hand, therefore, an annual charge of 9,726,090*l.* was incurred to enable the Sinking Fund Commissioners to go to market; and, on

* Hamilton on the National Debt, p. 237, &c.

† 584,874,557 : 30,174,364 :: 188,522,350 : 9,726,089 $\frac{15817827}{584874557}$.

the other, they bought stock which yields 9,168,233*l*. a-year; so that, on the whole, their operations during the war occasioned a dead loss to the country of 557,857*l*. a-year, equivalent to a 3 per cent. capital of 18,595,233*l*., exclusive of the expenses of the office, which amounted to above 60,000*l*.! Such is the practical result of that sinking fund so long represented as the palladium of public credit and the sheet-anchor of the nation!

This striking discrepancy between the sums borrowed on account of the sinking fund, and those which it paid off, depends principally on the fact of the loans having been uselessly augmented by the whole amount of the sums transferred to the account of the Commissioners. Every body knows that a large loan is always negotiated on worse terms than a small one; for, to be in a condition to make a large purchase, intending contractors must sell a comparatively large amount of stock before the day on which the biddings are taken, and this, of course, depresses the market prices of that day, by which the terms of the loan are mainly regulated. In most cases, however, the depression caused by the preparation for a loan is but of short duration, so that, speaking generally, it may be said that during the war the Sinking Fund Commissioners were supplied with money borrowed when the funds were unnaturally depressed, with which they were sent to buy up stock that had recovered its full value! The discrepancy is in some degree, also, owing to the premium usually received by the contractors being paid on that part of the loans transferred to the Commissioners, and consequently deducted from the sums laid out by the latter. The wonder in truth is, not that a very heavy loss was incurred by keeping up the sinking fund machinery during the French war, but rather that that loss was not considerably greater.

It has sometimes been contended that, admitting all that has been previously stated to be true, the sinking

fund was, notwithstanding, advantageous, from the confidence inspired by the belief in its powerful agency!
We doubt, however, whether much stress can justly be
laid on its operation in this respect.   But, supposing
that such was the case, and (which is more doubtful) that
Government was warranted in encouraging a delusion
of this sort, the deception might have been equally well
kept up, and all the heavy expenses that have been
incurred been saved, by making the Sinking Fund Commissioners subscribe to the different loans the amount of
the sums that were otherwise to be borrowed on their
account.   By this simple and obvious device the amount
of the loans to be contracted for would have been lessened,
and they would consequently have been negotiated on
better terms, at the same time that the premiums on the
sums paid to the Commissioners would have been saved.
But though the advantages of this mode of keeping up
the sinking fund are all but obvious, and were set in the
clearest point of view by Mr. Grenfell many years previously, it was not adopted till 1819, when it was successfully introduced into the loan of that year.

There was only one part of Mr. Pitt's plan that was
really calculated to afford the means of reducing the
debt; and that was, the clause, enacted in 1792, which
ordered that taxes should be imposed, not only to defray
the interest of such loans as might be contracted in future,
but also to provide a sinking fund of 1 per cent. on the
stock so created.   Had this clause been scrupulously
observed, a fund would undoubtedly have been formed,
which, had it been exclusively applied to that object,
would ultimately have extinguished the debt contracted
during the war; but it is essential to bear in mind, that it
would have done this, not by the operation of compound
interest, but simply by raising a larger amount of taxes
than was required to pay the dividends on the loans, and
applying the surplus to buy up the principal.   A new
capital of 879,289,943*l.* of funded debt was created in

the interval between 1793 and 1817,* 1 per cent on which, exclusive of accumulations, would have been 8,792,943*l*. But, instead of having a surplus income of this amount at the end of the war, when the nominal sinking fund amounted to about fifteen millions, the clear real surplus did not amount to *two* millions; the taxes imposed to form a sinking fund on the capital of the loans having been mostly anticipated and mortgaged, by charging them with the interest of loans made in 1807, 1809, and 1813. It is indeed idle to suppose, that a surplus revenue, existing in the shape of a sinking fund, will ever be unceasingly applied to the extinction of debt. It may be so applied for a few years; but, whenever any considerable difficulty is experienced in raising taxes to defray extraordinary expense, it is all but certain that it will be diverted, as all such funds have ever been, from its proper and peculiar object.

Dr. Hamilton's book was published in 1813; but such is the vitality of error, that it was not till 1829 that the triumph of principle and common sense over quackery and folly was consummated by the act 10 Geo. IV. c. 27. This statute made an end of sham sinking funds, and enacted that thenceforth the sum to be applied to the reduction of the national debt should be the actual annual surplus revenue over the expenditure.

There is, perhaps, reason to think that the indirect operation of a real sinking fund of five or six millions, supposing it could be maintained, might be of material importance; and that by keeping, for a while, the price of the three per cents. at above par, it might enable the interest of the debt to be further reduced to two and a-half or even two per cent. But this result would depend, in a great degree, on the influence of circumstances which cannot be determined *à priori*: if the pressure on the national resources should diminish, and the profits of stock,

* Table, p. 445.

or of capital employed in industrious undertakings, be increased, the rate of interest would rise, and the funds fall below par; and, were such the case, it would be better, certainly, to remit taxes than to employ their produce in reducing the public debt. It is impossible, indeed, to form estimates beforehand of what may be the effect of any given financial operation, as any unforeseen change in the channels of industry, or in the situation of the country, may alter all the results that were anticipated. On the whole, however, we confess we are little sanguine in regard to any considerable direct reduction of the debt ever being effected; and we trust for the diminution of our burdens more to the increasing wealth and ability of the country to sustain them, than to anything else.

It has been said, and probably with no inconsiderable degree of truth, that a revenue but little above, or, perhaps, rather below the expenditure, is the best security for economy and moderation, and that the possession of a considerable surplus would be apt to bring on occasions for its misapplication. Mr. Ricardo was of opinion that a really efficient sinking fund would operate rather to encourage expenditure than to diminish debt: " There cannot," said he, " be a greater security for the continuance of peace, than the imposing on ministers the necessity of applying to the people for taxes to support a war. Suffer the sinking fund to accumulate during peace to any considerable sum, and very little provocation would induce them to enter into a new contest. They would know that, by a little management, they could make the sinking fund available to the raising of a new supply, instead of being available to the payment of the debt. The argument is now common in the mouths of ministers when they wish to lay on new taxes, for the purpose of creating a new sinking fund in lieu of one which they have just spent, to say, ' It will make foreign countries respect us; they will be afraid to insult or pro-

voke us, when they know that we are possessed of so
formidable a resource.' What do they mean by this
argument, if the sinking fund be not considered by them
as a *war fund*, on which they can draw in support of the
contest? It cannot, at one and the same time, be employed to annoy an enemy, and to pay debt. If taxes
are, as they ought to be, raised to defray the expenses
of a war, what facility will a sinking fund give to the
raising of them? None whatever. It is not because
the possession of a sinking fund will enable them to raise
new and additional taxes that ministers prize it, for they
know it will have no such effect, but because they know
that they will be enabled to substitute the sinking fund
in lieu of taxes, and to employ it, as they have always
done, in war, and in providing for the interest of fresh
debt." *

Besides the projects that have been set on foot for
paying off the national debt by means of sinking funds
and such like devices, it has been proposed to effect this
object by assessing the capital of the country. A scheme
of this sort was proposed in the reign of George I., and
strongly recommended by Mr. Archibald Hutcheson, an
intelligent member of the House of Commons. Mr. H.
estimated that a contribution of 10 per cent. on all fixed
and moveable property, including, of course, the debt
itself, would be sufficient for the extinction of the latter.
And to carry the measure into effect he proposed that
power should be given to the proprietors of estates to sell
as much of them as might be required to defray their
share of the assessment, notwithstanding any disability
arising from settlements or entails; and they were also
to be entitled to deduct 10 per cent. from all mortgages
and other burdens with which they might be affected.

Were a project of this sort practicable and just, the
stimulus it would give to industry and economy by making

* Art. Funding System, Encyclopædia Britannica.

that which is now the debt of the public the debt of individuals, and the many advantages that would result from the abolition of the taxes required to defray the interest, should make it be adopted at least to some considerable extent. But it is needless to dwell on these considerations; for there can be no doubt that the project is wholly impracticable, and that, supposing it to be practicable, it would be most unjust to attempt to carry it into effect. This has been shown briefly but conclusively by Hume in his 'Essay on Public Credit:'—" Mr. Hutcheson," says he, "appears not to have considered that the laborious poor pay a considerable part of the taxes by their annual consumptions, though they could not advance at once a proportional part of the sum required. Not to mention that property in money and stock in trade might easily be concealed or disguised; and that visible property in lands and houses would really at last answer for the whole, an inequality and oppression which never would be submitted to. But though this project is not likely to take place, it is not altogether improbable, that when the nation becomes heartily sick of their debts, and is cruelly oppressed by them, some daring projector may arise with visionary schemes for their discharge: and as public credit will begin by that time to be a little frail, the least touch will destroy it, as happened in France during the regency; and in this manner it will *die of the doctor*."

Even had a project of this sort been practicable in 1720, when the public debt was little more than *fifty* millions, it is now quite out of the question. The proportion of monied and other moveable and all but intangible property, as compared with that which is fixed, has increased *ten-fold* since the accession of George I.; and having previously shown that it is not practicable to make the holders of such property contribute their fair share of a moderate tax on income, we may be excused if we take it for granted that it would be still more impracticable to make them contribute anything like their fair share of a very heavy tax on capital! The reasons which justified Hume in condemning this scheme in 1750 have, therefore, incomparably greater weight at this moment. The chances, indeed, are ten to one that any *bonâ fide* attempt on the part of government to carry it into effect would end either in bankruptcy or revolution.

It will, we apprehend, be found that the best way of lessening the national debt is not by making attempts to pay it off either by sinking funds or otherwise, but by adopting such measures as may seem best fitted to give additional vigour to the productive energies of the people. Every increase of these proportionally diminishes the pressure of the debt. Although taxation were kept up for ten or a dozen years, so that there were annually *five* or *six* millions to apply to the redemption of stock, the progress made in the reduction of the debt would not be very considerable. But it is most unlikely that any government should make such an attempt, and it is still more unlikely, supposing it were made, that it should be persevered in. The desire of immediate relief from the pressure of existing burdens is too great, and the advantages to be derived from submitting to them too remote and uncertain, to allow us to suppose that any effectual progress will ever be made in the diminution of the debt by applying surplus revenue to its purchase. Even if the preference of immediate to future and contingent advantages were less certain, the occurrence of a war would at once swallow up the surplus revenue, and make it be employed to defray the interest on the loans contracted to carry it on. The imposition of new taxes entails privations, and is always unpopular; but the suspension of the payment of the debt by mortgaging the surplus revenue or sinking fund, occasions no inconvenience to any one; and is too obvious and too tempting an expedient for getting out of the present difficulty, not to be resorted to.

2 H

And we much doubt, supposing it were practicable to maintain a surplus revenue of five or six millions for a few years, whether it would be expedient. On the contrary, we incline to think that the popular is in this instance the preferable plan; and that the national interests will be best promoted by reducing taxation to the sum necessary to meet the public exigencies, leaving it to the contributors to employ the sums remitted in taxes in any way they think best. The increase of wealth and population will be promoted by this policy. Opportunities will, most likely, be found for reducing, or it may be repealing, some of the more objectionable taxes; and according as the pressure on the national resources is lightened, industry will gain more strength; the rate of profit will be increased; and the temptation to withdraw capital from the kingdom will be diminished. The greater productiveness of industry and the greater well-being of the community, are the real sinking funds which a wise government should exert itself to build up and encourage. And this will be best done by giving all that freedom to industry that is consistent with right and justice; and by reducing taxation to the amount necessary to make adequate provision for the public service, and assessing it on impartial principles, in the manner best suited to advance the public interests.

APPENDIX.

No. I.—LOCAL TAXATION.

BY LOCAL TAXES are usually meant taxes levied in particular districts of the country, and expended for the purposes of those districts. The existing taxes of this description in England and Wales are thus enumerated in the recent Report of the Poor Law Commissioners on Local Taxation :*—

" Rates of Independent Districts :—

" Poor Rate Series—Taxes on the basis of the Poor Rate.
1. Poor Rate.
2. Workhouse Building Rate.
3. Survey and Valuation Rate.
4. Jail Fees Rate.
5. Constables' Rate.
6. Highway Rate.
7. Ditto additional rate for purchase of land.
8. Ditto additional rate for law expenses.
9. Lighting and Watching Rate.
10. Militia Rate.

" Miscellaneous Taxes—Each on an independent basis.
11. Church Rate.
12. Ditto, for new churches, and repairs.
13. Burial Ground Rate.
14. Sewers Rate.
15. General Sewers Tax.
16. Drainage and Enclosure Rate.

" Rates of Aggregated Districts—

" County Rate Series—Taxes imposed originally on aggregated districts by some general authority, but ultimately assessed on the basis of the Poor's Rate.
17. County Rate.
18. Ditto for Lunatic Asylums.
19. Ditto for Building Shire Halls.
20. Burial of Dead Rate.
21. Hundred Rate.
22. Police Rate.
23. Borough Rate.
24. Watch Rate in Boroughs."

* Report made by the Poor Law Commissioners to the Secretary of State for the Home Department, and presented to both Houses of Parliament in 1843. This elaborate and valuable Report, which, with its Appendices, comprises much important information in regard to local taxation, was, we understand, compiled by George Coode, Esq., assistant-Secretary to the Commissioners.

The local taxes leviable in England and Wales thus appear to be twenty-four in number. Practically, however, there are not twenty-four collections. Some of the rates are furnished from the funds of other rates; some are incapable, or too difficult of collection; some are required only on few occasions, or in limited localities. The Workhouse Building Rate was apparently intended to be levied as a separate impost; but owing to the inadequacy of the enactment on the subject, this has been found to be impracticable, and the payments necessary for attaining its objects have been made directly from the poor rate. The Survey and Valuation Rate is likewise incapable of distinct enforcement; and as the statute admits of an alternative resort to the poor rate, no attempt has been made to enforce it. The Jail Fees Rate seems to have been designed merely to compensate persons in office at the time of its passing (May, 1815), and to be leviable only in "cities, towns corporate, and places not contributing to the county rate, and having no town rate or public stock." Moreover, if the smallness of its amount render its separate levy inconvenient, it is to be paid out of the poor rate. The Constables' Rate has, with very few exceptions, fallen into disuse; the constables' charges (though with doubtful legality) being usually defrayed out of the poor rate, under colour of the provision in the 18 Geo. III. c. 19, § 4. The Militia Rate is of course suspended, as the militia itself is not now embodied. Drainage and Enclosure Rates are applicable only to certain places under local acts. The Burial of Dead Rate, for defraying the expenses of burying dead bodies found on the sea-shore, is necessarily confined to maritime districts. It is to be raised in the same manner as the county rate.

The law establishes three distinct imposts in regard to the Highways: one for repairing the roads, another for purchasing land, and a third for defraying law expenses. The Poor Law Commissioners observe,[*] however, that " the separate highway rate for the purchase of land, and the separate highway rate for law expenses, appear, so far as we can learn, never to have been made on those occasions where the law enabled them to be raised; but the purposes have been more conveniently attained by the use of the common highway rate, even in cases where the amount of the latter rate has, by this addition, been made to exceed the limit fixed by law." That limit is, ten-pence in the pound at any one time, or two shillings and sixpence in the pound in any one year. A limit is also set to the rate for purchasing land, but the ambiguous phraseology of the statute renders it difficult to discover the precise amount intended. The Highway Rate is to be assessed upon the same property which was liable to contribute to the relief of the poor on 31st August, 1835: and also upon woods, mines, stone-quarries, and other hereditaments, usually rated to the highways before that date. Personal property, however, has been subsequently exempted from poor rate; but this exemption does not appear to extend legally to the highway rate. These two rates, therefore, are not altogether identical in the mode of their imposition.

Any parish may adopt the provisions of the Lighting and Watching Act (3 and 4 Will. IV. c. 90), either as to lighting, or as to watching, or as to both lighting and watching; and in the event of such adoption, the rate is to be levied on the same property that is liable to the poor rate, though houses, buildings, and property other than land, are to contribute, as com-

---

* Report, 8vo. ed., p. 24.

pared with land, in the proportion of three to one. This provision necessarily prevents the operation of the Act in places not maintaining their own poor.

The Poor Rate is raised under the 43 Eliz. c. 2, " by taxation of every inhabitant, parson, vicar, and other, and of every occupier of lands, houses, tithes impropriate, propriations of tithes, coal-mines, or saleable underwoods," in the parish. The importance of this tax has rendered it a subject of frequent litigation; and the terms of the statute of Elizabeth have been explained by numerous judicial decisions, affecting the liability of particular properties to contribute to the rate. The personal property of inhabitants was thus declared rateable, by implication of the courts; but this liability is suspended for the present, by a temporary enactment. It will be perceived that the statute of Elizabeth imposes the rate upon two descriptions of persons,—inhabitants and occupiers; but owners of small tenements may be assessed, instead of the occupiers, under the 59 Geo. III. c. 12, § 19; and owners, instead of the occupiers, of tithe commutation rent-charge, under 1 Vic. c. 69, § 8. The various irregularities which had crept into the mode of assessing property to the poor rate, induced the legislature, in 1836, to make provision for "establishing one uniform mode of rating for the relief of the poor throughout England and Wales;" for which purpose the Parochial Assessments Act, 6 and 7 Will. IV. c. 96, was passed. It defines the principle upon which the properties subject to the rate shall be assessed; but this definition itself is so loosely expressed, as to occasion much difficulty in its construction. It directs the rate to be made "upon an estimate of the nett annual value of the several hereditaments rated thereunto; that is to say, of the rent at which the same might reasonably be expected to let from year to year, free of all usual tenants' rates and taxes, and tithe commutation rent-charge, if any, and deducting therefrom the probable average annual cost of the repairs, insurance, and other expenses, if any, necessary to maintain them in a state to command such rent." The statute further provides for the appointment of a professional valuer, to survey the parish, and value the rateable hereditaments, where the overseers or guardians desire it; thus leaving the most material means of correcting the previous irregularities entirely in the discretion of the parties in fault. A recent decision, moreover (Reg. v. Lord Yarborough, 12 A and E 416), has established that the overseers are not bound to adopt the professional valuation, even when obtained.

The Church Rate, it is said by the canonists, should be laid upon lands, houses, and the like property, according to the stock which the parishioners have within the parish; and if the usage of the place sanction such a course, it should include personalty and stock in trade. But a church rate made according to the poor rate, appears to have been considered just and prudent. The 3 Geo. IV. c. 72, § 20, seems to require that a separate rate should be levied for the repair of churches and chapels acquired or appropriated under that Act, or under the 58 Geo. III. c. 45, or the 59 Geo. III. c. 134; but this object, as well as the purposes of the burial-ground rate, authorized by 3 Geo. IV. c. 72, § 26, would probably be found in practice to be usually provided for out of the ordinary church rate.

The Sewers Rate, as directed by the statute 23 Hen. VIII. c. 5, is to be charged by the Commissioners of Sewers, upon the persons through whose default the annoyances to be removed have happened, or who hold any lands or tenements, or common of pasture, or profit of fishing, or who have, or may have, any hurt or loss through such annoyances; and to be assessed "after the quantity of the lands, tenements, and rents" of such persons, "by the number of acres and perches, after the rate of every person's portion, tenure, or profit, or after the quantity of their common of pasture, or profit of fishing, or other commodities there." Both the persons and the properties subject to this impost are therefore in some degree different from those liable to the poor rate. The General Sewers Tax (4 and 5 Vic. c. 45) is to be laid upon the "lands and hereditaments" within the jurisdiction of the several Courts of Sewers; and to be apportioned among the occupiers of the lands and hereditaments, in such proportions and upon such individuals as of right ought to pay the same. This tax, consequently, differs in its incidence from the sewers rate, which is not restricted to occupiers. It is difficult to assign a precise meaning to the words—" such individuals as of right ought to pay the same."

The " messuages, lands, tenements, and hereditaments" rateable to the relief of the poor, form the basis of the County Rate. These terms do not include the personal property of inhabitants, which was formerly liable to poor rate; but the temporary exemption of that kind of property from the latter rate, removes the incongruity. Where, however, rates are raised for the relief of the poor, the county rate is to be collected as part of the poor rate; but where no poor rate is made, or where the poor rate does not apply separately and distinctly to any parish or place, or in the northern counties, the Justices may require the Petty Constables to collect the county rate. The levy is thus conducted: the Justices issue their warrant for the amount required to the High Constables, who collect it from the Overseers or Petty Constables of the several parishes or other places, and then pay it into the hands of the County Treasurer. The required amount is to be apportioned by the Justices among the several parishes and places within the county, rateably and equally, according to a certain pound rate, upon the full and fair annual value of the property which is rateable (or which, if there were a poor rate, would be rateable) to the relief of the poor; and, for the purpose of making this apportionment, the Justices are invested with powers enabling them to obtain valuations of the several parishes and places. There is, however, much obscurity and some inconsistency in the various statutes relating to the county rate; and it is not always easy to reconcile their provisions, or determine their exact effect. Special county rates may be levied for providing county lunatic asylums and shire-halls, on the same properties and persons, and in the same manner, as the ordinary county rate.

The Hundred Rate, for affording compensation for damages sustained in riots, ought to be levied on the same property as the county rate, or where there is no county rate, on the same as any rate in the nature of a county rate, or where there is no such fund, then on the same as the poor rate. The hundred rate is not liable in hundreds alone; but in any hundred, wapentake, ward, or other district in the nature of a hundred,—any liberty, franchise, city, town, or place, not being part of any hundred, but contributing to a county rate,—any county of a city, county of a town, liberty, franchise, city, town, or place, wherein there is any rate raised in the nature of a county rate, or fund applicable to similar purposes,—or any parish, township, district, or precinct, not contributing to a county rate, or any similar fund, but having a rate for the relief of the poor.

Where the provisions of the County and District Constabulary Acts (2 and 3 Vic. c. 93, and 3 and 4 Vic. c. 88) have been adopted, the Police Rate is to be levied on the same properties and persons as the county rate, but limited to the police districts.

The Borough Council may order the Overseers of the parishes wholly or partly within the borough, to pay the Borough Rate out of the poor rate, or else to collect it by a pound rate upon the occupiers or possessors of all rateable property within such parishes, or parts of parishes, respectively. The Borough Watch Rate may be imposed at the discretion of the Borough Council, and is leviable from the occupiers of all lands, messuages, tenements, and hereditaments, within those parts of the borough which are watched by day and by night. The persons and properties liable to this rate differ, as will at once be seen, from those subject to the poor rate.

The foregoing summary will show that the law creates or contemplates variations, more or less considerable, in the incidence of several, at least, of these different local taxes. Thus, the properties legally liable to the poor and the highway rates, though substantially similar, are not altogether the same. The church rate, probably, in strictness of law, differs partially from both; and the sewers rate, if properly imposed, would deviate still more widely from them. Nevertheless, the Poor Law Commissioners remark, as the result of their inquiries into the subject, that " these legal differences have very little operation in practice," and "that it may be generally affirmed, that the whole of our local taxation is imposed, either by law, or by usages regardless of the law, on the same basis as the poor rates."

We regret there are no means of forming any accurate estimate of the local sums annually raised under the various rates enumerated above, but it is abundantly certain that their aggregate amount must be very large. Thus the

	£
Sum levied as poor rate in 1842 amounted to . . .	6,552,890
County rate in 1842, exclusive of payments from other rates and from the Treasury	703,526
Highway rate (probably)	1,200,000
Church rate (1839)	506,812
Total of the above rates	8,963,228

But to these rates have to be added the sums levied by tolls, &c., on highways, amounting, in 1841, to 1,574,518l., with the various sums paid for light and harbour dues, corporation rates, fees on account of the administration of justice, &c. Hence the local taxation of England and Wales, exclusive of tithe, will probably not fall short of 12,000,000l. a-year, if it do not exceed that amount. And if to this we add the local taxation of Scotland and Ireland, the aggregate amount of the local taxes of the United Kingdom will certainly not be under 14,000,000l. a-year, being little short of double the amount of the entire revenue of the Prussian monarchy!

This vast amount of local taxation is a most important feature in the economical condition of the kingdom. The Poor Law Commissioners estimate that in England only no fewer than 180,000 individuals are connected one way or other with the levy of the local taxes. Many of these render their services gratuitously; but vast numbers are paid, some by salaries, and some by a per centage on the sums collected. And there are good grounds for thinking that in many cases the accounts of the parties so employed are not subjected to any very efficient check or control, and that, consequently, there is considerable room for abuse. But the point of paramount importance in the reform of local taxation is the selection of a proper and invariable basis on which to raise the assessment; and we have already endeavoured to show how this may be best effected (see p. 65).

The purposes to which the local taxes are lawfully applicable (amounting to about 200) are so numerous and various, that a detailed catalogue would be tediously lengthy, and a general description almost useless. The names of the rates, as given above, usually indicate with sufficient distinctness the primary purpose of each; but this primary purpose is not always the only one to which the tax is even by law devoted. The poor rate, perhaps, is the most multifarious in its objects; comprising, besides the relief of the poor, such general measures as the registration of births and deaths, the vaccination of all classes of the community, the prosecution of certain kinds of criminals (such as the keepers of disorderly houses), the preparation of the lists of jurymen and parliamentary voters, and so forth. The county rate, again, provides for the repair of bridges, the maintenance of jails, the relief of prisoners, the payment of coroners, the prosecution of felons, and a long list of purposes besides. It may be observed generally that the several rates are designed to deal with exigencies of a most important public character; and it is therefore highly desirable that they should not only be levied with fairness, but expended with fidelity.

No. II.—Indian Revenue Systems.

" The land-tax constitutes the principal source of the revenue of British India, as it has always done of all Eastern states. The governments of such countries may, in fact, be said to be the real proprietors of the land; but in India, as elsewhere, the cultivators have a perpetual, hereditary, and transferable right of occupancy, so long as they continue to pay the share of the produce of the land demanded by the government. The value of this right of occupancy to the rural population depends on the degree of resistance which they have been able to oppose to the exactions of arbitrary governments. In Bengal and the adjacent provinces of India, from the peculiarly timid character of the inhabitants, and the open and exposed nature of the country, this resistance has been trifling indeed, and, consequently, the value of the right of occupancy in the peasant, or *ryot* (an Arabic word meaning subject), has been proportionally reduced. This also may be considered, though with some modifications, as being nearly the condition, in this respect, of the inhabitants of every part of the great plain of the Ganges, comprising more than half the population of Hindostan. But where the country is naturally difficult, the people have been able more effectually to resist the encroachments of the head landlord, or state, and to retain a valuable share in the property of the soil. This has been particularly the case along the ghauts, as in Bednore, Canara, Malabar, &c.; the inhabitants of which provinces not only lay claim to a right of private property in the soil, but have been generally ready to support their claim by force of arms. There can be no question, indeed, that the same modified right of property formerly existed everywhere; and it is indeed impossible that otherwise the land should ever have been reclaimed from the wilderness. But in those parts of India which could be readily overrun by a military force, the right of property in the soil has long been little else than the right to cultivate one's paternal acres for behoof of others, the cultivators reserving only a bare subsistence for themselves.

"Under the Mogul emperors, the practice in Bengal was to divide the gross produce of the soil, on the *métayer* principle, into equal shares, whereof one was retained by the cultivator, the other going to government as rent or tax. The officers employed to collect this revenue were called *zemindars;* and in the course of time their office seems to have become hereditary. It may be remarked that, in Persian, zemindar and landholder are synonymous; and this etymology, coupled with the hereditary nature of their office, which brought them exclusively into contact with the *ryot,* or occupier, as well as with the government, led many to believe that the zemindars were in reality the owners of the land, and that the ryots were their tenants. This, however, it is now admitted on all hands, was an incorrect opinion. The zemindars in reality were tax-gatherers, and were, in fact, obliged to pay to the government *nine-tenths* of the produce collected from the ryots, retaining only one-tenth as a compensation for their trouble; and, so long as the ryots paid their fixed contribution, they could not be ousted from their possessions, nor be in anywise interfered with.

" But notwithstanding what has now been stated, the perpetual or zemindary settlement established by Lord Cornwallis in Bengal in 1793, was made on the assumption that the zemindars were the proprietors of the soil. His lordship, indeed, was far from being personally satisfied that such was really the case; but he was anxious to create a class of large proprietors, and to give them an interest in the improvement and prosperity of the country. It is clear, however, that this wish could not be realised without destroying the permanent rights of the ryots, for, unless this were accomplished, the zemindars could not interfere in the management of their estates. The interests of the zemindars, and the rights of the ryots, were plainly irreconcileable; and it was obvious that the former would endeavour to reduce the latter to the condition of tenants at will. But this necessary consequence was either overlooked or ineffectually provided against. The zemindars became, under condition of their paying the assessment or quit-rent due to government, proprietors or owners of the land. The amount of the assessment was fixed at the average of what it had been for a few years previously, and it was declared to be *perpetual* and *invariable* at that amount. When a zemindar fell into arrear with government his estate might be either sold or resumed.

" That the assessment was at the outset, and still is, too high, cannot well be doubted; and it must ever be matter of regret that the settlement was not made with the ryots or cultivators, rather than with the zemindars; but, notwithstanding these and other defects, the measure was, on the whole, a great boon to India. Until the introduction of the perpetual system into Bengal, the revenue was raised in it, as it continues to be in the rest of India down to the present day, by a *variable* as well as a most oppressive land-tax. We all know what a pernicious influence tithe has had in this country; but suppose that, instead of amounting to 10, tithe had amounted to 50 per cent. of the gross produce of the soil, it would have been an effectual obstacle to all improvement; and the country would now have been in about the same state as in the days of Alfred, or of William the Conqueror.

"In France, Italy, and other parts of Europe, where the *métayer* system is introduced, the landlord seldom or never gets half the produce, unless he also furnish the stock and farming capital, and, in most cases, the *seed*. But in India, neither the government nor the zemindars do anything of the sort: they merely supply the land, which is usually divided into very small portions, mostly about six, and rarely amounting to twenty-four acres. A demand on the occupiers of such patches for half the produce is quite extravagant, and hence the excessive poverty of the people, which is such as to stagger belief. Still, however, the perpetual system is vastly preferable in principle, and also in its practical influence, to any other revenue system hitherto established in India. It set limits to fiscal rapacity, and established, as it were, a rampart beyond which no tax-gatherer dared to intrude. The enormous amount of the assessment, and the rigour with which payment was at first enforced, ruined an immense number of zemindars. But their lands having come into new and more efficient hands, a better system of management was introduced, and the limitation of the government demand gave a stimulus to improvement unknown in any other part of Hindostan. This, in fact, was the grand desideratum. A land-tax that may be increased should the land be improved, is all but certain to prevent any such improvement being made. This has been its uniform operation in every country in the world that has had the bad fortune to be cursed with such a destructive impost. But a heavy land-tax, provided it be fixed and unsusceptible of increase, is no bar to improvements, unless in so far as it tends to deprive the proprietors and occupiers of land of the means of making them. There is, in such a case, no want of security, and the cultivator is not deterred from attempting improvements, or of bringing superior enterprise and industry to operate on his estate, by the fact that the tax will, in consequence, be increased.

"The truth of what is now stated has been fully evinced in Bengal during the last twenty or thirty years; for both the population and the land-revenue of that part of our Indian empire have greatly increased. A great deal of waste land has been cultivated, and various works have been undertaken that would not be so much as dreamed of in any other part of our empire in the East. But, with all this, there has been but little, if any, improvement in the condition of the people of Bengal under our government. They in fact are practically excluded from at least all direct participation in the benefits resulting from the limitation of the assessment. They have merely exchanged one taskmaster for another. It is their landlords who have been the great gainers. The occupiers still, generally speaking, hold under the *métayer* principle, paying half or even more of their produce as rent; so that their poverty is often extreme, and their condition not unfrequently inferior even to that of the hired labourer, who receives the miserable pittance of two annas, or about 3*d.* a-day as wages.

"It seems, however, as if there were some strange fatality attending the government of India; and that the greatest talents and the best intentions should, when applied to legislate for that country, produce only the most pernicious projects. The perpetual settlement carried into effect by Lord Cornwallis in Bengal was keenly opposed by Lord Teignmouth, Colonel Wilkes, Mr. Thackeray, Sir T. Monro, and others, whose opinions on such subjects are certainly entitled to very great respect; and it would seem that the Board of Control became at length favourable to their views. In consequence of this change of opinion it was resolved to introduce a different system, under the superintendence of its zealous advocate, Sir Thomas Monro, into the presidency of Madras, or Fort St. George. This new system has received the name of the *ryotwar* settlement. It proceeds on the assumption that government possesses the entire property of the soil, and may dispose of it at pleasure : no middlemen or zemindars are interposed between the sovereign and the cultivators ; the ryots being brought into immediate contact with the collectors appointed by government to receive their rents. It is impossible, however, to enter fully into the details of this system. They are in the last degree complicated, which of itself would be enough to show their inexpediency. The land is taxed, according to its quality, at rates varying from 6*d.* up to 70*s.* an acre. Thus, for example, if the land were mere *dry field*, without artificial irrigation, the land-tax would be about 3*s.* an acre. If it have a supply of water capable of growing rice, the tax rises to 23*s.*, or to nearly eight times the former rent ; and if the irrigated land be a garden or an orchard, the tax rises to 40*s.*, or above thirteen times the tax on dry land ! In the first instance, the natural and inherent fertility of the soil only is taxed ; in the second, to that tax is added one on the capital and labour which the peasant or his ancestor laid out in reservoirs, canals, trenches, or wells. In the third, not only are all these taxed, but there is imposed besides an excise on fruits, garden-stuffs, and pot-herbs. But the radical vice of the system is, that the lands are not let for a considerable number of years, or for ever. On the contrary, there is a constant tampering and interference with the concerns of the ryots. It is enacted, for example, that " at the end of each year the ryot shall be at liberty either to throw up a part of his land, or to occupy more, according to his circumstances." When, owing to bad crops, or other unforeseen accidents, a ryot becomes unable to pay his rent or assessment, it is declared that " *the village to which he belongs shall be liable for him to the extent of* 10 *per cent. on the rent of the remaining ryots, but no more.*" And to crown the whole, the tehsildars, or native officers, employed in collecting the land-rents or revenue, have been vested with powers to act as officers of police, to impose fines, and even to inflict corporal punishment almost at discretion !

" It is really astonishing how acute and able men should have dreamed of establishing a system in an extensive and only half civilised country, that every one must see would be destructive of the industry of the tenants, and would lead to the grossest abuses, were an attempt made to introduce it into the management even of a single estate in Great Britain. Mr. Tucker, a gentleman who resided long in India, and now occupies a place in the Company's direction, has animadverted on this plan as follows :—' My wish,' says he, ' is not to exaggerate ; but when I find a system requiring a multiplicity of instruments, surveyors and inspectors, assessors ordinary and extraordinary ; potails, curnums, tehsildars, and cutchery servants ; and when I read the description given of these officers by the most zealous advocates of the system, their periodical visitations are pictured in my imagination as the passage of a flight of locusts, devouring in their course the fruits of the earth. For such complicated details, the most select agency would be required ; whereas the agency we can command is of the most questionable character. We do not merely require experience and honesty to execute one great undertaking ; the work is ever beginning and never ending, and calls for a perennial stream of intelligence and integrity. And can it be doubted that the people are oppressed and plundered by these multiform agents? The principle of the settlement is to take one-third of the gross produce on account of government; and, in order to render the assessment moderate, Sir T. Monro proposed to grant a considerable deduction from the rates deducible from the survey reports. But if it be moderate, how does it happen that the people continue in the same uniform condition of labouring peasants? Why do not the same changes take place here as in other communities? One man is industrious, economical, prudent, or fortunate; another is idle, wasteful, improvident, or unlucky. In the ordinary course of things one should rise and the other fall: the former should, by degrees, absorb the possessions of the latter—should become rich while his neighbour remained poor: gradations in society should take place; and, in the course of time, we might naturally expect to see the landlord, the yeoman, and the labourer. And what prevents this natural progression? I should answer, the *officers of government*. The fruits of industry are nipped in the bud. If one man produce more than his fellows, there is a public servant at hand ready to snatch the superfluity. And wherefore, then, should the husbandman toil, that a stranger may reap the produce?

" ' There are two other circumstances which tend to perpetuate this uniform condition. The ryots have no fixed possession; they are liable to be moved from field to field: this they sometimes do of their own accord, for the purpose of obtaining land supposed to be more lightly assessed; at other times the land is assigned by lot, with a view to a more equal and impartial distribution of the good and the bad among the different cultivators. But these revolutions tend to destroy all local attachments, and are evidently calculated to take away one great incentive to exertion.

" ' The other levelling principle is to be found in the rule which requires that the ryot shall make good the deficiencies of his neighbour to the extent of 10 per cent.; that is to the extent, probably, of his whole surplus earnings. Of what avail is it that the husbandman be diligent, skilful, and successful, if he is to be mulcted for his neighbour's negligence or misfortune? A must pay the debt of B. If a village be prosperous it matters little, for the next village may have been exposed to some calamity; and from the abundance of the one we exact wherewithal to supply the deficiency of the other. Is it possible to fancy a system better calculated to baffle the efforts of the individual, to repress industry, to extinguish hope, and to reduce all to one common state of universal pauperism.'—(*Review of the Financial Policy of the E. I. Company*, p. 134.)

" This system is understood to have been adopted by the authorities in India and England, in the expectation of enabling the government to participate in the advantages resulting from the improvement of the old lands, and from the bringing of new or waste land into cultivation. But it is clear, as well from the experience of Madras itself as of all other countries in which it has been tried, that a continually varying land-tax is an insuperable barrier to all improvement; and that it is, in fact, a powerful cause, not of advancement, but of poverty and barbarism. But the power of periodically revising the assessment might be retained without perpetually tampering with the occupiers. The only effect of this is to paralyse industry, to make those who are not poor counterfeit poverty, and to hinder any outlay of capital on the land. To obviate these disastrous consequences, the proper plan would be to assess the occupiers at a reasonable rate, and to make the assessment invariable for a period of at least forty or fifty years. An arrangement of this kind would give the ryots that security of which they are now wholly destitute; and would, we are bold to say, do ten times more to improve the Presidency than all the other measures it is possible to adopt, save that of making the assessment perpetual. This plan is, in fact, beginning to be tried in some parts of India; and it has, we are assured, been attended with the best results.

" The land revenue in most parts of British India is assessed under one or other of the systems now described; but in some parts of the Bengal provinces, in the ceded districts on the Nerbudda, and in the greater number of the native states, a different plan is adopted, which has received the name of the *village system*. This system, though defective in many respects, is incomparably superior to the ryotwar system, and, in some points, is even preferable to the perpetual system. It is a settlement made between the government and the cultivators, through the medium of the native village officers, who apportion the assessment without any direct interference on the part of the government functionaries. (See Art. BOMBAY PRESIDENCY, GEOG. DICT., for a short notice of this system of assessment.) It is difficult to state the proportion of the produce of a village paid to government. The authorities know little of the precise property of any of the proprietors: it is not the interest or the wish of the village that they should; and if any member of the community fail to pay his share, that is a matter for the village at large to settle, and they usually come forward and pay it for him. These, however, are private arrangements; and the *mocuddim*, or headman, through whom the government settles with the cultivators, has no power from government to enforce the assessment on the particular defaulter. The tax to be paid by each villager is settled by the villagers amongst themselves; the total assessment being calculated after inquiry into the property of the village—what it has paid and what it can pay—regular surveys of the village boundaries, and of its lands, having been previously made by government. The *mocuddim* or *potail* (headman) is elected by the villagers; and if the latter become dissatisfied with him they turn him out of office. This system may have, and doubtless has, its disadvantages: the potails may, from various motives, unequally assess the villagers; and the tendency to cultivate waste lands will not be so strong as under the perpetual settlement; but the latter effect is much more likely to be brought about under this than under the ryotwar system; nor does the village system involve the same inquisitorial acts on the part of government. If the amount of the tax charged on a village under this system were not too high, and if the amount when once fixed were made perpetual or invariable, for a period of at least forty or fifty years, it would probably be as good a plan as could be devised for the assessment of the land-tax.

" We may in this place compare the respective results which have followed under the different revenue systems, but especially where the permanent and ryotwar systems of taxation have been established. In 1793-94, the total gross revenue of the four provinces of Bengal, Bahar, Orissa, and Benares, was 4,129,948*l.*, of which 3,012,580*l.* consisted of land-tax, only 2,873,714*l.* being, however, actually collected. In 1837-38, the total *gross* revenue amounted to 8,842,723*l.*, or to more than double its amount in 1793-94. The land-tax in 1837-38 amounted to 3,377,903*l.*, which was almost all collected. The produce of the other branches of revenue amounted, in 1837-38, to no less than 5,464,820*l.*, being nearly *five* times the produce in 1792-93, when the perpetual settlement was organised! It should also be observed, that Bengal, which but a short time previously to 1793 had been the theatre of a most frightful famine, has not since been afflicted with even a year of remarkable scarcity; while both famines and scarcities have been frequent in every other part of our dominions in Hindostan. In 1793, the highest estimate of the population of these provinces, exclusive of Benares, was 24,000,000; in 1825 it had risen to 37,500,000, or increased by more than a half in thirty-two years.

"In the Madras presidency, the land-tax, in 1805-6, amounted to 3,469,977*l.*; in 1814-15 to 3,439,193*l.*; and in 1837-38 to only 3,149,781*l.*! being a decline of 320,000*l.* a-year; whereas the land-tax in Bengal during the same period had increased more than half a million! But how could it be otherwise? In Madras, the tax, besides being assessed in the worst possible manner, is oppressively high; indeed, the land-tax paid by that Presidency is almost equal to that paid by the far richer and wealthier country of Bengal, Bahar, Orissa, and Benares, with more than double its population! The other taxes in Madras are also more onerous than in Bengal; and several, such as a monopoly of tobacco, a tax on fruit-trees, on cow-dung used as fuel, and on arts and professions, are unknown in the latter. But notwithstanding, while in Bengal the land-tax amounts to little more than a third, it amounts in Madras to fully three-fourths of the total revenue of the Presidency.

"In the upper provinces of Bengal, now forming the government of Agra, where both the ryotwar and village systems prevail, and where the population is estimated to be about 18,000,000, or not quite half that of the four provinces of Bengal, Bahar, Orissa, and Benares, the land-tax, in 1806-7, was 2,103,410*l.*; in 1811-12 it was raised to 2,665,484*l.*; in 1819-20 to 3,061,932*l.*; and in 1829-30 to 3,766,566*l.* In the short space of twenty-two years, the tax had therefore been augmented by *the enormous sum* of 1,663,156*l.* But this augmentation proved to have been a great deal too rapid; for in 1834-35 the land-tax realised in the upper provinces sank to 3,398,024*l.*, at the same time that the other branches of revenue amounted to only 796,867*l.*, making the land-tax 81 parts in 100 of the whole revenue. Two years afterwards a dreadful famine broke out in the Agra provinces; and not only was little or no revenue collected, but the tax-receivers had to dole out relief to the tax-payers. In the Bombay presidency, where fluctuating assessments prevail, the land-tax, in 1837-38, amounted to 1,727-717*l.*, collected at an expense of 284,717*l.*, or about 1-6th part of its gross produce. The gross amount of all the other branches of the Bombay revenue amounted, during the same year, to only 389,119*l.*

"These statements conclusively demonstrate the vast superiority of the perpetual settlement, not merely as respects the prosperity of the country and the inhabitants, but also as a financial engine. Had the perpetual settlement been adopted in Madras when it was adopted in Bengal, we venture to say that the revenue of the former, instead of remaining stationary, or retrograding, would have advanced quite as rapidly as in the latter, while the population and wealth of the Presidency would have been proportionally increased.

"Besides the lands subject to the foregoing systems of assessment, a considerable extent of land in India is held rent-free. Throughout Hindostan, and indeed, we believe, throughout Asia, China perhaps excepted, a considerable portion of the land-tax is assigned to a great variety of parties, and for various purposes. Lands have been given to public officers as the reward of their services; to men of learning; to the favourites of sovereigns; for the maintenance of civil and military public establishments; and for the endowment of charitable, educational, and religious institutions. The grants, especially those for the use of temples, mosques, and shrines, were in perpetuity; and others became so through the usage of India. Inscriptions on stone and brass, found in most parts of India, attest the antiquity of these grants. One of them is supposed to be nearly coeval with the invasion of Britain by Julius Cæsar, and hundreds are of dates antecedent to the Norman invasion.—(*Asiat. Researches*, i.; *Trans. of the Royal Asiat. Soc.*, passim.) The extent of these free-tenure lands throughout India is very great. In the ceded territory under the Madras Presidency, comprising an area of 26,000 square miles, they amount, as estimated by Sir T. Monro, to one-fifth part of the entire surface. In the N.W. provinces of the Bengal Presidency (now Agra), embracing an area of 66,000 square miles, the free-tenure lands were ascertained by the British commissioners to amount to 44,951,770 begahs, the land-tax of which, if assessed in the usual manner, would have amounted to 1,236,000*l.* From an inquiry made in 1777, it appeared that the rent-free lands in Bengal Proper amounted to 8,575,942 begahs, or 2,164,554 acres, which would have yielded a tax of 1,256,390*l.* a-year. It is deserving of notice, that the rent-free lands under the Agra Presidency were at the very threshold, as it were, of the Mohammedan power; and the territory in which they are included was in the possession of the Mohammedans *for six centuries.* But, notwithstanding their bigotry and despotism, they respected the free tenures. They also, much to their honour, respected them in a singular degree in Bengal, where most of them had originally consisted of tracts of waste or wild land, reclaimed by the labour and capital of the grantees, or their heirs and successors. Lord Cornwallis, and the Indian council of his day, confirmed the possession of the rent-free lands to their holders, on the same perpetual tenure as the taxed lands; and it was enacted that those that held under a free tenure prior to 1765 should remain untaxed 'for ever.' It has been said that the present Indian government has manifested a strong disposition to seize upon the rent-free lands, or to subject them to a system of taxation; but, as a proceeding of this sort would be a flagrant violation of a solemn engagement, we do not believe that there is any real foundation for the statement."—(GEOGRAPHICAL DICTIONARY, Art. INDIA, BRITISH.)

No. III.—THE CASE OF THE MESSRS. FIELDEN.

THE following extracts from the Parliamentary report of the 'Times' of the 26th February, 1844, and from a Manchester paper, will explain the allusion to the case of the Messrs. Fielden, p. 124 :—

"Mr. Fielden said, before voting supplies, it had become necessary to inquire how the sums to be voted had been raised, who were taxed and made to pay them, the manner in which taxes were levied, and whether or not a mode of levy, legal, fair, and impartial, was carried on, or one of great oppression and injustice? and it was particularly necessary to ascertain whether or not wrong had been committed by official persons in carrying into effect the avowedly arbitrary enactment called the Property and Income

Tax Act? He believed that a considerable part of the money raised under that Act was forced out of the pockets of tradesmen and others by the most arbitrary process of assessment this country had ever known. The injustice towards the poor done by indirect taxation on the articles of necessity they purchased, and on which the duties were so much higher per cent. than on the articles consumed by the rich, had been so ably exposed by the honourable member for Coventry, that he would not say more upon it than that the case had shown so great an injustice to the poor as to warrant the withholding of supplies unless an assurance were given by Ministers that these glaring irregularities should be corrected. The stamp taxes and many others were also unfairly imposed and enforced, and equally required revision; but, on that occasion, he proposed to make known to the house the iniquitous and oppressive mode in which the income-tax was assessed and exacted. He had heard of many cases in which persons had been assessed by the district commissioners, and made to pay on profits derived from trade and manufactures, when, so far from profit having accrued for the three years previous to the year of assessment, considerable loss had been sustained. These assessments had been acted on, and the goods of the parties seized and sold, although they had tendered proof on oath to the fact that no profit existed. He concurred in an observation of the honourable and gallant colonel the member for Lincoln, that this country was governed, not by law, but by commissioners, who swarmed over the land, whose powers were almost unlimited, and against whom there was no appeal. He was reluctant to speak on his own affairs, but he felt that he was performing a public duty in illustrating a great public grievance by reference to his own case. He was speaking now, not of the property-tax, but of the income-tax, and he would detail to the house what had happened, he believed, to many manufacturers of his own class by showing what had happened to himself. In his business, as a manufacturer, he was, of course, subject to a tax on his property; but with respect to income from that business, he was subject or not according as the business returned profit or not. He and his partners had received a letter, which he would read:—'Stamps and Taxes, Somerset-House, February 14, 1844. Gentlemen,—Her Majesty's Commissioners of Stamps and Taxes having directed immediate process to be issued for your arrear of income-tax due the 20th of March last, amounting to 350*l.*, and returned into the Exchequer, I beg to inform you that, in order to save the expenses of a levy by the sheriff, the amount must be paid to Mr. Peter Ormerod, of Todmorden, the collector, before the 24th instant. I am, gentlemen, your most obedient servant, J. TIMM, Solicitor for Stamps and Taxes. To Messrs. Fielden.' Now, he would wish the house to mark that that letter informed him and his partners that the Commissioners of Stamps and Taxes had directed process to issue for arrears of income-tax due the 20th of March last, that was, more than 11 months ago. Why had not that demand been enforced before? He had asked for no credit. If the debt was due from him and his partners they ought to have been made to pay it long ago. He denied the debt. He feared that many who could less afford to lose the money had been assessed with equal injustice, but made to pay because too weak to offer resistance. He would now go into details, for it was right that the house and the country should know the vexatious and unjust manner in which the taxes were wrung from those who paid them. If he and his brothers had been the only parties unjustly treated under the income-tax, the house would not have heard a word from him of their case ; but when he knew that great numbers complained of the same grievance, and having been again and again applied to to take up the question, and expose the injustice and arbitrary proceedings of the officials and commissioners, he should incur the charge of negligence if he did not do so. As the case of himself and his partners would probably be the case of thousands, and was, of course, familiar to himself, he would state it. In the autumn of 1842 he received a printed form, requiring him to make a true return of the profits of his trade, under schedule D, for the year ending the 5th of April, 1843. He filled up the paper with the word 'Nothing,' as the fact was. On the 24th of January, 1843, he received a notice that the commissioners had made an assessment on him for the year ending the 5th of April, 1843, in these words —'To duties granted by schedule D on profits on trade, professions, foreign property, casual profits, 12,000*l.* Duty payable, 350*l.* Dated this 31st of December, 1843. J. Woods, Clerk to the Commissioners.' He gave notice that he should appeal, and on the 16th of February, 1843, attended the commissioners at Rochdale, and being, as they required, first sworn, was examined by them, and stated that he had made a true return, that the business of himself and partners had not yielded a profit, but had caused a loss. The chairman asked, if there was no profit on the average of the then three last years ? He answered, no; that he had been required to make a true return, and any other than the one he had made would not have been true. One of the commissioners said, 'Mr. Fielden should understand that in ascertaining profits no interest is allowed to be deducted for the capital employed in their business.' He answered, that he had so understood the Act, and that the capital he and his partners had employed in their business had been entirely unproductive, and had diminished in amount during the three years. Other questions and answers followed, after which the chairman of the board said, that the commissioners were invested with extraordinary powers of inquiry, and a precept was handed to him to fill up and return to Mr. Woods within six days. He (Mr. Fielden) said he would see what return he could make to it, and on rising to leave the room he was informed by the surveyor of taxes, then present, that he would be wanted there again after the precept was returned. He assented, and was told he should know when and where. The precept required a debtor and creditor account of profits on an average of the then last three years, and of gross profits, which were to be very full and particular. Within the six days he returned the precept as required, and stated in it ' that we had no means of making out a debtor and creditor account of profit and loss on an average of the last three years, nor of our gross profits, otherwise than by an account in the following form, which would require an estimate of stock on hand both at the beginning and end of that period, and the result would show a heavy loss without any interest charged on capital employed :—

" Profit and Loss.

Dr.	To stock three years ago .	.	.	.	.
	To materials purchased since	.	.	.	.
	To wages and expenses paid	.	.	.	.
	To rent of premises charged with property-tax
		under schedule A	.	.	.	.	.
Cr.	By stock now	.	.	.	.	.	.
	By sales	.	.	.	.	.	.	.

> By bad debts and other losses in trade   · ·
>
> Balance, showing a heavy loss on the last three
>
>   years · · · · · · ·

To this notification no answer was returned from the commissioners, but he and his partners were served with a notice, dated March 30, 1843, by the collectors of the district, that they were returned in a schedule to the commissioners of the district as defaulters in the sum of 175*l.* then due, and that, unless paid, process would issue against them. On receiving this he applied to the Chancellor of the Exchequer, who received him most courteously, and listened to him with attention. (Hear.) The right honourable gentleman made inquiry, and the result was, that he received from him a copy of a letter which had been addressed to the commissioners, through Mr. Woods, their clerk, by the Commissioners of Stamps and Taxes, through Mr. Pressley. This was the letter:—' Stamps and Taxes, London, 27th of March, 1843.—Sir, I have laid before the board your letter of the 15th, relative to the case of Messrs. Fielden, under the Property-tax Act, and in reply I am directed to state that, in their opinion, the proper course to be pursued is for the commissioners to direct another precept to the parties, under the authority of section 120, requiring them to deliver within a reasonable but limited time a schedule containing certain specific particulars, such as the amount of the several items set forth respectively under the head of 'debtor and creditor,' in their letter of the 21st ultimo addressed to you, and any other particulars which the commissioners may think requisite to enable them to determine the appeal; and that, in default of the parties delivering such a schedule within the time limited, the commissioners will be justified in confirming the assessment; or, if such a schedule should be delivered, the commissioners may, in like manner, call for any further information that they may deem requisite, and so on from time to time until they are satisfied; and further, that they may call upon the parties to be examined *viva voce* before them, but not upon oath; and lastly, that they may require the parties to verify on oath the statements contained in the schedules delivered, and also the substance of their answers taken down in writing on their *viva voce* examination (the parties having liberty previously to amend such schedules and statements, provided by section 122); but that if the parties do so verify the same on oath the commissioners are bound to decide the appeal according to the result of the schedules and examination. I am to add, that the board think that a precept calling upon the parties for a debtor and creditor account of profits and loss is too general and vague to justify the commissioners in confirming the assessment in the present stage of the proceedings. I am, Sir, your obedient servant, C. PRESSLEY. To J. Woods, Esq., Clerk to Commissioners, Rochdale.' This letter suggested two things to the commissioners; first, that they should require of him and his partners a schedule containing certain particulars, such as the amount of the several items set forth respectively in the form which he had sent them, to be delivered within a reasonable time; and, secondly, that the account called for by the commissioners was too general and vague, and that they were not justified in confirming their assessment. He had never since been called upon for the account suggested by himself, and thus plainly approved by the Board of Stamps and Taxes, and yet he had now received the notice that his goods were to be seized by the sheriff to satisfy a demand that he had the authority of the board at Somerset-House for saying was not legally due. He and his partners had resolved to resist this arbitrary and illegal act of the commissioners, and though they would suffer the Government, if it liked, to come and seize upon their property, they would never pay a tax on profit that had not accrued to them, and which they had already sworn they had not realized. So much for the year 1842; the year 1843 he also returned 'Nothing' as profits of trade, as before. On the 27th of December, 1843, he received notice that the commissioners had again assessed him for profits, 12,000*l.* This notice was dated 15th of December, 1843, and signed ' J. Woods, Clerk to the Commissioners.' He again appealed, and on the 11th of January went before the commissioners and stated to them that he and his partners, instead of a profit on the three years preceding, had sustained a heavy loss,—that they held a heavy stock of goods which had been accumulating over that period, and that the value of their stock upon the same quantity of goods had been less and less every succeeding stock-taking during that period,—that the raw material used in their manufacture had fallen lower and lower until July last, when it was at the lowest,—that they had kept up wages, which, had they been reduced, would have caused much suffering among their work-people,—that they had made bad debts to a considerable amount,—that the accumulated stock at the end of the three years was not worth what it had cost, and that the capital employed under schedule D at the commencement of the three years had diminished in amount at the end of that period. After many questions on these points, a precept was put into his hand requiring answers to these questions :—

" 'State each trade or profession you are engaged in, where they are respectively carried on, and who are the partners in each ; state the capital employed in each concern, distinguishing the amount belonging to each partner.

" ' State the amount of interest on your banking account.

" ' State the income from Ireland, or from any of Her Majesty's dominions, or from any foreign securities or possessions.

" ' State the amount of the balance of profits in each concern, separately, for each of the three last years.

" ' State the particular deductions made in forming the above balances,—

" ' For rent, or taxes, or other expenditure of or connected with the dwelling-house.

" ' For rent, or taxes, or other expenditure of or connected with buildings used for the purposes of trade.

" ' For bad debts, specifying whether the parties are bankrupts, or compounding, or how otherwise.

" ' For wages or board of servants.

" ' For improvements or repairs of premises, or depreciation in value thereof.

" ' For average losses.

" ' For repairs or supply of utensils or machinery, or depreciation in value thereof.

" ' Have you made any and what deductions for losses by bank or railways, or mining adventures, or any other not connected with your trade ? or from capital withdrawn from trade ? or from sums employed or to be employed as capital therein, or on account or pretence of interest of capital ? or on account of the maintenance of yourself, family, or establishment ? or for any annuity, interest of money, or other payment gratuitously allowed or otherwise? or on account of any moneys, property, or unappropriated credits, reserved or set apart, being portion of or appertaining to your capital or undivided profits, not elsewhere assessed?

" ' You will bear in mind that the account is to embrace the period of three years, notwithstanding any change or succession of a firm, or of the partners therein.'

" The 20th of January was fixed on as the day for a further hearing on this subject, and on that day he attended the board again, and, having looked over the questions, told the commissioners that he could not possibly answer them, and he did not believe any one carrying on such a business as his could do so; but that he had made out a statement showing the amount of capital in his business at the beginning of the period for which they had asked for a return, and the amount of the same at the termination of it, which showed a great loss. A long examination followed on this document, in which he informed the commissioners that these amounts were obtained by valuations made by him and his brothers at their stock-takings, not to meet any demands for profits on income, but to determine each partner's share and interest in their joint property at the time, and what the representatives of any one or more, dying before the next stock-taking, would be entitled to receive out of the concern; that he and his partners signed a balance-sheet at every stock-taking. He asked the commissioners what more they required of him? Whether they disbelieved him? They answered, ' No.' He desired to know if they wished to see his books? They again answered, ' No.' He told them that, if they did, and he did not force from them the truth of what he said, and that he had a losing business, he would submit to the charge. He was then asked to withdraw; and, being called in again, was told by the chairman that they had confirmed the assessment, but that if on the 5th of April next he could prove to them that he had had no profit in his trade on the year ending that day, they would make a return of the duty as directed by the 133rd section of the act. He told the commissioners that they had done him injustice, and that he would not pay, upon which the chairman observed, that the commissioners had been instructed by the officials present. With respect to the first year he had, he thought, clearly shown that the commissioners had not acted in accordance with the law, nor in accordance with the suggestions from Somerset-House. He called on the Government to inquire into his own and other cases of the like kind, before he could sanction the vote of supply. As to the second year in which he had been assessed, he called on the Government here to interpose and prevent an equal violation of this law, sufficiently odious when administered in its letter, but intolerable as administered by the present commissioners. What right had they to require him to attend there again on the 5th of April next, and prove whether or not he had made any profit on the year ending on that day? None. It was a stretch of power which he called on the Government to look into at once, for he could tell them that, although this had been borne once or twice, there were murmurs arising that would burst forth on a repetition of this injustice. The act itself contained a rule for the computation of profits on an average of three years preceding the year of assessment. The words were these :—
' Rule 1. The duty to be charged in respect thereof shall be computed on a sum not less than the full amount of the balance of the profits or gains of such trade, manufacture, adventure, or concern, upon a fair and just average

of three years, ending on such day of the year immediately preceding the year of assessment on which the accounts of the said trade, manufacture, or concern shall have been usually made up, or on the 5th day of April preceding the year of assessment.' Looking at that rule, he thought the commissioners were prohibited from any inquiry as to profits accruing in the year of assessment, and this he told them, and that when that year came to charge he would deal honestly by them, and make a return on that, unless, indeed, they drove him, by their acts of injustice, to follow the example of a neighbour of his and make no return at all."—*Times.*

" The circumstances attending the distraint on the property of Messrs. Fielden, Brothers, of Todmorden and Manchester, having transpired, and been published in other journals, we may briefly notice and correct some of the statements. It seems that Messrs. Fielden had returned the papers which they were required to fill up with their trade profits, &c., with the word 'nil.' The commissioners not being satisfied with the return, assessed them in about 350*l.* Mr. John Fielden, M.P., the senior partner, appealed against the decision of the commissioners, when the assessment was confirmed. Messrs. Fielden having refused to pay the amount, the commissioners issued a warrant of distress, with which a sheriff's officer proceeded to Todmorden, to demand the money. He was, however, met with a peremptory refusal of payment, and was told that he might distrain; the partners who were on the premises declaring that they would turn out all their hands, and close their works when he did so. However, it having incidentally transpired that there were goods in the warehouse of the firm in Manchester, supposed to be sufficient to satisfy the claim, the sheriff's officer said that he would first see the stock there, and if he found it adequate he would withdraw the man he had brought with him, and whom he then left in possession. The Messrs. Fielden immediately stopped their works, and turned out all their hands; thus causing considerable excitement in Todmorden, and the bailiff in possession was for a time in no very enviable position. The sheriff's officer finding that there was property enough in the warehouse at Manchester to satisfy the amount claimed, sent immediately to Todmorden, and withdrew the man. On the officers proceeding to the warehouse, No. 21, Peel-Street, Manchester, Mr. Thomas Fielden gave orders that no more business should be transacted until the affair was settled; and refused to allow any goods to pass either in or out of the premises. He refused all information to the officers, and when one of them asked for the key of a locked door in the upper story, it was refused, and upon this the officer broke it open. In our paper of Wednesday was advertised the sale by auction of a quantity of grey domestics and sheetings, on the following Monday. The sale, under such circumstances, attracted various parties and it was well attended. We should state that though the original amount due from the firm as income-tax was about 350*l.*, this had been increased by costs and expenses to nearly 400*l.*, and to this extent the auctioneer was authorised to sell. The sale commenced shortly after eleven o'clock on Monday; and Mr. Joseph Gale, the auctioneer, sold forty-one lots, consisting of grey domestics and sheetings, of various lengths, widths, &c. at prices from 2½*d.* a-yard for 27-inch grey domestics, to 9½*d.* a-yard for 82-inch sheetings; being, we believe, a little, but not much, under the market prices of the goods. The forty-one lots realised 407*l.* 13*s.* 5*d.*; and though there were six more lots in the catalogue, the auctioneer, having sold sufficient to cover the required amount, closed the sale."—*Manchester Paper.*

No. IV.—An Account of the Public Income and Expenditure

INCOME.	1841		1842		1843	
	£	£	£	£	£	£
CUSTOMS AND EXCISE:						
Spirits { Foreign	1,361,453	..	1,262,094	..	1,210,154	
Spirits { Rum	1,063,087	..	978,959	..	981,906	
Spirits { British	5,178,175	..	5,041,773	..	4,958,223	
Malt	5,263,363	..	4,385,221	..	4,659,636	
Hops	69,055	..	260,979	..	908,366	
Wine	1,721,281	..	1,335,412	..	1,703,721	
Sugar and Molasses	5,307,675	..	5,130,271	..	5,290,406	
Tea	3,973,668	..	4,088,957	..	4,407,642	
Coffee	887,723	..	768,886	..	697,376	
Tobacco and Snuff	3,550,825	..	3,577,224	..	3,711,227	
		28,376,305		26,929,776		27,928,659
Butter	262,614	..	187,921	..	151,614	
Cheese	134,622	..	98,112	..	90,888	
Currants and Raisins	410.827	..	375,464	..	482,942	
Corn	568,341	..	1,363,977	..	758,293	
Cotton Wool and Sheep's imported	664,576	..	566,700	..	843,244	
Silks	257,785	..	245,080	..	263,949	
Hides and Skins	79,119	..	49,566	..	27,871	
Paper	586,219	..	591,263	..	642,338	
Soap	815,864	..	829,977	..	893,170	
Candles and Tallow	205,839	..	170,834	..	194,735	
Coals, sea-borne	11,925	..	57,415	..	131,304	
Glass	682,192	..	594,815	..	599,444	
Bricks, Tiles, and Slates	443,018	..	393,050	..	355,281	
Timber	1,500,315	..	948,070	..	667,536	
Auctions	311,788	..	294,836	..	282,863	
Excise Licences	1,036,592	..	1,014,899	..	1,019,947	
Post-Horse Duties	199,864	..	179,457	..	166,434	
Miscellaneous of Customs and Excise	1,570,477	..	1,350,402	..	1,069,369	
		9,741,917		9,311,138		8,641,222
Total Customs and Excise	..	38,118,222	..	36,140,914	..	36,569,881
STAMPS:						
Deeds and other Instruments	1,665,297	..	1,604,672	..	1,622,557	
Probates and Legacies	2,132,473	..	2,163,564	..	2,143,127	
Insurance { Marine	284,496	..	251,490	..	253,529	
Insurance { Fire	964,146	..	284,726	..	987,359	
Bills of Exchange, Bankers' Notes	743,312	..	680,671	..	673,873	
Newspapers and Advertisements	377,471	..	381,215	..	391,653	
Stage Coaches	460,733	..	444,215	..	388,928	
Receipts	174,747	..	180,059	..	174,756	
Other Stamp Duties	473,685	..	449,171	..	441,190	
		7,276,360		7,139,783		7,076,752
ASSESSED AND LAND TAXES:						
Land Taxes	1,214,431	..	1,172,842	..	1,159,149	
Windows	1,664,053	..	1,569,344	..	1,545,281	
Servants	215,844	..	205,727	..	200,252	
Horses	464,592	..	388,181	..	376,002	
Carriages	414,676	..	442,880	..	428,904	
Dogs	172,190	..	159,326	..	151,357	
Additional 10 per cent.	311,357	..	296,342	..	289,403	
Other Assessed Taxes	258,210	..	250,768	..	234,220	
		4,715,353		4,485,410		4,385,068
Property and Income Tax	..		582,088		5,387,455	
Post-Office	..	1,495,540	..	1,578,145	..	1,535,216
Crown Lands	..	488,298	..	368,161	..	409,377
Other Ordinary Revenue and other Resources	..	271,660	..	825,589	..	256,065
Money from China, under Treaty of August, 1842	..	..	..	..	..	1,815,208
Total Income	..	52,315,433	..	51,120,040	..	56,935,022
Excess of Expenditure over Income	..	2,149,885	..	4,075,119	..	
	£	54,465,318	..	55,195,159	..	56,935,022

of the United Kingdom in 1841, 1842, and 1843.

EXPENDITURE.	1841		1842		1843	
	£	£	£	£	£	£
REVENUE—Charges of Collection :						
Civil Departments { Customs	623,267		610,754		617,321	
{ Excise	798,883		776,784		774,489	
		1,422,150		1,387,488		1,391,810
Preventive Service, Land Guard, Revenue Police, } Cruisers and Harbour Vessels }		561,990		566,957		572,655
Stamps		1,984,140		1,954,445		1,964,465
Assessed Taxes		149,952		147,440		144,754
Other Ordinary Revenues		174,712		183,867		252,218
Superannuation and other Allowances		56,964		57,727		57,270
		858,278		363,018		364,685
Total Revenue	...	2,724,046	..	2,705,497	..	2,783,512
PUBLIC DEBT :						
Interest on Permanent Debt	24,333,352		24,489,291		24,512,753	
Terminable Annuities	4,076,776		4,071,530		3,924,184	
Management	135,669		134,158		135,991	
	28,545,797		28,694,979		28,572,928	
Interest on Exchequer Bills	896,465		725,010		688,084	
Total Debt		29,442,262		29,419,989		29,261,012
CIVIL GOVERNMENT :						
Civil List—Privy Purse ; Salaries and Tradesmen's } Bills	371,800		371,800		371,800	
The Allowances to Branches of the Royal Family, including King of Belgians	318,000		318,000		308,423	
The Lord Lieutenant of Ireland's Establishment	32,465		30,554		26,317	
Salaries and Expenses of Houses of Parliament } (including Printing)	122,717		123,847		106,001	
Civil Departments, including Sup. Allowances	498,551		524,773		510,894	
Other Annuities, Pensions, and Sup. Allowances	319,299		312,641		297,977	
Pensions, Civil List	4,022		5,120		5,307	
Total Civil Government		1,666,854		1,686,735		1,626,219
JUSTICE :						
Courts of Justice	533,761		551,540		580,516	
Police and Criminal Prosecutions	571,805		595,945		566,438	
Correction	497,060		493,117		635,515	
Total Justice		1,602,626		1,640,602		1,782,469
DIPLOMATIC :						
Foreign Ministers' Salaries and Pensions	185,770		183,470		178,456	
Consuls' Salaries and Superannuation Allowances	128,890		118,649		125,708	
Disbursements, Outfit	36,671		42,156		57,262	
Total Diplomatic		351,331		344,275		361,426
FORCES :						
Army . { Effective ; Charge	3,971,425		3,596,222		3,633,471	
{ Non-effective ; Charge	2,446,996		2,391,699		2,363,685	
Total Army	6,418,421		5,987,921		5,997,156	
Navy . { Effective ; Charge	5,103,358		5,231,164		5,199,446	
{ Non-effective ; Charge	1,385,716		1,408,999		1,406,611	
Total Navy	6,489,074		6,640,163		6,606,057	
Ordnance { Effective ; Charge	1,655,893		2,008,474		1,748,346	
{ Non-effective ; Charge	159,739		166,199		162,359	
Total Ordnance	1,815,132		2,174,673		1,910,704	
Total Forces		14,722,627		14,802,757		14,513,917
Army and Ordnance, Insurrection in Canada	117,153		253,843		25,300	
China Expedition	400,000		830,008		416,056	
China and India, Army, Navy, and Ordnance Services			272,921			
Opium Compensation					1,245,823	
Bounties, &c., for promoting Fisheries	13,604		19,410		11,286	
Public Works	356,424		419,519		405,246	
Payments out of the Rev. of Crown Lands for Improvements, &c.	213,815		193,607		211,561	
Post Office ; Charges of Collection and other Payments	981,372		967,195		966,834	
Quarantine and Warehousing Establishments	121,326		127,941		130,586	
Miscellaneous, not classed under the foregoing Heads	1,802,378		1,511,360		1,760,463	
Total Expenditure . . . £	54,465,319		55,195,159		55,501,740	
Surplus of Income over Expenditure	..	..	..	..	..	1,433,283
						56,935,022
MEMORANDUM :						
The Amount of Terminable Annuities, on 5th January, was	4,096,952		3,989,788		3,924,723	
In corresponding Perpetuities, as estimated by Mr. Finlaison	1,664,695		1,597,685		1,550,762	
Difference . . . . £	2,432,257		2,392,148		2,373,961	

No. V.—An Account of the Quantities of Tea imported into the United Kingdom during each of the Ten Years ending with 1842; specifying the Quantities re-exported, the Quantities annually entered for Home Consumption, the Rates of Duty, and the annual Produce of the Duties.

Years.	Quantities imported into the United Kingdom.	Quantities re exported from the United Kingdom.	Quantities retained for Home Consumption in the United Kingdom.	Amount of Duty received thereon.	RATES OF DUTY.
	Lbs.	Lbs.	Lbs.	£	
1833	32,057,832	254,460	31,829,620	3,444,102	{ If sold at or under 2s. per lb., 96l. per centum ad valorem. At or above 2s. per lb., 100l. ditto.
1834	33,643,980	1,181,005	34,969,651	3,589,361	{ Bohea, 1s. 6d. per lb.; Congou, Twankay, Hyson Skin, Orange Pekoe, and Campoi, 2s. 2d. per lb.; all other sorts, 3s. per lb. (from 22nd April).
1835	44,360,550	2,158,029	36,574,004	3,832,427	,,
1836	49,307,701	4,269,863	49,142,236	4,674,535	All sorts, 2s. 1d. per lb. (from 1st July).
1837	36,973,981	4,716,248	30,625,206	3,223,840	,,
1838	40,413,714	2,577,877	32,351,593	3,362,035	,,
1839	38,158,008	3,318,912	35,127,287	3,658,803	,,
1840	28,021,882	2,383,384	32,252,628	3,472,864	{ All sorts, 2s. 1d. per lb. (from 1st July); 5l. per cent. additional thereon from 15th May.
1841	30,787,796	4,490,363	36,675,667	3,973,668	,,
1842	40,742,128	5,710,127	37,355,912	4,088,957	,,

No. VI.—A Return of the Quantities and Prices of the several sorts of Tea sold by the East India Company, in each Year from 1814-15 to 1831-32 (1st of May to 1st of May).

Years.	BOHEA.		CONGOU.		CAMPOI.		SOUCHONG.		PEKOE.	
	Quantity.	Average Sale Price per Pound.	Quantity.	Average Sale Price per Pound.	Quantity.	Average Sale Price per Pound.	Quantity.	Average Sale Price per Pound.	Quantity.	Average Sale Price per Pound.
	Lbs.	s. d.	Lbs.	s. d.	Lbs.	s. d.	Lbs.	s. d.	Lbs.	s. d.
1814-15	397,909	2 10·20	21,283,549	3 2·55	1,002,000	3 4·67	1,520,035	3 7·51	22,625	6 10·62
1815-16	839,198	2 1·57	17,908,827	2 11·02	823,507	3 4·94	982,816	3 6·55	30,700	5 8·95
1816-17	1,597,276	2 5·56	14,895,681	2 10·39	925,550	3 1·73	1,862,135	3 0·47	98,562	4 2·53
1817-18	1,972,736	2 5·73	15,736,003	2 11·82	866,304	3 3·12	2,018,058	3 2·88	76,302	4 4·36
1818-19	1,441,636	1 4·78	18,441,066	2 11·22	533,821	3 4·49	1,183,051	3 0·11	69,760	4 4·37
1819-20	1,497,592	1 9·25	17,661,433	2 7·94	479,081	3 4·64	1,168,605	3 2·01	27,802	4 2·41
1820-21	2,522,927	2 1·88	15,939,795	2 7·31	319,775	3 6·04	1,285,496	3 2·96	133,964	4 2·53
1821-22	3,583,486	2 5·28	17,249,982	2 8·59	121,293	3 7·00	1,397,931	3 1·25	92,957	3 10·69
1822-23	1,873,881	2 5·43	18,822,848	2 7·82	323,063	3 6·30	1,391,668	2 10·62	44,757	4 4·73
1823-24	1,853,394	2 4·92	19,006,594	2 8·06	242,562	3 6·36	1,322,326	2 11·82	46,005	5 0·74
1824-25	2,093,276	2 4·59	20,598,958	2 7·90	227,722	3 0·88	473,476	3 4·74	86,051	4 3·26
1825-26	2,713,011	2 0·50	21,034,635	2 6·75	207,971	3 1·77	547,128	3 1·28	148,038	4 0·84
1826-27	2,588,124	2 7·02	20,472,625	2 4·73	166,701	2 9·04	475,796	3 2·17	165,842	3 6·01
1827-28	3,759,199	1 7·44	19,389,392	2 3·95	297,346	2 9·31	448,163	3 0·53	280,308	3 6·61
1828-29	3,778,012	1 6·65	20,142,073	2 3·88	284,187	2 9·14	601,739	2 10·38	131,281	3 9·23
1829-30	4,845,826	1 6·32	18,402,118	2 3·26	474,735	2 2·24	298,819	3 3·60	129,554	3 9·23
1830-31	6,096,153	1 10·03	17,857,208	2 3·15	431,455	2 3·17	277,067	3 0·76	253,101	3 9·92
1831-32	6,474,833	1 10·65	17,734,257	2 2·77	273,289	2 1·92	447,799	2 10·68	545,775	2 10·23

No. VI.—Return of the Quantities and Prices of the several sorts of Tea, &c.—*continued.*

Years.	TWANKAY.		HYSON SKIN.		YOUNG HYSON.		HYSON.		GUNPOWDER.	
	Quantity.	Average Sale Price per Pound.	Quantity.	Average Sale Price per Pound.	Quantity.	Average Sale Price per Pound.	Quantity.	Average Sale Price per Pound.	Quantity.	Average Sale Price per Pound.
	Lbs.	*s. d.*	*Lbs.*	*s. d.*	*Lbs.*	*s. d.*	*Lbs.*	*s. d.*	*Lbs.*	*s. d.*
1814-15	3,646,048	3 6·11	795,907	3 9·57	...	...	1,008,948	5 9·15	9,189	7 6·50
1815-16	3,784,868	3 3·06	708,280	3 5·26	...	...	1,059,225	5 5·75	15,425	5 0·93
1816-17	3,239,210	2 11·92	554,270	3 0·76	...	...	882,820	4 11·61		
1817-18	3,763,123	3 0·69	451,904	3 1·97	...	...	992,439	4 10·34		
1818-19	4,730,297	2 11·87	193,852	3 2·78	...	...	909,637	4 11·83		
1819-20	4,288,345	3 0·83	161,919	3 4·38	...	...	700,312	5 3·66		
1820-21	4,900,764	3 0·33	343,995	3 0·84	...	...	782,482	5 6·04		
1821-22	4,401,778	3 1·48	225,636	3 1·89	...	...	1,044,256	4 8·53		
1822-23	4,165,896	3 4·77	205,658	3 3·99	...	...	816,872	4 3·24		
1823-24	3,967,206	3 5·71	259,209	3 4·72	...	...	980,753	4 3·23		
1824-25	3,754,120	3 5·17	324,987	3 3·29	9,055	4 3·68	985,566	4 2·71		
1825-26	3,768,406	3 4·88	229,961	3 4·57	...	...	932,099	4 5·38		
1826-27	4,424,262	2 1·94	298,960	3 2·26	51,421	4 0·75	801,724	4 8·72		
1827-28	4,537,672	2 7·04	242,313	2 7·19	...	...	1,013,771	4 5·58		
1828-29	4,101,845	2 5·72	213,993	2 3·84	...	...	1,014,923	4 1·75	645	6 6·51
1829-30	3,852,443	2 4·04	228,016	2 4·60	...	...	1,071,278	4 1·40		
1830-31	4,560,562	2 3·72	196,791	2 6·39	...	...	1,047,748	4 1·56		
1831-32	4,463,352	2 3·02	169,909	2 6·78	1,065	2 6·87	1,243,758	3 10·31		

No. VII.—A Return of the Rates of Duty on Glass in 1813, with the Quantities of each kind of Glass retained for Home Use, and the aggregate Nett Revenue, in each Year from 1813 to 1842, both included, noting the Periods when any Alteration of the Duty took place, and the Amount of such Alterations.

Years. Rate of Duty in 1813, per Cwt.	Flint. 98s.	Plate. 98s.	Crown. 73s. 6d.	German Sheet. 73s. 6d.	Broad. 30s.	Common Bottle. 8s. 2d.	Total.	Period and Amount of Alteration of Duty.	Aggregate Nett Revenue.
	Cwts.	Cwts.	Cwts.	Cwts.	Cwts.	Cwts.	Cwts.		£
	Quantities of Glass retained for Home Use.								
1813	23,370	9,398	84,441	•	6,994	47,350	171,553		500,850
1814	24,227	6,778	84,251	•	8,628	140,252	264,136		530,791
1815	24,911	419	77,485	•	8,452	129,461	240,728		473,780
1816	20,011	•	56,151	•	6,140	160,221	242,523		353,188
1817	22,117	1,739	76,561	•	8,374	123,881	232,692		461,849
1818	26,978	6,391	88,893	•	8,319	201,795	332,376		584,399
1819	28,809	6,473	90,726	•	8,267	238,463	372,738	From 5th July, 1819, the duty on plate glass reduced from 4l. 18s. to 3l. per cwt.	606,176
1820	24,745	8,735	74,183	•	7,782	171,495	286,940		500,595
1821	21,927	9,718	86,384	•	8,035	137,117	263,181		521,075
1822	21,400	9,562	95,510	•	8,353	154,492	289,317		559,029
1823	21,829	11,607	101,392	•	9,172	198,456	342,456		607,378
1824	24,954	13,543	123,845	•	9,295	238,725	410,362		728,342
1825	34,184	15,082	140,298	•	8,347	251,932	449,843	From 5th July, 1825, the duty of 4l. 18s. on flint glass repealed, and a new duty of 12l. 10s. for every 1,000 lbs. of fluxed materials for flint glass imposed.	772,303
1826	47,090	12,527	115,731	•	8,113	282,512	465,973		720,920
1827	46,688	14,209	114,381	•	7,611	239,794	422,683	•	699,726

No. VII.—Return of Rates of Duty on Glass in 1813, &c.—*continued.*

Years.	Quantities of Glass retained for Home Use.							Period and Amount of Alteration of Duty.	Aggregate Nett Revenue.
	Flint.	Plate.	Crown.	German Sheet.	Broad.	Common Bottle.	Total.		
	Cwts.	*Cwts.*	*Cwts.*	*Cwts.*	*Cwts.*	*Cwts.*	*Cwts.*		£
1828	54,255	17,096	121,158	.	6,970	254,787	454,266	From 5th July, 1828, the duty on common bottle glass reduced in Great Britain from 8s. 2d. to 7s. per cwt., and the duty on every description of glass assimilated throughout the United Kingdom.	752,097
1829	50,869	13,925	92,252	.	6,864	218,901	382,811		609,406
1830	49,353	12,677	80,926	.	4,845	180,945	328,746		542,261
1831	49,608	14,373	88,688	.	5,915	150,520	299,104		531,718
1832	51,586	11,554	86,007	179	5,304	158,719	313,349	From 10th October, 1832, the duty on fluxed materials for flint glass reduced from 12l. 10s. per 1,000 lbs. to 20s. for every 100 lbs.	558,423
1833	54,818	13,893	105,134	.	6,306	164,000	344,151		645,781
1834	52,890	16,306	106,389	.	6,766	194,143	376,494		664,391
1835	43,936	16,941	111,651	4,248	5,847	201,613	384,236	From 10th October, 1835, the duty on fluxed materials for flint glass reduced from 20s. to 6s. 8d. per 100 lbs.	640,149
1836	86,866	19,993	117,041	.	7,629	249,145	480,674		663,162
1837	78,121	21,640	101,309	707	7,190	247,446	456,413		608,993
1838	81,594	23,992	113,756	2,262	6,575	243,046	471,225		667,998
1839	82,309	26,465	113,340	5,170	8,514	252,808	488,606		691,467
1840	82,486	31,200	111,316	7,914	9,049	232,834	473,799	From 15th May, 1840, the duty on every description of glass increased 5 per cent.; and from 15th August, 1840, the duty on broad glass increased from 1l. 10s. to 3l. 13s. 6d. per cwt.	724,343
1841	74,444	22,088	93,033	11,298	.	190,257	391,120		613,588
1842	68,098	18,396	81,715	17,117	.	161,537	346,863		563,437

No. VIII.—ACCOUNT of the QUANTITIES of MALT charged with Duty in
ENGLAND and WALES, of the Revenue received thereon, and of the
Rates of Duty, in each Year from 1702.

Years.	Number of Bushels of Malt.	Amount of Duty.			Rate of Duty per Bushel.
		£.	s.	d.	
1702	12,166,778	313,907	5	0	6½d.
1703	26,754,505	691,577	4	11	,,
1704	19,765,042	512,735	4	4	,,
1705	27,120,982	702,957	11	1	,,
1706	23,099,630	599,477	3	7	,,
1707	25,002,855	648,846	15	2	,,
1708	23,209,966	602,837	5	0	,,
1709	20,275,335	527,355	19	10	,,
1710	19,671,021	511,954	10	6	,,
1711	22,263,126	578,839	19	1	,,
1712	22,313,483	580,168	16	7	,,
1713	25,060,639	650,932	14	4	,,
1714	20,019,767	520,771	7	0	,,
1715	24,472,610	635,330	18	6	,,
1716	26,643,119	691,293	18	3	,,
1717	28,859,926	748,583	19	6	,,
1718	26,862,157	697,166	1	3	,,
1719	28,228,627	732,535	7	8	,,
1720	25,625,844	665,527	1	9	,,
1721	28,587,391	741,901	0	6	,,
1722	32,999,688	855,860	18	7	,,
1723	30,655,498	795,352	8	0	,,
1724	24,227,667	629,502	12	2	,,
1725	27,265,172	707,467	12	3	,,
1726	27,016,303	700,933	19	1	,,
1727	25,401,576	659,331	15	3	,,
1728	20,951,269	544,457	12	8	,,
1729	23,032,216	597,847	5	11	,,
1730	28,410,421	736,815	8	0	,,
1731	25,833,240	670,180	4	3	,,
1732	26,980,568	699,381	8	7	,,
1733	29,795,100	772,109	2	9	,,
1734	27,087,437	702,291	16	3	,,
1735	25,494,686	661,259	17	3	,,
1736	23,661,561	613,919	1	0	,,
1737	24,491,366	635,278	9	4	,,
1738	26,145,413	677,866	0	2	,,
1739	26,716,197	692,787	2	0	,,
1740	22,074,674	573,059	9	7	,,
1741	20,141,254	523,182	5	4	,,
1742	25,879,389	671,011	6	3	,,
1743	26,298,391	681,740	7	11	,,
1744	31,776,789	822,943	12	5	,,
1745	24,917,869	645,998	13	5	,,
1746	23,955,350	621,048	17	10	,,
1747	24,886,567	645,029	4	1	,,
1748	26,422,650	684,653	10	8	,,

No. VIII.—Account of the Quantities of Malt charged with Duty in England and Wales, &c.—*continued.*

Years.	Number of Bushels of Malt.	Amount of Duty.			Rate of Duty per Bushel.
		£.	s.	d.	
1749	24,966,250	646,946	18	5	$6\frac{16}{21}d.$
1750	29,284,786	758,396	18	1	,,
1751	26,994,880	699,318	11	8	,,
1752	24,280,058	629,314	13	7	,,
1753	25,240,816	654,430	16	1	,,
1754	27,347,890	708,255	4	1	,,
1755	27,916,402	722,732	2	5	,,
1756	24,120,284	624,851	4	9	,,
1757	17,640,926	457,719	16	8	,,
1758	25,027,614	648,173	14	6	,,
1759	28,090,252	727,158	15	7	,,
1760	27,810,971	999,818	11	11	$6\frac{16}{21}d.—9\frac{12}{421}d.$
1761	28,928,960	1,123,040	17	2	$9\frac{12}{421}d.$
1762	25,951,676	1,007,851	13	11	,,
1763	19,557,812	760,388	16	4	,,
1764	26,331,702	1,023,554	9	3	,,
1765	25,631,086	996,756	19	8	,,
1766	20,823,576	810,544	16	10	,,
1767	21,894,498	851,648	11	10	,,
1768	27,124,938	1,054,188	0	10	,,
1769	26,546,052	1,031,799	11	2	,,
1770	24,452,960	950,827	12	6	,,
1771	21,961,057	854,344	11	6	,,
1772	27,538,150	1,070,125	14	9	,,
1773	21,467,926	835,713	9	10	,,
1774	23,949,905	931,968	14	2	,,
1775	24,967,360	971,085	8	2	,,
1776	23,336,298	1,024,336	2	5	,,
1777	25,814,436	˙1,004,050	9	3	,,
1778	26,318,736	1,022,950	9	1	,,
1779	26,273,405	1,028,083	1	6	$9\frac{12}{421}d.—9\frac{14}{23}d.$
1780	30,805,100	1,534,454	14	5	$9\frac{14}{23}d.—1s.\ 4\frac{1}{4}d.$
1781	26,718,048	1,817,556	7	4	$1s.\ 4\frac{1}{4}d.$
1782	27,159,104	1,846,108	11	10	,,
1783	16,712,114	1,138,782	16	0	,,
1784	25,796,105	1,745,953	19	8	,,
1785	26,269,439	1,777,917	15	2	,,
1786	22,074,334	1,493,548	2	3	,,
1787	26,439,578	1,789,780	3	9	,,
1788	26,048,072	1,763,277	17	8	,,
1789	23,509,592	1,591,463	15	6	,,
1790	21,976,959	1,487,775	6	0	,,
1791	27,070,363	2,092,191	15	10	$1s.\ 4\frac{1}{4}d.—1s.\ 7\frac{1}{2}d.$
	Stock in hand	46,716	18	3	
1792	27,789,166	2,142,950	12	10	$1s.\ 7\frac{1}{2}d.—1s.\ 4\frac{1}{4}d.$
1793	23,706,765	1,604,717	9	9	$1s.\ 4\frac{1}{4}d.$
1794	24,813,341	1,679,222	8	6	,,
1795	23,960,822	1,620,515	7	6	,,
1796	27,282,973	1,846,819	5	9	,,
1797	29,979,110	2,029,349	7	11	,,
1798	26,143,432	1,769,476	13	11	,,

No. VIII.—Account of the Quantities of Malt charged with Duty in England and Wales, &c.—*continued.*

Years.	Number of Bushels of Malt.	Amount of Duty.			Rate of Duty per Bushel.
		£.	s.	d.	
1799	30,805,822	2,083,701	14	0	1s. 4d¼.
1800	14,049,740	950,296	18	5	,,
1801	18,005,786	1,218,455	16	7	,,
1802	29,432,584	2,175,406	18	4	1s. 4¼d.—2s. 5d.
Stock in hand		466,633	8	7	
1803	29,562,038	3,555,906	18	0	2s. 5d.—4s. 5¾d.
1804	21,854,111	4,858,056	9	4	4s. 5¾d.
Stock in hand		914,356	0	0	
1805	21,665,204	4,841,066	15	0	,,
1806	26,652,425	5,955,716	0	0	,,
1807	24,158,843	5,397,635	6	4	,,
1808	21,726,415	4,854,698	2	4	,,
1809	22,120,984	4,942,771	7	8	,,
1810	23,546,346	5,261,362	12	0	,,
1811	25,982,749	5,806,251	15	0	,,
1812	18,092,965	4,042,716	16	4	,,
1813	21,701,356	4,849,419	5	0	,,
1814	25,320,615	5,657,228	8	4	,,
1815	26,246,795	5,865,606	18	8	,,
1816	21,158,348	4,217,259	13	1	4s. 5¾d.—2s. 5d.
1817	20,855,566	2,509,817	18	4	2s. 5d.
1818	24,629,838	2,964,024	12	10	,,
1819	22,612,290	3,268,881	3	2	2s. 5d.—3s. 7¼d.
Stock in hand		420,263	8	8	,,
1820	25,884,242	4,311,446	5	1	3s. 7¼d.
1821	26,138,437	4,718,360	10	0	,,
1822	26,688,512	3,624,242	8	0	3s. 7¼d.—2s. 7d.
1823	24,845,152	3,203,502	17	6	2s. 7d.
1824	27,615,383	3,560,693	0	0	,,
1825	29,572,741	3,813,072	7	6	,,
1826	27,335,971	3,530,895	10	8	,,
1827	25,096,337	3,241,610	3	11	,,
1828	30,517,819	3,941,884	19	1	,,
1829	23,428,135	3,026,133	19	6	,,
1830	26,900,902	3,474,699	16	10	,,
1831	32,963,470	4,257,781	10	10	,,
1832	31,669,771	4,090,678	15	1	,,
1833	33,789,010	4,364,413	15	10	,,
1834	34,449,646	4,449,745	0	0	,,
1835	36,078,855	4,660,185	0	0	,,
1836	37,196,998	4,804,612	0	0	,,
1837	33,692,356	4,351,929	8	3	,,
1838	33,823,985	4,368,931	8	8	,,
1839	33,826,016	4,369,193	14	8	,,
1840	36,653,442	4,841,229	18	0	2s. 7d.—2s. 7d. and 5 per cent.
1841	30,956,394	4,198,460	18	4	2s. 7d. 5 p. cent.
1842	30,796,262	4,176,742	19	0	,,

No. IX.—Account of the Quantities of Malt charged with Duty in Scotland, of the Revenue received thereon, and of the Rates of Duty, in each Year from 1793.

Years.	Number of Bushels of Malt.	Amount of Duty.	Rate of Duty per Bushel.	
		£.		
1793	1,715,381	58,164	8⅓*d.*	
1794	1,675,741	56,823	,,	
1795	1,692,946	57,419	,,	
1796	1,203,023	40,829	,,	
1797	2,085,672	79,670	,,	
1798	1,934,396	65,560	,,	
1799	2,365,897	80,075	,,	
1800	876,598	29,670	,,	
1801	607,384	20,560	,,	
1802	1,716,278	70,527	1*s.* 8⅔*d.*	
	Stock in hand	20,389		
			From Barley.	From Bigg.
1803	1,594,284	137,878		
1804	1,091,377	197,587	3*s.* 9½*d.*	3*s.* 1¼*d.*
	Stock in hand	34,808	,,	,,
1805	1,136,112	206,935	,,	,,
1806	1,244,104	225,642	,,	,,
1807	1,259,298	226,647	,,	,,
1808	1,048,946	189,934	,,	,,
1809	772,758	139,852	,,	,,
1810	820,294	149,206	,,	,,
1811	1,012,236	184,882	,,	,,
1812	934,452	169,870	,,	,,
1813	685,244	123,705	,,	,,
1814	1,266,852	231,776	,,	,,
1815	1,297,777	236,839	3*s.* 9½*d.*	3*s.* 1¼*d.*
1816	1,162,024	164,743	3*s.* 9½*d.* to 1*s.* 8¾*d.*	3*s.* 1¼*d.* to 1*s.* 8¾*d.*
1817	1,093,678	94,599	1*s.* 8¾*d.*	1*s.* 8¾*d.*
1818	1,390,515	120,274	,,	,,

Years.	Number of Bushels of Malt.	Amount of Duty.	Rate of Duty per Bushel.	
		£.	From Barley.	From Bigg.
1819	1,454,320	179,266	1*s.* 8¾*d.*—3*s.* 7½*d.*	1*s.* 8¾*d.*—3*s.* 7¼*d.*
	Stock in hand	17,739		
1820	1,182,208	212,282	3*s.* 7¼*d.*	3*s.* 7¼*d.*—3*s.* 1*d.*
1821	1,305,659	231,606	,,	3*s.* 1*d.*—2*s.* 10*d.*
1822	1,403,177	183,032	3*s.* 7¼*d.*—2*s.* 7*d.*	2*s.* 10*d.*—1*s.* 9½*d.* —2*s.*
1823	1,616,590	198,696	2*s.* 7*d.*	2*s.*
1824	2,788,608	335,505	,,	,,
1825	3,925,847	462,144	,,	,,
1826	2,726,555	335,574	,,	,,
1827	2,714,073	335,489	,,	,,
1828	3,867,159	478,508	,,	,,
1829	3,712,563	457,588	,,	,,
1830	4,101,946	505,651	,,	,,
1831	4,186,955	515,579	,,	,,
1832	3,714,334	458,096	,,	,,
1833	4,302,036	530,358	,,	,,
1834	4,491,292	553,567	,,	,,
1835	4,459,553	551,096	,,	,,
1836	4,903,187	611,910	,,	,,
1837	4,563,045	578,515	,,	,,
1838	4,419,141	557,913	,,	,,
1839	4,360,363	552,107	,,	,,
1840	4,397,304	572,544	2*s.* 7*d.*—2*s.* 7*d.* and 5 per cent.	2*s.*,—2*s.* and 5 per cent.
1841	4,058,249	539,572	2*s.* 7*d.* & 5 p. cent	2*s.* and 5 p. cent.
1842	3,786,476	503,829	,,	,,

No. X.—ACCOUNT of the QUANTITIES of MALT charged with Duty in IRELAND, of the Revenue received thereon, and of the Rates of Duty, in each Year from 1790.

Years.	Number of Bushels of Malt.	Amount of Duty.	Rate of Duty per Bushel.
1790	4,607,953	£.135,496	7d.
1791	4,775,390	140,412	,,
1792	4,676,835	137,522	,,
1793	5,039,899	148,197	,,
1794	4,873,984	186,315	9¼d.
	Stock in hand	17,672	
1795	4,697,153	290,051	1s. 3d.
	Stock in hand	36,761	
1796	4,956,584	306,070	,,
1797	4,672,989	288,558	,,
1798	4,413,817	313,661	1s. 5d.
	Stock in hand	19,768	
1799	3,311,463	253,170	1s. 6¼d.
	Stock in hand	12,226	
1800	681,340	52,090	,,
1801	1,030,175	78,760	,,
1802	3,611,579	276,115	,,
1803	3,553,762	283,584	1s. 6¼d.—1s. 9½d.
	Stock in hand	31,162	
1804	2,807,535	270,036	1s. 9½d.—2s. 9½d.
	Stock in hand	28,698	
1805	2,766,867	317,299	2s. 3½d.
1806	2,814,418	334,105	2s. 3½d.—2s. 6¾d.
	Stock in hand	22,220	
1807	2,372,293	302,281	2s. 6¾d.
1808	2,597,758	331,010	,,
1809	2,958,617	376,991	,,
1810	2,522,543	321,425	,,
1811	2,681,842	341,723	,,
1812	2,206,206	281,117	2s. 6¾d.
1813	2,967,603	428,830	2s. 6¾d.—3s. 3¾d.
	Stock in hand	63,406	

Years.	Number of Bushels of Malt.	Amount of Duty.	Rate of Duty per Bushel.	
1814	3,156,175	522,813	3s. 3¼d.	
1815	2,664,466	482,685	3s. 3⅜d.—4s. 5d.	
	Stock in hand	122,233		
1816	1,879,721	359,809	4s. 5d.—2s. 4½d.	
1817	1,385,486	164,771	2s. 4½d.	
1818	1,783,636	211,930	,,	
1819	1,742,444	207,096	,,	
1820	1,793,671	319,684	3s. 6¾d.	
	Stock in hand	43,974		
1821	1,949,315	347,424	,,	
1822	1,756,391	275,614	3s. 6¾d.—2s. 7d.	
1823	1,702,395	217,302	2s. 7d.	
1824	2,107,752	276,255	,,	
1825	2,706,862	356,108	,,	
1826	2,406,253	310,808	,,	
1827	1,803,091	232,899	,,	
1828	2,409,228	311,192	,,	
1829	2,012,079	259,894	,,	
			From Barley.	From Bigg.
1830	1,959,606	251,646	2s. 7d.	2s.
1831	2,101,844	263,308	,,	,,
1832	2,006,350	250,278	,,	,,
1833	1,984,849	245,987	,,	,,
1834	2,204,653	272,291	,,	,,
1835	2,353,645	288,602	,,	,,
1836	2,287,635	283,357	,,	,,
1837	2,275,347	286,470	,,	,,
1838	2,262,440	284,954	,,	,,
1839	1,744,550	218,503	,,	,,
1840	1,406,116	178,703	2s. 7d.—2s. 7d. and 5 per cent.	2s.—2s., and 5 per cent.
1841	1,149,692	151,210	2s. 7d. & 5 p. cent.	2s. and 5 per cent.
1842	1,268,656	168,009	,,	,,

No. XI.—An Account of the Articles subject to the Excise Duties in England and Scotland in 1815, specifying the Rates of Duty on each, and the Nett Produce of the Duties (omitting the Articles that have been since transferred to the Customs).

[By contrasting this account with that ou page 234 the reader will see the reductions effected in the Excise Duties since 1815.]

Articles.	RATES OF DUTY.	Nett Produce of Duty in England.	Nett Produce of Duty in Scotland.	Nett Produce of Duty in GreatBritain.
		£.	£.	£.
Auctions....	Estates, Houses, &c. . . . . .7d. in the £ Furniture, &c. . . . . 1s. ditto Sheep's Wool . . . . 2d. ditto First Sales of Foreign Produce ¼ per cent.	263,848	14,779	278,627
Beer	Strong . . . . 10s. per barrel Table . . . . 2s.　　,,	3,235,847	94,013	3,329,860
Bricks...... and Tiles	Common. . . . . 5s. 10d. pr. 1000 Large . . . . 10s.　　,, Polished . . . . 12s. 10d.　,, Ditto, exceeding 10 inches } same as 　long and 5 inches wide . } paving tiles Plain . . . . 5s. 8d. per 1000 Pan or Ridge . . . . 12s. 10d.　　,, Paving, small . . . . 2s. 5d. per 100 Ditto, large . . . . 4s. 10d.　　,, All other . . . . 4s. 10d. per 1000	262,065	6,949	269,014
Candles	Tallow . . . . 1d. per lb. Wax and Spermaceti . . 3½d.　,,	335,044	19,323	354,367
Cyder, Perry, and Verjuice	Cyder and Perry . . . . . 1l. 10s. per hhd. Verjuice . . . . 7s. 8d.　　,,	19,302	3	19,305
Glass.......	Flint. . . . . 4l. 18s. per cwt. Crown or German Sheet . . 3l. 13s. 6d. ,, Plate (materials used) . . . . 4l. 18s.　　,, Broad . . . . 1l. 10s.　　,, Common Bottles . . . . . . 8s. 2d. ,,	366,678	57,466	424,144
Hides and Skins.......	_Tanned._ All Hides whatsoever . . . . 3d. per lb. Calf-skins, Dog-skins, &c. . . 3d.　　,, Goat-skins with Shumack . . 8s. per doz. Sheep-skins for roans . . . 4s. 6d.　,, Ditto for gloves . . . . 3d. per lb. Other Skins, & parts & pieces 1s.　　,, _Tawed._ Horse-hides. . . . . 3s. per hide Cow hides . . . . 6s.　　,, Calf-skins, Kip, & Seal-skins 3d. per lb. Slink Calf with hair . . . . . 6s. per doz. Ditto without hair, &c.. . . . 2s.　　,, Buck and Doe-skins. . . . . 1s. per lb. Goat and Beaver . . . . . . 4s. per doz. Sheep and Lamb . . . . . 2¼d. per lb. Other Skins, & parts & pieces 1s.　　,, _Dressed in Oil._ Buck, Deer, and Elk-skins. . 1s. per lb. Sheep and Lamb-skins. . . . 6d.　　,, All other Hides . . . . 6d.　　,, All other Skins, & parts & pieces 1s.　,, Vellum. . . . . 7s. per doz. Parchment . . . . 3s. 6d. ,,	637,771	60,375	698,146
Hops. . . Licences....	. . . . 2d. per lb. Iuserted at the end	222,025 693,354	・ ・ 85,486	222,025 778,840
Malt	From Barley . { England . 4s. 4d. per bush. 　　　　　　{ Scotland . 3s. 8d.　　,, From Bear or Bigg, Scotland 3s.　　,,	5,830,588	235,807	6,066,395
Paper	First Class . . . . 3d. per lb, Second Class . . . . 1½d.　,, Glazed Paper, &c.. . . . . 1l. 1s. per cwt.	418,248	47,958	466,206
	Carried forward . . ⸱.	12,284,770	622,159	12,906,929

Articles.	RATES OF DUTY.	Nett Produce of Duty in England.	Nett Produce of Duty in Scotland.	Nett Produce of Duty in Great Britain.
		£.	£.	£.
	Brought forward	12,284,770	622,159	12,906,929
Printed Goods	British Manufactures . . . . 3½d. per yard Foreign Calicos . . . . 7d. ,, Linens and Stuffs . . . . . . 3½d. ,, Silks. . . . . 6d. ,, Stained Paper. . . . . 1½d. ,,	280,482	107,317	387,799
Salt.	Salt in England. . . . . . . 15s. per bushel Ditto in Scotland . . . . . . 8s. 6d. ,, Salt imported . . . . 20s. ,, Mineral Alkali . . . . 30s. per ton.	1,471,312	100,167	1,571,479
Soap	Hard . . . . 2¼d. per lb. Soft . . . . 1¾d. ,,	625,039	86,612	711,651
Spirits......	*England.* From Corn . . . . 9s. 2½d. per gall. From Scotland . . . . 9s. 5½d. ,, From Ireland . . . . 9s. 10½d. ,, *Scotland.* From Corn . . . . 8s. 1 . ,,	2,179,832	752,039	2,931,871
Starch......	. . . . 3½d. per lb.	45,308	2,006	47,314
Stone Bottles	. . . . 2s. 6d. per cwt.	1,887	2	1,889
Sweets and	Mead . . . . 2l. 9s. per barrel	20,803	213	21,016
Vinegar	. . . . 15s. ,,	46,686	891	47,577
Wire	Gilt . . . . 1s. 8d. per oz Silver . . . . 1s. 2d. ,,	10,047	. .	10,047
	Total	16,966,166	1,671,406	18,637,572

Rate per cent. at which the Nett Produce was collected, £3 12s.

RATES OF DUTY ON LICENCES.

	Per Annum. £.	s.
Auctioneers.	0	12
Common Brewers of Table-beer only	2	0
Common Brewers (according to the quantity brewed) . . . from	2	5
to	75	0
Retailers of Beer, Cyder, or Perry . .	4	4
Makers of Wax or Spermaceti Candles	12	0
Sellers of ditto	1	1
Makers of Candles other than Wax or Spermaceti	2	0
Dealers in Coffee, Tea, Cocoa-nuts, or Chocolate	0	11
Glass Makers, for every Glass-house	20	0
Tanners within the Bills of Mortality	10	0
Ditto elsewhere	5	0
Tawers	2	0
Oiled Leather Dressers	4	0
Curriers	4	0
Makers of Vellum or Parchment . . .	2	0
Maltsters (according to the quantity made). from 7s. 6d. to	4	10
Makers of Mead or Metheglin . . .	2	0
Paper Makers	4	0
Paper Stainers	4	0
Dealers in Plate, under 2 ozs. of Gold and 30 ozs. of Silver	4	12
Ditto, above that weight, Pawnbrokers and Refiners	11	10
Calico, &c. Printers	20	0
Printers of Silks	20	0

	Per Annum. £.	s.
Soap Makers	4	0
Distillers . . . . England . .	20	0
Scotland . .	10	0
Rectifiers . . . . England . .	10	0
Scotland . .	5	0
Spirit Dealers	10	0
Retailers of Spirits (according to the Rent of the Premises) from	7	1
to	10	13
Starch Makers	10	0
Makers of Sweets or made-Wines . .	10	0
Retailers of ditto	4	8
Manufacturers of Tobacco and Snuff . . . . from	3	0
to	30	0
Dealers in ditto within the limits of the Chief Office in London or Edinburgh	0	10
Ditto elsewhere	0	5
Vinegar Makers	20	0
Dealers in Foreign Wine, not having a Licence to retail Spirits or Beer . .	10	8
Ditto, having a Licence to retail Beer but not Spirits	8	8
Ditto, having a Licence to retail Beer and Spirits	4	8
Wire Drawers	4	0
Dealers in plain Aqua vitæ only, (Scotland)	6	0
Retailers of ditto In the Highlands	2	0
In the Lowlands .	4	0

Excise-Office, London,
30 *November*, 1844.

No. XII.—An Account of the Articles subject to the Excise Duties in Ireland in 1815, specifying the Rates of Duty on each, and the Nett Produce of the Duties (omitting the Articles that have been since transferred to the Customs).

Articles.	RATES OF DUTY.	Gross Produce of Duty in Ireland.
		British Currency. £.
Auctions....	Estates, Houses, &c.. . . . . 6d. in the £ Furniture, &c. . . . . 10d. ,, Sheep's Wool . . . . 2d. ,,	6,802
Glass.......	Bottles. . . . . 3d. per doz.	388
Hides and Skins.	*Tanned.* All Hides and Skins tanned with Bark . 9d. per annum, per cubic foot of or tan pit. . . . . Goat and Sheep-skins tanned with Shumack 1d. per lb. Bazil Sheep and Lamb-skins . . . . . . ½d. ,, Horse Hides. . . . . 1s. each Veal and Hog-skins . . . . 5s. per dozen. Shoe and Seal-skins . . . . 2s. 6d. ,, Skins for Bookbinders . . . . 1s. ,, Vellum . . . . 6d. ,, Parchment · . . . . 3d. ,, *Dressed in Oil.* Deer, Goat, and Beaver . . . . 3d. per lb. Calf-skins. . . . . 2d. ,, Sheep and Lamb-skins . . . . ½d. ,, All other and parts and pieces . . . . 2d. ,,	40,694
Licences....	Nearly the same as in England	85,297
Malt	. . . . 17s. 4d. per barrel	604,918
Paper	First Class . . . . 3d. per lb. Second Class . . . . 1d. ,, Glazed Paper . . . . 5s. per cwt. Pasteboard . . . . 20s. ,, or For every Engine, Vat, and Wet Press . . 10s. per annum per cubic foot	16,852
Printed Goods	Stained Paper . . . . 1½d. per squ. yard or · For every Table used. . . . . 4l. 3s. 4d. p. month	1,438
Spirits......	Home made . . . . 6s. per gallon	1,312,908
Sweets and Mead	Mead or Metheglin . . . . 4d. per gallon Wine, Home made . . . . 2l. 7s. per barrel	250
Vinegar.....	. . . . 3s. per barrel	304
Wrought Plate ...	. . . . 1s. per ounce	3,524
	Total Gross Produce.	2,073,375
	Deduct Drawbacks and other Repayments . .	38,444
	Nett Produce of Duty in Ireland	2,034,931

Note—The Nett Produce of the respective Duties cannot be ascertained from the Accounts made up at this period.

Excise Office, London,
  30th November, 1844.

No. XIII.—STATEMENT of the QUANTITIES of the Different Descriptions of WINE entered for Consumption, the RATES of DUTY, and the TOTAL AMOUNT of the DUTY, in each YEAR from 1784 to 1843 inclusive.—(From the Circular of Messrs. Shaw and Maxwell.)

Year.		Years.	Portuguese.		Spanish.		Madeira.		Teneriffe.		Sicilian.		Cape.		French.		Rhenish.		Total Gallons.	Revenue.
			Gallons entered for Consumption.	Rate of Duty.	Gallons entered for Consumption.	Rate of Duty.	Gallons entered for Consumption.	Rate of Duty.	Gallons entered for Consumption.	Rate of Duty.	Gallons entered for Consumption.	Rate of Duty.	Gallons entered for Consumption.	Rate of Duty.	Gallons entered for Consumption.	Rate of Duty.	Gallons entered for Consumption.	Rate of Duty.		
From	To			s. d.		s. d.		s. d.		s. d.		s. d.		s. d.		s. d.		s. d.		£.
1784	1785	2	2,602,110	4 2½	619,920	4 10	. .	..	. .	..	. .	..	. .	..	97,230	9 2	31,080	5 2½	. .	625,454
1786	1794	9	4,180,890	3 1¾	921,270	3 1¾	196,140	3 1¾	20,370	3 1¾	5,460	3 1¾	. .	..	179,970	4 10	20,790	—	5,524,890	889,031
	1795	1	5,161,170	5 0½	1,610,280	5 0½	122,430	5 0½	27,930	5 0½	2,730	6 5	. .	..	96,180	7 8½	1,050	7 1¼	7,021,770	1,430,722
	1796	1	2,909,970	6 11	1,123,290	6 11	78,330	6 11	25,410	6 11	18,270	8 3	. .	..	34,020	10 6¾	420	9 0¼	4,189,710	1,159,523
1797	1802	6	4,136,580	—	1,058,820	—	167,790	—	22,050	—	—	—	. .	..	53,760	—	10,710	—	5,449,710	1,723,339
	1803	1	5,616,240	8 4	1,319,010	8 4	311,220	8 4	23,310	8 4	34,860	—	. .	..	135,450	12 7½	7,770	10 2	7,447,860	2,141,356
	1804	1	1,821,540	8 10	1,287,510	8 10	186,690	8 10	34,650	8 10	—	—	. .	..	16,170	13 9	1,260	10 11	3,347,820	2,814,323
1805	1814	10	3,773,070	9 1	1,464,120	9 1	353,050	9 2½	200,340	9 1	123,690	9 1	. .	..	90,930	—	9,030	11 3	6,015,030	1,974,102
1815	1820	6	2,525,460	—	828,540	—	359,940	—	175,770	—	55,020	—	441,630	3 0	156,450	—	21,420	—	4,564,140	1,931,865
	1821	1	2,343,509	—	959,834	—	400,476	—	160,350	—	69,102	—	572,131	—	159,462	—	21,991	—	4,686,885	1,797,491
	1822	1	2,375,210	—	967,149	—	341,916	—	129,620	—	66,025	—	538,847	—	168,732	—	19,500	—	4,606,999	1,704,013
	1823	1	2,492,212	—	1,078,922	—	323,734	—	123,036	—	79,686	—	555,119	—	171,681	—	25,670	—	4,845,060	1,907,466
	1824	1	2,512,343	—	1,217,034	—	297,479	—	117,428	—	77,085	—	595,299	—	187,477	—	25,976	—	5,030,091	1,967,953
	1825	1	4,200,719	4 10	1,830,975	4 10	372,524	4 10	167,108	4 10	134,609	4 10	670,639	2 5	525,579	7 3	107,299	4 10	8,009,542	1,815,053
	1826	1	2,833,688	—	1,622,580	—	286,275	—	134,445	—	140,318	—	630,436	—	343,707	—	66,994	—	6,058,443	1,270,118
	1827	1	3,222,192	—	1,908,331	—	300,295	—	152,938	—	156,721	—	698,434	—	311,289	—	76,161	—	6,826,361	1,426,550
	1828	1	3,307,921	—	2,097,628	—	272,977	—	137,553	—	186,537	—	652,286	—	421,469	—	86,905	—	7,162,376	1,506,122
	1829	1	2,682,084	—	1,964,162	—	229,322	—	101,699	—	219,172	—	579,744	—	365,336	—	76,396	—	6,217,652	1,292,402
	1830	1	2,869,608	—	2,081,423	—	217,138	—	101,892	—	252,513	—	535,255	—	308,294	—	63,322	—	6,434,445	1,351,607
	1831	1	2,707,734	5 6	2,089,532	5 6	209,127	5 6	94,803	5 6	259,916	5 6	539,584	2 9	254,366	5 6	57,888	5 6	6,212,264	1,356,208
	1832	1	2,617,405	—	2,080,099	—	159,898	—	72,803	—	254,251	—	514,262	—	228,627	—	38,197	—	5,965,542	1,519,643
	1833	1	2,596,530	—	2,246,085	—	161,042	—	69,621	—	312,993	—	545,191	—	232,550	—	43,758	—	6,207,770	1,629,219
	1834	1	2,780,303	—	2,279,854	—	150,369	—	62,186	—	372,744	—	524,081	—	260,630	—	50,377	—	6,480,544	1,705,520
	1835	1	2,780,024	—	2,230,187	—	139,422	—	52,862	—	374,549	—	522,941	—	271,661	—	48,696	—	6,420,342	1,691,522
	1836	1	2,878,359	—	2,388,413	—	133,673	—	54,584	—	403,155	—	541,511	—	352,063	—	59,454	—	6,811,212	1,793,963
	1837	1	2,573,157	—	2,297,070	—	119,873	—	42,146	—	373,458	—	500,727	—	440,322	—	44,807	—	6,391,560	1,687,097
	1838	1	2,900,457	—	2,497,538	—	110,294	—	97,979	—	370,610	—	538,528	—	417,281	—	57,584	—	6,990,271	1,846,056
	1839	1	2,921,422	—	2,578,997	—	118,715	—	35,178	—	369,417	—	534,182	—	378,636	—	63,937	—	7,000,486	1,849,699
	1840	1	2,668,534	5 9	2,500,760	5 9	112,555	5 9	29,489	5 9	383,774	5 9	456,773	2 11	341,841	5 9	60,056	5 9	6,553,992	1,872,799
	1841	1	2,387,017	—	2,412,821	—	107,701	—	25,772	—	401,439	—	441,238	—	353,740	—	55,242	—	6,184,960	1,800,127
	1842	1	1,288,953	—	2,261,786	—	65,209	—	21,169	—	393,028	—	370,800	—	360,692	—	53,585	—	4,815,222	1,409,205
	1843	1	2,517,709	—	2,311,639	—	95,589	—	20,597	—	416,643	—	332,369	—	326,498	—	49,943	—	6,068,987	1,704,434

REMARKS ON PRECEDING TABLE.

Until 1814, Duties were charged per Tun, in accordance with which our calculations have been made, and the rate per Tun, and per *old* Gallon, reduced to the rate per *Imperial* Gallon, throughout; and, although differing at the earliest periods from other statements, will, we believe, be found perfectly correct.

The Official Documents of the years 1784 and 1765, are evidently so imperfect, that we do not state the "Total Gallons."

The years from 1784 to 1820 include only England and Scotland. From 1821 Ireland is included.

We believe the amounts of Duty in 1842 and 1843 to be correctly calculated, but we cannot make them agree with the official statements.

The Consumption of Wine in Ireland was—In 1790, 1,117,556; 1800, 1,238,512; 1810, 1,127,200; 1815, 608,000; 1824, 467,000 Gallons.

From 1790 to 1814, Duties in Ireland were raised on "French" from 3s. 2d. to 13s. 9d. per Gallon, upwards of 400 per cent.; and on Port, &c. from 2s. 1d. to 9s., being 450 per cent.

The Population was in 1790, 3,000,000; and in 1824, 7,000,000. Duty received in 1790, 138,000l.; in 1824, 185,000l.

Prior to 1821, the quantities are calculated from the annual Importations, deducting the Exportations; after, and including 1821, from the Customs Returns of "Quantities retained for Home Consumption."

The Customs Records of 1813 were destroyed by fire.

The great apparent increase in "French" in the years 1836-7-8, is owing to the large quantity of Masdeu (a Wine resembling Port) introduced in those years.

Champagne, and various cheap sparkling Wines, now form a large proportion of " French," and appear to be displacing " Rhenish."

If a reduction on other Wines takes place, " Cape " will no longer be imported.

In the South of Europe sobriety may be said to be universal; but, even in those parts of the North where Wine and Spirits are extremely cheap, there is but little intemperance compared with that which still prevails in this kingdom, where the rates of the Duty on Spirits, and the per centage on the respective cost of each, according to quality, are as follows:—

United Kingdom .. {	Brandy and Geneva ...	22s. 10d.	from 300 to 1000 per cent.
	Rum	9s. 9d.	from 200 to 400 ,,
	Liqueurs ...:....... .	30s. 4d.	
Ireland and Scotland	Whisky—Corn Spirit...	3s. 8d.	About 200 per cent.
Ireland	Whisky—Malt Spirit...	5s. 0d.	About 330 ,,
Scotland	Whisky—Malt Spirit...	4s. 4d.	About 300 ,,
England......... {	Whisky—Corn Spirit...	7s. 10d.	About 500 ,,
	Whisky—Malt Spirit...	9s. 2d.	About 600 ,,

(Per Gallon.)

The consequence of such unequal, and (on Brandy and Geneva especially) such enormous Duties, is only what might be anticipated, extensive smuggling, illicit distillation, and every kind of fraud against the Revenue, the consumer, and the honest dealer.

Many yet remember the time when few Cellars in Scotland and Ireland were not filled with Wine (especially Claret), as well as Brandy and Geneva, little or none of which had paid duty. The Isle of Man was then a great smuggling dépôt for these and other parts of the kingdom.

RATES of DUTY per Gallon on all WINES, and DIFFERENTIAL DUTY per CENT. between FRENCH and other WINES, since 1671.

Years.	Duty on French.	Duty on Portuguese.	Duty on Spanish.	Duty on Rhenish.	Differential Duties per Cent. on French and other Wines.
	s. d.	s. d.	s. d.	s. d.	
1671	0 4	0 4	No Acct.	No Acct.	Equal.
1678	0 8	0 8	No Acct.	No Acct.	Equal.
1688	1 4	1 8	1 8	1 8	French 20 per Cent. less.
1693	2 1	1 8	1 8	1 8	,, 25 ,, more.
1697	4 10	2 0	2 1	2 5	,, 136 ,, ,,
1707	5 3	2 5	2 5	2 11	,, 115 ,, ,,
1745	6 0	2 9	2 9	3 4	,, 113 ,, ,,
1782	9 2	4 8¼	4 10	5 2	,, 109 ,, ,,
1786	4 10	3 1	3 1	5 2	,, 55 ,, ,,
1824	13 9	9 1	9 1	11 3	,, 50 ,, ,,
1825	7 3	4 10	4 10	4 10	,, 50 ,, ,,
1831	5 6	5 6	5 6	5 6	Equal.
1840	5 9	5 9	5 9	· 5 9	Equal.

AVERAGE ANNUAL REVENUE from WINE, with the NUMBER of GALLONS CONSUMED, the POPULATION, and the CONSUMPTION per INDIVIDUAL, during the last Fifty-nine Years, ending with 1843.

	From	Years.	Revenue.	Gallons.	Average Population	Average Consumption per Individual per Ann.
			£.			
England and Scotland.	1785 to 1794	10	889,031	5,524,890	9,300,000	3½ Bottles.
	1795 to 1804	10	1,788,595	5,470,542	10,400,000	3 do.
	1805 to 1814	10	1,974,102	6,015,030	12,100,000	3 do.
	1815 to 1820	6	1,931,865	1,564,140	12,900,000	2 do.
England, Ireland, and Scotland.	1821 to 1824	4	1,866,730	4,792,258	21,500,000	1 1-3rd do.
	1825 to 1840	16	1,600,843	6,608,925	25,400,000	1 3-5ths do.
	1841	1	1,800,127	6,184,960	26,715,920	1 2-5ths do.
	1842	1	1,409,205	6,815,222	26,965,900	1 1-9th do.
	1843	1	1,704,434	6,068,987	27,215,900	1 1-3rd do.

No. XIV.—AMOUNT of TAXES to be levied in FRANCE in 1842.

DIRECT TAXES.

The total of the Direct Taxes for the Year 1842 is 396,054,610 francs, divided as follows :—

FOR THE STATE :

	Francs.		£	s.	d.
On Land	187,509,600	=	7,500,384	0	0
Moveables	40,800,000	=	1,632,000	0	0
Doors and Windows	26,454,510	=	1,058,180	8	0
Patents (a direct tax on the exercise of a trade or profession)	31,066,000	=	1,242,640	0	0
	285,830,100	=	11,433,204	8	0

FOR THE PROVINCES :

	Francs.		£	s.	d.
On Land	52,606,280	=	2,104,251	4	0
Moveables	10,887,000	=	435,480	0	0
Doors and Windows	2,426,000	=	97,040	0	0
Patents	2,659,000	=	106,360	0	0
	68,578,280	=	2,743,131	4	0

FOR THE COMMUNES :

	Francs.		£	s.	d.
On Land	25,901,710	=	1,036,028	8	0
Moveables	3,808,340	=	152,333	12	0
Doors and Windows	1,300,040	=	52,001	12	0
Patents	1,699,500	=	59,620	0	0
	32,499,590	=	1,299,983	2	0

The taxes above stated should give the amount required ; but an additional sum to make good deficiencies is levied as follows :—

	Francs.		£	s.	d.
On Land	2,252,560	=	90,102	8	0
Moveables	740,000	=	29,600	0	0
Doors and Windows	745,350	=	29,814	0	0
Patents	4,710,000	=	188,400	0	0
	8,447,930	=	337,916 · 8	0	

When the taxes are collected, a sou is added to each charge to defray the expenses of the paper on which the demand is made; the total of this tax amounts to 698,700 *fr.* = 27,948*l.*

RECAPITULATION OF DIRECT TAXES:	Francs.	£	s.	d.
State .	285,830,110 =	11,433,204	8	4
Provinces .	68,578,280 =	2,743,131	4	2
Communes .	32,499,590 =	1,299,983	12	0
Additional Tax .	8,447,950 =	337,918	0	0
Charge for Paper	698,700 =	27,948	0	0
	396,054,610 =	15,842,184	8	6

INDIRECT TAXES.

FOR THE STATE:	Francs.	£	Francs.	£	s.	d.
Registration of Acts .	191,363,000 =	7,654,520				
Stamps . . .	34,475,000 =	1,379,000				
	225,838,000 =	9,033,520	230,882,500 =	9,235,300	0	0
Domains (sale and produce of) . .	5,044,500 =	201,780				
Woods and Fisheries	34,700,000 =	1,388,000	34,700,000 =	1,388,000	0	0
Customs . . .	117,848,000 =	4,713,920	123,629,000 =	4,945,160	0	0
Navigation . .	5,781,000 =	231,240				
Excise on — Salt . .	65,904,000 =	2,636,160				
Wine, Beer, &c. .	90,468,000 =	3,618,720				
Sugar .	7,425,000 =	297,000	264,413,000 =	10,576,520	0	0
Tobacco . .	95,000,000 =	3,800,000				
Gunpowder. .	5,616,000 =	224,640				
Miscellaneous Taxes			33,646,000 =	1,345,840	0	0
Postage			47,025,500 =	1,881,020	0	0
Derived from Property belonging to the Ministry of Public Instruction			4,349,082 =	173,563	5	7
Total of Indirect Taxes . .			738,605,082 =	29,544,203	5	7
Direct Taxes			396,054,610 =	15,842,184	8	0
Indirect Taxes			738,605,082 =	29,544,203	5	7
Miscellaneous Items			11,343,450 =	453,738	0	0
Total of Budget . .			1,146,003,142 =	45,840,125	13	7
Departmental Taxes, not in general Budget . .			11,200,000 =	448,000	0	0
Algiers			2,390,000 =	95,600	0	0
India			1,050,000 =	42,000	0	0
Total . . .			14,640,000 =	535,600	0	0

General Total . . . 1,160,643,142 *fr.* = 46,425,725*l.* 13*s.* 7*d.*

London : Printed by WILLIAM CLOWES and SONS, Stamford Street.

Printed in the United States
By Bookmasters